D1725156

Developments in Glocal
Language Testing

New Approaches to Applied Linguistics

Volume 3

Edited by

Mark Garner

Annabelle Mooney

Barbara Fennell

PETER LANG

Oxford • Bern • Berlin • Bruxelles • New York • Wien

Developments in Glocal Language Testing

The Case of the Greek National Foreign Language Proficiency Exam

Evdokia Karavas and Bessie Mitsikopoulou (eds)

PETER LANG

Oxford • Bern • Berlin • Bruxelles • New York • Wien

Bibliographic information published by Die Deutsche Nationalbibliothek.
Die Deutsche Nationalbibliothek lists this publication in the Deutsche National-
bibliografie; detailed bibliographic data is available on the Internet at http://
dnb.d-nb.de.

A catalogue record for this book is available from the British Library.

Library of Congress Cataloging-in-Publication Data:

Names: Karavas, Evdokia, 1967- editor. | Mitsikopoulou, Bessie, editor.
Title: Developments in glocal language testing : the case of the Greek
    national foreign language exam system / Evdokia Karavas and Bessie
    Mitsikopoulou (eds).
Description: First edition. | Oxford ; New York : Peter Lang, [2019] |
    Series: New approaches to applied linguistics ; 3 | Includes
    bibliographical references and index.
Identifiers: LCCN 2017027967 | ISBN 9783034322416 (softcover : acid-free
    paper)
Subjects: LCSH: Language and languages--Ability testing--Greece. | Language
    and languages--Examinations--Greece. | Language and languages--Study and
    teaching (Higher)--Greece. | Educational tests and measurements--Greece. |
    Glocalization--Greece.
Classification: LCC P57.G7 D38 2017 | DDC 418.0076--dc23 LC record available
at https://lccn.loc.gov/2017027967

Cover design by Peter Lang Ltd.

ISBN 978-3-0343-2241-6 (print) • ISBN 978-1-78707-692-1 (ePDF)
ISBN 978-1-78707-693-8 (ePub) • ISBN 978-1-78707-694-5 (mobi)

© Peter Lang AG 2019

Published by Peter Lang Ltd, International Academic Publishers,
52 St Giles, Oxford, OX1 3LU, United Kingdom
oxford@peterlang.com, www.peterlang.com

All rights reserved.
All parts of this publication are protected by copyright.
Any utilisation outside the strict limits of the copyright law, without the permission
of the publisher, is forbidden and liable to prosecution.
This applies in particular to reproductions, translations, microfilming, and storage
and processing in electronic retrieval systems.

This publication has been peer reviewed.

Printed in Germany

Contents

Figures

Tables

Abbreviations

Adv	Adverbial
ANOVA	Analysis of Variance
CALT	Computer Adaptive Language Testing
CDA	Critical Discourse Analysis
CEFR	Common European Framework of Reference for Languages
CESOL	Cambridge ESOL exams
CLD	Curriculum Language Database
CLC	Cambridge Learner Corpus
CMS	Content Management System
EFL	English as a Foreign Language
ELIUM	Michigan Language Exams
ELL	Early Language Learning
EPP	English Profile Programme
ESL	English as a Second Language
EU	European Union
FAQs	Frequently Asked Questions
FL	Foreign Language
IELTS	International English Language Testing System
IFLC	Integrated Foreign Languages Curriculum
IMS	Inventory of Mediation Strategies
KPG	Kratiko Pistopiitiko Glossomathias
L1	First Language
L2	Second Language
LPI	Language Proficiency Interview
MDA	Multimodal Discourse Analysis
MMA	Multimodal Analysis Image
NP	Noun Phrase
OPI	Oral Proficiency Interview
PP	Prepositional Phrase
RCeL	Research Centre for Language Teaching, Testing and Assessment

SFL	Systemic Functional Linguistics
TGI	Test Gist Item
TSRP	Test Taking Strategies Research Project
TWE	Test of Written English
V	Verb
WCMS	Web Content Management System

ELANA SHOHAMY

Foreword

It is a special honour to be asked by Evdokia Karavas and Bessie Mitsikopoulou, the editors of this volume, to write a foreword to this special book in honour of Professor Bessie Dendrinos. The book, entitled *Developments in Glocal Language Testing: The Case of the Greek National Foreign Language Proficiency Exam*, represents the state of the art in language testing, since it integrates language testing with multiple societal and educational perspectives, that is, the political, the social, language policy, linguistics and psychometrics. This integration is manifested through the case of the Greek National Foreign Language Proficiency Exam, an examination battery that Professor Dendrinos devoted her work to in the past two decades. Thus, the findings reported in the chapters of this book are derived from research and development within the Greek testing system. Yet, the implications of these findings go far beyond the Greek case as they are relevant to the language testing field at large in many worldwide systems. Hence, the word 'glocal' in the title implies both the local and the global. The other unique dimension of the chapters is that the research described in the volume was conducted with, and/or under the direction of Professor Dendrinos, with her creative and critical thinking.

I would like to acknowledge and recognise the special contribution that Professor Dendrinos made to the Applied Linguistics field and to my own thinking and academic growth. Bessie is a scholar who affected many researchers and had an influence on their critical views, seeking language justice in relation to English and other languages.

In the mid-1990s, I attended a lecture delivered by Professor Dendrinos at one of the GURT conferences held at Georgetown University in Washington DC, organised by the late Professor James Alatis. I had the privilege of listening to Professor Dendrinos addressing issues which at the time were very new to me and required great courage to discuss. This was an era when the number of people learning English was growing exponentially, especially in the third-world countries where governments and Ministries of Education were introducing English in school systems, in the belief that knowledge of English would improve the economy and status of their counties. It was during that lecture that Professor Dendrinos delivered the message about the power of the English language and the inequalities it produced, especially in relation to the western world. Bessie demonstrated this in a number of ways, but the one I recall best was how the contents included in the English textbooks gave false ideas to the people of the third world that learning the English language would make them success-ful in life. She argued that English textbooks portray those who know the English language as wealthy, rich, smart and having endless opportuni-ties and possibilities. Quite often, according to Dendrinos, the English language textbooks equated speakers of English with the 'haves', leading the learners in the third world to believe that if they were proficient in the English language, they would be able to attain the same status and wealth.

One example I recall from that talk was that of a speaker of English, often a native speaker of the language, who had many available alternatives about where to live, where to go, what to eat, and his only concern would be to choose one of the available options. The false illusion was that, despite their knowledge of English, most third-world learners would probably still have limited options and would continue to be poor. For most of these learners, English opened a gate to another world that was not reachable even with the knowledge of the English language. Not only did those third-world English learners not have such options; they could gradually adopt false expectations, fantasies and illusions by equating knowledge of the language with wealth and by assuming that the English language redeems learners from poverty and introduces them to the world of the privileged. From this perspective, English textbooks may become political and ideological tools for domination, resulting in the marginalisation of the learners and the widening of the gap between the haves and the have-nots. For me, working on language testing at the time, the misleading messages that English language textbooks gave to third-world learners were similar to those created by the domination of tests; the political and social mes-sages of textbooks were perpetuated in the testing arena and transformed tests into powerful political tools. The critical view I adopted over the years was rooted in the talk and the follow-up readings by Professor Dendrinos. I feel I am indebted to Bessie for planting in me the first seeds of critical language testing, which has accompanied me since then. I only met Bessie personally years later at the University of Athens, when she was deeply involved in the KPG test, developing and conducting research with her colleagues from that critical and constructive perspective. It was a very meaningful meeting for me as I realised that Bessie inspired much of my academic work.

A few years later, I was invited by Bessie to Athens to evaluate the work on the KPG; I was amazed by the extensive work of the team on different dimensions of the test. It was especially revealing to see Bessie, as the president of the KPG Central Examination Board, running the project and having the responsibility of designing and implementing the examination and certification system, as well as integrating assessment with learning, teaching and evaluation. The chapters in this book address multiple dimensions of this connection and as such they are not limited to testing; rather, testing is directly related to all other dimensions of a full expanded view of assessment that is not an isolated event.

It is thus a special opportunity to write this foreword, given the critical nature of the chapters. Even today, it is still not very common to find in mainstream language testing and teaching publications a substantial number of articles which address critical issues, although the field is expanding. It has become imperative to examine issues related to formative testing, dynamic assessment, multilingual testing, and the impact of language tests and those who do critical work are taking initiatives to look deeply and understand the connection between textbook materials and testing and their effect on learning. The work on the KPG reminds us about the difficulties and complexities of test development and validation.

The chapters in this volume address various issues of the KPG and in these studies we are able to see the complexity of tests. Professor Dendrinos provided the inspiration and the legitimacy.

The book consists of eleven chapters, and an introduction, each reporting on a different research dimension related to the KPG test. Using solid research designs, the chapters present different aspects of the test's construct, the test-takers' perspective of text difficulties, the behavior of the testers, the interviewer in an oral test and more. The book, written by Bessie's colleagues and previous students in her honour, shows great respect for her leadership and captures the social and educational with the psychometric.

These chapters are extremely comprehensive and broad, yet at the same time provide useful details that can be used by others outside Greece. Each chapter addresses major questions about the test and its validity and explores deeper issues related to the construct validity of the test. In fact, the large repertoire of research questions about testing are rarely asked and researched, and together they provide an excellent picture of a broader dimension of test validity. These questions are by no means an exhaustive list. Additional and varied questions may be asked about how KPG is being used, its consequences over time, the differentiation among different students and teachers, with implications for many other systems worldwide. The book as a whole is an excellent example of serious validation where evidence is continuously being collected; only in that way can construct validity be achieved.

This masterwork is a reflection of Professor Dendrinos' thoughtful approaches to validity, where validity is an unending process in which questions need to be asked and answered so as to create reliable tests that can be used by human beings with trust and confidence.

Preface

The purpose of this volume is twofold. First, it aims to disseminate information regarding a most innovatory examination system – the Greek State Certificate in Language Proficiency (hence KPG) – and related research which constitutes a significant contribution to the field of testing and assessment internationally. Second, it celebrates the substantial work of the 'mastermind' and 'heart' of the KPG system, Professor Bessie Dendrinos. The inspiration for this volume came from two of Bessie Dendrinos' mentees, colleagues at the Department of English Language and Literature of the National and Kapodistrian University of Athens and close associates, Associate Professors Bessie Mitsikopoulou and Evdokia Karavas. We consider it a great honour and pleasure to dedicate this volume to Bessie Dendrinos as a small token of gratitude for all she has selflessly and tirelessly offered us and the foreign language community in Greece for more than thirty years.

Bessie Dendrinos was the initial president of the KPG Central Examination Board, which had the responsibility of designing and implementing the examination and certification system, as well as managing the first exam administration on a trial basis in 2003. Since then she has been a key player and a visionary for the KPG exams. The contribution of Professor Dendrinos was decisive as she articulated the aims of this new institution and its social perspective, and was primarily responsible for setting the content and the theoretical framework of the examination battery. She served as president up to 2006 and then again from 2014 until today and hopefully for many years to come. Since 2003 she has also been the Scientific Director of the KPG exams in English, shaping the format of the separate test papers, and giving the exams in English their theoretical grounding, ideological orientation and sociolinguistic character.

According to Professor Dendrinos, tests are not value-free or ideology-free products. The texts and images used in tests carry ideological meanings which, until recently, were not systematically investigated. She believes that exam systems serve as ideological apparatuses involving processes of

ideologisation, just as the discursive practices in the texts of language textbooks do (as she demonstrated in her 1992 book *The EFL Textbook and
Ideology*), and just as language teaching practices do. Embracing a multilingual paradigm, in which people learn to make maximum use of all the
semiotic resources they have available in order to communicate effectively
in situational contexts, she strongly supported the development of a multilingual exam suite which views languages not as compartmentalised, but
as equal, interrelated meaning-making, semiotic systems. In this context,
she argues, localised tests through a glocalised language testing system can
cater to the needs of local job markets and can serve as counter-hegemonic
alternatives to the monolingual, profit-driven international language exam
systems.

Consistent with these views, Professor Dendrinos has directed the
multifaceted KPG-related research being carried out at the University of
Athens and specifically at the Research Centre for Language Teaching,
Testing and Assessment (RCeL), which she founded in 2004 and of which
she has been the director ever since. The RCeL is a fully equipped research
unit at the School of Philosophy of the University of Athens (<http://
www.RCeL.enl.uoa.gr/>) whose main purpose is to carry out research in
language teaching, testing and assessment, to develop teaching and testing materials, to produce relevant publications and to develop data bases
which facilitate linguistic research. In addition, it supports research and
education projects of the Greek Ministry of Education and of educational
and research institutions in Greece and abroad and has developed into a
reputable organisation.

The RCeL has been responsible for the development of the KPG exams
in English and in its first years of operation it concentrated exclusively on
carrying out research with a team of young scholars on issues relating to
testing and the development of the KPG exams. This entailed preparing
exam specifications and test paper guidelines, developing testing materials
for the exam item bank, conducting particular types of analysis related to
the quality of the exams and to test-taker performance, conducting research
related to KPG test strategies and to features of the exams, examiner training, script rater training, writing, translating and publishing information about the KPG exams, producing exam-related materials, building

mechanisms for internal and external evaluation of KPG subprojects and developing measurement and evaluation tools for the assessment of test papers, exams, materials and human resources.

At the same time, the RCeL developed a variety of corpora and supported postgraduate research at MA, doctoral and postdoctoral levels, some of which is reported in this volume. One of the most significant projects undertaken by the RCeL is the development of the KPG English Corpus, which comprises collections of written texts (scripts) produced by candidates in the KPG examinations in English, totalling approximately 4 million words. The KPG script collections have been systematised in a Script Database which is being enriched on an ongoing basis, maintaining a balance across proficiency levels, types of tasks which candidates are asked to perform, as well as communicative environments to which they are asked to respond using the target language.

Because of its interest in corpus-based work, the RCeL has become a member of SLATE, a European-wide research network brought together through a common interest in the relationship between second/foreign language development, levels of second language proficiency, and language testing research. It has also collaborated with other European organisations and taken part in European projects such as Language Rich Europe, for which the RCeL became a dissemination partner, and SurveyLang, for which the RCeL staff conducted extensive data analysis of information collected through the European Survey of Language Competences. In addition to this, the RCeL has participated in international workshops organised by the Council of Europe with a view to validating a set of descriptors of language proficiency to complement those already available in the CEFR. Another project of the Council of Europe in which the RCeL took part was 'The CEFR Reading and Listening Items and Tasks Project (2015–16)'. KPG reading and listening items and tasks illustrating the European reference levels in English, French, German, Italian and Spanish were selected to be published on the Council of Europe's website.

Through her work as director of the RCeL and the KPG Central Examination Board, Professor Dendrinos has been responsible for major innovations in foreign language teaching in Greece such as the Young Learner Programme which involved the introduction of English in the first and second grade of primary school (<http://rcel.enl.uoa.gr/peap/>) and the development of the new Integrated Foreign Languages Curriculum for primary and secondary education in Greece (<http://rcel.enl.uoa.gr/xenesglosses/sps.htm>). In addition, due to her keen interest in socially accountable applied linguistics and her expertise in language politics and policies in the European Union, she has also been very active in a number of European associations and projects supporting multilingualism and plurilingualism in Europe and in 2014 she was elected president of the Civil Society Platform for Multilingualism.

Above all though, Professor Dendrinos has been an outstanding educator, as the authors of this volume can verify. She is inspiring, open-minded, caring and with a unique ability to affect people's lives in the most positive way. The idea behind this volume has been to put together and present some of the PhD work and research projects on KPG she has supervised all these years, expressing in this way our love and gratitude to Professor Bessie Dendrinos.

Evdokia Karavas
Bessie Mitsikopoulou

EVDOKIA KARAVAS AND BESSIE MITSIKOPOULOU

Introduction
Issues and challenges in glocal language testing: The case of the Greek State Certificate in Language Proficiency

This edited collection focuses on research and developments in the Greek 'State Certificate in Language Proficiency', nationally and internationally known as the KPG (an acronym for the Greek title *Kratiko Pistopiitiko Glossomathias*). The KPG exams represent a 'glocal' multilingual examination battery, the first of its kind in Europe,[1] whose main purpose is to cater for the linguistic needs of the domestic job and education market, as well as for other regional social demands. Given that publications in language testing and assessment address research and developments of international, monolingual exam suites, this book aims at presenting research studies of a locally developed multilingual exam suite which, however, uses the knowledge and responds to standards developed through international proficiency testing. In this sense, the papers which are included in the volume highlight the innovative features and specifications of the KPG as a local exam suite but with important implications for global language testing and practices. A brief overview of the KPG as a national project is presented in the Appendix at the end of this chapter.

The KPG system: A glocal multilingual examination suite

The KPG is an examination system which is based on the belief that degrees of literacy in several languages help people face the challenges of globalisation, increased mobility and immigration. Acknowledging that in

---

1   But also see the Finnish language examination system (Dendrinos 2013)

a multicultural Europe, with its linguistic diversity and variety of institutions, it is essential for citizens to have language qualifications which are recognised by all, the KPG exam suite aims at the certification of different levels of language proficiency in various European languages. It is therefore grounded on an appreciation of languages which are considered essential for employability, and on the conviction that multilingual people acting as intercultural mediators are a precious asset to Europe. For this reason, the primary objective of the KPG exam from B1 level onwards is to respond to candidates' social needs, by granting them certification which can be of use for occupational purposes. Certification at levels A1 and A2 level aims mainly to assess knowledge and skills developed by candidates in the course of their language training within or outside the state educational system.

Within the KPG exam battery, language is viewed as social practice embedded in the sociocultural context by which it is produced.[2] The system adheres to a functional approach to language use and sets out, throughout all its tests (modules), to evaluate socially purposeful language use, which entails a certain amount of social and school literacy (Dendrinos 2004). As a result, the KPG exams aim at assessing how well candidates use the language to understand oral and written texts and to produce socially meaningful messages. They do not aim to assess candidates' knowledge about the foreign language or about grammar and vocabulary. More specifically, the KPG exams measure candidates' ability to: (1) comprehend and produce oral and written discourse, (2) act as mediators across languages, and (3) use the target language to produce socially purposeful meanings. Using a language for such purposes presupposes that candidates have developed not only a relative level of competence in a language, but also language awareness which involves knowledge of the way a language functions, the ability to make appropriate language choices, and the skills to understand and communicate in the foreign language.

The KPG exam suite takes into account local needs, global conditions of knowledge and international concerns regarding testing and

---

2   Dendrinos, B. (2009). Rationale and ideology of the KPG exams. *ELT News*. Available at: <http://rcel.enl.uoa.gr/kpg/gr_kpgcorner_sep2009.htm>.

assessment. In this sense it can be characterised as a 'glocal' examination system (Dendrinos 2009). Glocal, a portmanteau word deriving from 'global' and 'local', refers to the 'integration of local cultural differences and practices in initiatives, programs, or projects that are based on a globalization framework' (Francois 2015: 62). The term was initially associated with the business, technology, and sociology disciplines in order to emphasise that the globalisation of a product is more likely to succeed when the product or service is adapted specifically to each locality or culture it is marketed in. Glocalisation generally refers to the merger of global and local perspectives on the socio-economic and political impact of all phenomena that affect local and global communities. Within the higher education context, glocalisation refers to the respectful exchange of cultural wealth among learners and teachers to inform and enhance higher education pedagogical practice (Patel & Lynch 2013: 225). In education, glocal-oriented pedagogies are learner-centred and context-sensitive and infuse global content into local curricula, which are seen as too locally focused and parochial and not meeting the needs of society or the economy (Mannion 2015).

Within the area of language testing, glocal language assessment involves locally operated schemes, set up to serve domestic social conditions and needs, which are informed by international research and assessment practices (Dendrinos 2005, 2013). In contrast to globally administered language tests, which feature a 'standard' variety of a language (e.g. in the case of English, that could be a British or an American standard variety), a 'western' sensitivity to appropriateness of topics, as well as a contextualisation within a native-speaker language environment, one of the main aims of glocal tests is to cater for the linguistic needs of the domestic job and education markets, as well as for other regional social demands. While international language proficiency testing aims at sustaining the position of the national language and the culture in which the language is immersed, in glocal testing attention is turned from the language itself (as an abstract meaning system devoid of ideological inscriptions and disconnected from its cultural context) to language users (as meaning makers) taking into account their experiences, literacies and needs. Therefore, decisions regarding the test papers are meaningful for the specific society for which they are developed.

The global character of the KPG exams can be ascertained by the fact that the system issues certificates to those candidates who pass the exams with a view to using language in a global context. Thus, despite the localisation of the exams, they have an international orientation. The KPG exams use international experience for the organisation of the system and development of resources (material and item banks, data bases for tools evaluation, etc.), for the development of instruments of language proficiency measurement and tools, for quality assessment, as well as for approaches to examiner and rater training.[3] Moreover, research studies conducted within the context of the KPG system constitute significant contributions to the field of testing and assessment internationally. In addition, the KPG examination system does not follow a code of ethics or code of practice developed by an external international organisation, but it has seriously considered international codes of ethics and practices in order to develop a glocal code of ethics and practices. This code adheres to principles of accountability, professionalism and transparency and makes attempts to follow democratic principles. It is itself a glocal artefact in the sense that it follows the models proposed by International Language Testing Association and Association of Language Testers in Europe, but makes adjustments and alterations appropriate to the context (Karavas 2011).

Another international/global feature of the KPG exam system is that it has used the supranational structure of the CEFR as a basic reference for the design of the examination battery, adopting the six levels of proficiency set by the CEFR and the recommendations of the Education Committee of the Council of Europe, which had been announced for the first time in 2002. On the scale set by the Council of Europe and in line with the overall aims of the Common European Framework of Reference for Languages, illustrative descriptors for levelled performance have been produced indicating the communicative abilities candidates are expected to have acquired. As a result, the KPG responds to social needs of citizenry in Greece as an EU member state and its action plan is compatible with the European Union Multilingualism Policy as articulated in 2007

---

3   See *The KPG handbook* at <http://www.rcel.enl.uoa.gr/fileadmin/rcel.enl.uoa.gr/uploads/texts/KPG_Handbook_17X24.pdf>.

by the Directorate General of Education and Culture and with the EU Commission's Multilingualism Action Plan 2007–13. Moreover, since the KPG certificate is issued by a public organisation of a member state and is under the auspices of the Greek Ministry of Education, it is recognised in all other EU member states.

Apart from these international and global features, the KPG exam system is emphatically local. The exam suite is linked with education and social life in Greece while the selection of topics and tasks seriously takes into account the candidates for whom they are constructed, that is, their interests, lived experiences, linguistic and cultural knowledge, as well as the types of competences, skills and strategies they need to develop. The exams focus on the socially located use of language and not on language as an autonomous system of notions and structures – independent of their socially construed meanings. Besides testing awareness of how language operates to create meanings, the exams also indirectly test levels of literacy and intercultural awareness. The exams systematically test language functions and specifically the ideational, the interpersonal, the creative and mediatory function. Systematic research which has been carried out since the launch of the system (reported in the chapters of this volume) has demonstrated that in relation to other language certification systems, in the KPG exam system:

- there is a greater variety of discourses, genres and registers than in the tests of other exam systems;
- the higher the level being tested, the higher the demands as to appropriate language use according to genre and context;
- test items are motivated by multimodal texts;
- listening and reading comprehension is tested on the basis of authentic texts;
- scripts are rated by two trained evaluators on the basis of instruments constructed for this purpose;
- there is transparency regarding the language theory behind KPG testing and what candidates are expected to do at each level of proficiency.

Another major difference between international language testing batteries and the KPG system is that the former are essentially monolingual as examination suites (i.e. they are intended to test a single language) and as assessment systems (i.e. they are constructed to measure monolingual competence), whereas the later is essentially multilingual (Dendrinos 2013). Despite the fact that within the European Union the promotion of multilingualism has been a consistent endeavour over the last fifteen years and 'although dynamic, diverse, and constructive discussions of multilingual teaching and learning are currently taking place within the language education field, the phenomenon is completely overlooked in the assessment field that continues to view language as a monolingual, homogenous, and often still native-like construct', as Shohamy (2011: 419) asserts. Even though language tests need to build on an updated language construct of what it means to know a language in order to achieve high construct validity, international language exams and curricular artefacts are still based on monolingual approaches, viewing language as a closed and finite system that does not enable other languages to 'smuggle in'. They endorse the idea that effective communication is monolingual and that proficient users of a language do not use 'hybrid' forms; they do not mix languages or codes. This monolingualism is in stark contrast to the current understanding of multilingual competencies for which various languages and aspects 'bleed' into one another in creative ways (Dendrinos 2010).

The KPG exam system from its inception has been built on the principle of multilingualism, recognising that it is important for groups and individuals to communicate with more than one languages in public and privately. In this paradigm, as Dendrinos (2013: 15) explicitly argues, 'people learn to make maximum use of all their semiotic resources so as to communicate effectively in situational contexts, which are often bi-, tri- and multilingual. In such settings, people use code switching and "translanguaging" techniques, drawing upon the resources they have from a variety of contexts and languages. They use different forms of expression in multimodal texts to create socially situated meanings. Often they also resort to intra- and inter-linguistic as well as intercultural mediation'.

Multilingualism is operationalised in the KPG exam system by viewing all languages assessed as equal. Any innovation introduced concerns and is applied to all languages tested. Exams for all levels and languages are based on a common theory of language and are designed on the basis of common specifications. More specifically, across languages, the exams

- test common competences and strategies;
- are regulated by common specifications;[4]
- use a common test-task typology.

The theory of language permeating assessment criteria and the design of tasks, as well as the rating scale for assessing oral and written production, is common across levels and languages. Criteria for the assessment of oral or written production, derived from the theory of language, are also common across languages, as is the training or oral examiners and script raters.

The assessment of mediation performance is a unique characteristic of the KPG exams in relation to all the other international examination batteries. Mediation involves a 'hybrid practice of languaging' or translanguaging (Garcia, 2011) an interplay of languages highlighting the fact that there are no clear-cut boundaries between the languages employed (Stathopoulou 2013, 2015). Translanguaging describes the use of literacy practices to 'move back and forth with ease and comfort between and among different languages and dialects, different social classes, and different cultural and artistic forms' (Guerra 2004: 8). The KPG candidates are required to prove that they are able to act as mediators and, more specifically, produce written or oral discourse in the foreign language on the basis of a text in Greek. Mediation activities are included in the writing and speaking tests of the B (B1/B2) and C (C1/C2) level exams in all languages and they assess the candidates' ability to move back and forth between languages and to simultaneously draw on different linguistic and cultural resources from a variety of contexts. As a result in order to take part in the KPG exams, candidates are expected to be independent users of the Greek language.[5]

---

4   Find them at: <http://rcel.enl.uoa.gr/kpg/exam_specif.htm>.

5   KPG exams at B and C levels are designed for candidates over fifteen years of age, who are EU citizens, and candidates from other countries who are living, studying and/or working in Greece, whereas the A1 and A2 levels are mainly addressed at young learners, although older candidates also sit for the exam at these levels. Greek is

Additional innovatory features of the KPG exam system

Unlike international proficiency testing with its overpriced fees, a concern of the KPG Central Examination Board, especially in these times of severe financial crisis that Greece is experiencing, has been how to make the exams as affordable as possible for the average Greek candidate. Thus, apart from the fact that testing fees are about half the price of commercial international exams, it was decided to develop and administer graded, intergraded paper-based exams for which a candidate pays a single exam fee, sits for one exam, but may be certified in one of two levels of proficiency. Each test paper includes tasks for two levels of language proficiency (A1+A2, B1+B2 and C1+C2) and candidates have a double shot for a certificate – for either the higher or the lower of the two levels, depending on the level of their performance. Thus, currently, three intergraded exams are being offered, which contain an equal number of items at each level.

Moreover, KPG is linked with school education. It is linked directly with the newly introduced Integrated Foreign Languages Curriculum for primary and secondary education in Greece (see <http://rcel.enl.uoa.gr/xenesglosses/>). In addition, language exams in schools are based on similar specifications as the KPG exams while preparation for the KPG exams has already been introduced in school support programmes. Connecting KPG to Greek state school education has been a multifaceted endeavour. The KPG e-school, an online platform addressing different stakeholders involved in the KPG exams, such as candidates, teachers, assessors and parents, was developed in an attempt to provide educational materials for all its stakeholders in a systematic way (see also Chapter 11 in this volume).

In addition, the KPG exam system takes additional measures to help candidates with special needs. It adapts the tests to cater for different types

considered the common language of the candidates since they are required to understand instructions and rubrics in Greek, for the A level exam, and to function in the role of mediator transferring information from Greek in the TL for the B and C level exams.

of learning difficulties and disabilities, depending on the candidate applications, and provides two special Examination Centres, one in Athens and one in Thessaloniki. Examiners trained in dealing with special needs are used in the two examination centres and specially trained script raters are also used in the Rating Centres to grade the written scripts of candidates with special needs.

Finally, since 2010, teams of experts from the universities of Athens and Thessaloniki have been working towards developing the e-KPG, in collaboration with the Computer Technology Institute of the University of Patras. The three universities in partnership have produced a platform for an electronic version of the exams to be administered online (alongside the pen-and-paper exams) and a platform with a distance learning scheme for off-line training of examiners and script raters. The Computer Adaptive Language Testing (CALT) platform for e-KPG exams contains a common proficiency scale for all languages (aligned to the six-level scale of the Council of Europe) and common illustrative descriptors (aligned to the CEFR). It is based on a constructivist view of language in use, like the paper-based exams, and it is task-based, not item-based.

Researching the KPG English exam

This volume reports on research studies conducted within the context of the KPG English exams under the supervision of Professor Bessie Dendrinos from 2004–2016, which have developed into full PhD projects and have led to international publications of books, book chapters and research articles in academic journals. Honouring their professor, the authors of this volume present aspects of their work using diverse methodologies and drawing on systemic functional grammar and linguistics, critical discourse analysis, multimodal discourse analysis, corpus linguistics and research covering topics on listening, speaking, reading and writing.

The first chapter of the collection, 'The sociosemiotic language view underlying the design of the KPG exams' by Bessie Mitsikopoulou, Evdokia

Karavas, and Christina Lykou, offers an account of the theory of language adopted in the KPG exam. It exemplifies how the view of language as social practice and as a meaning-making source, interrelated with the sociocultural context in which it is produced, permeates the rationale and design of the KPG examination suite and is illustrated in its glocal and multilingual character, in the selection of texts or materials, in task design in all different modules and proficiency levels, as well as in the applied evaluation criteria. In this chapter special attention is given to socially purposeful language use presenting tasks from the different modules. Consistent with the contextual view of language, the chapter moves to explicate the genre-based approach adopted by the KPG examination suite in designing, evaluating and assessing written and oral production activities and it provides examples from written and oral production modules. Through this language approach, the KPG exam battery views candidates as meaning-making producers with the ability to make appropriate language choices and the knowledge of the functional role of language.

The next two chapters deal with research on the KPG English listening and speaking modules. In 'Oral text difficulty in foreign language listening comprehension testing', Elizabeth Apostolou focuses on the listening comprehension test of the KPG exams in English and discusses the results of an investigation into oral text variables (linguistic, paralinguistic, and cognitive) that contribute to text complexity and listener incomprehensibility. The findings reported in this chapter are particularly original and useful since they stem from candidates themselves who were asked to evaluate the difficulty of oral texts in the listening exam. Motivated by a lack of similar empirical research, the study examines the listener's perspective (i.e. test takers' and EFL learners') using two main methodological tools, namely candidate feedback questionnaires and learners' verbal reports. An important finding of this study, of particular importance to test designers, concerns the interactive relationship of the linguistic and paralinguistic features of audio texts in influencing test difficulty, as well as the role of background knowledge in listening test comprehension.

Xenia Delieza's chapter, 'The impact of oral examiners' conduct on candidates' performance in the KPG exam', reports findings of the innovatory observation project of oral examiners' on-the-job performance, focusing specifically on the extent to which oral examiners intervene in candidates' language output while conducting the KPG speaking test in English. The project, which was launched in November 2005, involved on-site observation of oral examiners as a means of evaluating and monitoring the KPG oral exams for English, thus gathering information about, inter alia, the conditions of the oral exam administration, examiner discourse practices, examiner efficiency and conduct. The project involved the design of structured observation schemes used by trained observers during each exam administration. Specific observation categories were developed focusing on the changes examiners/interlocutors made to task rubrics and their interventions to candidates' language output. Delieza in her chapter presents the findings which are related to the types and frequencies of examiners' involvement in the candidates' oral performance in the B2 and C1 levels of the English KPG speaking test, highlighting the effect of task type on examiner involvement and discusses the implications of these results for examiner training as well as the types of tasks used in oral tests.

The following three chapters deal with research on the reading module. In 'Investigating ideologies in texts used in global and "glocal" language testing', Amalia Balourdi explores representations of the world in B2-level reading texts of three examination suites (KPG, Cambridge ESOL and Michigan) in order to investigate the ideologies these texts are invested with. Attempting a close linguistic analysis of transitivity following principles of systemic functional grammar, she focused on two material process sub-types, the processes of 'giving and taking', and found that each exam suite construes a different reality and worldview with its own values and beliefs. Very briefly, in KPG texts, people are active citizens of the world who care about the environment, promote public health and protect human rights; through its texts Cambridge ESOL construes a world of artistic and intellectual interests, in which emphasis is placed on feelings, ideas, experiences and opportunities; Michigan texts, on the other hand, construe a market-oriented world which places emphasis on the exchange of goods and services, customer-supplier relationships and compliance with market rules. This groundbreaking research brings to the foreground the issue of embedded ideologies in reading texts used for reading comprehension in international language proficiency assessment suites.

In 'Visual matters in language testing: Exploring intersemiotic meaning making in reading comprehension source texts', Stella Karatza turns to multimodal discourse analysis and explores the impact of the visuals in KPG reading comprehension texts at B1 level. Acknowledging that unlike other exam-oriented reading comprehension texts, KPG reading texts are multimodal, with the verbal and the visual modes working synergistically to construe meaning, she argues that KPG candidates are required to 'read' and make sense of both the verbal and the visual elements of the reading texts in order to respond to reading comprehension questions. Her main aim is to research the extent to which the visuals contribute to the meaning-making potential of the KPG multimodal reading texts through an analysis of intersemiotic features which examine verbal/visual interaction. For the analysis of how the visual and verbal components work together, she has used the Multimodal Analysis Image (MMA) interactive software. Quite interestingly, the high frequency of intersemiotic cohesive ties in her findings verifies the contribution of the visuals in the meaning-making potential of the source texts, something that leads her to the realisation that KPG candidates need to develop not only verbal language awareness but also visual and intersemiotic awareness in order to comprehend a multimodal source text sufficiently.

Trisevgeni Liontou, in 'Test-takers' strategies in responding to the KPG English language reading comprehension tasks: Evidence from retrospective think-aloud protocols', explores the ways in which reading and test-taking strategies are used by advanced learners when they prepare themselves for the KPG C1 reading comprehension test in English. Adopting the methodology of retrospective think-aloud protocols to investigate 'main idea' and 'factual' reading items, she found that participants in the study repeatedly used a limited number of planning and identifying strategies while they hardly used any monitoring strategies or evaluating strategies (e.g. predicting or inferring unknown words from context) to regulate reading comprehension. She concludes that successful completion of reading comprehension items involves effective use of a wide repertoire of strategies, for which learners should be trained. The findings of the study are important in that they add to the construct validity of the KPG English language exams and also provide practical guidance for EFL teachers, material developers and test designers regarding the kind of reading comprehension strategies EFL learners develop depending on their language competence level and the difficulty specific text features impose on them.

In the next three chapters of the volume, research into the writing module of the KPG English exams is reported. In 'A comparative study of cohesion in L2 candidates' texts', Virginia Blani uses a corpus of C1 level rated scripts produced under exam conditions in order to investigate the extent to which cohesion affects writing quality. As in previous studies, she found that overall the frequency of cohesive devices in her corpus cannot be considered an indication of high-quality writing. However, her statistical analysis confirms the use of some types of cohesive devices which indicate writing quality and are types of lexical rather than grammatical cohesion. Her study is significant in that it points out the complex ways in which cohesion operates at advanced levels of language proficiency and the need for including lexical cohesion descriptors in rating scales. It also demystifies the role of explicit grammatical cohesive devices which are overemphasised in foreign language textbooks and instruction.

Vasso Oikonomidou, in 'The effect of source text on read-to-write task difficulty', explores a particular type of writing task in the KPG English B1 level exam, the read-to-write tasks, which contain text-based prompts that candidates should use as models in order to construct a similar text on another topic. She investigates the effect of the source text on read-to-write task difficulty by analysing the tasks and by comparing them to candidates' scores. Through her analysis, she illustrates several of the complexities involved in the specific task type and she concludes that difficult source texts increase the difficulty of the writing task and result in low-scored scripts. In addition, she points to the need to investigate other aspects of read-to-write tasks, including the instructions given to the candidates, the text type of the source and target text, the level of discourse formality and topic familiarity. Finally, the chapter reflects on the usefulness of the findings for test task writers and the language testing community.

Maria Stathopoulou's chapter, 'Assessing cross-language mediation in the Greek national multilingual exam suite: Test-takers' language performance and strategy use', deals with one of the most significant and profound innovations of the KPG exam system: the notion and assessment of cross-language mediation. Drawing data from the KPG English writing test and using candidates' scripts on mediation tasks as a source of analysis, the study seeks to identify which mediation strategies differentiate successful from less successful mediation scripts (and to what extent) by comparing those which were rated by trained KPG assessors as fully satisfactory with others which were rated as moderately satisfactory. After extensively discussing the notion of cross-language mediation and how it is operationalised in the KPG exams, Stathopoulou presents the most frequent and popular mediation strategies used by candidates in successful and less successful scripts drawing on a corpus of approximately 50,000 words, that is, 600 mediation scripts produced by KPG candidates sitting for the B1, B2 and C1 level exams over a period of six years (2008–13). Her findings reveal that it is not only the nature of the task and the proficiency level that differentiates strategy use, but also the test-takers' language performance. Evidence, in other words, shows that specific mediation strategies seem to discriminate between texts written by low- and high-performance writers.

Finally, the last two chapters of this volume deal with electronic developments of the KPG exam suite. Voula Gotsoulia's chapter, entitled 'Documenting language proficiency levels using learner data from the KPG examinations suite', focuses on another innovatory and groundbreaking project carried out by the Research Centre for Language Teaching, Testing and Assessment, which used the KPG corpus as a main data source: the Language Learner Profile project. The aim of this project is to describe the linguistic profile of the Greek learner/user of foreign languages, adding details to the CEFR levelled descriptors of language proficiency across languages. In other words, proficiency scaling is specified in terms of the use of target language properties exhibited by learners with coherent L1 characteristics. Bringing together different strands related to the study of languages (applied and theoretical linguistics, foreign language studies, computational linguistics), Gotsoulia's chapter reports on the findings of an extensive and ongoing empirical study of the use of three European languages (English, German and Spanish) by Greek learners, in various communicative and discursive contexts. Drawing on corpus data collected on the basis of the KPG multilingual examination suite (i.e. the

KPG English Corpus and similar corpora for German and Spanish) and using advanced natural language processing techniques for automated text analysis, a generic methodological framework (portable across languages) has been developed, suitable for describing the contextual use of language in terms of features pertaining to distinct levels of linguistic analysis. The project, as reported in this chapter, will eventually deliver lists of lexical, semantic, grammatical/morpho-syntactic, and functional features that characterise Greek learners' language production, at different levels of proficiency. The results of this research will be valuable for practitioners working on foreign language teaching, testing and assessment, especially on a local level, for language education policy and language curriculum planners and for foreign language learning and second language acquisition scholars studying the relationships between acquired/ learned languages.

The last chapter of the volume, 'KPG e-school: The diffusion and implementation of an educational innovation' by Bessie Mitsikopoulou, Evdokia Karavas and Smaragda Papadopoulou, describes a recent innovation of the KPG exam system, the KPG e-school. The KPG e-school is a multipurpose and multifunctional educational website developed by members of the RCeL whose main goal is to link the KPG language exams with the state compulsory education system and to give primary and secondary school students the opportunity to prepare in school for the KPG exams in English, German, French, Italian and Spanish. The final outcome was the presentation of a 'Uniform KPG exam preparation programme', which is open to the public and can be visited at <http://rcel.enl.uoa.gr/ kpgeschool/>. The KPG e-school acts as an awareness-raising tool for students, teachers and parents alike, facilitating the diffusion of information regarding the nature, validity, structure and content of the KPG exams and also represents a strategic move to facilitate the link between the KPG exam system and the national Integrated Foreign Languages Curriculum (IFLC). This last chapter presents the rationale permeating the development of this educational resource, describes the selected design process of the educational resources produced and discusses the potential and the contribution of these resources and materials for the preparation of language learners in the foreign languages taught in Greek schools.

Conclusion

Until the introduction of the KPG exams, language testing in Greece was dominated by international examining bodies (i.e. Cambridge ESOL Examinations, University of Michigan, and Educational Testing Service) which

> offered a variety of language certificates of different status and value, yielding significant symbolic and material profit for the testing organizations who administered them, and promoting and assessing linguistic and cultural knowledge that was not always compatible with the needs of the Greek language users. (Eckes et al. 2005: 360)

With the introduction of the KPG exam system in 2003, Greece established a national system of assessment building on local expertise that for so many years had been suppressed by the existence of foreign language examinations. Ever since its introduction, it has gained widespread acceptance at a national level judging not only from the increasing number of candidates who decide to take part in the exams at various levels, but from the number of private language institutions that have introduced KPG exam preparation classes in their curricula and the number of local and international commercial publishers that have produced special teaching materials (textbooks, practice test materials, etc.) to help KPG candidates prepare for the exams (particularly for the English test). It has also had a positive washback effect on public foreign language education since it is recommended that language exams in schools be based on similar specifications as the KPG exams, while preparation for the KPG exams has been introduced in school support programmes. It has also acted as a springboard for the production of a wealth of research studies and projects with significant implications for global language testing and practices, which the papers in this volume attest to.[6]

6   Detailed information about test papers (and past papers), the examination suite and how it is organised, about the multilevel research that has been carried out in the last 10 years, M.A. dissertations, Ph.D. theses, publications which have appeared in English, Greek and other languages and presentations in Greece and abroad concerning the KPG multilingual examination suite can be found at <http://rcel2.enl.uoa.gr/kpg/en_index.htm>.

Bibliography

Dendrinos, B. (2004). 'Multilingual Literacy in the EU: Alternative Discourse in Foreign Language Education Programmes'. In B. Dendrinos and B. Mitsikopoulou (eds), *Politics of Linguistic Pluralism and the Teaching of Languages in Europe*, pp. 60–70. Athens: Metaichmio Publishers and University of Athens.

——(2005). 'Certification de Competences en Langues Etrangeres, Multilinguisme et Plurilinguisme'. In *Langue Nationales et Plurilinguisme: Initiatives Grecques*, pp. 95–100. Athens: The Ministry of National Education and Religious Affairs & Centre for the Greek Language.

——(2010). 'Language issues and language policies in Greece'. In G. Stickel (ed.), *National and European Language Policies. Duisburg Papers on Research in Language and Culture*, 53–70. Frankfurt: Peter Lang.

——(2013). 'Social Meanings in Global-glocal Language Proficiency Exams'. In C. Tsagari, S. Papadima-Sophocleous & S. Ioannou-Georgiou (eds), *Language Testing and Assessment around the Globe: Achievements and Experiences*, pp. 47–67. Vienna: Peter Lang.

Eckes, T., et al. (2005). 'Progress and problems in reforming public language examinations in Europe: cameos from the Baltic States, Greece, Hungary, Poland, Slovenia, France and Germany', *Language Testing* 22 (3): 355–77.

Francois, E. J. (2015). *Building Global Education with a Local Perspective: An Introduction to Glocal Higher Education*. New York: Palgrave Macmillan.

Garcia, O. (2011). 'Theorizing Translanguiging for Educators'. I Celic and K. Seltzer (eds), 1–6. *Translanguaging: A CUNY-NYSIEB Guide for Educators*. New York: CUNY-NYSIEB.

Guerra, J. C. (2004). 'Emerging Representations, Situated Literacies and the Practice of Transcultural Repositioning'. In M. H. Kellis, V. Balester and V. Villanueva (eds), *Latino/a Discourses: On Language, Identity and Literacy in Education*, 7–23. Portsmouth, NH: Heinemann.

Karavas, K. (2011). 'Fairness and Ethical Language Testing: The Case of the KPG', *DIRECTIONS in Language Teaching and Testing*. RCeL Publications, University of Athens, 1 (1).

Mannion, G. (2015). 'Towards Glocal Pedagogies: Some Risks Associated with Education for Global Citizenship and How Glocal Pedagogies Might Avoid Them'. In John Friedman, Vicki Haverkate, Barbara Oomen, Eri Park, Marcin Sklad (eds), *Going Glocal in Higher Education: The Theory, Teaching and Measurement of Global Citizenship*, pp 19–34. Middleburg: University College Roosevelt.

Patel, F., & Lynch, H. (2013). 'Glocalization as an Alternative to Internationalization in Higher Education: Embedding Positive Glocal Learning Perspectives', *International Journal of Teaching and Learning in Higher Education* 25 (2): 223–30.

Shohamy, E. (2011). 'Assessing Multilingual Competencies: Adopting Construct Valid Assessment Policies', *The Modern Language Journal*, 95 (3), 418–29.

Stathopoulou M. (2013). *Task Dependent Interlinguistic Mediation Performance as Translanguaging Practice: The Use of KPG Data for an Empirically Based Study.* PhD Thesis, University of Athens.

—— (2015). *Cross-Language Mediation in Foreign Language Teaching and Testing.* Bristol: Multilingual Matters.

Appendix: Introducing the KPG as a national project

The KPG is a foreign language proficiency language exam system instituted by law in 1999 which uses the Common European Framework of References for Languages (CEFR) as a springboard for content specifications and which adopts the six-level scale of the Council of Europe for certification purposes. The KPG exams represent a 'proficiency assessment' (rather than diagnostic or competences measurement) examination system which aims to test the candidates' ability to make socially purposeful use of the target language. It is an exam system governed by the Greek Ministry of Education, Research and Religious Affairs, who is the legal copyright owner of all documents containing information about the KPG assessment system and is responsible for the administration of the exams. Test paper development and research related to test validity and reliability are carried out by groups of foreign language specialists and testing experts from the language departments of the National and Kapodistrian University of Athens and the Aristotle University of Thessaloniki, who are appointed by the Ministry of Education. The administration of the exams is directed and regulated by the Central Examination Board (CEB), which consists of university professors who are experts in the field of foreign language teaching and testing and is also appointed by ministerial decree. The CEB, functioning in an expert consulting capacity, is responsible for the development of specifications regarding exam format and structure and scoring regulations and advises the Ministry of Education on matters regarding the development and growth of the system, exam policies and law amendments, new and revised regulations. Starting off with the assessment of B2 level in four languages (English, French, German and Italian) in 2003, the system has grown to include the assessment of two more languages (Spanish and Turkish) and exams on the basis of which all six levels of language proficiency may be certified (A1 to C2).

The development of the KPG exam system would not have been possible without substantial funding from the EU. More specifically, although the KPG in its initial stages was funded exclusively by the state, in 2007, upon approval of the grant proposal prepared by Professor Bessie Dendrinos, it received a substantial grant from the European Social Fund (75 per cent) and the Greek State (25 per cent). The project with the acronym SAPiG was implemented by three institutional bodies: (a) the Special Office for the Programmes of the European Support Framework of the Ministry of Education, (b) the National and Kapodistrian University of Athens, and (c) the Aristotle University of Thessaloniki. The aim of the project was to develop the exam battery for the four most commonly taught languages in Greece (English, French, German and Italian) and to introduce exams in a fifth major language (Spanish). Funded from March 2007 to December 2008, the project aimed at securing the necessary human and material resources for the system, producing a series of electronically supported data banks and operational programmes to safeguard and manage the data, as well as a comprehensive information system to be used by all involved or interested in the KPG exams. Building on the products and services produced as a result of the SAPiG project, a new project entitled 'Differentiated and (Inter)Graded National Foreign Language Exams' (with the Greek acronym DiaPEG) was secured for 2010–13. Funded also by the European Union and the Greek State through the operational programme 'Education and Lifelong Learning', it was carried out by the National and Kapodistrian University of Athens in partnership with the Aristotle University of Thessaloniki and in collaboration with the Computer Technology Institute of the University of Patras. Its aims, in brief, were to develop further the KPG exam system in order to include:

- differentiated exams which cater to the needs of candidates of different age groups, candidates with special needs, etc.;
- (inter)graded pen-and-paper exams for the three basic levels of language competence, that is, the A level exam (Basic User), the B level exam (Autonomous User), and the C level (Proficient User);
- (inter)graded adaptive electronic tests for all levels of language proficiency in all KPG languages;
- exams in two additional levels of language competence for Turkish, the most recently introduced language in the KPG system;
- distance learning and training opportunities to KPG examiners and script raters of all the KPG languages;

- connection of the KPG exams with the foreign language learning taking place in Greek schools;
- dissemination of information about the KPG exams to the general public and to special interest groups;
- evaluation and assessment of the quality of the system through internal and external procedures.

The structure and content of the KPG exams for all levels assessed are presented in the Appendix at the end of this volume.

PART I

Understanding and producing oral texts

BESSIE MITSIKOPOULOU, EVDOKIA KARAVAS AND
CHRISTINA LYKOU

1   The sociosemiotic language view underlying the design of the KPG exams

ABSTRACT

This chapter presents the sociosemiotic theory of language permeating the KPG exam suite and discusses the principles of this theory which have been used in test design. The KPG test papers in English view language as a meaning making system interrelated with the textual and cultural context in which it is produced. Influenced by this functional view of language, the KPG tests aim primarily at measuring candidates' ability to use the English language effectively in specific communicative situations and contexts. The chapter discusses some of the main features of the KPG exam in English which have resulted from this conceptualisation of language and illustrates its effects on various aspects of test design such as the types of activities and the choice of texts used in the activities.

A sociosemiotic view of language

The KPG test papers in English ascribe to a sociosemiotic view of language, and thus approach language as a social phenomenon that people use for a variety of purposes in order to take part in social practices. According to this view, language is always processed and understood in the form of texts produced by individuals in social contexts in order to serve specific social needs and requirements. Within this paradigm, language is seen as a social semiotic and a meaning-making system inextricably interrelated with textual and broader sociocultural contexts. Influenced by this functional view of language, the KPG modules are primarily aimed at measuring candidates' abilities to use the English language effectively in specific communicative situations and contexts.

According to the adopted sociosemiotic language orientation, words and sentences do not have meaning on their own, but their meaning is shaped according to the use of language in a particular communicative situation and under specific social circumstances. In other words, meanings are developed by the way in which language is used in specific instances of communication, and may also include non-verbal forms of communication such as images, diagrams, signs, and sound effects. Consequently, comprehension and production of meanings require knowledge of the various uses of language in different social situations and contexts of communication, as well as in different oral, written or multimodal texts (see *KPG Handbook* 2013). Therefore, KPG candidates are expected to show that they can use language to understand or construct meaning from different types of oral and written texts.

This view of language as a system of meanings accompanied by forms through which the meanings are realised (Halliday & Matthiessen 2004) prioritises the semantic level of language and approaches the relationship between the semantic and lexicogrammatical level as a relationship of realisation. Language becomes the most important means for construing and exchanging meanings in order to understand the world, ourselves and our relationships. As claimed by Halliday (1993: 7),

> it is the grammar – in the sense of lexicogrammar, the grammar plus the vocabulary, with no real distinction between the two – that shapes experience and transforms our perceptions into meanings. The categories and concepts of our material existence are not 'given' to us prior to their expression in language.

Thus, language is viewed as a theory of human experience[1] and as a principle of social action. The relationship between the act of meaning (Halliday 1993), that is the instance of meaning making, and the language system itself is crucial, as it assumes that the language system provides the semantic

---

[1]   Halliday (1998) has shown how the grammar of pain is construed in the English language. He claims that the vast variety of ways in which pain is construed in grammar shows the complexity of this domain of human experience and humans' attempt to comprehend and control this domain of experience, which is not only complex but is itself painful and often relentless.

dynamic for the ideological construction of a society in its entirety. Still, the argument goes, the acts of meaning determine which ideas, worldviews and ideologies are reproduced, depending on the lexicogrammatical elements chosen from the whole language system. In other words, the acts of meaning construe the language system, and the system defines the dynamic for each instance of meaning making.

Therefore, the notion of choice plays a significant role since it is acknowledged that the choices made from the semantic system of the language are socially and ideologically meaningful. The underlying assumption here is that each choice in the system acquires its meaning against the background of all the other choices which could have been made (Halliday & Matthiessen 2004). Consequently, different ways of using language are associated with different ways of meaning making which in turn construe different representations of reality (Halliday & Hasan 1989). Following this semiotic interpretation of the language system, KPG exams consider the appropriateness of different linguistic choices in relation to their contexts of use, and view language as a resource which we use to make meanings in various contexts.

Subscribing to the constructivist interpretation of language, whereby 'it is through our acts of meaning that we transform experience into the coherent patchwork that we learn to project as "reality"' (Halliday 1993: 46), the KPG exam suite follows the view that language and social reality co-evolve and that their relationship is a relationship of realisation. Hasan (1996: 22) argues that the categories of language correspond to what has already been construed by language and that 'whatever aspect of raw reality has not been articulated semiotically remains unknown'. This is the reason for suggesting that reality is not *found* but *shaped*, not *mirrored* but *constructed*. Ideology, therefore, is not viewed as a pre-existing entity but as construed in language and by language through its semiotic process. Given the semogenic power of language in construing beliefs, ideas ideologies, etc., in the KPG exam suite tests are not treated as value-free or ideology-free products but as apparatuses involving processes of ideologisation, just as, according to Dendrinos (1992), language textbooks do. The assumption here is that the texts and images which are included in the language proficiency tests have ideological inscriptions which linguistically construe different worldviews and social realities creating particular subject positions for the implied reader or test-taker. An illuminating illustration of this approach is provided by a critical study of the reading comprehension texts of three proficiency exams (two international ones, an American and an English, and KPG) by Balourdi (2012, see also this volume) in which different worldviews and task takers' positions are construed. As highlighted in Balourdi's study, contrary to a market-oriented world promoted by the American proficiency exam (Michigan), or a world of individualism and inner experience promoted by the English one (Cambridge ESOL Exams), the KPG exam suite promotes a more collectivised view of the world, as its texts construe a world that has special concern for environmental, health and social issues. What is more, in this world text participants are socially active citizens, members of national and international social groups and interested in environmentally friendly practices. The implied reader or test-taker is positioned as a seeker of truth and knowledge, in need of valid information, advice and guidance.

The sociosemiotic language theory which underpins KPG and its approach to language use also relate to the two unique characteristics that differentiate KPG from other international language proficiency exams: its glocal and multilingual dimension.[2] The view of language as a meaning-making system inextricably linked with the sociocultural context is in tune with one of the most important characteristics of glocal testing, namely the relocating of attention to language as an autonomous system socially and culturally decontextualised, to language users themselves as constant meaning-making agents who make choices from the semantic dynamic of language. Through such a perspective, as argued by Dendrinos (2013), the candidates' cultural experiences, areas of life-world knowledge, types of literacies and social needs are always taken into account. As a result, the topics chosen to assess candidates' written or oral productions and the

---

2   See the Introduction of this volume for a detailed account of the glocal and multilingual characteristics of the KPG exam suite.

topics of texts in the reading comprehension and listening comprehension modules are drawn from Greek users' life-world knowledge and experiences.

Moreover, viewing languages and cultures that people experience in their immediate and wider environment as interrelated meaning-making semiotic systems relates to the multilingual dimension of the KPG. It has been acknowledged that people use all their semiotic resources so as to communicate effectively in situational contexts, which are often bi-, tri- and multi-lingual. In such settings, people use code-switching (Shohamy 2011) and 'translanguaging' techniques, drawing on the resources derived from a variety of contexts and languages in order to create socially situated meanings. Thus multilingualism, as viewed in the KPG exams, not only refers to the endorsement of testing and assessing multiple languages in the same exam suite, but also, as Dendrinos (2012) points out, to allowing the disruption of the boundaries between the language, codes and semiotic modes and to facilitating the development of interlingual strategies and intercultural performance This is realised in the KPG exam suite through the inclusion of intra- and inter-linguistic mediation activities in the written and oral production modules (Dendrinos 2006, Stathopoulou in this volume).

Besides glocality and multilingualism, another aspect which differentiates KPG from other international language proficiency exams is its emphasis on multimodal communicative performance. Meaning making not only requires knowledge of the various uses of language in different social situations and contexts of communication, but also various multimodal texts (see *The KPG Handbook* 2013), since the texts used in the KPG exam, which can be either written or oral, include non-verbal forms of communication such as images, diagrams, signs, and sound effects. Thus, candidates function as meaning-making agents able to produce meanings from different semiotic modes. In particular, the visual mode is quite important. As claimed by Karatza (this volume), the visuals that accompany the KPG reading comprehension texts co-produce the meanings of the texts. In her multimodal discourse analysis of KPG reading comprehension texts, Karatza found a frequent use of intersemiotic cohesive ties and concluded that meanings in these texts are made through the interplay of verbal and visual modes.

The impact of the sociosemiotic approach on test tasks

The view of language described above is realised in the KPG English test. In particular, it is realised in the modules of oral and written production which measure candidates' ability to use the English language effectively in specific communicative situations and contexts. In addition, because the KPG English test is a localised test addressing people living and working in Greece, the preparation of its test tasks and items takes into account the various types of literacies, such as school and social literacies, that candidates living in the specific socio-cultural context are expected to develop. Thus the tasks in the KPG exams require that candidates be aware of the forms that the English language takes in the contexts in which it is used, and of the grammatical structures that make up these forms. This actually implies an awareness of what is appropriate and inappropriate within a sociocultural context and calls for the development of cultural knowledge, in addition to knowledge about how to operate the language system. As a result, appropriacy (i.e. whether the linguistic choices made by the candidate are on the whole appropriate for the context of situation as set by the task rubrics) constitutes one of the criteria in the rating scale for assessing candidates' oral and written production in the KPG exams. Consequently, comprehension and production of meanings in the KPG English test require knowledge of the various uses of language in different social situations and contexts of communication, as well as in different types of texts. Overall, it is expected that candidates have developed varying degrees of language, cultural and intercultural awareness.

Language awareness refers to 'the use of language through items and tasks that require candidates to make suitable and appropriate choices in terms of language use, genre, style and register' (*The KPG Handbook* 2013: 27). For example, candidates are expected to be aware that there would be a difference in style (i.e. in terms of formality, language forms used, strategies, etc.) between a summary of an issue written to be published in a newspaper and a summary of an issue presented verbally to friends, or a conversation with a teacher and a conversation with a friend. Language awareness is assessed directly through tasks in the Reading

Comprehension and Language Awareness test (Module 1) and indirectly through the Written and Oral Production tests (Modules 2 and 4 respectively). Example 1 below is characteristic of a language awareness activity in a B2 level reading comprehension test. In this example, based on their knowledge of various expressions containing the word 'good', candidates are required to demonstrate awareness of the use of these expressions in different communicative contexts.

Example 1: Language awareness activity (B2 level)

Use expressions A-F to complete utterances 1–5 so that they make sense. Use each option only once. There is one option you do not need.

A. as good as my word
B. for my own good
C. it's no good
D. make good time
E. have a good time
F. as good as gold

1. Speaker A: *I know that taking that awful medicine is ... ..., but this doesn't make it any easier.*
   Speaker B: *You know you have to follow doctor's orders.*
2. Speaker A: *If we ... ..., we should reach the airport by 11.30.*
   Speaker B: *I really doubt that.*
3. Speaker A: *Why don't you try to ... ...? Don't just sit there sulking!*
   Speaker B: *I can't help it. I feel really bad about hurting her. Maybe if she'd speak to me ...*
4. Speaker A: *.......... trying to apologise for what you did. The harm is done now!*
   Speaker B: *But I really didn't mean to hurt you.*
5. Speaker A: *I always try to be ... ... If I promise to do something, I'll do it!*
   Speaker B: *We'll just see about that. We'll just see about that.*

Cultural awareness requires knowledge of the sociocultural context in which the target language is used, since the way language is used is indissolubly linked to the culture in which it is produced, as language and culture co-evolve. In the KPG exams, cultural awareness is tested indirectly, from the way in which candidates are asked to use the target language; in other words, candidates are expected to demonstrate, according to their age and level of proficiency, a certain degree of familiarity with basic textual and communication practices, since language production depends on the context in which it is produced. In Example 2 below from a C1 level exam test task in English, candidates are asked to draw on their language and cultural knowledge of different ways of writing in different genres and communication practices and match extracts to possible publications. Grammatical and lexical choices, tone and formality, even typeface and ordering of information in a text, and generally ways of talking and behaving in a particular communicative situation function as indicators of the specific contexts in which these extracts may appear and thus guide candidates in their decision.

Example 2: Language and cultural awareness activity (C1 level)

Read the following extracts (1–7) and decide in which publication they might appear. Use each of the options below (A-H) only once. There is one option you do not need.

A. A book of quotations
B. Small ads section of a newspaper
C. A horoscope
D. An autobiography
E. An official United Nations document
F. A manual for electrical equipment
G. An encyclopaedia
H. Stage directions

1. At the beginning of the 19th century, the Balkan peninsula was ruled entirely from Constantinople, the centre of a multi-racial empire.
2. There is a continuous cold war between me and my clothes'. Malcolm Lowry.
3. Article 5. No one shall be subjected to torture or to cruel, inhuman or degrading treatment.
4. The wall, right, is almost entirely taken up by a pair of doors which open into another room. Upstage, left, a small door leads to a bedchamber.
5. Short term Volunteer
    Work overseas on development projects
    India, Nepal, Sri Lanka
    See www.HelpCamps or call Mario on 0210 8291 6181
6. *Warning*: this appliance must be earthed.
7. With the Moon in the relationship sign of Libra, romance can flourish on Friday and Saturday. A spirit of adventure grows as loving Venus enters excitable Aries on April 5th.

Moreover, it is taken for granted that KPG candidates are conscious of the ways the Greek and the foreign languages are used, since the exams are directed at individuals who live or have lived in Greece, know the Greek language, and are familiar with Greek culture. Thus, candidates' intercultural awareness is assessed indirectly from the way in which they use the target language to perform mediation tasks and relay information from Greek into English, thus acting as mediators. These activities are related to the specific social environment and draw on familiar, real-life contexts from Greek reality. The KPG exams assess mediation skills at B and C levels through writing and speaking tasks, and at A level through reading and listening comprehension tasks (see also Stathopoulou, in this volume). For instance, in Example 3 below – a C1 level writing mediation task – candidates are asked to adopt the role of a journalist who works on an online magazine and by using information from the Greek text about 3D printing to write their own text in English for the online magazine *Cutting Edge*. The same pattern is followed in the rubrics of speaking tasks. In Example 4 below from a B1 level oral mediation activity, candidates have been provided with a text in Greek on the topic of 'fengshui' and are asked to imagine that they are speaking to a friend who has just moved house and wants advice on how to decorate it. They are expected to choose pertinent information from the Greek text and try to persuade their friend that following principles of fengshui is important in setting up a new home.

> Example 3: Activity rubrics of a writing mediation activity (C1 level)
>
> Imagine you are a journalist for the online magazine *Cutting Edge*. Using information from the text below, write an article to inform readers about what 3D printing is and to present its practical applications.
>
> Example 4: Activity rubrics of an oral mediation activity (B1 level)
>
> I am your English friend who has just moved to a new house and wants to decorate it. Based on Text 1, tell me (*try to persuade me*) why 'fengshui' is important.

The underlying theoretical assumption here is that although texts are produced by individual candidates, these individuals always produce texts as social subjects who function within a specific social environment. KPG candidates taking the exams in English are therefore assumed to be informed social subjects, who interact with the world around them, and who have been exposed in their everyday lives and through their formal (first and foreign) language education to a variety of text types which they can actively analyse, reconstruct and reflect upon, when required. This view of the ideal candidate is very different from the one found in some international language exams, whose performance should resemble that of a native speaker of the language.[3]

Besides the deconstruction of the notion of the native speaker paradigm, the KPG exam suite also promotes the view of English language as a 'contact language', detached from its internationalisation and its view as a service and a marketable product (see also Pennycook 1994, Dendrinos 2013). Generally, an important point to keep in mind is that KPG candidates are expected to understand the standard form of the target language, in our case English, which the KPG exam views as pluricentric. To this end, it uses written and oral texts that are not exclusively in British English or American English. On the contrary, considering the impact of English as a global language today and its role as a lingua franca, or contact language, all level exams include texts which may be in standard Australian or Canadian English, standard English spoken in the USA or England but also perhaps in Ireland, Wales and New Zealand, India or South Africa, etc.

A genre-based approach to writing

The view of language followed in the KPG exam has also led to the adoption of a genre-based approach to assessing writing which stresses the social nature of language and builds on the understanding that while language is produced by individuals, speech and writing production and

---

3   See Dendrinos (1998, 1999) and Phillipson (1992) for the economic and political dimensions of English language teaching based on the native-speaking paradigm.

comprehension are socially governed. The underlying assumption of the genre-based approach adopted in the KPG exam in English is that people do not simply write to express their ideas but that they write as members of specific communities, producing texts which conform to different social conventions and rules. These conventions and rules depend on a variety of contextual factors, such as who is writing to whom and for what purpose, and in what discourse environment a text is to appear. The rules are institutionally bound and determine what kind of language is appropriate in each instance and how language is organised into text. Consequently, the adopted genre-based approach brings together language, content and context, and focuses on the ways words and structures are used to make coherent and socially meaningful texts. KPG writing activities create real conditions for language use and require that candidates use language that is both correct and appropriate to (a) the type of text candidates are exposed to, and (b) the communicative event in which they are asked to engage.

In particular, the KPG exam in English adopts the view of genres as both products (i.e. text types) and processes (linguistic courses of action).[4] On the one hand, genres as socially situated products are classified according to their social purpose and are identified according to the stages they move through to attain their purpose (Martin 1989, 1992). Each text type is viewed as encoding the functions, purposes and meanings of the social institutions of a particular culture (e.g. news report, letter, interview, promotional leaflet, novel, office memo, political speech, editorial, etc.) and is characterised by a relatively stable structural form (e.g. a particular beginning, middle and end) and a consistent way of organising information (e.g. in paragraphs or in bullet forms), which are shared by members of a community.

On the other hand, genres are processes: the result of the ongoing process of choices from the semantic potential of the language system in order to grammatically construe the social purpose of the text. Here there is an acknowledgment that what also differentiates one text from another is its

---

4   This view draws on Halliday & Hasan (1989).

social (generic) process, what it actually does.[5] In each text specific lexical and grammatical features and patterns are chosen which grammatically realise the social purpose of the text. For instance, a newspaper article that reports an event employs different lexical and grammatical features from a newspaper article that argues in favour of a particular policy. Viewing texts as formed out of the dynamics of social processes rather than just being determined by an overall social purpose, KPG approaches texts as variable and complex, as always in engagement with the potential for variation and change.

In fact, this notion of genre as both text type and process enables us to view writing as an attempt by the writers to communicate with readers, and raises our awareness of the ways language patterns are used in order to achieve a communicative purpose. It also suggests that texts are not viewed as products produced *ab initio* each time by individuals expressing an inner meaning, but are the effects of the actions of individual social agents acting within the boundaries of their social history, the constraints of the context in which they are operating, and their awareness of existing generic types (Kress 1989).

The underlying assumption here is that every time we come into contact with a new text (written, oral, visual, multimodal), we bring with us the knowledge we have developed from the interaction with all the previous texts we have encountered in our life – whether in our mother tongue or in another language; for instance, texts we have read, commented on or written. The familiarity we develop with different types of texts allows members of a community to identify similarities and differences among text types and to recognise relatively easily the type a text belongs to, such as whether it is a recipe, an office memo, a letter or a comic strip; or, to recognise the generic features of a specific generic process, for example, of describing as opposed to arguing.

5   Knapp & Watkins (2005) identify five main generic processes: describing (the process of ordering things into commonsense or technical frameworks of meaning), explaining (the process of sequencing phenomena in temporal and/or causal relationships), instructing (the process of logically sequencing actions or behaviours), arguing (the process of expanding a proposition to persuade readers to accept a point of view) and narrating (the process of sequencing people and events in time and space).

In addition, it is assumed that the lexical and grammatical features of a text are inextricably linked to its contextual features, since texts are the products of the contextual environment within which they are produced. Consequently in the KPG writing test in English, a text is always viewed as interrelated with its context, and it is suggested that one cannot be interpreted without reference to the other. For this reason, contextual features are always explicitly described in the rubrics (i.e. the instructions) of the writing activities. The contextual information given in the rubrics of the activity to a great extent determines the content, the organisation of the text and the kind of language to be used. For instance, in order to perform a writing task, candidates are asked to assume a specific role and address specific readers to convey a specific meaning through a particular type of text (genre) for specific communicative purposes. The aims of the writing activity are then to identify the degree to which candidates can use English in a socially meaningful way, and the extent to which they can effectively and appropriately address in writing a variety of different audiences (individuals, groups, organisations, a broader reading public).

For instance, in the C1 writing activity in Example 3 presented in this chapter (see previous section), KPG candidates are asked to use information from a Greek text given to them about 3D printing and some of its practical applications (topic) in order to write an article for the online magazine *Cutting Edge*. The communicative purpose of the article is twofold; first, the candidates are expected to inform readers about what 3D printing is and, second, they must present the practical applications of 3D printing, referred to in the text. Therefore, candidates are expected in their text to get involved in two processes: to inform their readers and to present some information, using a semi-formal style that is typical of articles of this type. In terms of text organisation, they are expected to produce a well-organised article to be presented in an online magazine with (a) a title, (b) an appropriate introduction, (c) a main body which begins with information about what 3D printing is and continues with a presentation of its practical applications with great detail and accuracy, and (d) an appropriate conclusion, possibly referring to the fact that 3D printing is a great technological advancement. In terms of cohesion, candidates are expected to use connective words and cohesive devices appropriately. Ideas in and across paragraphs should be coherently linked and flow smoothly. In terms of sentence grammar, candidates' lexical choices should be conducive to the content and the communicative purpose of the text. Given the advanced level, a wide range of vocabulary and complex grammatical and syntactic structures are expected, as well as the use of informative language. These expectations are drawn from the instructions given to candidates and constitute elements of the communicative situation and the context of the text to be produced by the candidates. They are also given as guidelines to writing assessors in order to help them in their evaluation of the writing activities.

The genre-based view also permeates the evaluation criteria of writing assessment.[6] In the rating scales for writing assessment, the first criterion is 'task completion', which evaluates the extent to which candidates have responded to the requirements of the task and have selected appropriate content, organisation, grammar and lexis depending on the situation in which they are writing. In other words, the first criterion, task completion, considers how a text or script, through appropriate lexicogrammatical features, responds to generic and contextual requirements in relation to the social purpose, the generic process, the theme or topic, the participants, and the text structure or channel of communication. For example, a newspaper article whose purpose is to report a racist event employs different language features from an article whose purpose is to argue against racism.

The second part of the rating scale includes criteria that relate to sentence and text grammar. At the level of text grammar, there are criteria which relate to cohesion, coherence, and text organisation. These criteria consider how all parts of the text are structured, organised and coded in order to produce a coherent and cohesive text, effective for the purposes of a particular communicative and social context. Candidates are expected to produce coherent texts by drawing on knowledge of how to organise and present their ideas from their previous experience as text producers and

6   For an account of the criteria for written production, see Mitsikopoulou (2013). Readers interested in the assessment criteria and marking grids may visit the KPG site for the exam in English at <http://rcel.enl.uoa.gr/kpg/script_train.htm>.

from their experience as readers. For instance, they know that events in a story are presented in chronological order, while arguments in an essay are often presented in terms of their importance (starting from the less important and moving to the most important arguments, or the opposite).

Finally, at the level of sentence grammar, the written production rating scale (which is common across all levels) includes criteria relating to accuracy, appropriacy and range of lexical choices. These criteria focus on how language is organised within sentences, dealing with grammatical features (e.g. appropriate use of prepositions, plurals, articles, agreement) and lexis. As stated in Mitsikopoulou (2013), different text types require the use of different types of vocabulary as well as a different range of vocabulary (or repetition), depending on determining categories such as topic, purpose and audience. For example, an academic report will use a range of technical vocabulary including nominalisations and technical noun groups; a literary description, on the other hand, will use descriptive verbs, adjectives and adverbs, and affective language in order to create an emotive effect on the reader. Raters should assess vocabulary appropriacy in terms of a specific text type and lexical range (for more advanced levels).

Conclusion

This chapter presented an overview of the adopted view of language as background reading for the chapters that follow. It also illustrated how the sociosemiotic view of language adopted in the KPG exam is materialised in the design of the tasks, the choice of texts and the assessment criteria for written production. The underlying language theory constitutes a unique characteristic of the KPG exam suite, which differentiates it from the other international language proficiency examinations. In fact, this view of language is in contrast to most international exam suites, which approach language as an autonomous, culturally and ideologically neutral system cut off from ideological inscriptions and disconnected from its cultural and social context – a view that promotes the internationalisation of the

English language and its export as a service and a product (see Dendrinos 2001, 2002 and also Pennycook 1994).

From the above description it becomes clear that the adopted view of language does not focus solely on rules of correctness but also on rules of appropriacy, by assessing a candidate's ability to comprehend and produce appropriate to the situation meaning. In doing so, it requires that candidates are aware of the forms that the English language takes in the contexts in which it is used, and of the grammatical structures that make up these forms. This actually implies an awareness of what is appropriate and inappropriate within a sociocultural context and calls for the development of cultural knowledge, in addition to knowledge about how to operate the language system. As we have seen, the KPG exam requires from the candidates the development of three kinds of awareness: language, cultural, and intercultural awareness. This entails a number of important effects: it makes candidates sensitive to the fact that in addition to accurate use of language, effective communication also involves appropriate use of language; it enables them to pay attention to features of language in use, and to understand that language use involves making choices about lexis, grammar, discourse structure etc; and, most importantly, it informs their selection of textual and lexicogrammatical features. Overall, by following a social view of language, the KPG test tasks focus on candidates' active and negotiated understanding, interpretation, and construction of meanings.

Bibliography

Balourdi, A. (2012). *World Representations in Language Exam Batteries: Critical Discourse Analysis of Texts Used to Test Reading Comprehension*. PhD thesis, submitted to the Faculty of English Language and Literature, National and Kapodistrian University of Athens, November 2011.

Dendrinos, B. (1992). *The EFL Textbook and Ideology*. Athens: Grivas Publications.

——(1998). 'Una Aproximacion Politica a la Planificacion de la Ensenanza de Lenguas Extranjeras en la Union Europea'. In L. Martin-Rojo & R. Whittaker (eds), *Poder-decir o el poder de los discursos*, pp. 149–68. Madrid: Arrefice Producciones, S. L.

——(1999). 'The Conflictual Subjectivity of the EFL Practitioner'. In A. F Christidis (ed.), *'Strong' and 'Weak' Languages in the European Union: Aspects of Hegemony, vol. 2.*, pp. 711–27. Thessaloniki: Centre for the Greek Language.

——(2001). *A Politicized View of Foreign Language Education Planning in the European Union. The Politics of ELT*. Athens: Athens University Press.

——(2002). 'The Marketisation of (Counter)Discourses of English as a Global(ising) Language'. In M. Kalantzis, G. Varnava-Skoura & B. Cope (eds), *Learning for the Future: New Worlds, New Literacies, New Learning, New People*, pp. 241–55. The UniversityPress.com (Australia): Common Ground Publishing.

——(2006). 'Mediation in Communication, Language Teaching and Testing', *Journal of Applied Linguistics*, 22, 9–35.

——(2012). 'Multi- and Monolingualism in Foreign Language Education in Europe'. In G. Stickel & M. Carrier (eds), *Language Education in Creating a Multilingual Europe*, pp. 47–60. Duisburg Papers on Research in Language and Culture, vol. 94. Frankfurt, New York, Oxford & Vienna: Peter Lang.

——(2013). 'Social Meanings in Global-glocal Language Proficiency Exams'. In C. Tsagari, S. Papadima-Sophocleous & S. Ioannou-Georgiou (eds), *Language Testing and Assessment around the Globe: Achievements and Experiences*, pp. 47–67. Vienna: Peter Lang.

Halliday, M. A. K. (1993). 'The Act of Meaning'. In M. A. K. Halliday, *Language in a Changing World, Occasional Paper, 13*, pp. 42–61. Canberra, ACT: Applied Linguistics Association of Australia.

——(1998). 'On the Grammar of Pain', *Functions of Language*, 5 (1), 1–32.

Halliday, M. A. K., & Hasan, R. (1989). *Language, Context and Text. Aspects of Language in a Social Semiotic Perspective*. Oxford: Oxford University Press.

Halliday, M. A. K., & Matthiessen, C. M. I. M. (3rd edn) (2004). *An Introduction to Functional Grammar*. London, New York: Arnold.

Hasan, R. (1996). 'What Kind of Resource is Language?' In C. Cloran, D. Butt & G. Williams (eds), *Ways of Saying, Ways of Meaning: Selected Papers of R. Hasan*, pp. 13–36. London, New York: Cassell.

Knapp, P., & Watkins, M. (2005). *Genre, Text, Grammar: Technologies for Teaching and Assessing Writing*. New South Wales: UNSW Press.

The KPG Handbook: Performance Descriptors and Specifications (2013). Athens: RCEL Publications.

Kress, G. R. (1989). 'Texture and Meaning'. In R. Andrews (ed.), *Narrative and Argument*, pp. 9–21. Milton Keynes: Open University Press.

Martin, J. R. (1989). *Factual Writing: Exploring and Challenging Social Reality*. Oxford: Oxford University Press.

——(1992). *English Text: System and Structure*. Philadelphia and Amsterdam: John Benjamins.

Mitsikopoulou B. (2013). 'Evaluation Criteria for the KPG Writing Test in English'. *Directions in Language Teaching and Testing*, 1. RCeL Publications: <http://rcel.enl.uoa.gr/directions/issue1_2e.htm>.

Pennycook, A. (1994). *The Cultural Politics of English as an International Language*. London: Longman.

Phillipson, R. (1992). *Linguistic Imperialism*. Oxford: Oxford University Press.

Shohamy, E. (2011). 'Assessing Multilingual Competencies: Adopting Construct Valid Assessment Policies', *The Modern Language Journal*, 95 (3), 418–29.

ELISABETH APOSTOLOU

2 Oral text difficulty in foreign language listening comprehension testing

ABSTRACT

This chapter reports on a study which investigated the role of specific text variables (i.e. linguistic, paralinguistic, and cognitive) in influencing test-taker comprehension in FL listening comprehension assessments. To this end, the listener's perspective was considered through an examination of quantitative and qualitative data elicited from actual test-takers and learners of English with reference to the oral texts included in the KPG listening comprehension test papers. The findings of the study revealed the combined effect of specific linguistic and non-linguistic variables on EFL users' perceptions of text difficulty. In this sense, they seem to bridge the gap with previous research which has elicited inconclusive or contradictory findings regarding the role of these variables in overall oral text difficulty. Implications are drawn for test developers and item writers of listening comprehension tests as well as for language teachers. Regarding the KPG exams, the findings could be of particular help to item writers of listening test tasks in making appropriate text selection decisions.

Introduction

This chapter draws on a broader research study which explored the effect of specific factors (item-related, text-related, linguistic and non-linguistic) on FL listening comprehension test difficulty. Its main stimulus has been the lack of empirical findings into the aspects of task design that can influence listening comprehension test performance and the ensuing need to highlight possible ways of improving listening comprehension exam materials, namely comprehension test items and the audio texts accompanying them.

This area of study is closely linked to Bachman's (1990) and later Bachman and Palmer's (1996) proposed framework of factors that can affect performance in language tests. They recognised three central categories of factors: test method characteristics, language ability and the characteristics of test-takers. The findings reported in this chapter seek to provide empirical evidence in terms of the first set of factors in Bachman and Palmer's (1996) framework (i.e. test method). In particular, it embraces their view that

> since we cannot totally eliminate the effect of task design characteristics, we must learn to understand them and control them so as to ensure that the tests we use will have the qualities we desire and are appropriate for the uses for which they are intended. (1996: 46)

Language testers have long held an interest in the factors that affect foreign language test performance, and several empirical studies (e.g. Buck, Tatsuoka, Kostin & Phelps 1997; Buck & Tatsuoka 1998; Freedle & Kostin 1999; Spelberg, de Boer & van de Bos 2000) have demonstrated the way that specific aspects of the listening test can be associated with overall listening comprehension difficulty. These studies have mainly drawn their findings from examining test scores through psychometric measurement tools, such as item analysis. There is, however, a dearth of research focusing on the investigation of task and text difficulty from the EFL user's perspective.

The present study focuses on the investigation of factors affecting the difficulty of oral texts as perceived by candidates and future test-takers. More specifically, it seeks to provide empirical evidence in terms of the role of specific linguistic, paralinguistic and cognitive variables in contributing to text complexity and listener incomprehensibility. Motivated by a lack of similar empirical research, the study examines the listener's perspective (i.e. test-takers and EFL learners) using two main methodological tools, namely candidate feedback questionnaires and learners' verbal reports.

In the following section, research relevant to this study is reviewed. This includes a discussion of the complex nature of the listening comprehension process and the effect of text-related factors on listening test difficulty. The research methodology section describes the procedure that was used to collect and analyse the data in this study. The two sections that follow offer a discussion of results from the analysis of the questionnaires and the verbal reports respectively. The final section discusses the implications of the study's findings for test designers and teachers and reflects on the strengths and limitations of this study.

Background to the study

Researchers agree that listening is a complex, active procedure that requires simultaneous use of knowledge, processing skills and strategies. They argue that it is an inferential process, in which the listener must use a wider variety of knowledge sources, both linguistic and non-linguistic, to interpret rapidly incoming data (Anderson & Lynch 1988; Buck 2001; Rost 1990). Buck (2001) explains that listening comprehension involves discrete elements of language such as phonology, vocabulary and syntax, but it also involves interpretation. Rost (1990) further argues that listening involves background knowledge and listener-specific variables, as meaning is constructed within the listener's background and in relation to the listener's purpose. What is more, the listening input is characterised by such features as speech rate, accent, elision, the placement of stress and intonation, redundancy and hesitation, which are unique to listening and different from one language to another (Buck 2001).

Regarding oral text difficulty, which is the main area of interest in the present study, the review of the relevant literature reveals the existence of a small number of studies which have looked into the effects of specific text linguistic and paralinguistic difficulty factors on overall task performance. The findings of these studies are presented below.

Linguistic variables affecting oral text difficulty: Syntactic complexity and lexical difficulty

Taking into consideration the findings of the relevant reading research, the body of FL listening comprehension research examining oral text difficulty from a linguistic perspective has mainly focused on discussing text length in terms of two related difficulty factors, namely syntactic complexity and lexical difficulty.

Blau's (1990) and Pica, Young & Doughty's (1987) investigation of the effect of syntax modification on listening comprehension showed that sentence structure is less significant in affecting text difficulty when the input is oral rather than written (Blau 1990: 748). In other words, simplifying the syntax of the oral texts did not have any effect on the performance of foreign language listeners. The specific finding comes in contradiction with the findings of the relevant reading research (Cook 1975; Lee 1964; Shiotsu & Weir 2007) which proved text syntax simplification an important predictor of test performance.

Regarding lexical knowledge and text comprehensibility, few studies (Bonk 2000; Nissan, DeVincenzi & Tang 1996; Stæhr 2009; Van Zeeland & Schmitt 2013) have explored the relationship of the two factors and their contribution to successful listening comprehension. The results of these studies showed a positive correlation between lexical familiarity and comprehension ratings, but the researchers concluded that listening comprehension requires less lexical coverage than reading comprehension. The notion that there is a difference between the role of vocabulary in reading and listening was also supported by Mecartty (2000), who found vocabulary knowledge to be more highly correlated with reading than with listening in a study of Spanish as a foreign language (cited in Saehr 2009: 583).

Paralinguistic variables affecting oral text difficulty:
The role of speech rate and accent

Regarding the paralinguistic features of the oral texts as unique characteristics of the listening test construct, speech rate has been the most researched variable in the relevant literature. In terms of the effect of speech rate on text difficulty, there has been a growing body of studies focusing on the effect of speech rate modification on L2 listening comprehension (Blau 1990; Griffiths 1990; Rader 1991; Zhao 1997). The specific studies elicited their findings by comparing test scores obtained under different listening conditions, after participants had been exposed to oral texts delivered at different speech rates. However, the derived evidence as to whether speech rate modification can have an impact on text difficulty was quite contradictory leaving this area of investigation rather incomplete.

In terms of accent and its potential effect on L2 listening comprehension in assessment contexts, there has been very little empirical research, the findings of which have been equally inconclusive. Pertinent research on this issue has explored the hypothetical advantage of L2 listeners who share a speaker's first language over others who do not. In other words, these studies investigated the role of non native L2 accents in listening comprehension (Ortmeyer & Boyle 1985; Smith & Bisazza 1982; Tauroza & Luk 1997; Yule, Wetzel, & Kennedy 1990). Across these studies, while a shared-L1 advantage was observed for particular L1 speaker-listener pairs, the phenomenon was inconsistent (Harding 2012: 166). Thus, some L1 groups find their own accent more comprehensible, while for other L1 groups, a particular native speaker variety was found to be equally as familiar as a shared-L1 accent.

As is clear from the research review above, the importance of the linguistic and paralinguistic text features in influencing FL listening comprehension is far from settled. Moreover, the majority of these investigations discuss difficulty on the basis of text analysis, by isolating and examining specific text characteristics. However, as far as language test performance is concerned, we would ideally want to see whether these or other characteristics are also related to the EFL user's perceptions of text difficulty.

Cognitive variables: The role of background knowledge[1]

A point of convergence among language theorists and researchers regarding the discussion about the complex nature of listening comprehension has been the role of background knowledge activation in enabling language understanding. Therefore, they have claimed that linguistic knowledge alone is not enough for achieving comprehension (Anderson & Lynch 1988; Buck 2001; Rost 1990).

By now, most research studies on the effect of background knowledge on language comprehension have been conducted in foreign language reading comprehension and to a lesser extent in listening comprehension. Therefore,

---

1   The identification of background knowledge as a cognitive type variable follows Purpura's (1999) conclusion that linking new information with prior knowledge constitutes a cognitive process-type variable representing the storing or memory processes in human information processing.

few empirical studies (Chang & Dunkel 1992; Hayati 2009; Jennings, Fox, Graves and Shohamy 1999; Jensen and Hansen 1995; Othman & Vanathas 2004; Sadighi & Zare 2002; Samian & Dastjerdi 2012; Schmidt-Rinehart 1994) have investigated the effect that background knowledge may have on listening comprehension task performance.

Most of the elicited evidence has indicated a positive correlation between background knowledge and successful performance leading researchers to support the facilitating role of prior knowledge activation in enhancing text comprehensibility and task performance. However, little is known as to how background knowledge can be used by listeners to facilitate the listening comprehension procedure. Buck's research (1991) was one of the few that confirmed the influential role of background knowledge by investigating learners' thought processes in understanding oral texts as elicited from verbal protocols. He maintained that listeners used background knowledge in two ways: either in order to understand unknown vocabulary and/or the syntactic relationships within sentences, or in order to draw inferences about text parts they had not understood.

Without doubt, additional studies are required to establish the relationship between background knowledge and listening comprehension in an EFL testing context. The current study, expanding on this line of research, tried to discover the effect of background knowledge on the listening comprehension of Greek users of English with reference to test material drawn from the KPG English exams. The following section turns to the present study, addressing the employed data collection methods and research procedure.

Research methodology

The main purpose of this study was to investigate the listener's perspective regarding the variables – linguistic (i.e. syntactic and lexical complexity, information density), paralinguistic (i.e. rate of speech) and cognitive (i.e. background knowledge) – that can influence oral text difficulty in listening comprehension assessment. It thus combined quantitative and qualitative data derived from three different groups of informants: candidates of the KPG B2 English exams, undergraduate university students, and B2 level learners of English preparing for the KPG exams.

Quantitative data: Candidates' questionnaires

Feedback questionnaires were administered to KPG B2 level candidates between the examination periods of May 2006 and November 2011 as part of a national survey conducted by the KPG university team with the support of the Greek Ministry of Education aiming at investigating the profile of the KPG candidates and their attitudes towards the exams. In total, 9,212 questionnaires were collected, processed and analysed. Table 2.1 illustrates the distribution of the analysed questionnaires per examination period to give the reader a clearer picture of the research sample investigated:

Table 2.1: Questionnaire survey sample

Exam period	May 2006	Nov 2006	May 2007	Nov 2007	May 2008	May 2009	May 2010	Nov 2010	May 2011	Nov 2011
Number	500	500	1000	750	750	2505	733	1079	888	513
Percent	10%	13%	13.5%	23%	11.2%	31.4%	10.4%	30%	12.2%	19%

$N = 9212$.

The questionnaires were in the form of Likert scales and were provided in the candidates' first language (i.e. Greek). They were administered on the day of the exams – right after the end of the exams and before candidates left the examination room – in examination centres throughout Greece. The questionnaires invited respondents to evaluate, among other things, the level of difficulty of the oral texts included in the KPG listening comprehension test papers. They asked them to rate the effect of certain text difficulty variables, linguistic and non-linguistic (i.e. lexical difficulty, information comprehensibility, speaker accent and rate of speech, topic unfamiliarity and lack of background knowledge and topic interest) on their understanding of oral texts.

The specific questionnaire data were made available to me through the Research Centre for Language Teaching, Testing and Assessment (henceforth RCeL). RCeL is a unit of the Faculty of English Language and Literature, National and Kapodistrian University of Athens, which, among other things, is responsible for the development of the KPG exams in English. Statistical and data analyses were performed using the Statistical Package for Social Science (SPSS), version 20.0 for Windows.

Qualitative data: Interviews and verbal reports

The qualitative data of the study were elicited in two successive studies, the first contributing to the design and development of the following one. More specifically, as part of the first study, interviews were conducted by the researcher using a controlled group of seven university students, whereas in the second study, self-perception open-ended questionnaires were distributed to a random group of 28 B2 level learners of English preparing for the KPG exams. The two qualitative studies aimed at shedding further light into the EFL listeners' perceptions of text difficulty by providing them with the opportunity to explain the kind of difficulties they are facing in responding to test items. Such evidence was needed to support and elaborate on the quantitative findings of the study derived from the questionnaire analysis.

Table 2.2 shows the profile of the research subjects used in the two studies. All participants were adults. In particular, the interviewees were undergraduate students of the Faculty of English Language and Literature, National and Kapodistrian University of Athens, who were attending a workshop on Teaching and Assessing Listening offered by the researcher as part of the Faculty's programme of studies. Their age ranged from twenty-two to thirty years and there was one participant who was over thirty. All of the interviewees were women.

In terms of the second group of research subjects, they were all learners who were attending a B2 level exam-oriented course of English at the Foreign Language Teaching Centre of the National and Kapodistrian University of Athens. Their age ranged from eighteen to sixty-seven years. There was an equal distribution between men and women ($n = 14$).

Table 2.2: Subjects' profile

Interviewees				B2 Learners			
Sex		Age		Sex		Age	
Male	0	18–21	0	Male	14	18–21	8
Female	7	22–25	6	Female	14	22–25	5
		26–30	0			26–30	4
		Above 30	1			Above 30	11
No. of interviewees			7	No. of B2 learners			28

The fact that the research subjects were all adults was considered to be an advantage for the purposes of this study as their high level of literacy was expected to facilitate the process of reasoning regarding their perceived difficulties. More specifically, the interviewees, as a result of their participation in the researcher's workshop, were expected to be aware of the variety of factors possibly influencing their performance, and thus provide meaningful explanations regarding the difficulties they encountered in the given listening test. On the other hand, due to their exposure to a variety of listening test tasks and audio texts as part of the exam preparation procedure, the B2 learners were expected to have enough experience so as to be able to evaluate the listening test material used in the study in terms of its degree of difficulty.

The data collection procedure employed in both studies was quite similar. It involved a test of listening comprehension the participants were requested to respond to, followed by the verbal report procedure eliciting their perceived difficulties in responding. In other words, the listening comprehension test served as a stimulus for the interviews and the open-ended feedback questionnaires which invited the participants to comment on and explain the specific text difficulties they experienced while responding.

The listening comprehension tests used in both studies contained listening material (i.e. test items and audio texts) derived from the KPG listening comprehension past papers. The specific material was selected on the basis of post-administration item analysis data. In other words, 'problematic' test items (either too easy or too difficult) were included along with their associated audio texts.

In the case of the first study, semi-structured interviews were conducted by the researcher individually with each interviewee. Since the interviews were not carried out on the day of the listening test, but a few days later, the interviewees had their listening test paper in front of them while being interviewed, so that they could recall the test material and consult the notes they had taken during the listening procedure. The interviews were carried out in the participants' first language, namely in Greek, as a means of ensuring a non-threatening environment in which the interviewees would express their thoughts spontaneously without considering the language errors they may make. The participants were invited, among other things, to explain what they found difficult or confusing about the audio texts included in the test and why. Moreover, they were encouraged to reveal the reasoning they engaged in when responding and the processes they went through. Each interview lasted approximately 30 to 45 minutes and was recorded. The recordings were transcribed and translated into English.

In the second study, the qualitative data were derived through completion of open-ended questionnaires associated with two listening comprehension tests. The decision to use questionnaires instead of interviews was mainly dictated by the efficiency of the first instrument in terms of researcher time and effort since information can be collected from a larger group of people in less than hour (Dörnyei 2007: 115). The test and questionnaire completion procedure lasted approximately one hour. Each subject was given the listening comprehension test along with the questionnaire and was instructed to use both of them during the listening process. The test procedure was kept exactly the same as in the actual exams as it was the researcher's intention to secure that the testing conditions would be as real-life as possible. The only difference was that the recording was stopped after each activity so that the participants were given some extra time to answer the questions in the questionnaire in terms of the test items they had just responded to.

Regarding the data analysis procedure, the verbal reports, either in the form of interview transcripts or in the form of responses to open-ended questions, were imported in N-Vivo 8 and analysed qualitatively. The analysis was carried out by selecting and coding (tagging) relevant parts of text in the verbal reports specifying the participants' perceived difficulties. With regard to text difficulty, the analysis specified a variety of difficulty variables which were organised under the following broader categories: linguistic factors (involving variables of difficulty associated with the language used in the audio texts), paralinguistic factors (involving features of spoken language such as accent, rate of speech, background noise, pronunciation, etc.) and finally cognitive factors (i.e. lack of background knowledge, memory and processing load).

In the following two sections, the results from the quantitative and qualitative analyses of the study are presented, while in the last section of the paper the conclusions along with the implications and possible limitations of the study are discussed.

Presentation of findings and discussion

Candidate questionnaire data

For the purposes of this chapter, audio texts from the examined KPG listening comprehension test papers that were rated higher (i.e. above 50 per cent) in terms of lexical difficulty, information density, rate of speech or accent and lack of background knowledge have been isolated and grouped in Table 2.3. In the exam administrations between May 2006 and May 2007, the dash (-) in the 'speaker's rate of speech/accent' and 'information density' columns indicates non applicability of the variables in the questionnaire data. Speaker's rate of speech/accent was evaluated as a difficulty variable in the exam periods from November 2007 and onwards, whereas the information density variable in the exams from November 2010 and onwards. On the other hand, the 'X' symbol in the columns indicates that

Table 2.3: Questionnaires' high difficulty rates

Exam periods	Audio texts	Lexical difficulty	Background knowledge	Speaker's rate of speech / accent	Information Density
May 2006	Language Museum	48.2%	53.2%	-	-
	South England	53%	55.2%	-	-
	Movie Extract	56.4%	52.6%	-	-
Nov. 2006	Robinson Crusoe	60.8%	59.7%	-	-
	Notting Hill	66.2%	68.6%	-	-
May 2007	Stonehenge	61.1%	53.2%	-	-
	August Wilson	66.3%	60.7%	-	-
Nov. 2007	Interview with a film producer	X	X	52.5%	-
May 2008	Brief audio messages	53.3%	49.9%	60.6%	-
	USA's Multilingualism	54.8%	52.4%	66.3%	-
	Aesop's fable	58.3%	54%	70.8%	-
May 2009	Three instances of talk	X	54.6%	X	-
	Cyberbullying	X	62%	X	-
	Aunt moves to Italy	X	58.7%	X	-
	Dislike doing	X	64%	X	-
Nov. 2010	Objects	X	X	X	52.1%
May 2011	What are they talking about	54.4%	X	58.4%	72.7%

the specific audio texts were not rated as difficult in terms of the specific variables corresponding to each column.

Starting from the text variables of lexical difficulty and background knowledge for which data have been available from all or at least the majority of questionnaires, the respondents' ratings showed consistency. As is evident in Table 2.3, many of the audio texts that were perceived as difficult in terms of lack of background knowledge were also rated highly in terms of lexical difficulty (i.e. South England, Movie Extract, Robinson Crusoe, Notting Hill, Stonehenge, August Wilson, USA's Multilingualism, Aesop's fable). This seems to suggest the interaction of the two difficulty variables in affecting text difficulty. An interesting observation to make based on the titles of the above texts concerns the association of many of these texts with specialised, less familiar topics.

Thus, the August Wilson text, perceived as the most difficult in terms of vocabulary use (66.3 per cent), concerned a specialised topic linked to American literature. More specifically, its content focused on the work of an eminent literary figure in American drama. Its language was expected to cause difficulty to the average Greek B2 level candidate, who as pupils aged between twelve to fifteen years were less likely to have been acquainted with foreign, that is, American, literature or art.

Cases considered to be similar to August Wilson were the texts Stonehenge, USA's Multilingualism and Language Museum. They were all scientific texts, providing specialised information and were normally expected to include more sophisticated language. Moreover, they were more likely to address the knowledge and experiences of a specific group of people (i.e. older, educated candidates). Taking into consideration that the number of adults taking the KPG English exam at B2 level is small as compared to candidates between twelve to eighteen years of age, the respondents' evaluations of the specific texts as very difficult in terms of language seems to be largely justified.

In contrast to the preceding texts, it was not the specialised content of the audio texts Notting Hill and South England that affected candidates' perceptions of high text difficulty in terms of lack of background knowledge and lexical difficulty, but rather their reference to topics that were not within a Greek context. Given the fact that the KPG examination battery is mainly addressed to Greek FL learners, it seems quite justifiable that both texts were rated so high in terms of background knowledge (68.6 per cent and 55.2 per cent respectively). It can therefore be assumed that audio texts which do not address the experiences of the FL listeners are equally difficult to process and understand. The similar high difficulty ratings in terms of lexical use (66.2 per cent and 53 per cent respectively) also provide support for the interaction of linguistic and non-linguistic knowledge in enhancing comprehensibility. Indeed, relevant research has shown that FL listeners need to learn to become more reliant on guessing from contextual or prior knowledge in order to compensate for difficulties with processing audio input (O'Malley, Chamot & Küpper 1989; Olsen & Hucklin 1990; Tsui & Fullilove 1998). Obviously, this assumption has clear implications for FL pedagogy. It suggests that language teachers will be able to enhance their learners' FL listening skills if they encourage them to activate strategies related to the use of their prior knowledge (i.e. inferencing, elaborating, etc.).

Exceptions to the above conclusions were provided by the audio texts Robinson Crusoe and Aesop's fable. The paradox in the results of Table 2.3 with regard to the two texts concerned the high percentage of respondents claiming lack of background knowledge for texts that they were expected to be familiar with. Indeed, with regard to the Robinson Crusoe audio text, almost 60 per cent of the respondents perceived lack of topic familiarity as a source of text difficulty. However, it was rather unexpected that neither the younger nor the older candidates had heard the story of Robinson Crusoe before. A similar conclusion can be drawn as regards the respondents' perceived lack of background knowledge for the audio text Aesop's fable. Considering that this text originates from Greek culture it is surprising that 54 per cent of the respondents claimed to have found the text difficult in terms of lack of background knowledge.

These discrepancies seem to reflect Vandergrift's (2006) claim that L2 learners are either unable to transfer inferencing ability from the L1 drawing on nonlinguistic knowledge resources (e.g. world knowledge), or are unaware that they are actually doing it. In our case, the candidates' inability to activate their presumed prior knowledge about the two audio texts, that is, Robinson Crusoe and Aesop's fable could be attributed to the high rates of lexical difficulty attached to them. Following Yi'an's (1998) finding that processing of linguistic knowledge is a more basic constraint to the activation of non-linguistic knowledge, it can be concluded that the respondents' linguistic deficiency had a constraining impact on the activation of their background knowledge.

Regarding the paralinguistic features of speech rate and accent, higher difficulty ratings were observed in the audio texts Brief audio messages, USA's multilingualism, Aesop's fable and What are they talking about. As is evident from Table 2.3, candidates' ratings of text difficulty in terms of these two variables correlated positively with their ratings in terms of lexical difficulty. In other words, the more difficult the audio texts were perceived to be due to speaker accent or fast rate of delivery, the harder they were to process from a linguistic perspective.

Finally, with regards to the feature of information density, the candidates were requested to rate their perceived difficulty in processing and understanding the audio texts they were exposed to. The introduction of the specific variable in the questionnaires was based on the assumption that the denser a text is, the harder it is for listeners to comprehend its content. The questionnaire data analysis provided evidence of increased perceived difficulty in terms of two audio texts (i.e. Objects and What are they talking about). Obviously, this finding cannot be used to make valid conclusions as to the role of this linguistic factor. An interesting observation though regarding the two audio texts perceived as dense in terms of content was that they were part of the short response comprehension activity of the KPG listening tests.[2] Provided that the specific activity is an inference one, requiring from the candidates to guess the requested lexical item based on text content rather than identify it in the text, this finding seems to suggest

2   The types of tasks used in the KPG listening comprehension test papers are divided into two broader categories, namely choice test tasks involving selection of the correct response on the basis of provided options and text comprehension and completion test tasks requiring production of a word or number of words on the basis of the listening input (short response comprehension activity). The short response comprehension activity was mainly an inference activity. This means that candidates, instead of having to listen carefully to a text in order to understand what word was missing in given sentences, were asked to infer the required word or words on the basis of their general understanding of specific aspects of the audio texts (e.g. guess where the speakers are, what each speaker's profession is, etc.).

that information explicitness has an important role to play on inference-making. However, further evidence on this issue was elicited from the learner's verbal reports which allowed a deeper insight into the listeners' perceptions of the specific attribute.

Learners' verbal reports

Despite the fact that an initial investigation of the quantitative data elicited from the KPG candidate feedback questionnaires provided some evidence of the effects of specific text difficulty variables, it was the qualitative information obtained from the analysis of the interviews which allowed a more comprehensive understanding of their role in listening comprehension. The elicited findings confirmed the combined effect of certain text-related factors, as the quantitative data indicated, but also demonstrated their interaction with specific listener attributes – such as processing skills, memory capacity and ability to activate background knowledge – in influencing overall listening comprehension test difficulty.

PERCEIVED PARALINGUISTIC DIFFICULTIES

Rate of speech was the most commonly reported difficulty in the learners' verbal reports affecting their text comprehensibility. More specifically, absolute unanimity was observed regarding the important role of fast speech delivery in text comprehensibility. Therefore, all the participants in the two qualitative studies claimed that due to the fast pace of speech of the audio texts, they could not retain in their memory the necessary information to choose the correct response.

> Q1: *Very fast rate of speech. You couldn't remember all the information you needed in order to respond.*
>
> Respondent B7

> Q2: *It confused me. The speaker spoke very fast, and I couldn't follow the information, so I responded using my common sense.*
>
> Interviewee 1

In these excerpts, the participants reflected on their inability to follow the speakers of the audio texts due to their fast rate of speech and half of the participants attributed this to their inadequate listening comprehension practice in the learning classroom and lack of exposure to everyday language being spoken naturally. They pointed out the following:

> Q3: *Oral speech was very fast and I found it difficult to understand due to lack of practice in listening to the foreign language.*
>
> Respondent B22

> Q4: *I have problem with fast speech rate because I'm not well acquainted with fast, everyday, authentic language.*
>
> Respondent B23

Similar explanations were provided with reference to the effect of other paralinguistic features (i.e. accent, intonation, stress) on text comprehensibility. Therefore, it was revealed that the participants' perceived difficulties in terms of the paralinguistic features of the oral texts were mainly due to their lack of exposure to authentic language being spoken naturally.

These findings seem to reflect the generally agreed assumption among researchers (Anderson and Lynch 1988; Arnold 2000; Lund 1991; Rost 1990; Ur 1984) that FL learners' insufficient exposure to authentic native-like speech serves as an additional obstacle to oral speech perception. Given the fact that the KPG listening comprehension test component involves authentic or semi-authentic material replicating real-life circumstances of communication, the research subjects' reported difficulties seem justified.

Interestingly, however, perceived difficulties were reported in terms of the combined effect of speech rate with the linguistic factor of information density. In other words, there was a consensus among the research subjects that what affected them most was the amount of information they had to process at a rather rapid rate, as determined by the speaker of the audio text. The problem was intensified in the case of text types densely packed with new information, that is, News reports, or by the presence of comprehension test items focusing on locating and understanding specific information in the texts, which involved the candidates in focused, detailed listening comprehension.

Q5: *In general, all these texts were loaded with information and this in association with the fact that the speaker spoke very fast caused difficulty.*

Interviewee 4

Q6: *A combination of fast speech rate and information load. You had to process a lot of information in very little time.*

Interviewee 2

Q7: *You had to be very focused because you did not have enough time to process the information so as to respond [...] and as new information is added you forget what you have already listened to and it's difficult to decide.*

Interviewee 5

Q8: *He spoke very fast and I couldn't focus on the specific information he provided. For example, I couldn't understand if he referred to an exhibition in general or to an exhibition taking place in Athens.*

Interviewee 2

From these excerpts it is evident that the participants emphasise the ephemeral nature of oral speech as an explanation for the effect of information density in combination with fast speech rate on comprehensibility. More specifically, they state that processing conditions (i.e. processing a lot of information at a rather fast pace) were a problem due to the time restrictions of oral communication. Consequently, the continuous flow of new information that they had to understand while at the same time combining it with the test items they were given increased memory load leading to information loss.

The participants' perceptions of text difficulty did not just pertain to the paralinguistic features of the audio texts, as, on the contrary, difficulties were also reported regarding specific linguistic text characteristics. In particular, many of the participants' comments (70 per cent) concerned the variables of information density and lexical difficulty. Interestingly, however, the verbal reports highlighted the joint effect of more than one variable, linguistic and/or non-linguistic.

PERCEIVED LINGUISTIC AND COGNITIVE DIFFICULTIES

Information density was perceived as one of the main factors causing difficulty to learners. As the learners' verbal reports illustrated, two main conditions intensified the problem. The first was that of text type and topic. More specifically, the participants suggested that informative texts (Language Museum, August Wilson, USA's Multilingualism, News reports, etc.) containing factual information about a topic were the most difficult to process as a result of their information density and non-linear rather abstract sequencing of ideas. In addition, they stated that the specialised topics (i.e. cultural, socio-political, economic, etc.) of some of these texts was an additional factor of difficulty rendering their content less easy to process and understand. Interviewee 1 explained as follows:

> Q9: *Density is experienced differently within different text types. For example, a narrative in which the events follow some sequential order, in other words the story has a beginning and an end, is easier than an informational text in which new information is built on previous one through less straightforward relations.*

The second condition concerned item type and the amount of reading work induced on the listener. Therefore, choice test items containing a lot of written information that had to be processed along with the listening input enhanced the processing and memory load leading to information loss and response failure.

> Q10: *The test items were comprehensible. However, the fact that you had to read them more than once at the same time as listening to the audio text and process all that information made them complex. Definitely in Greek it's easier because it is our native language, but in English, I don't know, it's more difficult to remember and choose on the spot as you have to move on to the following test item.*
>
> Interviewee 2

Focusing on the above excerpt it is evident that the respondents tended to associate their perceived difficulties as a result of text information density with their memory and processing abilities (Buck 2001). Therefore, they claimed that processing the incoming information at a rather fast pace as determined by the natural speech rate of the speaker of the text and at the same time retaining this information in memory in order to respond to the test items was the most challenging part of the listening procedure:

> Q11: *it was not only that information density impeded text comprehensibility. The fact that you had to think of the incoming information in terms of the answer options you were presented in the multiple choice test items and reach a conclusion as to*

> *which one was a more appropriate response was the hardest part of the listening procedure.*
>
> Interviewee 2

Q12: *As this was a continuous stretch of speech, you had to locate and isolate the pieces of information that were relevant to item response. However, recalling all this information is very difficult especially when the number of test items linked to this text is large.*

Respondent B15

Besides content density and information load, the participants in the studies identified specific problems with the language included in some audio texts. Sixty per cent of the learners reported lexical difficulty as an important problem in the audio texts. However, the analysis of their verbal reports indicated the joint effect of this difficulty variable with other text characteristics. Speed of delivery was one such characteristic for impeding meaning making even in the case of familiar words:

Q13: *Perhaps the words themselves were known but due to the speaker's way of talking and the text's unfamiliar topic, I couldn't understand them.*

Interviewee 4

The specialised topic of some audio texts was another factor reported to affect text lexical difficulty. In other words, it was found that the participants perceived those audio texts with which they were less familiar as more demanding in terms of vocabulary. With reference to the audio texts August Wilson, USA's Multilingualism and Language Museum, the following were reported:

Q14: *... there were words you hear once in 1000 years ...*

Interviewee 7

Q15: *... this text was full of unknown book names.*

Respondent B15

On the other hand, topic familiarity seemed to enable their linguistic resources and helped them anticipate the kind of language and the lexis expected in the text. As a result, the audio texts were easier to process and more comprehensible.

Q16: *Knowing that it [the text] was a narrative and that Robinson Crusoe was a shipwrecked who spent many years in a desert island, I expected to hear about this hero and his adventures, about ships, flags, clothes made from animals, etc.*

Interviewee 3

Q17: *I believe that the topics of these texts were much easier. And because the concerned everyday matters, they contained easier vocabulary. So yes it played an important role.*

Respondent B9

Q18: *It definitely helped, because I knew the words and it was a lot easier for me to answer.*

Respondent B7

Evidently, regarding the interactive relationship of lexical difficulty with the factors of fast speech rate and lack of background knowledge in influencing listener text comprehensibility, the verbal report findings coincided with the questionnaire data presented in the previous section. Thus, the learners' beliefs were concomitant in all three studies.

Discussion and conclusion

The quantitative and qualitative data analysed in this research provided evidence that FL learners attributed their problems in listening comprehension to the joint effect of several factors rather than to a single contributing factor. This seems to reflect the multi-dimensional nature of learner's beliefs towards listening in the foreign language. In this sense, earlier studies which have also investigated the FL learners' perspective towards listening comprehension are confirmed (Goh 1999, 2000; Graham 2006; Hasan 2000). Moreover, the complexity of listening comprehension text difficulty was reinforced. Specific text characteristics (i.e. speech rate, accent, text type, topic, information density and lexical frequency) were found to interact with specific listener attributes such as their background knowledge and processing skills in influencing text comprehensibility and response difficulty.

An important finding of this study concerns the interactive relationship of the linguistic and paralinguistic features of audio texts in influencing test difficulty. Therefore, KPG candidates' consistent ratings of text difficulty in terms of specific linguistic (i.e. lexical difficulty, information density) and paralinguistic variables (i.e. accent, speed of delivery) were further supported by the learners' verbal reports on text difficulty. This finding suggests that both categories of factors jointly affect text difficulty in listening comprehension. Therefore, although speech rate was found to influence candidates' text comprehensibility more than any other paralinguistic feature, its effect was intensified under certain conditions. One such condition was text information density. In other words, candidates' ability to understand was mostly impaired in cases of audio texts densely packed with information which they had to process at a rather fast rate. As was claimed in the learners' verbal reports, the continuous flow of new information, which they had to combine with the test items, increased memory load leading to information loss. In addition, the ephemeral nature of oral speech along with their limited exposure to authentic native-like speech in the classroom was found to intensify the problem. This finding warrants further investigation as it bridges the gap with previous research (Blau 1990; Griffiths 1990; Rader 1991; Zhao 1997) which has elicited contradictory evidence regarding the effect of speech rate on text comprehensibility. In other words, it can be suggested that the contribution of speech rate to listening comprehension task difficulty depends on the amount of information processing necessary for responding.

Moreover, the elicited findings regarding the role of background knowledge in listening test comprehension seem to merit special attention. Indeed, the learners' beliefs towards the role of this non-linguistic variable were concomitant suggesting that texts including culturally familiar content schemata were better comprehended and linguistically easier to process than texts whose topics were beyond the listeners' background knowledge. In other words, lexico-grammar, and as a result, text meaning are easier to deal with provided that the topic is familiar. On the reverse side, specialised texts referring to uncommon topics were associated with processing difficulties and had a significant impact on the listeners' ability to utilise their linguistic resources. As a consequence, many reported encountering unfamiliar vocabulary in texts they had no prior knowledge about. This seems to validate earlier considerations of listening comprehension as an interactive process between the listener and the text, presupposing use of linguistic as well as of non-linguistic resources (Anderson & Lynch 1988: 6; Buck 2001: 29; Rost 1990: 62).

Regarding the usefulness of the current study, its outcomes are expected to be particularly useful for item writers and test developers, who, being aware of the combined effect of specific text difficulty factors, that is, linguistic and non-linguistic, can take them into consideration in order to best exploit the audio texts they select for a specific exam level and, as a result, maximise the usefulness of the tests they design. In this sense, the findings are bound to be of particular usefulness to the KPG test designers of all languages tested in the KPG exam suite, that is, English, French, German, Italian, Spanish and Turkish.

More specifically, the learners' emphasis on speech rate as a factor of text difficulty is a finding that warrants test developers' attention and should be considered a criterion for text selection. What is more, the findings in support of the combined effect of speech rate with specific linguistic factors (i.e. information density) and listener attributes (i.e. processing and memory skills) can help item writers determine the degree of difficulty of a task based on the assessed exam level. For example, test items focusing on shorter stretches of speech that require processing of straightforward information are expected to be easier to answer as compared to items associated with texts densely packed with information requiring fast processing skills from the listener. Obviously, test items of the second category seem to increase the processing and memory load imposed on the listener resulting in response difficulty. Moreover, acknowledgement of the determinant role of text topic and background knowledge in text linguistic complexity can help item writers control the difficulty of the selected audio texts with regard to exam level and roughly estimate their appropriateness for the test's purposes.

On the other hand, the results of the study will be a valuable source of information for English language teachers who need to become aware of the factors that impede comprehensibility in order to enhance their students listening comprehension abilities. One such factor concerns the FL learners' limitations towards processing spoken language delivered at a natural speed. As language teachers are responsible for presenting learners with materials that will enhance their listening comprehension abilities, they should include audio texts that use spoken discourse likely to be found in real-life situations of listening comprehension. In other words, the classroom should provide learners with opportunities for authentic listening practice that will expose them to the language as it is spoken naturally.

Additionally, the findings of the study reinforcing the combined effect of many linguistic and non-linguistic factors seem to allude to the significance of strategy instruction in the EFL learning classroom. Hence, rather than depending on their language resources only, learners need to learn how to use contextual or prior knowledge to compensate for information they failed to understand or for information not explicitly stated, but implied. Without doubt, EFL teachers should draw their attention towards the teaching of test-taking strategies that will help learners be adequately prepared to achieve the best of their performance.

Unlike previous similar research on text difficulty focusing on text analysis, the originality of the present study lies in the fact that it considered the listener's perspective using three different groups of informants, that is, actual candidates of the KPG English exams, university students and B2 learners of English. However, there were certain limitations as well. The less standardised questionnaire content of the KPG Candidate Questionnaire Survey following the university test development team's range of research purposes over an extensive period of time led certain variables to be investigated less than others, thus resulting in less conclusive evidence with regard to them. However, the specific limitation was counterbalanced with the collection and analysis of introspective data focusing on the research subjects' perceptions of difficulty.

In the future, similar efforts to unveil what is difficult and why are bound to prove helpful for the improvement of listening comprehension testing practices in language proficiency examination suites as well as for the development of effective teaching practices. In this way, different groups of learners/candidates will learn how to effectively utilise test-taking strategies in order to overcome the difficulties involved in listening comprehension tests.

Bibliography

Anderson, A., and Lynch, T. (1988). *Listening*. Oxford: Oxford University Press.

Arnold, J. (2000). 'Seeing through Listening Comprehension Exam Anxiety', *TESOL Quarterly*, 34 (4), 777–86.

Bachman, L. F. (1990). *Fundamental Considerations in Language Testing*. Oxford: Oxford University Press.

Bachman, L. F., and Palmer, A. (1996). *Language Testing in Practice*. Oxford: Oxford University Press.

Blau, E. K. (1990). 'The Effect of Syntax, Speed and Pauses on Listening Comprehension', *TESOL Quarterly*, 24 (4), 746–53.

Bonk, W. J. (2000). 'Second Language Lexical Knowledge and Listening Comprehension', *International Journal of Listening*, 14 (1), 14–31.

Buck, G. (1991). 'The Testing of Listening Comprehension: An Introspective Study', *Language Testing*, 8 (1), 67–91.

——(1992). 'Listening Comprehension: Construct Validity and Trait Characteristics', *Language Learning*, 42, 313–57.

——(1994). 'The Appropriacy of Psychometric Measurement Models for Testing Second Language Listening Comprehension', *Language Testing* 11, 145–70.

——(2001). *Assessing Listening*. Cambridge, UK: Cambridge University Press.

Buck, G., and Tatsuoka, K. (1998). 'Application of the Rule-space Procedure to Language Testing: Examining Attributes of a Free Response Listening Test', *Language Testing*, 15 (2), 119–57.

Buck, G., Tatsuoka, K., and Kostin, I. (1997). 'The Sub-skills of Reading: Rule Space Analysis of a Multiple-choice Test of Second Language Reading Comprehension', *Language Learning*, 47 (3), 423–66.

Chang, C. A., and Dunkel, P. (1992). 'The Effect of Speech Modification, Prior Knowledge, and Listening Proficiency on EFL Lecture Learning', *TESOL Quarterly*, 26, 345–74.

Cook, V. D. (1975). 'Strategies in the Comprehension of Relative Clauses', *Language and Speech*, 18 (3), 204–12.

Dörnyei, Z. (2007). *Research Methods in Applied Linguistics: Quantitative, Qualitative and Mixed Methodologies*. Oxford: Oxford University Press.

Freedle, R., and Kostin, I. (1999). 'Does Text Matter in a Multiple-choice Test of Comprehension? The Case for the Construct Validity of TOEFL's Minitalks', *Language Testing*, 16 (1), 2–32.

Goh, C. (1999). 'What Learners Know About the Factors that Influence their Listening Comprehension', *Hong Kong Journal of Applied Linguistics*, 4, 17–42.

——(2000). 'A Cognitive Perspective on Language Learners' Listening Comprehension Problems', *System*, 28, 55–75.

Graham, S. (2006). 'Listening Comprehension: The Learners' Perspective', *System*, 34 (2), 165–82.

Green, A. (1998). *Verbal Protocol Analysis in Language Testing Research: A Handbook*. Cambridge, UK: Cambridge University Press.

Griffiths, R. T. (1990). 'Speech Rate and NNS Comprehension: A Preliminary Study in Time-benefit Analysis', *Language Learning*, 40 (3), 311–36.

Harding, L. (2012). 'Accent, Listening Assessment and the Potential for a Shared-L1 Advantage: A DIF Perspective', *Language Testing*, 29 (2), 163–80.

Hasan, A. (2000). 'Learners' Perceptions of Listening Comprehension Problems', *Language, Culture and Curriculum*, 13, 137–53.

Hayati, A. M. (2009). 'The Impact of Cultural Knowledge on Listening Comprehension of EFL Learners', *English Language Teaching*, 2 (3), 144–52.

Jennings, M., Fox, J., Graves, B., and Shohamy, E. (1999). 'The Test-takers' Choice: An Investigation of the Effect of Topic on Language-test Performance', *Language Testing*, 16 (4), 426–56.

Jensen, C., and Hansen, C. (1995). 'The Effect of Prior Knowledge on EAP Listening-test Performance', *Language Testing*, 12, 99–119.

Lund, R. J. (1991). 'A Comparison of Second Language Listening and Reading Comprehension', *The Modern Language Journal*, 75, 196–204.

Mecartty, F. (2000). 'Lexical and Grammatical Knowledge in Reading and Listening Comprehension by Foreign Language Learners of Spanish', *Applied Language Learning*, 11, 323–48.

Nissan, S., DeVincenzi, F., and Tang, L. (1996). 'An Analysis of Factors Affecting the Difficulty of Dialogue Items in TOEFL Listening Comprehension', *TOEFL Research Reports 51*. Princeton, NJ: Educational Testing Service.

Olsen, L. A., and Hucklin, T. N. (1990). 'Point-driven Understanding in Engineering Lecture Comprehension'. *English for Specific Purposes*, 9, 33–47.

O'Malley, J. M., Chamot, A. U., and Küpper, L. (1989). 'Listening Comprehension Strategies in Second Language Acquisition'. *Applied Linguistics*, 10, 418–37.

Ortmeyer, C., and Boyle, J. P. (1985). 'The Effect of Accent Differences on Comprehension', *RELC Journal*, 16 (2), 48–53.

Othman, J., and Vanathas, C. (2004). 'Topic Familiarity and its Influence on Listening Comprehension', *The English Teacher*, 8, 19–32.

Pica, T., Young, R., and Doughty, C. (1987). 'The Impact of Interaction on Comprehension', *TESOL Quarterly*, 21, 737–58.

Purpura, J. E. (1999). *Learner Strategy Use and Performance on Language Tests: A Structural Equation Modeling Approach*. Cambridge, UK: Cambridge University Press.

Rader, K. E. (1991). *The Effects of Three Different Levels of Word Rate on the Listening Comprehension of Third-quarter University Spanish Learners*. Columbus: Ohio State University.

Richards, J. C. (1990). *The Language Teaching Matrix*. Cambridge, UK: Cambridge University Press.

Rost, M. (1990). *Listening in Language Learning*. London and New York: Longman.

——(2002). *Teaching and Researching Listening*. Great Britain: Pearson Education.

Sadighi, F., and Zare, S. (2002). 'Is Listening Comprehension Influenced by the Background Knowledge of the Learners? A Case Study of Iranian EFL Learners', *The Linguistics Journal*, 1 (3), 110–26.

Samian, S. H., and Dastjerdi, H. V. (2012). 'The Relationship Between Prior Knowledge and EFL Learner's Listening Comprehension: Cultural Knowledge in Focus', *Mediterranean Journal of Social Sciences*, 3 (1), 361–70.

Schmidt-Rinehart, B. (1994). 'The Effects of Topic Familiarity on Second Language Listening Comprehension', *Modern Language Journal*, 18, 179–89.

Shiotsu, T., and Weir, C. J. (2007). 'The Relative Significance of Syntactic Knowledge and Vocabulary Breadth in the Prediction of Reading Comprehension Test Performance', *Language Testing*, 24 (1), 99–128.

Smith, L. E., and Bisazza, J. A. (1982). 'The Comprehensibility of Three Varieties of English for College Students in Seven Countries', *Language Learning*, 32 (2), 259–69.

Staehr, L. S. (2009). 'Vocabulary Knowledge and Advanced Listening Comprehension in English as a foreign language', *Studies in Second Language Acquisition*, 31, 577–607.

Spelberg, H. C., de Boer, P., and van de Bos, K. P. (2000). 'Item Type Comparisons of Language Comprehension tests', *Language Testing*, 17 (3), 311–22.

Tauroza, S., and Luk, J. (1997). 'Accent and Second Language Listening Comprehension', *RELC Journal*, 28 (1), 54–71.

Tsui, A., and Fullilove, J. (1998). 'Bottom-up or Top-down Processing as a Discriminator of L2 Listening Performance'. *Applied Linguistics*, 19 (4), 432–51.

Ur, P. (1984). *Teaching Listening Comprehension*. Cambridge, UK: Cambridge University Press.

Van Zeeland, V. H., and Schmitt, N. (2013). 'Lexical Coverage in L1 and L2 Listening Comprehension: The Same or Different from Reading Comprehension?', *Applied Linguistics*, 34 (4), 457–79.

Vandergrift, L. (2004). 'Listening to Learn or Learning to Listen', *Annual Review of Applied Linguistics*, 24, 3–25.

——(2006). 'Second Language Listening: Listening Ability or Language Proficiency?', *The Modern Language Journal*, 90 (1), 6–18.

Yi'an, W. (1998). 'What Do Tests of Listening Comprehension Test? A Retrospection Study of EFL Test-takers Performing a Multiple-choice Task', *Language Testing*, 15 (1), 21–44.

Yule, G., Wetzel, S., and Kennedy, L. (1990). 'Listening Perception Accuracy of ESL Learners as a Function of Speaker L1', *TESOL Quarterly*, 24 (3), 519–23.

Zhao, Y. (1997). 'The Effects of Listeners' Control of Speech Rate on Second Language Comprehension', *Applied Linguistics*, 18 (1), 49–68.

XENIA DELIEZA

3   The impact of oral examiners' conduct on
     candidates' performance in the KPG exam

ABSTRACT

One of the major research foci in oral language proficiency testing has been oral examiner's differential enactment of their role, since variation in examiner conduct has been found to result in unfair testing and assessment. This chapter presents findings from a large-scale study which investigated the frequency and nature of oral examiner involvement in the KPG B2 and C1 level speaking tests in English. It sheds light on and evaluates different types of examiner involvement at two levels of proficiency testing focusing on the effect of the test task on involvement. As such it aims to show how examiner involvement should be fully monitored so it does not pose a threat to the reliability and validity of the testing procedure.

Introduction: Oral language assessment and the KPG oral exam in English

Research on oral language assessment has been the centre of attention for test designers, applied linguists, language teachers and language researchers in the second language learning arena for more than fifty years. This is because oral language assessment is exceptionally complex and its complexity resides in the very nature of oral language, that is, speaking, which is critically dependent on context, fleeting, ephemeral and is 'essentially transitory' (Brown & Yule 1983: 14).

Despite the difficulties these features create, experts who are involved in second language oral assessment have tried to measure in a valid and reliable way the quality of oral production in a foreign language. Such measurement has been seen as a multifaceted undertaking entailing the definition of a construct, that is, the language ability expected in a particular testing situation, which also forms the basis for the inferences one can make from performances in a test (Bachman & Palmer 1996: 66).

In oral language proficiency testing the social dimension of interaction (McNamara & Roever 2006) plays a crucial role. Performance is jointly constructed or co-constructed (Kramsch 1986; Jacoby & Ochs 1995) by the many factors or facets which interact within the oral testing procedure, namely the candidate, the examiner, the task, the rater and the rating criteria (McNamara 1995, 1996, 1997). The examiner's principal role as interlocutor in the KPG oral exam in English is the focal point of the study presented here.

This oral exam is an unexplored area of research for various reasons. First of all, it differs in format from the traditional language or oral proficiency interview (LPI or OPI), which has been adopted by most high-stakes proficiency exam batteries and has been studied by many researchers. It is not an interview in the strict sense that the LPI is and has been defined through its own specific theoretical framework for language use (for details on this issue, see Dendrinos 2009, 2013). Second (and consequently), the KPG English oral exam has been developed on the basis of a particular language theory which views language as social practice, where language is used for a variety of purposes, that is, to perform certain functions. Thus, the context in which interaction takes place plays a determining role for the linguistic choices participants make (Karavas 2009: 24). Third, one of the most important results of early research on this oral exam had been the indications that examiners varied in the way they conducted the test, as they were then inexperienced and insufficiently trained. Further research into KPG examiner practices indeed revealed inconsistencies in the way examiners conducted the oral test, which were then largely amended through systematic training (Karavas & Delieza 2009). However, a variation in examiners' approaches remained detectable and one of the goals of the KPG training programme has always been to reduce the threat this variation may pose to the fairness of the testing procedure.

The findings reported in this chapter are part of a large scale research project focusing on the examiner variable[1] in the KPG oral exam in English.

1   Research on the KPG speaking test was conducted at the Research Centre for Language Teaching, Testing and Assessment (RCeL) of the Faculty of English

The study investigated what it calls examiner 'involvement' (as opposed to the term examiner 'variation') to see if, when and how examiners operate according to training instructions and guidelines, acting out the role assigned to them as 'silent interlocutors' or if they interfered or involved themselves unduly in candidates' oral performance. Moreover, it explores the consequences of such involvement in assessment so as to ascertain what sort of impact different degrees and types of involvement have on how a candidate's oral performance is evaluated and assessed.

After a brief review of relevant studies, a presentation of the two speaking tests, the oral examiners' training and observation programme, this chapter presents results per level-test with a view to highlighting the effect of task type on examiner involvement. Implications of these results will also be discussed for examiner training as well as the types of tasks used in oral tests.

Literature review

The examiner variable in oral language proficiency testing

As indicated above, studies on various testing systems and oral examinations (Bachman et al. 1995; Brown 2003; 2005; Brown et al. 2005; Brown & Hill 2007; Brown & Hill 1997; Brown & Lumley 1997; Kasper & Ross 2007; Lazaraton 1996a, 1996b; Malone 2003; Malvern & Richards 2002; Merrilees & McDowell 1999; Reed & Halleck 1997; Young & Milanovic 1992; to name just a few) mostly investigate what they call interviewer or examiner 'variation'.

Most of this examiner 'variation' research is conducted with LPIs or oral tests where examiner conduct is to some extent uncontrolled. Since

Language and Literature, National and Kapodistrian University of Athens where the author worked as a researcher and member of the team responsible for developing the English KPG exam and also conducted the relevant PhD study.

interviewers are also mostly teachers (as well as native or near-native speakers) of the language being assessed, they often take the liberty of developing parts of the interview in different ways; as a result, there may be a variation in the way, for instance, they ask questions or set tasks or provide help. In one of the many relevant studies, Lazaraton (1996b) draws attention to findings that prove the existence of inconsistency in the amount of support given by interlocutors to candidates and raises concerns about both the impact of such support on a candidate's language production and the evaluation of such production. Brown (2003: 3) lists different aspects of behaviour in which interlocutors have been found to vary, for example, speech accommodation, topic development and expansion, and level of rapport with the candidates; she explains that designers of oral tests which utilise conversational interviews of 'unscripted and relatively unstructured format' (2003: 1) boast about their efficiency as valid measures of conversational communicative competence and then she argues that 'the unpredictability and dynamic nature of the interaction' (2003: 2) taking place therein sacrifices reliability in favour of validity. Ross (2007: 2042), using the OPI in a Japanese context, found different interaction styles and variation in the way examiners were inclined to 'backchannel, accommodate, [and] audit candidate language'. Brown (2005: 244) explored the IELTS speaking test and found variations in examiners' behaviour along a number of dimensions, namely, topic, functional challenge, questioning technique, accommodation and rapport. Brown and Lumley (1997: 146) refer to 'reformulation' or 'syntactic simplification' as a feature of examiner behaviour which may render the test easier for examinees. Similarly, Lazaraton (1996b: 159, 160) refers to 'supplying vocabulary or engaging in collaborative completions' as a form of support which may make the candidates' 'proficiency appear artificially inflated'. Alderson et al. (1995) recognise uncontrolled variation in examiners' performance as an issue of test validity on the grounds that such variation interferes with the capability of the test to appropriately measure what it is supposed to measure.

As already stated, many studies are conducted with LPIs or oral tests which are to some extent unstructured, thus allowing improvisation on the part of the interviewer. Such a characteristic enhances their validity as measures of conversational skills because it allows them to better reflect the free nature of real-life conversations. However, in his very influential study, van Lier (1989) supports the idea that by definition there are significant differences between LPIs and real-life conversations and that the kind of discourse produced in LPIs is a unique product of the interview situation. In other words, interview discourse does not reflect non-test interaction, due to the asymmetrical nature of the examiner-candidate communication, resulting in what has frequently been classified as 'test genre' (van Lier 1989; Perret 1990; Lazaraton 1991, 1992; Johnson 2001). For example, in an oral test there might be no conversational interaction similar to real-life conversations, at least between examiner and candidate. This proposition further enhances the view that examiners should be somewhat controlled and restrict themselves to their institutional role of delivering questions and/or tasks. It is also one reason why researchers and test designers have increasingly looked into and used the paired or group interview or paired activity within oral tests (Fulcher 1996; Iwashita 1998; Csépes 2002; O'Sullivan 2002; Bonk & Ockey 2003; Nakatsuhara 2006; Brooks 2009; Ducasse and Brown 2009; May 2006, 2009, 2010), where the role of examiners is reduced to that of a listener and monitor and where peer-peer interaction can take place. Finally, the interlocutor script has been introduced in oral examinations as a means of controlling examiner variation (Galaczi and ffrench 2011; May 2010; Roshan 2013; Delieza 2014; De Jong and Banerjee 2016).

Background of the study

The KPG speaking test

The research has drawn data from Module 4, Oral Production and Mediation, of the KPG exam in English at B2 and C1 levels. In this exam, examiners are mainly non-native speakers of English (but well qualified EFL teachers). Their role has been specifically defined and described separately for each level of the speaking test procedure. Table 3.1 presents the content and structure of the KPG B2 and C1 speaking tests.[2] In terms of

2   Table 3.1 describes the content and structure of the two levels as these were administered when the study was conducted and the data collected. Today, B2 is administered together with B1 as an intergraded exam, but has not changed in terms of

Table 3.1: The content and structure of the KPG B2 and C1 speaking tests

B2	C1
Duration of the test	
15–20 minutes	20–25 minutes
Pattern of participation	
Candidates are tested in pairs but do not converse with each other.	Candidates are tested in pairs and converse with each other.
Content of the test	
Warm-up (not assessed – 2 minutes): examiner asks each candidate a few ice-breaking questions (eg. age, studies/work, hobbies)	Warm-up (not assessed – 2 minutes): examiner asks each candidate a few ice-breaking questions (eg. age, studies/ work, hobbies)
Activity 1: Dialogue (3–4 minutes) between examiner and each candidate individually, who answers questions posed by the examiner about him/ herself and his/ her environment.	Activity 1: Open-ended response (4 minutes): ehe candidate responds to a single question posed by the examiner, expressing and justifying his/ her opinion about a particular issue /topic.
Activity 2: One-sided talk (5–6 minutes) by each candidate individually, who develops a topic on the basis of a visual prompt.	Activity 2: Mediation (15 minutes): candidates carry out a conversation in order to complete a task, using input from a Greek text.
Activity 3: Mediation (5–6 minutes) by each candidate individually, who develops a topic based on input from a Greek text.	

examination procedure, in both level tests two candidates enter the examination room and are examined by one examiner, the interlocutor, while another examiner, the rater, is also present.[3]

According to Table 3.1, apart from the obvious differences in the test tasks between the speaking tests at the two levels, what is important for

_____

format, while C1 is administered as an integrated exam with C2 and has changed considerably. For the specifications of the two oral tests at the time the study was conducted, please see KPG B2 Level Exam Specifications (2007) and KPG C1 Level Exam Specifications (2007) or visit <http://rcel.enl.uoa.gr/kpg/gr_exam_specif.htm>.

3   This second examiner observes the testing procedure and only assigns marks; s/he does not participate in the speech event. At the end of the test, the examiner who conducts the interview also marks the two candidates.

the purposes of this study is that the role of the examiner-as-interlocutor also differs. At B2 level, the examiner has been instructed to read out the questions (Activity 1) and tasks (Activities 2 and 3) to each of the two candidates, thus interacting with each one of them in turn. During the B2 level speaking test candidates do not speak to each other at all. On the other hand, at C1 level, while the examiner reads out one question (for each test-taker) in Activity 1, thus interacting with each of the two candidates in turn (as at B2 level), in Activity 2 s/he becomes a listener while the candidates interact in order to reach a decision or solve a set problem on the basis of input presented in reading texts in Greek.

Examiners as interlocutors are rather 'controlled' in that they are given specific questions and tasks to deliver without engaging in a process of discussion or taking initiative away from the instructions. An Interlocutor Script has also been introduced as a means of reducing variation in the talk of examiners as interlocutors. Towards this end, one more step has been taken based on the findings from the Observation Project (see below). Examiners were supplied with a list of 'acceptable' and 'non-acceptable' types of involvement, that is, discourse practices which may simply encourage candidates to speak or to complete their answer as opposed to practices that may affect the quality and/or quantity of the candidate's language output, thus threatening score interpretation and intra-candidate fairness.[4] (See Appendix I, Table 3.6 for the full, original list of acceptable and non-acceptable types of involvement.)

The Oral Examiner Training Programme

The Oral Examiner Training Programme for KPG Exams in English has been one of the most challenging projects undertaken by the RCeL (Karavas 2009). Since the launch of the KPG exam system, the training of examiners has been systematic and seminars take place all over Greece just before

---

4   In other words, a distinction was drawn between involvement which supports the candidates' efforts to produce language without providing or altering the language required by the question or task, and involvement which either makes language available to the candidates and/or makes some kind of change to the question or task as a whole.

each exam cycle, but also in between periods. By December 2015 more than 3,000 examiners were trained in assessing candidates' oral performance at A1/A2, B1/B2, C1/C2 levels.

Each seminar takes place with groups of a maximum of 18 to 20 people to enable dialogue, discussion and group work. For each round of training seminars a new, tailor made oral examiner training pack and accompanying videos with simulations of the oral test are developed by a group of experienced teacher educators from the RCeL who are also involved in designing the oral test. The oral examiner training seminars are conducted by this group and a body of 50 'multipliers' throughout Greece. Before each round of training seminars begins, multipliers are invited to a one day seminar in Athens or Thessaloniki during which they are informed of the aims, content and structure of the training seminar and are trained to use the seminar materials. Depending on where they live and their mobility, they are assigned groups of oral examiners and have the responsibility of setting a date and place for the seminar, contacting the oral examiners and photocopying the training material; after each seminar they are requested to provide an evaluation report on the seminar noting any cases of absence and providing details of problems and issues raised in the seminar.

The training programme has a series of stages presented below which all oral examiners need to go through:

- Recruitment (applications), initial screening, inclusion in database.
- Initial evaluation of oral performance and induction (applies once to an applicant oral examiner).
- Training seminars (recurrent and cyclical since the outcomes of monitoring and evaluation feed into training).
- Monitoring of the oral test and evaluation of examiners' performance by multipliers through specially designed observation schemes.

Thus, training seminars are recurrent and cyclical. Their content is constantly updated on the basis of findings and results from the monitoring of the speaking test (through Oral Examiner Feedback Forms completed after the end of speaking tests administration) and the evaluation of examiners' performance through real-time observation of speaking tests.

The Observation Project

On-site observation of the speaking test was launched in November 2005. 'The initial overall goals of the observation project were to gain information about the efficiency of the oral exam administration, the efficiency of oral examiner conduct, applicability of the oral assessment criteria and inter rater reliability' (Karavas & Delieza 2009: 8). Since then, it has been conducted in five more phases, providing invaluable information about organisational and procedural issues and most importantly about oral examiner conduct 'in an attempt to identify whether and to what extent examiners adhere to exam guidelines and the suggested oral exam procedure' (ibid. 8).

Observations were carried out in actual administrations of the KPG oral exam in English, in a random sample of examination centres throughout Greece, by multipliers who were especially trained to use observation forms and carry out observations. Observation forms are clearly defined, structured checklists which were designed on the basis of categories and subcategories related to the oral test rules and guidelines which concern both the procedure and examiner conduct. (For more information on the Observation Project, see Karavas 2008; Karavas & Delieza 2009; Delieza 2012, 2013, 2014).

Purpose of the study and methodology

As already stated, the study attempted to gain new insights into examiner involvement in all the test tasks of two different speaking tests and levels of the KPG oral exam in English. The rest of this chapter presents findings in response to a basic research question:

> What types of examiner involvement can be found during the KPG speaking tests?
> What is the frequency of occurrence for each type?

It also seeks to evaluate the impact of these types of examiner involvement on candidates' performance. This is achieved, more specifically, by identifying which types of involvement affect performance by helping candidates in their oral production and which types of involvement successfully resolve misunderstandings or problems or even add to the real-life-conversational nature (if any) of the speaking test without being a potential source of measurement error.

Furthermore, since the study was an in-depth investigation into and comparison of examiner involvement in two levels of foreign language proficiency, the findings are compared both within each level of proficiency individually – that is, each test task included in the two speaking tests – and among the test tasks of the two levels; thus, the chapter examines whether the level assessed and the types of test task impinge on the findings.

Data collection and analysis

In view of the complexity of oral assessment and the highly qualitative nature of the data used in the present research, a mixed- or multi-method approach (Cohen et al. 2011: 195; Dörnyei 2007: 164) to data collection and analysis was used to ensure the reliability of results. Three types of research methods were used, two of which are relevant to the findings presented in this chapter, namely observation of actual examinations and statistical analysis of the collected data, and combined discourse and conversation analysis of simulated speaking tests.

More specifically, this study initially drew data from the KPG English Oral Exam Observation Project (2005–8) (Delieza 2013). Observations carried out in two of these exam cycles (May and November 2007) were chosen as relevant to the objectives of the present research in terms of goals and content. In these two observation periods, the observation forms, that is, the tools for data collection, comprised questions relating to examiner intervention, which was the term used in the observation project and later replaced by examiner 'involvement'.

The May 2007 observation form and analysis shed light on the types of examiner intervention, focusing on their categorisation and evaluation, while the frequency of different types was also reported and commented.

On the basis of previous observation findings, 'intervention' had been defined to include two main categories of linguistic behaviour by the examiner: the linguistic change of questions or task rubrics and interruption of or the interference with the candidate's linguistic output. These two constituted the umbrella categories and each comprised several distinct types of intervention; for example, use of an introductory question or expansion of the original question or task under the first category and making a correction or repeating part of the question or task under the second category. Some of these types were acceptable, for example, repeating part of the question or task, while others were non-acceptable, for example, expansion of the original question or task. (See Appendix I, Table 3.6 for acceptable and non-acceptable types of involvement.)

Data from the November 2007 observation form and analysis was again collected about types of examiner intervention and their frequency. One of the differences from the May 2007 observation form was that while only the two umbrella categories were used, they were redefined to include only the non-acceptable types. Thus, observers were asked to record only non-acceptable changes to tasks or questions and interruptions or interferences, for example, correction or expansion but not repetition.

In the second stage of this study, the data used were drawn from a non-operational administration, that is, simulations, of the KPG speaking tests in English, in which 14 learners of English at B2 level and 15 at C1 level were interviewed in pairs by one examiner simulating the KPG speaking test procedure. The speaking tests (seven for the B2 level and seven for the C1) were video-taped and then transcribed. Thus, the discourse of actual examinations was available for analysis as opposed to the information from observations of actual examinations, as here it was only possible to access what observers had detected and noted. A combined method of discourse and conversation analysis was utilised with a view to studying examiner involvement. Thus, the two umbrella categories of examiner involvement from observation were abandoned, and ten distinct types were adopted for the analysis, for example, expansion, repetition, correction, etc. Also, exemplification was given for all types of involvement, which also allowed for further evaluation and sounder conclusions.

Findings: Types of examiner involvement: Quantity and quality

This section presents a synthesis of some of the findings from two of the phases of the Observation Project. These findings concern the different types of examiner involvement and the frequency of their occurrence per level and task type, and include comparisons and conclusions regarding the effect of task type on examiner involvement.

Results from observation

The B2 level oral exam

Based on the findings from the first two observation phases (May and November 2007), examiner involvement, called 'intervention', was analysed using two basic categories, namely changes of questions or task rubrics and interruption of or interference with a candidate's linguistic output. Table 3.2 presents the frequency of examiner intervention per category for each activity of the B2 level speaking test from both Observation Projects.[5] As explained in the data collection and analysis section, the observation tools and objectives of the two phases differed. However, comparisons and conclusions are possible.

In May 2007, acceptable or non-acceptable types of intervention were investigated and statistically analysed. In Table 3.2, the May 2007 results include the percentages for non-acceptable types (in italics) which have been set apart so that the comparison with November 2007 is easier.

Concerning the first main intervention category, *changes to the rubrics*, the vast majority of changes were non-acceptable (Appendix II, Table 3.7).

5   In Appendix II, Table 3.7 and Table 3.9 present frequencies for the sub-types of the two basic categories of intervention in May 2007.

Table 3.2: Frequencies of examiner intervention per test task in the B2 speaking test in May 2007 and November 2007 observation phases

May 2007 Intervention per test task	B2 (588 observed cases in total)		
	Activity 1	Activity 2	Activity 3
Changes to the rubrics	57.5% (338)	31% (184)	33% (194)
only non-acceptable types	*54%*	*27%*	*30.4%*
Interruptions and/or interferences	20.5% (121)	33.5% (198)	28.5% (168)
only non-acceptable types	*9.2%*	*15.8%*	*10.5*
November 2007 Intervention per test task *(only non-acceptable types)*	B2 (514 observed cases in total)		
	Activity 1	Activity 2	Activity 3
Changes to the rubrics	30% (155)	23% (117)	22% (112)
Interruptions and/or interferences	25% (128)	40% (204)	30% (152)

Most frequently, examiners in the B2 level speaking test were found to 'use an introductory question' and present an 'expansion' of the given question, in Activity 1;[6] there were also high percentages for 'expansion' in Activities 2 and 3, and 'changes of word(s)' in Activity 3. It was also found that in Activity 1, examiners made up entirely 'new questions'. Among the acceptable types of intervention, which were rather scarce (and are found under the type 'other') was 'repetition'.[7]

As regards the second umbrella category, interruption or interference with the candidate's language output, most types that were found were

6   For instance, for the question 'Tell us about a happy day or moment in your life'. *expansion* would be 'You can talk about people who were with you or a particular place or an anniversary'.

7   Under both umbrella categories in May 2007, except for specific sub-types given, there was a type called 'other', where observers noted types not already included in the given list. Such types were also analysed and counted, so as to be further classified as acceptable or non-acceptable types. Table 3.8 and Table 3.10, included in Appendix II, present frequencies for acceptable or non-acceptable 'other' types.

acceptable practices (Appendix II, Table 3.9). More specifically, 'redirect-ing the candidate by repeating part of the task' was the most frequent type found in all three activities. On the other hand, non-acceptable interven-tion was found in the type 'other', and its presence was not negligible: there was a somewhat frequent 'use of additional questions', mainly in Activity 2 (i.e. 10.05 per cent, see Appendix II, Table 3.10).

The second observation phase of November 2007 only addressed non-acceptable types of intervention, and did so solely in terms of the two umbrella categories, namely changes to rubrics and interruption of or interference with the candidate's language output, while no sub-types were included. With reference to changes to rubrics, the most frequent instances occurred in Activity 1; but they were also quite frequent in the other two activities as well. However, the highest percentage appears in the second general category in Activity 2.

Percentages in November 2007 can be compared with the percentages for non-acceptable practices in May 2007 (marked in italics in Table 3.2). Activity 1, where the examiner asks 2 to 4 personal questions to candidates, presents the highest frequency of changes to the rubrics in both phases (54 per cent in May and 30 per cent in November), Activities 2 and 3 fol-lowing with similar frequencies in the two observation data (27 per cent and 30 per cent in May and 23 per cent and 22 per cent in November, respectively). Also, Activity 2, where the candidate is asked to carry out a task on the basis of visual input, is the most popular context for inter-ruptions/ interferences: 15.8 per cent in May (as opposed to Activity 1, 9.2 per cent; and Activity 3, 10.5 per cent) and 40 per cent in November (as opposed to Activity 1, 25 per cent; and Activity 3, 30 per cent).

THE C1 LEVEL

In a similar manner to the B2 level, two basic categories of involvement were investigated in the two relevant observation phases in the C1 level oral test. The results are included in Table 3.3, where, as for B2, percentages for non-acceptable types have been separately presented.[8]

8   In Appendix II, Table 3.7 and Table 3.9 present frequencies for the sub-types of the
     two basic categories of intervention in May 2007 and also for the C1 level.

Table 3.3: Frequencies of examiner intervention per test task in the C1 level speaking
tests in May 2007 and November 2007 observation phases

May 2007 Intervention per test task	C1 (342 observed cases in total)	
	Activity 1	Activity 2
Changes to the rubrics	22.5% (77)	23.5% (80)
only non-acceptable types	*18.5%*	*18.2%*
Interruptions and/or interferences	36% (123)	55.5% (188)
only non-acceptable types	*17%*	*9.8%*
November 2007 Intervention per test task *(only non-acceptable types)*	C1 (232 observed cases in total)	
	Activity 1	Activity 2
Changes to the rubrics	21.5% (53)	13.5% (31)
Interruptions and/or interferences	34.5% (80)	21% (49)

In May 2007, both acceptable and non-acceptable types of intervention were investigated. At this level, percentages for rubric changes were much lower than at the B2 level, with the category 'other' (i.e. mainly 'repetition') having the highest percentage. The interventions involving 'expansion' in Activity 1 and 'change of word(s)' in Activity 2 had the same percentages of frequency (see Appendix II, Table 3.7).

Concerning interruption or interference with the candidate's language output, again, most types that were found were acceptable practices (Appendix II, Table 3.9). Non-acceptable intervention was found in the category 'other' in Activity 1, mainly including the 'use of additional questions' (i.e. 15.8 per cent see Appendix II, Table 3.10); but there was more frequent use of an acceptable type in Activity 2, namely 'reminding candidates to refer to all the texts given to them' (i.e. 16.4 per cent see Appendix II, Table 3.9).

In November 2007, and with reference to changes to rubrics, the most frequent instances occurred in Activity 1. Changes to rubrics were also less frequent in Activity 2. Nevertheless, the highest percentages appear in the second general category, namely interruption of or interference with the candidate's language output in C1 Activity 1.

As with B2, percentages in November 2007 can be compared to the percentages for non-acceptable practices in May 2007 (marked in italics in Table 3.3). It appears that in both phases changes to the rubrics are more frequent in Activity 1 (where the candidate is asked an opinion question by the examiner) than in Activity 2 (where the two candidates interact to complete a mediation task). The same is true for interruptions/ interferences. Also, the percentages for changes to the rubrics and interruptions/ interferences are significantly higher in Activity 1 than those in Activity 2. The only exception is the May changes to the rubrics, where the two percentages are very close (18.5 per cent and 18.2 per cent).

In general, by comparing the findings of both levels it seems that examiners tend to intervene less at C1 level than at B2 level. At C1 level, the findings of both exam administrations do not reveal differences in examiners' use of 'changes in rubrics'; regardless of exam period, examiners make changes to rubrics at a low frequency. On the other hand, at B2 level, the category 'changes to rubrics' seems to cover the most commonly employed type of examiner intervention while interruptions/interferences seem to be used more frequently in the November exam period than in May in the speaking tests at both levels.

Results from simulated tests

In the analysis of the transcribed simulated tests, the total number of involvement types identified was 280 for the B2 and 91 for the C1 speaking test, but the frequencies of involvement types varied for each of the test tasks, as shown in Table 3.4.

Table 3.4: Number of instances of involvement in the two levels per Activity

LEVEL	Activity 1	Activity 2	Activity 3
B2	135	78	67
C1	55	36	

As was the case in both of the real time observation phases, the B2 speaking test presents a much higher number of involvement instances, almost double those used at C1 level. It is also evident that Activity 1 in both levels is the most amenable to examiner involvement.

At this stage of the research, the categories of involvement were refined and redefined to produce ten categories in total, as shown in Table 3.5, which also shows frequencies for the various types in each activity of each level.

Table 3.5: Types of involvement as identified in the simulated speaking tests and percentages for each Activity

INVOLVEMENT	B2			C1	
The examiner-as- interlocutor-...	Act. 1	Act. 2	Act. 3	Act. 1	Act. 2
expands	45%	32%	47%	34%	37%
repeats	20%	40%	18%	14%	13%
explains	8%	2%	3%	12%	3%
comments or evaluates / draws a conclusion	13%	8%	8%	15%	18%
asks candidate whether s/he needs help/clarification/repetition etc.	0%	4%	1%	12%	8%
asks for clarification or confirmation	4%	0%	0%	3%	0%
corrects	4%	4%	1%	2%	3%
confirms / agrees	4%	5%	3%	0%	0%
uses 'anything else' or 'and' to get the candidate going	0%	2%	4%	2%	5%
other	1%	0%	10%	0%	0%

In B2 Activity 1, the most commonly found type of involvement was some form of 'expansion' made by the examiner. This term includes different kinds of linguistic information, in addition to the given question or the answer to it. For instance, in the following extract from the simulated speaking tests, the examiner expands on the question by adding two subsequent questions (as indicated by the arrows).

> I: Ok er and tell us about a good film that you saw recently either on TV or er at the
>   cinema.
> G: Mm er (...) one day that I have that I had er (...) sit with my parents [with my parents] =
> I: [uhm]
> G: = I watched I watched a (...) film good
> I: uhm
> G: It's a thriller
> I: uhm
> G: and I was scared very (...) er =
> → I: = and you liked it?
> G: yes-
> → I: was it a Greek one or an American?
> G: an American.
> → I: an American film and did you know any actors?
> J: Er no becau no

'Repetition' and 'Comments/Evaluation' rank second and third in this activity. On the other hand, 'repetition' presents the highest frequency in B2 Activity 2 (with 'expansion' following), while the opposite is true for B2 Activity 3 ('expansion' followed by 'repetition'). In C1 Activities 1 and 2, 'expansion' is again the most frequently occurring type of involvement, while all other types are a lot less common.

Comparisons and conclusions

Findings from observation and the simulated tests analysis show that B2 Activity 1 clearly presents the highest frequency of occurrence of involvement. In this test task, some examiners tend to adopt the freer role of a teacher or of a non-institutional interlocutor. This is something that probably derives from the nature of the test task as it resembles a dialogue and even though examiners have been given very specific questions that are to be posed verbatim, some may get carried away and change them or supply additional questions.

Involvement is also frequent in C1 Activity 1 where candidates are given opinion questions which seem to bear a cognitive and linguistic load as well as being a prerequisite for developing a long answer. Despite the candidates' expected level of proficiency (i.e. proficient user), examiners may violate their role as question deliverers in order to help candidates cope with situations they presumably deem 'tricky' or complicated.

In general it seems that examiners tend to intervene more at the start of the test in an effort perhaps to help the candidate and put him or her at ease and less as the test progresses. Examiner involvement also appears to be less frequent in tasks where there is a third factor, for example, in B2 Activity 2 there is a set of photographs, in B2 Activity 3 a Greek text, and in C1 Activity 2 a Greek text and a peer interlocutor (the examiner playing the role of a listener and monitor in the interaction of the two candidates). Especially in B2 Activity 3 and C1 Activity 2 (also a peer interlocutor), where there is some Greek text input, involvement is the least frequent.

Regarding the frequency of the various types of involvement it was found that in all activities of both levels the most frequently occurring type was 'expansion'. This involvement type may be a threat to the reliability and validity of the oral test result because it possibly alters the linguistic content anticipated by the test designers by potentially embedding the examiner's linguistic input in the candidate's answer.

Furthermore, there is some evidence of what has been called 'acceptable intervention' in observation. Some kind of 'repetition' was found in all the activities, with C1 Activity 2 presenting the highest frequency. In the simulated tests, 'repetition' was also found to occur in high frequency in the data, ranking second after 'expansion' in all activities of both levels, except for B2 Activity 2, where it was more frequent. This is presumably because Activity 2 tasks are rather long and contain more than one sub-question which candidates may forget to answer and need to be reminded about. Repetition is a 'legitimate' type of involvement as it is a technique which helps the candidate overcome trouble spots or hesitation, without providing him/her with the linguistic means to do so.

Thus, involvement appears to be affected by the test task, both in terms of frequency of occurrence and type. As shown by the findings, the quantity and quality of examiner involvement varies from one level to the other and/or from one task type to the other.

Discussion and implications

The findings of the present study support the claims of earlier research that an examiner may be 'implicated in the candidate's performance and in the construct of his or her competence' (Brown 2005: 258; He & Young 1998; McNamara 1997; McNamara & Roever 2006). More specifically, an examiner in the KPG oral exam in English takes on roles with specific characteristics which are defined by the requirements of the different test tasks of the two speaking test-levels reported on in this chapter. These requirements may affect his or her involvement in the candidate's performance both qualitatively and quantitatively. However, the fact that the KPG oral exam is very 'controlled' in terms of an examiner's practices (i.e. an Interlocutor Frame, specific questions and tasks are all provided), this does not nurture – and actually discourages – examiner initiative.

Despite this, the results of the present research show that there is evidence of variation in examiner conduct in the KPG oral exam in English. Some examiners may involve themselves in the candidate's performance in various ways, and they seem to do so more frequently in some test tasks rather than others, which appears to indicate that involvement is task-specific. Thus, examiners seem to involve themselves in Activity 1 in both speaking tests more often than in the other test tasks. One reason for this might be that at the beginning of the test examiners may have the wish to accommodate a candidate's needs and so create a safe environment for a procedure which to some can seem quite formal and stressful. But as shown in this research, it is also the nature of the test tasks themselves that appears to be responsible for increased examiner involvement. In B2 Activity 1, there are questions which are asked by examiners during a very controlled dialogue with the candidate, while in C1 Activity 1 the opinion questions are cognitively loaded and place a heavy demand on the candidate, who is expected to take a long turn and develop an answer on his or her own.

In addition, the type of involvement which examiners in the KPG oral exam most frequently employ is expansion of the given question or task. Such involvement challenges the fairness of the procedure and may affect the reliability of the specific test item and the validity of the assessment. Depending on its quantity and quality, such a practice may also detract from the examination time actually designated for a candidate's answer. On the other hand, examiners in both levels also use repetition, a type of involvement which is perfectly 'legitimate' in that it may help a candidate complete an answer without providing the linguistic means to do so.

All these data have been used to inform the oral examiner training programme, providing abundant material included in several training seminars. Oral examiners were instructed against involvement by being acquainted with the different types; they were also updated on their classification of what was acceptable and non-acceptable and trained to use the acceptable types through videotaped simulated tests. In parallel, the Interlocutor Frame was introduced and included in the Speaking Test Examiner Pack to be used by the examiners as a means of further diminishing variability. Finally, on the basis of these findings and in combination with other data from the KPG speaking test research, an Oral Examiner Evaluation form was composed with specific criteria, accompanied by an analytic evaluation scale. By using this, a number of examiners were evaluated as interlocutors by observers in real-time examinations.

Concerning the implications of the findings relating to the design of the oral exam, evidence emerged that the peer-peer type of test task (i.e. C1 Activity 2) can provide an excellent format for generating a candidate's unassisted language production. Without examining the pros and cons of this type of activity, it became obvious that examiners involved themselves in this task less frequently than in other types of test tasks. Furthermore, it was shown that test tasks with pictorial (B2 Activity 2) and textual (B2 Activity 3 and C1 Activity 2, both requiring mediation of Greek texts) input also displayed a lower frequency of involvement by examiners.

Conclusion

The present study has shed light on ways in which examiners involve themselves in a candidate's performance in the KPG oral exams in English, providing insights into the role of examiners in the KPG oral exam context. Also, by examining their role in two different speaking test-levels of the KPG oral exam, which involve different types of test tasks, it provides information on the ways examiners may vary their behaviour according to the test task.

Finally, many researchers and testers have investigated the role of examiner and are still searching for the most appropriate way of testing and assessing oral proficiency. Some argue in favour of a conversational type of oral test, where examiners have a freer role; while others promote the advantages of a controlled type of test. This chapter has provided data to support the application of the more controlled examiner role, as it enhances the reliability and validity of the test procedure and its outcome.

Bibliography

Alderson, J. C., Clapham, C., and Wall, D. (1995). *Language Test Construction and Evaluation*. Cambridge: Cambridge University Press.

Bachman, L. F., and Palmer, A. S. (1996). *Language Testing in Practice*. Oxford: Oxford University Press.

Bachman, L. F., Lynch, B. K., and Mason, M. (1995). 'Investigating Variability in Tasks and Rater Judgments in a Performance Test of Foreign Language Speaking', *Language Testing*, 12, 239–58.

Bonk, W. J., and Ockey. G. (2003). 'A Many-facet Rasch Analysis of the Second Language Group Oral Discussion Task', *Language Testing*, 20 (1), 89–110.

Brooks, L. (2009). 'Interacting in Pairs in a Test of Oral Proficiency: Co-constructing a Better Performance', *Language Testing*, 26 (3), 341–66.

Brown, A. (1995). 'The Effect of Rater Variables in the Development of an Occupation-specific Language Performance Test', *Language Testing*, 12 (3), 1–15.

——(2003). 'Interviewer Variation and the Co-construction of Speaking Proficiency', *Language Testing*, 20 (1), 1–25.

—— (2005). *Interviewer Variability in Oral Proficiency Interviews*. Frankfurt am Main: Peter Lang.

Brown, A., and Hill K. (2007). 'Interviewer Style and Candidate Performance in the IELTS Oral Interview'. In M. Milanovic and C. Weir (eds), *Research in Speaking and Writing Assessment Studies in Language Testing 19, IELTS Collected Papers*, pp. 37–62. Cambridge: UCLES/Cambridge University Press.

Brown, A., and Lumley, T. (1997). 'Interviewer Variability in Specific-purpose Language Performance Tests'. In A. Huhta, V. Kohonen, L. Kurki-Suonio and S. Luoma (eds), *Current developments and alternatives in language assessment: proceedings of* LTRC 96, pp. 173–91. Jÿvasskÿla: University of Jÿvasskÿla and University of Tampere.

Brown, A., Iwashita, N., and McNamara, T. (2005). 'An Examination of Rater Orientation and Test-taker Performance on English for Academic Purposes Speaking Tasks', *TOEFL Monograph Series, MS-29*. Princeton, NJ: Educational Testing Service.

Brown, G., and Yule, G. (1983). *Discourse Analysis*. Cambridge: Cambridge University Press.

Cohen, L., Manion, L., and Morrison, K. (2011). *Research Methods in Education* (7th edn). London: Routledge-Falmer.

Csépes, I. (2002). *Measuring Oral Proficiency Through Paired Performance*. Unpublished PhD Dissertation, Eötvös Loránd University, Budapest.

De Jong, N., and Banerjee, J. (2016). 'The Examiner as Interlocutor', *Presentation in the EALTA Summer School, Innsbruck*.

Delieza, X. (2012). '"Co-construction" in the B2 and C1 KPG Oral Exams: A Comparison of Examiners as a Factor Involved in Candidates' Performance', *Research Papers in Language Teaching and Learning*, 3 (1), 78–91.

—— (2013). 'Monitoring KPG Examiner Conduct', *Directions in Language Teaching and Testing*, 1. RCEL Publications, University of Athens.

—— (2014). *The Impact of Oral Examiners' Conduct on Candidates' Performance: The Case of the KPG Exam in English*. Unpublished PhD Thesis. National and Kapodistrian University of Athens, Athens.

Dendrinos, B. (2009). 'Rationale and ideology of the KPG exams'. <http://rcel.enl.uoa.gr/rcel/texts/Rationale_and_Ideology_of_the_KPG_Exams> accessed 10 April 2017.

—— (2013). 'Social Meanings in Global-glocal Language Proficiency Exams'. In C. Tsagari, S. Papadima-Sophocleous and S. Ioannou-Georgiou (eds), *Language Testing and Assessment around the Globe: Achievements and Experiences*, 47–67. Bern: Peter Lang Publishing Group.

Dörnyei, Z. (2007). *Research Methods in Applied Linguistics*. New York: Oxford University Press.

Ducasse, A. M., and Brown, A (2009). 'Assessing Paired Orals: Raters' Orientation to Interaction', *Language Testing*, 26 (3), 423–43.

Fulcher, G. (2003). *Testing Second Language Speaking*. London: Pearson Longman.

Galaczi, E., and Ffrench, A. (2011). 'Context Validity'. In L. Taylor (ed.), *Examining Speaking: Research and Practice in Assessing Second Language Speaking (LTRC), Studies in Language Testing*, pp. 112–70. Cambridge: Cambridge University Press.

Green, A. (1998). *Verbal Protocol Analysis in Language Testing Research: A Handbook*. Cambridge: Cambridge University Press.

He, A. W., and Young, R. (1998). 'Language Proficiency Interviews: A Discourse Approach'. In R. Young and A. W. He (eds), *Talking and Testing. Discourse Approaches to the Assessment of Oral Proficiency*, pp. 1–23. Amsterdam: John Benjamins.

Iwashita, N. (1998). 'The Validity of the Paired Interview Format in Oral Performance Assessment', *Melbourne Papers in Applied Linguistics*, 5 (2), 51–65.

Jacoby, S., and Ochs, E. (1995). 'Co-construction: An Introduction', *Research on Language and Social Interaction*, 28 (3), 171–83.

Karavas, E. (ed.) (2009). *The KPG Speaking Test in English: A Handbook*. University of Athens: RCEL Publications.

Karavas, E., and Delieza X. (2009). 'On-site Observation of KPG Oral Examiners: Implications for Oral Examiner Training and Evaluation', *Journal of Applied Language Studies*, 3 (1), 51–77.

Kasper, G., and Ross, S. J. (2007). 'Multiple Questions in Oral Proficiency Interviews', *Journal of Pragmatics*, 30, 1–26.

KPG B2 Level Exam Specifications (2007). <rcel.enl.uoa.gr/kpg/docs/B2_Προδιαγραφές_Greek.pdf> accessed 10 April 2017.

KPG C1 Level Exam Specifications (2007). <rcel.enl.uoa.gr/kpg/docs/C1_Prodia grafes_Greek.pdf> accessed 10 April 2017.

Kramsch, C. (1986). 'From Language Proficiency to Interactional Competence', *The Modern Language Journal*, 70, 366–72.

Lazaraton, A. (1991). *A Conversation Analysis of Structure and Interaction in the Language Interview*. Unpublished PhD Dissertation, University of California, Los Angeles.

——(1992). 'The Structural Organization of a Language Interview: A Conversation Analytic Perspective', *System*, 20, 373–86.

——(1996a). 'A Qualitative Approach to Monitoring Examiner Conduct in the Cambridge Assessment of Spoken English (CASE)'. In M. Milanovic and N. Saville (eds), *Performance Testing, Cognition and Assessment: Selected Papers from the 15th Language Testing Research Colloquium (LTRC), Studies in Language Testing*, pp. 18–33. Cambridge: Cambridge University Press.

——(1996b). 'Interlocutor Support in Oral Proficiency Interviews: The Case of CASE', *Language Testing*, 13, 151–72.

McNamara, T. F. (1995). 'Modelling Performance: Opening Pandora's Box', *Applied Linguistics*, 16 (2), 159–79.

——(1996). *Measuring Second Language Performance*. London: Longman.

——(1997). 'Interaction' in Second Language Performance Assessment: Whose Performance?', *Applied Linguistics*, 18, 446–66.

McNamara, T. F., Hill, K., and May, L. (2002). 'Discourse and Assessment', *Annual Review of Applied Linguistics*, 22, 221–42.

McNamara, T. F., and Lumley, T. (1997). 'The Effect of Interlocutor and Assessment Variables in Overseas Assessment of Speaking Skills in Occupational Settings', *Language Testing*, 14, 140–56.

McNamara, T. F., and Roever, C. (2006). *Language Testing: The Social Dimension*. Malden, MA and Oxford: Blackwell.

Malvern, D., and Richards, B. (2002). 'Investigating Accommodation in Language Proficiency Interviews Using a New Measure of Lexical Diversity', *Language Testing*, 19 (1), 85–104.

May, L. (2006). 'An Examination of Rater Orientations on a Paired Candidate Discussion Task through Stimulated Verbal Recall', *Melbourne Papers in Language Testing*, 1, 29–51.

——(2009). 'Co-constructed interaction in a Paired-speaking Test: The Rater's Perspective', *Language Testing*, 26 (3), 397–421.

——(2010). 'Developing Speaking Assessment Tasks to Reflect the 'Social Turn' in Language Testing', *University of Sydney Papers in TESOL*, 5, 1–30.

Merrylees, B., and McDowell, C. (2007). 'A Survey of Examiner Attitudes and Behaviour in the IELTS Oral Interview'. In M. Milanovic and C. Weir (eds), *Research in Speaking and Writing Assessment Studies in Language Testing 19, IELTS Collected Papers*, pp. 142–83. Cambridge: Cambridge University Press.

Nakatsuhara, F. (2006). 'The Impact of Proficiency-level on Conversational Styles in Paired Speaking Tests', *Cambridge ESOL Research Notes*, 25, 15–20.

O'Sullivan, B. (2002). 'Learner Acquaintanship and Oral Proficiency Test Pair-task Performance', *Language Testing* 19 (3), 277–95.

Perret, G. (1990). 'The Language Testing Interview: A Reappraisal'. In J. de Jong and D. K. Stenenson (eds), *Individualising the Assessment of Language Abilities*, pp. 225–38. Philadelphia, PA: Multilingual Matters.

Roshan, S. (2013). 'A Critical Review of the Revised IELTS Speaking Test', *International Journal of English Language Education*, 2 (1), 120–7.

Ross, S. (2007). 'A Comparative Task-in-interaction Analysis of OPI Backsliding', *Journal of Pragmatics*, 39, 2017–44.

van Lier, L. (1989). 'Reeling, Writhing, Drawling, Stretching, and Fainting in Coils: Oral Proficiency Interviews as Conversations', *TESOL Quarterly*, 23 (3), 489–508.

Young, R., and Milanovic, M. (1992). 'Discourse Variation in Oral Proficiency Interviews', *Studies in Second Language Acquisition*, 14, 403–24.

Appendix I

Table 3.6: List of acceptable versus non-acceptable intervention

☺ ACCEPTABLE INTERVENTION	☹ NON–ACCEPTABLE INTERVENTION	
To take action or intervene in order to:	To change or interfere with the rubrics in the following ways:	To interrupt the candidate(s) or interfere with his/her/their language output in order to:
<ul><li>repeat the rubric (more slowly) [if asked or if considered necessary],</li><li>repeat part of the rubric or the rubric in parts (eg. to remind the candidate(s) of something they have forgotten to answer) [if asked or if considered necessary],</li><li>supply a synonym for a word after being asked to do so,</li><li>remind the candidates of (part of) the task / their goal [using the wording of the rubric],</li><li>remind the candidate to use/relay information from their text(s),</li><li>help the candidate continue by repeating his/her last words,</li><li>give the candidates the opportunity to produce more output by saying 'is there anything else you want/would like to add?' or simply 'anything else' or even 'and?',</li><li>use fillers, such as 'aha', 'uhm', etc. to show that they are following the candidate,</li><li>direct the candidates to a picture they have not used (only at B2 level),</li><li>remind the candidates that they have to interact (only at C1 level),</li><li>remind the candidates to refer to all the texts (only at C1 level).</li></ul>	<ul><li>Change one-two words, add words to or expand the rubric.</li><li>Supply a synonym for a word without being asked to.</li><li>Paraphrase or use examples to explain the rubric.</li><li>Direct the candidates' answer using an introductory question or leading question.</li><li>Use their own questions.</li></ul>	<ul><li>make some kind of correction,</li><li>supply one or more words the candidate was unable to find,</li><li>ask a seemingly irrelevant question,</li><li>make suggestions, give options or examples, or add something,</li><li>explain a word by paraphrasing it and giving examples,</li><li>make personal comments or provide information about themselves,</li><li>finish the phrase for the candidate,</li><li>participate in the discussion (only at C1 level).</li></ul>

Appendix II

Table 3.7: Percentages of different types of changes of rubrics
in the B2 and C1 oral test in May 2007

Type of change to or interference with the rubric	B2			C1	
	Activity 1	Activity 2	Activity 3	Activity 1	Activity 2
used an introductory question	17.3%	2.0%	2.9%	4.7%	0.6%
changed one-two words and/ or supplied a synonym for a word	9.0%	7.1%	11.2%	2.3%	8.2%
expanded the question and/ or used examples to explain it.	16.8%	14.1%	10.4%	8.2%	4.7%
other	*14.3%*	*8.0%*	*8.5%*	*7.3%*	*9.9%*

Table 3.8: Percentages of 'other' types of changes of rubrics (in the B2
and C1 oral test in May 2007) classified as acceptable and non-acceptable

Type of change to or interference with the rubric – *'other'*	B2			C1	
	Activity 1	Activity 2	Activity 3	Activity 1	Activity 2
Non-acceptable	10.9%	4.4%	5.9%	3.3%	4.7%
Acceptable	3.5%	3.6%	2.7%	4%	5.2%

Table 3.9: Percentages of different types of interruption of candidates
in the B2 and C1 oral test in May 2007

The examiner interrupted the candidate or interfered with their language output in order to ...	B2			C1	
	Activity 1	Activity 2	Activity 3	Activity 1	Activity 2
redirect the candidate because s/he misunderstood something by repeating the question or part of it.	7.1%	10.0%	7.0%	7.6%	10.5%

help the candidate continue by repeating his/her last words.	3.4%	4.9%	5.8%	5.8%	-
make some kind of correction or add something (eg. supply one or more words the candidate was unable to find).	3.4%	5.3%	5.8%	1.2%	2.9%
remind the candidates of (part of) the task / their goal?	-	-	-	-	2.3%
remind them they have to interact?	-	-	-	-	4.7%
remind them to refer to all the texts?	-	-	-	-	16.4%
*participate in the discussion? * (Why?/ How? Please specify. ___)*	-	-	-	-	4.1%
other	6.6%	13.4%	10.0%	21.6%	14.6%

*These are the only two non-acceptable types of interruption/interference.

Table 3.10: Percentages of 'other' types of interruption of candidates (in the B2 and C1 oral test in May 2007) classified as acceptable and non-acceptable

The examiner interrupted the candidate or interfered with their language output in order to ... 'other'	B2			C1	
	Activity 1	Activity 2	Activity 3	Activity 1	Activity 2
Non-acceptable	5.62%	10.05%	4.7%	15.8%	2.8%
Acceptable	0.98%	3.35%	5.3%	5.8%	11.8%

PART II

Understanding written texts

AMALIA BALOURDI

4   Investigating ideologies in texts used in global and 'glocal' language testing

ABSTRACT

While many studies have used SFL analytical tools to investigate ideologies encoded in various text types, the ideological implications of texts used in English language certification exams have not been systematically investigated. This chapter presents a study which, informed by the theoretical principles of CDA and SFL and combining the methodological tools of SFL with those of corpus linguistics, applies transitivity analysis to a corpus of reading comprehension texts used by three different English language examination batteries (i.e. the KPG glocal exams and the global exams of Cambridge ESOL and Michigan) in order to explore the ideologies these texts are invested with. With the aid of a socio-semantic inventory of the social actants, the analysis focuses on the investigation of the experiential meanings realised in patterns of two material process sub-types (i.e. processes of giving and taking) in order to reveal how the world of 'giving and taking' is construed in each examination battery.

Introduction

> Anything that is said or written about the world is articulated from a par-
> ticular ideological position: language is not a clear window but a refracting,
> structuring medium. If we can acknowledge this as a positive, productive
> principle, we can go on to show by analysis how it operates in texts.
>
> — FOWLER (1991: 10)

This quotation clearly expresses the basis of the study of the ideological nature of texts related to language testing. As with all texts, those used in English examination systems are invested with particular ideologies, and these ideologies cannot fail to characterise the institutions which are responsible for the exams (Balourdi 2012).

This research project has been inspired by Bessie Dendrinos' perspectives on the ideological functions of texts (Dendrinos 1992, 2001) and on the use of high-stakes language proficiency exams 'as ideological apparatuses involving processes that produce, reproduce or resist specific forms of knowledge and communication exchange' (Dendrinos 2013: 2). In addition, it has also been largely motivated by Shohamy's critical perspectives on language policies (Shohamy 2006) and the powerful role of tests (Shohamy 2001), particularly her specific reference to the power of texts used in tests. In fact, Shohamy (2001: 123–4) sees tests both as a means for measuring knowledge and as a means for the implementation of specific language and educational policies, which implies their significant role in the promotion and maintenance of ideologies.

The study focuses on three language examination batteries which are popular in Greece (i.e. the KPG Exams, the Cambridge ESOL Exams, and the Michigan Exams) at the B2 level of competence, in order to explore the worlds they linguistically construe in the texts used for the assessment of reading comprehension. A preliminary investigation of a number of such texts had already shown distinct differences, not only in terms of text types and thematic choices, but also in terms of particular lexico-grammatical choices. As these choices appeared to systematically foreground certain aspects of reality, whereas other aspects of reality were either backgrounded or totally absent, it constituted a challenge to see how this contributed to the encoding of certain ideologies and consequently to the construal of a different world in each exam battery.

Taking into account the main principles of Critical Discourse Analysis (hereafter CDA) and Systemic Functional Linguistics (hereafter SFL), which will be briefly presented in the next section, a systematic and detailed lexico-grammatical analysis was carried out on a corpus of texts from each exam battery, in order to show how 'textual and syntactic elements of texts are ideologically loaded and how the use of different elements would construct a very different reality' (Dendrinos 1992: 99). To this end a transitivity analysis was combined with corpus linguistics techniques, while the CDA theory was used to interpret the results and discuss their implications.

This chapter is part of a broader research project aimed at developing a systematic model of analysis to investigate the experiential and interpersonal meanings the reading texts of the three aforementioned language examination batteries make, thus revealing the way the texts linguistically construe the world and the subject positions they create for their readers. The focus in what follows is on the use of a particular process type[1] (i.e. processes of 'giving and taking') and shows how, by means of a systematic lexico-grammatical analysis, the transitivity patterns involving these processes construe different experiential meanings in each examination battery, thus promoting different value systems and ultimately different ideologies, which are not always explicit to the reader.

Literature review

This section discusses the main principles of CDA and SFL which have largely informed the theoretical and methodological approach of the study and presents its approach to ideology and the representation of meanings through language. Finally it touches upon the basic points of Halliday's SFL concerning the experiential function of the clause and the system of transitivity which was employed for the purposes of the present study.

Ideology and discourse

The investigation of ideologies here draws on the basic principles of SFL and CDA. Placing his systemic functional approach within the context of a social semiotic approach, Halliday (1978: 111) views language as a

---

1   Processes in SFL terms being the verbs used in texts.

social semiotic system which encodes meanings through the process of representation, thus sustaining and facilitating cultural communication. Representation, as defined by Hall (1997: 61), is 'the process by which the members of a culture use language to produce meanings'. However, representation is conceived not merely as a reflection of the world but as 'entering into the very constitution of things' (1997: 5–6). Consequently, social reality is understood as a semiotic construct, in other words, a construct of meanings, while language is one of the semiotic systems that constitute a social reality. Furthermore, sociocultural meanings are not conceived as pre-existing but as constructed, that is, produced in discourse through the process of representation. Therefore, it is discourse and not simply language that has a constitutive role in the social realm. In fact this is one of the basic premises of CDA according to which discourse does not neutrally reflect the world, identities and social relations, but plays an active role in creating and changing them.

Hence, meanings cannot be communicated neutrally. More accurately, the sociocultural meanings texts encode by means of their lexicogrammatical choices are understood to be 'influenced by the sociocultural context in which they are exchanged' (Eggins 1994: 2). Thus, meanings are affected by different usages, different historical circumstances, different positions and perspectives. In fact, as Fairclough (2000: 23) points out, language is not just a transparent medium for reflecting the way things are, but it 'constructs the world in one way or another according to position or perspective'. Therefore, the way in which a meaning is chosen to be encoded in a text implies a particular viewpoint, thus contributing to the representation of the reality which best serves the interests of those who either write or use the texts for a certain purpose. Meanings are then understood to be ideologically invested and consequently ideologies are closely interwoven with the representation of sociocultural meanings. Interestingly, this may happen either consciously or unconsciously as the structure of a language is 'already impregnated with social values which make up a potential perspective on events' (Fowler 1991: 24).

On the basis of the above, CDA takes a critical perspective on language use and aims to investigate ideologies, which is actually what distinguishes it from mainstream discourse analysis. In this study the concept of ideology is central, given its particular concern in the representation of sociocultural meanings in texts with a specific use. The definition of ideology adopted in the present study is that of Kress and Hodge (1993: 6), according to whom ideology is 'a systematic body of ideas, organized from a particular point of view'. However, a point that should be made here is that taking into account the distinction between critical and neutral conceptions of ideology (Thompson 1990), the conception of ideology this study adopts is a critical one, which implies that it goes further than simply viewing ideologies as different systems of socio-cultural values and attitudes.

Moreover, a critical approach to ideology implies a close connection between ideology and power relations and therefore views language not only as an instrument of communication but also as an instrument of control, which is also among the main principles of CDA. Van Dijk (2000: 36) states that 'if there is one notion often related to ideology it is that of power', while Fairclough (1995b: 14) sees ideologies as 'propositions that generally figure as implicit assumptions in texts, which contribute to producing or reproducing unequal relations of power, relations of domination'. In the same line of thought, Dendrinos (1992: 99) proposes a critical analysis of discourse in order to understand how ideologies 'function as instruments to sustain relations of domination and, by extension, how they may function as instruments to transform these relations'. Ideologies are then perceived as constructions of meaning which contribute to the production, reproduction and transformation of power relations, often 'without being evident to participants' (Jaworski & Coupland 1999: 497).

The theoretical principles of SFL and CDA have thus informed the theoretical perspectives of this study on language and discourse. Yet SFL has also provided the methodological tools for the analysis of the corpus, as it establishes the relationship between the grammatical structures of language and their context of use thus providing the appropriate grounds for the kind of linguistic analysis this study is concerned with. In relation to this, Fowler (1991: 68) argues that the SFL model examines 'the connections between linguistic structure and social values', while Martin (2000: 275–6) points out that SFL provides CDA with the 'technical language for talking about language' and this is due to 'its ability to ground concerns with power and ideology in the detailed analysis of texts as they unfold, clause by clause, in real contexts of language in use'. In fact, the appropriateness of the SFL analytic tools for the purposes of CDA has been largely acknowledged by many critical theorists and researchers and subsequently many CDA works have drawn on systemic functional grammar (e.g., van Dijk 1991; Fairclough 1989, 1995a, 1995b, and 2000; Fowler 1991, 1996; Coulthard-Caldas, 1993; Young & Harrison 2004; Wodak & Wright, 2006; Fairclough & Fairclough 2011).

Transitivity analysis in SFL

According to the SFL model, language makes three types of meaning (i.e. experiential, interpersonal and textual), which are realised through a lexico-grammar (i.e. words and structures). Associated with the production of experiential meanings is the grammatical system of transitivity through which experiential meanings are realised. Transitivity analysis explores the experiential meanings in texts, namely the meanings which express the writer's experience as a member of a culture, and which, as Halliday (1978: 112) explains, 'express the phenomena of the environment: the things – creatures, objects, actions, events, qualities, states and relations – of the world and of our own consciousness'. According to the SFL paradigm, realities are constructed on the basis of 'who is doing what to whom'. Therefore, the two main elements in the process of representation are the 'processes' and the 'participants'. In traditional grammatical terms, the 'processes' are the verbs of the clauses and the 'participants' are the subjects and/or objects of the clauses.

The SFL model suggests seven major types of processes (Halliday & Matthiessen 2004: 170–5), namely material, mental, verbal, behavioural, existential, relational and causative. Material processes, with which this chapter is concerned, are understood as processes of doing and happening and along with mental and attributive processes make the three principle types in the English clause in that 'they are the cornerstones of the grammar in its guise as a theory of experience' (2004: 248). However, due to the vast range of experience they represent, material processes are sub-categorised by Halliday & Matthiessen (2004: 187–99) into two main types, which in turn are further categorised into distinct sub-types.[2] The main functional participant roles associated with material processes are the Actor (i.e. the doer of the action) and the Goal (i.e. the one to whom the action is extended). Yet, there is also the Beneficiary, that is, the one who benefits from the performance of the process and which SFL actually distinguishes between the Recipient (i.e. the one to whom something is given) and the Client (i.e. the one for whom something is done).

Purpose of the study and methodology

As stated above, transitivity analysis explores the experiential meanings in a text, namely the meanings which express what is happening (i.e. actions, events, qualities, states and relations) in the world construed therein. Transitivity patterns are then understood to constitute the map of reality a text construes. The focus here is on the system of transitivity and on the patterns of two particular transformative material process sub-types,

---

2   Creative processes are further categorised into creative/general (i.e. create, appear, develop, etc.) and creative/specific (i.e. compose, write, etc.) and transformative are further categorised into three major sub-types, that is, transformative/elaborating (i.e. burn, increase, paint, etc.), transformative/extending (i.e. give, rent, meet, etc.) and transformative/enhancing (i.e. shake, drive, go, etc.). In addition, for the transformative/elaborating processes Halliday & Matthiessen suggest fifteen further sub-types under the labels: state, make-up, surface, size, shape, age, amount, colour, light, sound, exterior (cover), interior, contact, aperture, operation, while for the transformative/extending processes they suggest two further sub-types, that is, transformative/extending possession (i.e. give, take, rent, buy, acquire, etc.), which are further divided into four unlabelled sub-categories, and transformative/extending accompaniment (i.e. meet, collect, separate, etc.). For the transformative/enhancing processes they also suggest two further sub-types, namely, transformative/enhancing motion: manner (i.e. shake, drive, fly, run, etc.) and transformative/enhancing motion: place (i.e. come, go, arrive, etc.). For a detailed table with examples, see Halliday & Matthiessen (2004: 187–8).

namely transformative/extending possession processes implying benefit and money transactions,[3] or put more simply, processes of 'giving and taking'. The particular process sub-types were selected due to their high frequencies in the corpus of the study, as indicated by the first stages of the analysis (see Table 4.1 and related section), along with the fact that the field of 'giving and taking' is interesting to explore on its own, since what is given and taken, whether material or not, implies the inherent values of a particular society or institution. Thus, the aim of the present study is to explore how 'giving and taking' is construed by the reading texts of three different language examination batteries, comprised in each of the three sub-corpora that constituted its research corpus.

The corpus of the study consists of ninety-three texts (42,400 words) which are included in reading comprehension language tests in three well-known language examination batteries, that is, the KPG Exams (hereafter KPG), the Cambridge ESOL Exams (hereafter CESOL), and the Michigan Exams (hereafter ELIUM) for the B2 level of competence. This corpus is divided into three sub-corpora (i.e. one for each examination battery), each consisting of thirty-one texts. The reading texts in the three sub-corpora come from official sources, that is, from the official tests given between November 2003 and November 2007 for KPG and CESOL and from official publications aimed at the candidates' preparation for the exams for ELIUM.[4]

Thus the main objective was to achieve an accurate description of how 'giving and taking' is construed in the texts of each sub-corpus, a description that would be obtained by studying how the particular processes are associated with certain participants. Specifically, by studying the most

---

3   As stated earlier, transformative/extending possession processes are further divided by Halliday & Matthiessen into four unlabelled sub-categories. In the present study these are differentiated in terms of their features and provided appropriate labeling as follows: implying use (i.e. use, wear, consume, eat, drink, etc.), implying money transactions (i.e. buy, pay, sell, rent, charge, etc.), implying benefit (i.e. offer, give, take, etc.) and implying effort and/or achievement and success (i.e. win, succeed, achieve, etc.). For more details, see next section.

4   Hellenic American Union Publications 2000, 2005 and 2007.

frequent types of participants the selected process sub-types are associated with as well as the functional roles these participants tend to occupy, the most prominent experiential meanings related to 'giving and taking' in the texts would be revealed. These meanings would in turn compose the particular worlds of values and beliefs related to 'giving and taking' as construed in each sub-corpus.

Since in the related literature there has been no systematic study of the experiential meanings in a corpus of texts, two analytical steps were considered essential. These actually turned out to play a key role in the analysis, as they provided the necessary socio-cultural context for the integration and interpretation of the findings in the qualitative part of the analysis. The analytical steps were: a) the sub-categorisation of the most frequent process types and b) the categorisation of the actants (i.e. the verb subjects and objects).[5]

The sub-categorisation of the processes was necessary in order to refine the findings from the initial distribution of the main process types across the three sub-corpora and understand which particular aspects of experience are foregrounded in each sub-corpus. Yet, although in sub-categorising material processes the present study draws on Halliday & Matthiessen's perspectives, the sub-categorisation of transformative material processes, that is the sub-type this chapter is concerned with, had to be differentiated from the more delicate sub-types suggested by Halliday & Matthiessen both in terms of their labeling and their features (see Table 4.1). Thus, here we focus on two sub-types of the Transformative/extending possession process type: (1) those implying benefit (i.e. offer, give, serve, get, take, accept, etc.), and (2) those implying money transactions (i.e. buy, pay, sell, charge, etc.).

The categorisation of the actants, on the other hand, could not be based on an existing methodology due to the absence of a systematic model for such categorisation in the relevant literature. In order to come up with appropriately labeled categories which would serve its analytic aims, this

---

5   The term 'actant' has been borrowed from the French linguist Tesnière, who defines actants as 'beings or things which in some capacity and in whatsoever manner, even in the capacity of mere onlookers and in the most passive manner participate in a process' (Tesnière 1959: 102).

study drew on Fowler's categorisation of people in the discourse of the press (Fowler 1991: 92) and proceeded with a manual analysis of all texts, recording the actants of all processes. This procedure provided two main actant categories, namely human actants and non-human actants (i.e. other living beings, concrete objects, abstract entities, etc.). Each of these two categories was further sub-divided into categories using a labeling system devised so that each sub-category would bear a characteristic label representing the particular social domain associated with the actants in this category. In this way the labeling of the categories could function as a 'sociosemantic inventory', borrowing van Leeuwen's (1996) term, which would serve as a map of the actants, viewed from a socio-cultural standpoint.

Thus the human actants were divided in nine major groups (see Table 4.2) and the non-human actants in eleven categories, each one labeled after the thematic field the listed actants were associated with (see Table 4.3). However, the different types of non-human actants each sub-corpus comprises did not always allow for the use of common labels across the three sub-corpora. Therefore, the category labels selected for the non-human actants were differentiated across the three sub-corpora, but there was an attempt to select the closest possible equivalent.

The next step in the analysis, after the sub-categorisation of material processes and the categorisation of the actants, was to study the distribution of the process sub-types and actant categories within each sub-corpus in order to identify the dominant processes and the dominant actants therein. To this end corpus linguistics techniques (i.e. word frequencies and concordancing) were applied using the Wordsmith software. More precisely, by using the wordlists of the Wordsmith software the frequencies of all occurring processes in each of the main process categories were obtained. Moreover, with the aid of the Wordsmith software concordancing tool, the concordance lines for all occurring processes in each process type and sub-type, actant category or group were studied in order to calculate the number of texts they occurred in.

It should be noted that the frequency counts obtained at this stage were determined by the number of texts in which each process sub-type or actant category was found to occur and not by the total number of occurrences counted within a sub-corpus. Hence, a process sub-type, actant group or category that occurred at least once in one text was given an equal value to another process sub-type, actant group or category that may have occurred in the same text several times. This was due to the fact that counting occurrences and not texts would make the findings misleading, such as if a process or actant had ten occurrences in one text, but not a single occurrence in the rest of the texts of the same sub-corpus.

Thus having obtained a clear picture of the dominant process sub-types and the dominant actants in each sub-corpus, the main body of transitivity analysis followed, that is, its actual qualitative part. This aimed at exploring the different transitivity patterns of the two transformative/extending possession processes in question in each sub-corpus in order to see how they construed different experiences of 'giving and taking'. Specifically, by using the Wordsmith software concordancing tool concordance lines were accessed for the individual occurrences of these processes, which also included the particular actants these were associated with. Then, by listing the concordance lines of the two transformative/extending possession process sub-types, the actant categories most frequently associated with them were revealed, thus providing the transitivity patterns concerning 'giving and taking'.

Quantitative analysis

The quantitative part of the analysis started with the study of the distribution of the main process types across the three sub-corpora. Material processes turned out to dominate all three sub-corpora, yet with different percentages across them, but this is not a concern of this chapter (see Balourdi 2012). However, the study of the distribution of their sub-categories indicated that of the thirteen material process sub-types the transformative/implying benefit sub-type, on which this chapter is focused, was among the three that shared the highest frequencies in all three sub-corpora. As stated earlier, throughout this analytic stage the focus is on the number of texts each sub-type occurs in. Thus, out of the thirty-one texts of each sub-corpus transformative/extending possession/implying benefit processes were found to occur in eighteen KPG texts, twenty-seven CESOL texts and twenty-four ELIUM texts, as shown in Table 4.1, which displays the frequencies of material process sub-types across the three sub-corpora.

Table 4.1: Types and sub-types of material processes across the three sub-corpora

Types	Subtypes	Number of texts they occur in		
		KPG (31 texts)	CESOL (31 texts)	ELIUM (31 texts)
Creative	General	12	16	18
	Specific	18	22	22
Transformative: elaborating	General	9	22	12
	Implying change	8	10	6
	Implying care	11	5	8
	Implying control and/or restrictions	13	11	9
	Implying damage and/or failure and accident	5	9	7
Transformative: extending possession	Implying use	16	17	15
	Implying money transactions	10	14	12
	Implying benefit	18	27	24
	Implying effort and/or achievement and success	7	16	7
Transformative: extending accompaniment		9	13	19
Transformative: enhancing motion		23	27	22

Considering the close association between processes of the transformative/implying benefit and the transformative/implying money transaction sub-types, the frequencies of the latter, though not particularly high and almost equally distributed across the three sub-corpora, added to those of the former, constituted an interesting finding that was worth further investigation in the qualitative stage of the analysis. Thus, the selection of these two particular sub-types, which can actually be merged under the label 'processes of giving and taking' and in which the participant functional role of the Recipient is significant, was due to the considerable number of instances in the three sub-corpora, a fact that made their presence distinct and interesting to explore.

Table 4.2: Frequencies of human actants across the three sub-corpora

Category	Number of texts it occurs in KPG	Number of texts it occurs in CESOL	Number of texts it occurs in ELIUM
Everyday people	21	23	23
Working people	8	17	7
Young people	4	18	14
The commercial world	8	17	22
Educated people and specialists	8	13	11
Activists	5	3	0
The authorities	8	3	7
Artists & celebrities	4	16	6
Human collectives & people in general	21	22	15
Total no. of texts	31	31	31

The categorisation of the actants, as mentioned earlier, provided two major groups (i.e. human actants and non-human actants) each of which was divided in nine and eleven categories respectively. Tables 4.2 and 4.3 present the inventory of human and non-human actants together with the distribution of each actant category in each sub-corpus, thus providing an initial understanding of the population and the main concerns of the world represented by each sub-corpus. Moreover, it shows the protagonists of these three worlds, as indicated by the foregrounding of certain human actant categories against others.

According to Table 4.2, 'everyday people' dominate all three sub-corpora, with roughly equal frequencies. The rest of the categories, that is, 'human collectives and people in general' are almost as frequent as 'everyday people' in KPG and CESOL, while in ELIUM they seem to occur in nearly half of the texts. Interestingly, 'young people', 'working people', and 'artists and celebrities' appear to be particularly foregrounded in CESOL. On the other hand, 'the commercial world' is quite prominent in ELIUM, while 'activists' make their presence distinct in KPG, especially when compared to their low ranking in CESOL and their total absence in ELIUM. Finally, 'the authorities' appear to have a distinct presence both in KPG and ELIUM, while 'educated people and specialists' seem to be more foregrounded in CESOL and ELIUM.

When exploring the individual occurrences of the different human actants that fall into each category (for details, see Balourdi 2012), it was observed that in the KPG sub-corpus there is a distinct presence of 'citizens' (five texts) in the category of 'everyday people', a group which appears only once in each of the other two sub-corpora. In fact, the same was observed with the group of 'activists' (e.g., environmental groups, conservation organisations, protesters, etc.), as despite their low frequency (i.e. five texts), in CESOL they count three occurrences and occupy the last position, whereas in ELIUM they do not occur. Interestingly, the type of citizen KPG appears to be mainly concerned with is that of the 'world citizen', as in KPG citizens from different parts of the world are equally present. Finally, in the category of 'human collectives and people in general' the group of 'human collectives' includes a considerable number of national (i.e. the Greek people, Greece, Athenians, the German people), international (i.e. the Mediterranean people, world countries, etc.) and major social groups (e.g., the world poor and rich). Hence the protagonists of the KPG world are 'world citizens', activists, national, international and major social groups.

In CESOL, which turned out to be almost exclusively concerned with British actants, young people appear to play a central part as indicated by their high frequency (i.e. eighteen texts) and also by the fact that CESOL contains the highest proportion of young actants across the three sub-corpora. Moreover CESOL shows a distinct preference for 'teenagers', given the frequent occurrences of 'teenagers', 'school leavers', 'university' or 'college students', their 'friends', their 'flatmates' and so on. On the other hand, 'travellers', who are characterised by a spirit of independence and a tendency for adventure, are the second most frequent group in the category of 'everyday people' as they appear in seven texts. Another group which turned out to play a central role in the CESOL world is that of successful professionals such as artists, writers and people in the media or the publishing world, as indicated by the prominence of the category of 'artists and celebrities' (e.g., actors and actresses, pop musicians, a pianist, painters, etc.). Within this group 'writers' has a distinct presence (i.e. six texts), along with the high frequency (i.e. six texts) of 'artistic jobs' in the category of 'working people' and the considerable frequency of the 'media group' (i.e. six texts) in the category of 'the commercial world'. Hence, British young people, adventure travellers and successful professionals such as artists, writers, publishers and people in the media constitute the protagonists of the CESOL world.

In ELIUM, which is almost exclusively concerned with American actants, the prominent 'commercial world' covers a wide range of business activity (e.g., a multinational car industry, USA coach companies, a toy-store chain, etc.), yet tourist businesses (e.g., tour operators, hotels, restaurants, children's camps, etc.) figure as its main representatives, occurring in ten texts. In addition, the group of 'tourists and travellers', of which ELIUM has the highest proportion (i.e. ten texts) across the three sub-corpora, figures as the most frequent in the category of 'everyday people' and is mainly represented by tour participants (i.e. tourists, visitors, travelers, etc.) in well-organised tourist activities. Also, ELIUM has the highest proportion of scientists across the three sub-corpora, as a wide range of scientists (e.g., anthropologists, biochemists, linguists, etc.) and researchers (eight texts) were found to dominate the category of 'educated people and specialists'. Thus, the commercial world mainly represented by American tour operators and their customers, as well as specialised scientists and researchers appear to be the main protagonists in the ELIUM world.

Table 4.3: Frequencies of non-human actants across the three sub-corpora

KPG		CESOL		ELIUM	
Category	No. of texts it occurs in	Category	No. of texts it occurs in	Category	No. of texts it occurs in
Ecological issues	10	The natural world	13	The natural world	7
Political issues	5	The press	4	Political issues	2
Social issues	2	Work issues	9	Social issues	1
Cultural issues	8	Arts & culture	9	History & culture	9
Financial matters	3	Financial matters	2	Financial matters	10
Education	2	Education	2	Education	5
Science	3	Science & technology	4	Science & technology	12
Health, fitness & diet	10	Sports & games	7	Sports & fitness	2
Tourism	4	Travelling	6	Tours, visits and holidays	9
Transport	4	-	-	Transport & ravelling	6
Abstractions	10	Abstractions	29	Abstractions	11
Total no. of texts	31	Total no. of texts	31	Total no. of texts	31

The distribution of non-human actants (Table 4.3) along with the study of their individual occurrences revealed the basic issues each sub-corpus world appears to be concerned with. Thus KPG indicated a high proportion of actants from the categories of 'ecological issues' and 'health, fitness & diet' as well as a prominent presence of the merged category of 'socio-political issues', which implies a particular concern for such issues. Furthermore, cultural issues seem to be of significance in the KPG world, while the Greek element is foregrounded, as implied by the considerable frequency of the category 'cultural issues' and the particular type of act-ants it is comprised of.

In CESOL, work appears to be the central social issue, yet arts and culture, nature, sports and certainly travelling are particularly prevalent. In addition, there is a distinct prominence of abstractions denoting cognitions, perceptions and feelings. Finally, in ELIUM the predominant category is that of 'science & technology', obviously implying great concern for such matters. Yet, organised activities such as tours, visits and holidays make their presence felt as does the category 'financial matters', the prominence of which along with its clear association with the 'commercial world' indi-cates that money plays a central role in the ELIUM world.

Thus, having obtained a clear picture of the protagonists of each sub-corpus world as well as the basic issues they are concerned with, the quali-tative part of the analysis was to explore how these are associated with 'giving and taking'.

Qualitative analysis: The construal of three different realities around 'giving' and 'taking'

This section presents the major findings of the analysis by exploring the patterns of 'giving and taking' processes in each sub-corpus with their associated participants. Starting with KPG, it was observed that the use of a considerable number of such processes contributes to the construal of citizens and people worldwide, as well as activists and scientists, as consist-ently involved in practices which imply an increased concern for ecological, socio-political and public health issues.

More precisely, through the frequent use of transformative/imply-ing benefit processes (i.e. offer, provide, give, contribute, benefit, send, donate, leave, take advantage, get, gain) nine KPG texts construe 'citizens' and 'human collectives' (i.e. the world, the Greeks, etc.) as the main par-ticipants involved in processes of 'giving' and 'taking', either in the role of the Recipient or in the role of the Actor, the Goals or Actors of which are non-human actants mainly chosen from the categories 'ecological issues' and 'health, fitness and diet'. For example:

(1) *The Way to Clean Air campaign* is designed *to provide you (citizens)* with resources to help reduce smog and lessen climate change (B604c)[6]

(2) ... *exercise benefits well-being* ... (B506c)

(3) It is also necessary *(citizens) to give (heat stroken people)* plenty of liquids ... (B1105c)

(4) ... and yet *each one of us* has the power *to contribute* to stop global warming (B1107c)

As shown in (1) and (2) above, citizens and people in various parts of the world appear to have benefited from environmental campaigns or physical exercise, which are then understood as basic benefit-gaining activities. This also indicates the significance of living in a healthy environment and maintaining a good physical condition. What is more, as illustrated in (3) and (4) above, citizens and people worldwide are not represented simply as passive receivers of the benefits of 'benefit providers' such as environmental campaigns and exercise, but also as active participants, that is, initiators of benefit gaining processes aimed at promoting public health or conserving the environment.

On the other hand, the use of processes implying money transactions (i.e. buy, pay, spend, rent, sell, earn) was found to contribute to the construal of similar experiential meanings. Thus in four texts 'consumers' appear to be the Actors of such processes, the Goals of which represent commodities that imply the participants' concern for a healthy life and environment. For instance:

(5) ... when *(consumers) buying* fresh *fruit and vegetables*? (B405b)

(6) ... when *(householders/citizens) buying* these products *(biodegradable products for house cleaning)* ... (B507c)

6   Text code number.

Interestingly, the 'commercial world' and even the 'authorities' appear to be involved in money transactions (i.e. pay fines or allowances) which imply their acceptance of responsibility for practices that have a negative impact on the environment, as shown below:

(7)   In Brussels *employers* can *pay an allowance* per kilometre to employees who cycle ... (B1105b)

(8)   After years of not caring about the environment, *the government* risks *paying* big *fines* ... (B506a)

Considering all the above patterns, the KPG sub-corpus sets out a picture of reality where the environment and public health are of the utmost importance. Thus, the KPG texts are understood to be particularly concerned with considerate world citizens, whose actions are aimed at improving their quality of life by limiting the harmful repercussions modern civilisation has inflicted upon the environment, their health and their social status.

Unlike KPG, in CESOL the analysis did not show any significant differentiation in the frequencies of 'giving' and 'taking' processes nor a clear distinction between actants exclusively associated with them, as there is an almost even distribution of such processes across all actant categories. Yet, in ten texts abstractions associated either with the world of conscience (i.e. feelings, ideas, challenges, experiences) or with the notion of 'opportunity' (i.e. chances, opportunities) consistently appear as the Goals of 'giving' and 'taking' processes (i.e. offer, put, contribute, donate, leave, provide, give, send, serve, take, get, accept, obtain, gain, be rewarded), the Actors or Recipients of which turned out to be frequently selected from the actant categories of 'working people', 'young people' and 'celebrities'. For instance:

(9)   ... to experience something new and different, and it's *a challenge* – one you (*British school students*) should *grab* (F604a)

(10)   ... a local writers' group which will help *you (an aspiring writer) to gain ideas and confidence* from mixing with other aspiring writers (F1204c)

(11)   *The experience gave Jo one of her first chances* of doing something on her own ... (F1203d)

In addition, considering processes implying money transactions in CESOL (i.e. buy, purchase, pay, earn, sell), an equal distribution was observed between 'buying' and 'selling' processes, with actants from different categories appearing as their Actors. Yet, their Goals are almost always selected from the category of 'arts and culture' (i.e. paintings, cartoons, stories, tickets for theatrical performances, etc.). Patterns such as these suggest that in the CESOL world money basically serves the participants' artistic and intellectual interests. The following are some typical examples:

(12)   *He* (an artist) also began to paint and *sell* pictures (F604c)

(13)   … and *as a student* in London *I* regularly *bought* cheap standing tickets for West End productions (F606c)

All the above findings thus indicate that the CESOL sub-corpus construes a world which is concerned with the exchange of feelings, ideas, experiences and, most significantly, of challenges and opportunities rather than being concerned with the exchange of material goods and services. In fact, the only material goods and services the CESOL world appears to show a clear preference for are associated with the arts. Notably also, the construal of experience as a provider of opportunities suggests its significance as a value in this world.

In ELIUM, the previous stages of the analysis indicated that 'giving' and 'taking' processes are the dominant material process type, which is an interesting finding on its own. The qualitative analysis then showed that the 'commercial world' and 'everyday people' were systematically used as their Actors, the former in processes of 'giving' (i.e. offer, give, serve, provide, send, return, cater to, benefit, back, contribute) and the latter in processes of 'taking' (i.e. accept, get, receive, obtain, take, entitle), while the Goals of 'giving' and of most of the 'taking' processes appeared to represent various commodities, mainly selected from the category of 'tours, visits and holidays'.

Specifically, in fourteen texts various representatives of the commercial world (i.e. hotels, restaurants, tour operators, private schools, etc.) occur as Actors, while in seven texts the Actors are selected from the category of 'everyday people', mainly represented by visitors and tour participants.

Thus, the predominance of the 'commercial world' in the role of the 'giver' and also the fact that 'giving' actions were found to dominate over 'taking' actions construe a consumers' world centered around various sorts of commodities, exclusively provided and controlled by the business world.

Findings concerning processes of the transformative/implying money transactions type (i.e. buy, purchase, spend, pay, rent, sell, charge, fine) indicate that the 'giving' and 'taking' relation construed between the 'commercial world' and 'everyday people' is consistently characterised by money transactions, thus lending further support to the above interpretation. More accurately, 'everyday people' were observed occurring in nine ELIUM texts as Actors in processes of 'buying', 'purchasing' and the like, the Goals of which represent various types of commodities (i.e. tickets, passes, souvenirs, meals, etc.). For instance:

(14)   *Visitors* can *buy* souvenirs from our shop (E6c)

(15)   *Cafe Groups* (museum visitors) can *purchase* lunch from the Café ... (E7c)

Moreover, various representatives of the 'commercial world' appear in four texts as Actors in processes such as 'sell', 'charge' and the like, their Goals representing commodities (i.e. *cars, tickets* etc.), as illustrated below:

(16)   *Greyhound USA Bus Lines sells* both one way and round trip tickets (E3b)

(17)   So far, *GM has sold* only 288 of these electric cars (E4a)

However, an interesting finding concerning the patterns of both process types in the ELIUM sub-corpus is the systematic use of certain strategies which serve to conceal the power of the commercial world. In fact, further indications of such strategies were found in the analysis of passive transformations and the use of agentless passives (see Balourdi 2012), though this is beyond the scope of this chapter. The strategies observed are as follows:

a)   The selection of a 'taking' process instead of its 'giving' process equivalent allows for the concealment of powerful participants, such as the commercial world. More precisely, 'everyday people' (i.e. citizens, visitors) appear mostly as Actors in 'taking' processes rather than Recipients in 'giving' processes, thus eliminating the role of the business world as 'provider'. What is more, the Goals of such 'taking' processes are associated either with some source of authority or with some sort of money transaction (i.e. permission, a discount, traffic tickets, tickets, etc.). In other words, 'taking' processes allow the omission of the participants who are in the powerful position to give traffic tickets, permission or discounts, whereas participants in the weak position of getting them are foregrounded by being construed as Actors. The following are some typical examples:

(18)   *Violators* (cyclists/tour participants) ... may *receive* traffic tickets (E5b)

(19)   ... *visitors* are required *to obtain* permission before entering the Hopi (E8c)

b) The systematic omission of the Recipients in patterns of 'giving' processes (i.e. customers), though we can easily understand their identity, appears to boost the significance of the role of the business world as a 'provider' of goods and services. For example:

(20)   *The Green Tortoise company offers* long leisurely trips throughout the US ... (E3b)

(21)   *We* (tour operators) also *provide* customised tours throughout the Southwest ... (E8c)

c) In contrast, there is a tendency to background the money receiver by eliminating the participants who have a powerful role in processes that imply money transactions and authority control. More accurately, when the Goals of 'giving' processes are associated with money and power the business world is rarely present as a salient Actor.

d) Among the processes of the extending possession/implying money transactions type, the 'buying' type dominates over the 'selling' type, thus foregrounding the customers, unlike processes of 'giving' in which the 'commercial world' is foregrounded.

Hence, the use of processes of the transformative/extending possession type implying benefit and money transactions in the ELIUM texts is understood to contribute to the construal of a market-oriented world in which, by means of various strategies, the supplier's role as a profit maker as well as the authority and power such a role implies are systematically and tactfully obscured.

Conclusion

Informed by the theoretical principles of CDA and SFL and combining the methodological tools of SFL with those of corpus linguistics, this study applied transitivity analysis on a corpus of reading comprehension texts used by three different English language examination batteries (i.e. the KPG 'glocal' exams and the global exams of Cambridge ESOL and Michigan) in order to explore the ideologies these texts are invested with. The analysis, which focused on the investigation of the experiential meanings realised in patterns displayed by two material process sub-types, namely the transformative/extending possession 'implying benefit' sub-type and the 'implying money transactions' sub-type, revealed in each examination battery sub-corpus the construal of different realities, that is, different worldviews, values and beliefs.

In summary, the underlying ideology in KPG texts is that human beings are active 'world citizens' whose actions are basically aimed at conserving the environment, promoting public health and protecting their human rights. On the other hand, Cambridge ESOL texts construe a world of particular artistic and intellectual interests, where the exchange of feelings, ideas, experiences, challenges and opportunities are of more significant value than the exchange of goods and services. Finally, in ELIUM the fact that almost everything appears to revolve around the customer-supplier relationship contributes to the construal of a strictly market-oriented world, where the obscure manipulations of those in power place the customer in the weak position of unwittingly accepting this role and complying with the rules set by those in power.

Thus, the present study shed light on a rather unexplored and neglected aspect of texts used in language certification exams by examining the ideologies promoted through their particular linguistic choices. It also provided a systematic model of analysis which proved rewarding both in terms of creating the necessary conditions for the linguistic analysis and in terms of providing a firm grounding for the interpretation and explanation of the findings. Moreover, a strong aspect of this model is the development of a socio-semantic inventory for the categorisation of the actants and the sub-categorisation of the processes, which neither the SFL tools nor the relevant literature provide. This inventory could be further developed and would prove particularly useful in the qualitative analysis of findings in similar future research projects.

One last point which should be made is that, although the linguistic and discursive choices in the analysed texts are understood to reflect the particular ideologies that characterise the institutions responsible for the particular exams, the aims and perspectives of this study are neither to criticise the testing policies and practices of these institutions nor to question the quality of the tests developed by the three examination batteries. It should also be noted that the experiential meanings the texts were found to encode are not understood as permanent features of the ideological positions of the institutions which design and administer the particular exams. They are simply indicative of the social, political and cultural trends and tendencies of the period between 2000 and 2007. Therefore, the particular institutions are not expected to always remain attached to the same values and perspectives, yet this should be examined in future research projects.

In conclusion, the usefulness of this study lies in the development of critical awareness on the part of language test developers, teachers preparing their students for the exams and exam candidates so that they will be able to choose for themselves whether or not to 'question and if necessary reject the view of the world represented there' or 'conform with open eyes and recognise the compromises they are making' (Janks & Ivanic 1992: 317–18). In fact, the development of critical awareness can be extended to the development of critical strategies in order 'to examine the uses and consequences of tests, to monitor their power, minimize their detrimental force, reveal their misuses, and empower the test takers' (Shohamy 2001: 132). This study can thus claim common ground between its interests and those of the wider field which Shohamy calls Critical Testing, which 'attempts to encourage testers, teachers, test takers and the public at large to question the uses of tests, the materials they are based on and to critique the values and the beliefs inherent in them' (2001: 132).

Bibliography

Balourdi, A. (2012). *World Representations in Language Exam Batteries: Critical Discourse Analysis of Texts Used to Test Reading Comprehension.* Unpublished PhD Thesis. Faculty of English Language and Literature. University of Athens.

Coulthard-Caldas, C. (1993). 'From Discourse Analysis to Critical Discourse Analysis: The Differential Re-Presentation of Women and Men Speaking in Written News'. In J. Sinclair, M. Hoey, and G. Fox (eds), *Technique of Description*, pp. 196–208. London: Routledge.

Dendrinos, B. (1992*). The EFL Textbook and Ideology.* Athens-Greece: N. C. Grivas Publications.

——(2001). *Readings in Language and Ideology.* Athens: University of Athens Press.

—— (2013). 'Social Meanings in Global-glocal Language Proficiency Exams'. In D. Tsagari, S. Papadima-Sophocleous and S. Ioannou-Georgiou (eds), *Language Testing and Assessment around the Globe: Achievements and Experience*, pp. 47–67. Frankfurt: Peter Lang.

Eggins, S. (1994). *An Introduction to Systemic Functional Linguistics.* London: Pinter.

Fairclough, I., and Fairclough, N. (2011). 'Practical Reasoning in Political Discourse: The UK Government's Response to the Economic Crisis in the 2008 Pre-Budget Report'. *Discourse & Society,* 22 (3), 243–68.

Fairclough, N. (1989). *Language and Power.* London: Longman.

——(1995a). *Critical Discourse Analysis. The Critical Study of Language.* London and New York: Longman.

——(1995b) *Media Discourse.* London: Arnold.

——(2000). *New Labour, New Language.* London: Routledge.

Fowler, R. (1991). *Language in the News. Discourse and Ideology in the Press.* London and New York: Routledge.

——(1996) *Linguistic Criticism.* Oxford: Oxford University Press.

Hall, S. (1997). *Representation: Cultural Representations and signifying practices.* London: Sage.

Halliday, M. A. K. (1978). *Language as a Social Semiotic: The Social Interpretation of Language and Meaning.* London: Edward Arnold.

Halliday, M. A. K., and Matthiessen, C. (2004). *An Introduction to Functional Grammar*. London: Edward Arnold.

Hodge, R., and Kress, G. (1993). *Language as Ideology*. London and New York: Routledge.

Janks, H., and Ivanic, R. (1992). 'Critical Language Awareness and Emancipatory Discourse'. In N. Fairclough (ed.), *Critical Language Awareness*, pp. 305–31. London: Longman.

Jaworski, A., and Coupland, N. (1999). *The Discourse Reader*. London and New York: Routledge.

Martin, J. R. (2000). 'Close Reading: Functional Linguistics as a Tool for Critical Discourse Analysis'. In L. Unsworth (ed.), *Researching language in Schools and Communities: Functional Linguistic Perspectives*, pp. 275–303. London and Washington: Cassell.

Shohamy, E. (2001). *The Power of Tests*. London: Pearson Education Ltd.

——(2006). *Language Policy: Hidden Agendas and New Approaches*. London and New York: Routledge.

Tesniere, L. (1959). *Elements d'une Syntaxe Structurale*. Paris: Klincksieck

Thompson, J. (1990). *Ideology and Modern Culture*. Cambridge: Polity Press.

Van Dijk, T. A. (1991). *Racism and the Press*. London: Routledge.

——(2000). 'Ideology and Discourse: a Multidisciplinary Introduction'. *English version of an internet course for the University Oberta de Catalunya (UOC)*, <http://www.discourses.org> accessed 10/05/2016.

Van Leeuwen, T. (1996). 'The Representation of Social Actors'. In C. Coulthard-Caldas and R. M. Coulthard (eds), *Texts and Practices. Readings in Critical Discourse Analysis*, pp. 33–70. London and New York: Routledge.

Wodak, R., and Wright, S. (2006). 'The European Union in Cyberspace'. *Journal of Language and Politics*, 5 (2), 251–75.

Young, L., and Harrison, C. (2004). *Systemic Functional Linguistics and Critical Discourse Analysis. Studies in Social Change*. London and New York: Continuum.

STYLIANI KARATZA

5   Visual matters in language testing: Exploring intersemiotic meaning making in reading comprehension source texts

ABSTRACT

This chapter presents the results of Systemic Functional Multimodal Discourse Analysis (SF-MDA) conducted on reading comprehension texts of KPG English exams at B1 language competence level. The main objective of the research is to investigate the contribution of the visual mode to the meaning potential of KPG source texts, which include both the visual and the verbal mode. Here the focus is on intersemiosis, the interplay between the visual and the verbal (O' Halloran et al. 2012, Holsanova 2012). It also examines visual–verbal interaction, reports on quantitative and qualitative data in regards to visual–verbal relations of similarity and difference and discusses how intersemiosis affects multimodal source text meaning potential. The chapter also concentrates on 'the range of meaning as content' (i.e. ideation) (Halliday 1979: 117) and examines the frequency of occurrence and the kinds of linkages between the visual and the verbal in terms of content. To analyse how visual and verbal components work together to create an impact and achieve the purposes of the texts (Tan, K. L. E., and O'Halloran 2012), Multimodal Analysis Image (MMA) interactive software (O'Halloran et al. 2012) was used. Additionally, there is a consideration of whether and to what extent the meanings provided by the visual input and the intersemiotic relations are important for test-taker's successful completion of test tasks.

Introduction

The current prevalence of the coexistence of visual and verbal modes in print and electronic media necessitates a reconceptualisation of the notion of literacy in the field of foreign language testing and assessment. It is assumed that 'meaning potential',[1] or the range of possible meanings, of multimodal texts differs from verbal text meaning potential due to the existence of the visual mode. Thus it is expected that readers' comprehension could be enhanced by some kind of visual literacy which could function in combination with the verbal. Despite the shift towards this combination in media texts, it seems that the multimodal nature of texts is often overlooked in language exam batteries. The absence of visuals typically creates a distance between texts included in large scale tests and texts found in real-life communication.

It is widely accepted that EFL language tests focus on the examination of the verbal, given that their priority is to test English language knowledge. But as Kress et al. (2001) point out, language is 'there' among other modes, which belong to the representational ensemble of communicative modes. The question arises of how language can be tested without being in a multimodal context as it is normally experienced. This study attempts to transcend the traditional language-based focus in language assessment by adopting a multimodal paradigm in testing reading comprehension, which nevertheless does not imply a devaluation of language.

From a multimodal perspective, each mode is seen to be doing a different thing, or the same thing in a different way. According to van Leeuwen (2008), there is 'a division of labour between word and image' (van Leeuwen 2008: 136). Kress (2010) also supports the idea that different modes serve different needs in different contexts and that each one lends itself to different semiotic work; writing names, image shows and colour highlights and frames. Thus, every mode has a different mission which it can accomplish effectively. Besides, according to one of the key premises of multimodality which Jewitt et al. (2016: 3) formulate, 'meaning is made with different semiotic resources, each offering distinct potentialities and limitations'. However, as well as making meaning in separation, modes also make meaning in

---

1   This is a term used by Halliday (1979, 1994) in the context of a social semiotic view of language which views grammar as a system of 'options' and the speaker as having the potential to 'mean'. Meaning potential is realised in language as lexico-grammatical potential, that is, what the speaker 'can say'.

combination and it seems that visuals and verbal texts work jointly for the creation of more meanings in new ways (Unsworth 2007). The interplay between various modes is often addressed as intersemiosis (O'Halloran et al. 2012; Holsanova 2012). Thus, besides the independent role each mode can play in meaning making, it is challenging to explore the contributions image and language make to multimodal texts in co-action. In terms of intersemiosis, the visual and the verbal co-act as they are related in various ways and multiply the meaning potential of the text.

This chapter is part of a larger research project which investigates the different kinds of literacies (verbal, visual, intersemiotic) that are required from a test-taker in order to comprehend a multimodal source text in the reading comprehension test of KPG English exams at different levels of language competence. Employing a view of 'language as social semiotic' (Halliday 1994) and operating in the context of Systemic Functional Linguistics (henceforth SFL), this study adopts the framework of systemic functional grammar for the analysis of the source texts. According to one of Halliday's (1994) main principles, three metafunctions simultaneously construe meaning in a text; the ideational (which is concerned with clauses as representations), the interpersonal (which is concerned with clauses as exchanges) and the textual (which is concerned with clauses as messages). According to SFL, analysis of any linguistic unit, for example a clause, can be conducted simultaneously in relation to 'the work it does to represent the world, the work it does to enact social relationships (e.g. asking questions, evaluating entities, etc.) and the work it does to contribute to an unfolding text or dialogue' (Bateman 2008: 39). Multimodal SFL analysis perceives visual presentations as multimodal artefacts which are presumed to manage meaning making in Halliday's three metafunctional domains in a similar way to linguistic units (ibid.). This chapter focuses on meaning as content (i.e. the ideational metafunction) (Halliday 1979: 117). Thus, it examines intersemiosis in terms of the representational domain and investigates how the experiential and logical meaning potential of B1 level source texts is influenced through the interplay between the visual and the verbal: are the modes connected ideationally and how? If a reader considers the visual as a source of meaning, will ideational meanings multiply and therefore will test-takers gain a better understanding of the source text? These are the questions this study aims to address by placing particular emphasis on the relations between the verbal and the visual with regard to content information. Moreover, taking into account that no similar publication is available in the literature that addresses the issue of intersemiotic relations in source texts of reading comprehension test tasks, it is important to investigate how modes are related to each other in language exam contexts.

Still, however, in the context of language testing test-takers purposefully read each source text in order to answer the accompanying test items successfully. The ultimate goal of this study is to verify the hypothesis that the visual truly matters in language testing. Therefore, apart from the investigation of the literacy requirements the source text itself poses, it would be very useful to analyse the literacy requirements of the items. The focus here is on the role of the visual in item processing. Are there items that require meanings of the visual mode in order to be answered? To what extent are B1 level test-takers invited to activate their visual and intersemiotic literacy in order to select the correct responses? These are the questions that will be addressed concerning the items which accompany the reading comprehension tasks.

SFL and image/text relations in terms of content: Intersemiosis

A research shift towards the employment of systemic functional approaches to multimodal discourse analysis (SF-MDA) can be observed during the last decades of the last century (O'Halloran 2007). Researchers have been interested in broadening the scope of systemic functional grammar by focusing on a variety of non-verbal semiotic resources (Liu & O'Halloran 2009). Recent research has focused on the nature of visual and verbal relations and particularly on the development of frameworks which utilise SFL metalanguage to describe intersemiotic relations, opting for a reconceptualisation of literacy and literacy education (Unsworth 2007; Liu & O'Halloran 2009). The expected coexistence of visual and verbal modes in print and electronic media necessitates the need to extend analysis from the focus on each mode separately, specifically 'mode specialization', to the analysis of modes which, working synergistically, result in the multiplicity of meaning (Royce 1998, 1999). O'Halloran et al. (2017: 163) use the term *semiotic interactions* to address 'linguistic and visual choices which co-contextualise each other to reinforce particular meanings' or 'achieve a purposeful contrast'.

As will be further analysed in the sections that follow, this research uses O'Halloran et al.'s (2012) and Tan et al.'s (2012) categories of visual–verbal relations of similarity (i.e. illustration, repetition, addition) and difference (i.e. contrast, displacement) to examine the source texts. These categories are similar to the ones employed in previous work which aimed at the construction of frameworks which include the different kinds of linkages between the verbal and the visual. These frameworks, which stem from SFL, have provided the current research with useful insights. For instance, Roth et al. (2005) investigated photographs in science books and identified four functions that relate pictures and their captions to the main text: the decorative function, aimed at engaging the reader interactively; the illustrative function, aimed at exemplifying the verbal content through the image; the explanatory function, providing an explanation or classification of what is depicted through the captions; and the complementary function, whereby the captions offer content information not included in the text. Overall, Roth et al.'s (2005) work provides useful insights into a possible classification of visual verbal relations in all kinds of multimodal texts including the KPG source texts. Similarly, another inspiring work by Unsworth (2007) on visual – verbal interaction for the construction of ideational meaning in school science texts and materials suggested the category of 'expansion', which identifies the features of concurrence, complementarity and enhancement. Used in concurrence images clarify or explain the verbal (i.e. clarification), re-express meanings of the verbal text (i.e. exposition), provide examples (i.e. exemplification) or co-exist with the verbal messages in a common multimodal space (i.e. homospatiality). Complementarity involves the addition of meanings that are either similar to the verbal ones through the image (i.e. augmentation) or different from the verbal (i.e. divergence), while enhancement is connected with circumstantial information such as space and time.

Some other studies have stressed the notion of multimodal coherence. Royce (1999), for instance, explored the function of the visual in relation to the verbal mode in economics discourse in order to study the visual–verbal interface in multimodal texts. Adopting a Hallidayan systemic functional framework, he concluded that the production of a coherent multimodal text is based on the complementarity and synergistic co-action of the intersemiotic semantic resources of the text. Taking on board Royce's notion of multimodal coherence, Liu and O'Halloran (2009) studied the visual–verbal relations in print media texts arguing that a coherent multimodal text ought to be distinguished from a mere co-occurrence of modes. They specified intersemiotic texture as the major feature of coherent multimodal texts and introduced a framework of intersemiotic cohesive devices that expanded on Hasan's (1985) work on linguistic texture. They also supported the efficacy of a discourse-based approach towards the logical relations between images and words.[2] Overall, their approach is based on Martin's (1992) and Martin and Rose's (2003) work, denoting comparative intermodal relations (when different modes share similar experiential meanings and one reformulates the other semiotically), additive (when a mode adds new pieces of information to the other), consequential (when a mode determines or enables the other) and temporal intermodal relations (when images display procedural steps, which are also presented in written form). Drawing on this body of multimodal coherence research, the study presented in this chapter endorses the perception that it is not enough for a multimodal text to be verbally coherent, but that it needs to be multimodally coherent as well. Hence, it attempts to discover whether and how the source text data achieve multimodal coherence.

---

2   Likewise, O'Halloran (2005) suggested that visual and verbal components are approached as covariate arrangements enhancing a bidirectionality of semantic relations between the two modes, supporting the variety of reading paths that could be followed in a multimodal text environment (Kress & van Leeuwen 1998).

Investigating intersemiotic visual–verbal relations through Systemic Functional Multimodal Discourse Analysis (SF-MDA)

The purpose of the current study is to examine the intersemiotic texture of KPG reading comprehension source texts and to explore the extent to which they function as coherent multimodal texts. It scrutinises whether the use of the visual and verbal modes results in a mere co-existence without ideational connections between them or in a co-action that contributes to the content meaning potential of the source text. Moreover, the study investigates whether visual and intersemiotic meanings are required by reading comprehension items. The underlying assumption of this investigation is that if the verbal and the visual prove to be systematically connected in terms of ideational meanings, both modes could be deemed equally important for the meaning potential of a source text. If so, then that would unveil a new parameter for the preparation of candidates for a specific exam and would require the development of test-takers' multimodal literacy as a precondition for a better understanding of the KPG reading comprehension source texts and an important parameter for the successful completion of the exam.

The corpus of the data used for this research consists of 24 source texts (6,102 words and 46 images) included in reading comprehension test tasks of KPG English exams covering twelve exam periods (2007–12) at B1 language competence level. The majority of the source texts contained from one to three visuals except for two marginal cases, namely, one text which contained six visuals and another one which contained no visuals. In order to guarantee consistency and reliability in the research, it was decided to only analyse articles and information leaflets quantitatively and qualitatively because they are non-fiction texts with quite similar structures, purposes and features in contrast to other text-types used in reading comprehension test tasks (e.g. a diary). Another decisive parameter for the selection of these text-types was the fact that they are the most frequently found text-types in reading comprehension test tasks at B language competence level.

Methodologically, the Multimodal Analysis Image (henceforth MMA) interactive software (O'Halloran et al. 2012) was used as a tool for annotation and analysis to conduct Systemic Functional Multimodal Discourse Analysis (SF-MDA) to discern how visual and verbal components work together to create an impact and achieve the purposes of the texts (Tan et al. 2012).[3] Although the synergistic co-action of the visual and the verbal mode is expected to contribute to meaning making in all strata of meaning (i.e. ideational, interpersonal, textual), this chapter will only focus on the ideational metafunction because the focus of the study is the visual-verbal relations in terms of content. From an ideational metafunction perspective, according to Kress and van Leeuwen (1996), visual messages can be divided into processes, participants in the processes and circumstances of the occurrence of those processes. As regards intersemiosis, which is the focus here, the MMA software provided a list of available visual-verbal relation option choices of similarity (namely, illustration, repetition and addition) and difference (namely, contrast and displacement), which could possibly be found in multimodal texts such as the source texts of the data used in this research. In terms of similarity, the words may describe the image through illustration or mirror the concepts and ideas in the visual through repetition or the image may add something new to what is expressed in the verbal text through addition. In terms of difference, the concepts expressed in the image might offer a contrast to the ones expressed in the text or be totally unrelated to them (Tan et al. 2012).

In relation to aforementioned research on intersemiosis, the MMA subgroup of *similarity* shares a common purpose with Unsworth's (2007) grammar-based expansion category (i.e. the augmentation subgroup from complemetarity). From a discourse-based perspective, both illustration and

---

3   Explaining the design of the software, O'Halloran et al. (2014) attest that social
     semiotic theory and advanced computer techniques of analysis are employed in
     order to link low-level features in media texts to higher order semantic information.
     The multimodal analysis image software was originally and primarily designed to be
     used by researchers and expert analysts but underwent simplifications and technical
     adjustments in order to be more approachable for teaching purposes as well (Lim-Fei
     et al. 2015: 919).

repetition offer a reformulation of experiential meanings expressed by one mode or the other, constructing comparative relations (Liu & O'Halloran 2009; Martin 1992). Illustration should be selected when a part of the source text is described in the visual, or a part of a visual is described in the source text. On the contrary, repetition should be chosen for straightforward cases of the visual mirroring the verbal, so that the two available MMA choices of comparative relations can be discerned. The MMA option of addition is considered to be compatible with the additive relations from Liu and O'Halloran's (2009) framework, which refer to the instances when new information is added from one mode to what is expressed by the other.

The second MMA subgroup termed *difference* is reminiscent of Unsworth's second complementarity subgroup, or so-called *divergence* (Unsworth 2007). The MMA difference encompasses instances of contrast or displacement. For the purposes of the current data analysis, contrast is selected when the visual and the verbal contain semantically contrastive elements, while displacement serves for the cases when ideas and concepts presented in the image are completely irrelevant to the ones included in the written text. From a discourse-based standpoint that Liu & O'Halloran (2009) prefer, the MMA contrast option can contribute to the coherence of the text by providing a contrastive cohesive tie between text and image. However, displacement does not seem to offer intersemiotic cohesive ties that promote intersemiotic texture coherence.

Moreover, this study attempts to discover whether and to what extent the meaning input from the visual mode and the intersemiotic relations is required from the test-takers in order to respond to test items successfully. To this end, forty-five gist items[4] were analysed which accompany the B1 level source texts of the same exam periods. The study classified gist items into types of gist items (henceforth TGIs) in order to examine them as groups of similar items in terms of their meaning requirements and to demonstrate whether there are TGIs which necessarily demand test-takers' visual or intersemiotic literacy in terms of the ideational metafunction.

---

4   Gist items require test-takers to respond on the basis of general rather than the spe-
     cific information in the source text.

Findings about visual-verbal relations of KPG reading comprehension source texts

Using the MMA software, specifically for visual–verbal relations, offers a number of system choices which relate to intersemiosis around the two main categories of similarity and difference (Tan et al. 2012).[5] These MMA system choices were applied to all texts in the data and the results are presented in Table 5.1 (ibid.). For reasons of consistency, since the number of visuals varied in every text, a study was made primarily of the intersemiotic relations between the main visual display of each source text and the linguistic messages in the headline, the lead paragraph or the main text/ story in order to draw conclusions on visual–verbal relations.

Table 5.1:   Instances of visual–verbal relations

Visual–Verbal Relations	No. of instances	No. of texts
SIMILARITY	57	24
ILLUSTRATION: 'if the words of the surrounding text describe what is shown in the image, the image functions as illustration'	22	17
REPETITION: 'if the concepts and ideas mirror those expressed in the text, the image functions as repetition'	27	18
ADDITION: 'if the image expands or adds something new to the concepts and values that are expressed in the text, the image functions as addition'	8	8
DIFFERENCE	2	2
CONTRAST: 'the concepts and ideas expressed in the image contrast with those expressed in the text'.	2	2
DISPLACEMENT: 'the concepts and ideas expressed in the image are not at all related to the concepts and ideas expressed in the text'.	0	0

5   See O'Halloran et al. (2012, 2014) for a detailed description of all the features included in the software.

As Table 5.1 illustrates, overall the main visuals of all source texts were clearly related to the verbal texts and represented similar ideas, concepts or things. This was proven by the fact that at least two instances of similarity were found on average in every source text. In particular fifty-seven instances of similarity were detected in twenty-four texts. The instances of illustration and repetition outnumbered those of addition. Therefore, there seems to be a pattern of using visual elements which either show what is described in the verbal text or mirror particular persons, animals or things referred to in the verbal part of the source text. In about one third of the data, the image added or expanded what was said in the written text through addition. It should be mentioned that although additions can have an aesthetic effect, their role should not be downgraded to the decorative level. On the contrary, they contribute to the content meaning potential of a multimodal text. On the other hand, just two instances of difference were found in the total of B1 level source texts in the sub-type of contrast and none in the sub-type of displacement. Consequently, visual and verbal elements that do not complement each other were highly infrequent in the source texts while thematically irrelevant visuals were not found. This indicates a synergistic role of the verbal and the visual modes in B1 reading comprehension texts, as they work jointly in order to present associated rather than incompatible concepts, persons, animals, things or ideas.

To exemplify how these visual-verbal relations were realised in the source texts, each one will be referred to using instances from the data. First, instances of the frequent and various occurrences of similarity will be addressed before elaborating on the two cases of difference (i.e. contrast) (see Figure 5.1). 'TEXT: workaholic' is a one-column article which talks about people who are addicted to work and expresses the author's opinion on this issue. The source text contains only one visual which is a cartoon that shows a person who is working intensively using a typewriter in order to do a great amount of work. By means of illustration, the concept of being a workaholic is described in the verbal text and shown in the main visual display. The visual illustrates a lot of parameters of being a workaholic, for example, working hard, for a long time and at a quick pace. Another instance of illustration is detected in 'TEXT: politeness' (Figure 5.2). This source text discusses the issue of treating other people with politeness and it draws on the writer's personal experience in relation to politeness in Germany and Britain. The source text is organised in two columns with one visual embedded in them. It is a three-dimensional picture representing two white figures standing on two puzzle pieces of different colours and shaking hands with each other. The idea of being polite is depicted through the illustration of a positive gesture of politeness, namely that of shaking hands with someone.

'TEXT: satellites' (Figure 5.3) is a factsheet which presents satellite system information and news. The source text is designed as an article found in a website about space. It is organised in one column and contains one visual, which is a photo of a satellite. Ideationally, the photo is clearly a visual of a satellite used primarily to display the appearance of a satellite, which is the main issue under discussion in the verbal text. Hence, the purpose of this visual is to mirror the main participant of the source text (i.e. a satellite) through the visual-verbal relation of repetition.

Apart from the frequently discovered relations of illustration and repetition, ideas or concepts were added to what was written through the visual mode by means of addition. For example, 'TEXT: women's history' (Figure 5.4) provides factual information about the different ways people have celebrated women's accomplishments by addressing historical events and presenting current information. A painting of a woman is placed on the left side of the one-column article. The depicted woman is wearing casual clothes (i.e. a denim shirt) and a headband. Her style of dress indicates a woman who is part of the workforce of society. The fact that she is raising the sleeve of her shirt with the intention to show the strength of her muscles is associated with her appearance as a working woman. The inclusion of the statement 'we can do it' in the visual contributes to a visual-verbal homospatiality effect, which directly enhances the meanings of the visual. This statement emphasises the woman's attitude, according to which women are deemed to be powerful and competent enough to accomplish their goals. Overall, the depiction of the woman constitutes a symbol, the addition of which intends to convey female strength and the constant fight for women's emancipation.

As mentioned previously, the vast majority of visual-verbal relations were instances of similarity but there were two instances where content information included in the headline contrasted with content information included in the main visual display. With regards to the first instance of contrast, 'TEXT: are we alone' (Figure 5.5) is a two-column magazine article which reports on a recent survey about people's beliefs in relation to life on other planets. It begins with a rhetorical question 'Are we alone in the Universe?' in its headline and contains two visuals. The main visual display is located at the beginning of the article and shows an alien. The second visual depicts planets in a solar system. The ideational meaning of the relational process of being and the adjective 'alone' in the universe contrasts the content information depicted in the main visual display, which illustrates an alien that is assumed to be the resident of another planet. Ideationally, the idea of being alone contrasts with the idea of being among aliens. Alternatively, if another headline was used which included the idea of alien life such as 'Aliens live with us' or 'We are not alone in the universe', the relation with the main visual display would be that of illustration since

Workaholic

'Workaholics anonymous' is for real. Membership is free and the only qualification you need is the wish to stop working all the time. My favourite thing about it is that they also have meetings online and by phone for people who are too busy to turn up in person!

What's so wrong with being a workaholic anyway? At least it's better-paid than being addicted to more dangerous habits. Instead of getting you into debt, it gets you promotion, extra money and more interesting work. Aren't these things what most people want? Like many who work late into the night, I am a workaholic and proud of it. I know it's not very healthy, but it is preferable to being lazy. It's the latter who are likely to develop more dangerous addictions.

But there is a difference between those who are workaholics because they love their work and can relax at some point and those who are workaholics because they have nothing better to do.

I once saw a colleague get promoted to a job she was not ready for and she began to work around the clock to cover up for the fact that she didn't know what she was doing. The more hours she worked, the worse things became. In six months, she had a nervous breakdown.

Anyway, the point is you have to know whether being a workaholic is good for you and those around you. If you can manage to be a bit of a workaholic and yet still lead an ordinary life outside work, you're fine. If not, maybe you need help.

Figure 5.1 TEXT: Workaholic.

Politeness

By Willy Wiedenmyer

It's really true what people say about English politeness: it's everywhere. When squeezing past someone in a narrow space, people say 'sorry'. When getting off a bus, English passengers say 'thank you' to the driver. In Germany, people would never dream of doing this: bus drivers are just doing their job!

I used to think the German way, until I was in Britain for a few years. I understood that there were more polite ways of treating people and I began to adopt some of those ways too!

When people buy something in a shop, both customer and shop assistant usually thank each other, twice or more. In Germany, it would be unusual to hear more than one 'thank you' in such a conversation. British students thank their lecturers when leaving the room. English employers thank their employees for doing their jobs, but Germans think that paying their workers money is already thanks enough!

But there is another side to British politeness. One word that comes to mind here is 'artificial'. Although it is enjoyable to talk with friendly people, it has often made me wonder what the English really think. In fact, this confused me throughout my stay in England. Everyone at the University I attended seemed to like me and people in my class were kind and friendly but I found it hard to understand who was really my friend and who was 'just being polite'.

I must say that British politeness is a little puzzling to me. For example, I often wonder why the English lose it when they drink too much. And then I think: maybe, drinking is a good excuse for being rude once in a while... After all, having to be polite all the time can be stressful, right?

WORLDtravel   15

Figure 5.2: TEXT: Politeness.

the idea of alien creatures existing in the universe would be both described in the verbal text and shown in the visual. The second example of contrast is found in the 'TEXT: pay attention' (Figure 5.6). The text is organised in paragraphs and sections. The article discusses the problems in terms of discipline in the classroom and offers possible solutions for the problem of not paying attention. On the right of the text there are three pictures. The main visual display is the central photo which shows a student who is not paying attention to the lesson and he is occupied with throwing an object, probably towards his classmates. The same idea of not paying attention is illustrated in the third visual as the central participant is not paying attention because she is looking out of the window. The first visual is thematically relevant as it depicts books but it mainly serves an aesthetic purpose. The visual-verbal relation between the headline 'Pay Attention' and the main visual display is one of contrast. The material process of throwing objects contrasts with that of paying attention to the lesson mentioned in the

SATELLITES

A satellite is defined as any object that orbits – that is, goes around – any other object. Satellites can be celestial bodies, such as a moon orbiting a planet in the solar system, or a planet in the solar system orbiting the sun. Satellites can also be constructed. Made up satellites are typically launched into outer space to collect data, photos and other information about the Earth and all the many things that exist around it.

From studying outer space and the atmosphere of the earth to tracking weather patterns and acquiring intelligence, satellites illuminate us with vital information and visual imagery that cannot be captured in any other manner. The first artificial satellite was Sputnik I launched by the Soviet Union on 4 October 1957. The largest artificial satellite currently orbiting the Earth is the International Space Station.

The United States Space Surveillance Network (SSN) began recording space objects with the launching of Sputnik I and since then, the SSN has tracked more than 26,000 space objects orbiting the earth. Nowadays more than 8,000 artificial objects move around the earth.

Stay up to date with the latest satellite system information and news. Whether you're interested in NASA and the Mars Renaissance Orbiter, which was the most recent satellite to visit the red planet, or the ongoing global race to further research and explore the moon, our diverse satellite images, articles and other news features will expose you to distant places, planets and infinite possibilities for learning more about this expansive galaxy we call home.

Figure 5.3: TEXT: Satellites.

WOMEN'S HISTORY MONTH

Every March, the country celebrates the accomplishments of women throughout American history

Interest in International Women's Day **(25)** remained pretty low until the 1960s, when the women's movement **(26)** motivated women to wonder why they weren't **(27)** included in the history books!

In 1978, a California school district began Women's History Week to promote the teaching of women's history. It was so popular that in 1981, the week **(28)** developed into a yearly event for the entire country!

In 1987, a group of women campaigned with representatives from museums, schools and libraries and **(29)** expanded the feeling, so that the entire Month of March was called National Women's History Month that very same year!

Two years ago, the first-ever national women's history museum opened in Dallas, Texas. "The Women's Museum: An Institute for the Future" pays tribute to women who **(30)** succeeded in the past, and **(31)** manages 'Girlstart', a program that **(32)** encourages young women to consider working in math, science and computer technology.

Figure 5.4: TEXT: Women's history.

DISCOVERmag   March 2012

Are We Alone In the Universe?

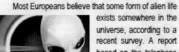

Most Europeans believe that some form of alien life exists somewhere in the universe, according to a recent survey. A report based on the telephone survey informs us that 60 percent of those asked believe that life exists on other planets. Most people agreed that they would be 'excited' if life was discovered on other planets. They also said that the Earth should reply to any message from another planet. The survey follows a TV documentary, *Life out there*, which has now been seen by millions of viewers worldwide.

'It is quite likely that there is life somewhere in our galaxy, and there's a real possibility that we will find evidence of life on other planets by the year 2025', said Paul Steiner, senior astronomer, who appeared in the programme *Life out there*. Most of the people who believed in life on other planets also said they thought it is likely that aliens are more intelligent than humans.

One argument put forward for the existence of life on other planets is based on the vast size of the Universe. According to this argument, supported by scientists such as Stephen Hawking, it would be improbable for life to exist only on Earth. On the other hand, the belief that some unidentified flying objects (UFOs) are from other planets is not taken seriously by most scientists. Most UFOs have been explained either as aircraft, or as a joke of some kind.

Figure 5.5:   TEXT: Are we alone.

Pay attention!

The problem

Teachers frequently complain about students who don't pay attention in class and often make a lot of noise. Having to tell students off all the time disrupts the class and wastes valuable time. 'Switching off' for a short time in class is quite natural in some children but attention problems can be quite serious if they carry on: such pupils fall behind the rest of the class.

What you can do

One solution to these problems is to ignore them and hope they go away. But they rarely do. So teachers usually punish students who behave badly. This strategy is often combined, sensibly, with 'rewards' for those who play the game according to the rules. Rewards can take the form of an amusing activity or something light, such as a song or a game, as a break from dull classroom routine. But getting students' attention can begin from the very first moments of the lesson. Like a good book or film, the first few minutes of a class should get your attention, so you follow the main part of the story with greater interest. For example, you can sometimes start the lesson in a way you haven't done before. Finally, one thing all teachers can do to get the attention of their students is to develop 'rapport' in class. Rapport is the good relationship we have with other people. Building an enjoyable atmosphere in class is more effective than any system of crime and punishment!

Figure 5.6:   TEXT: Pay attention.

headline. If the visual showed students looking at the board or participating in the lesson by raising their hands to answer a teacher's question, the visual-verbal relation between the headline and the main visual display would be one of illustration.

To facilitate test developers', teachers' and test-takers' attempts to understand the potential source text intersemiotic meaning, attempts were made to make visual-verbal relations more comprehensible through a more tangible sub-classification using examples from the data. An analysis was conducted of the intersemiotic relations between the visuals and the linguistic messages in the headline, the lead paragraph or the main text or story. In Table 5.2, the findings are grouped according to the MMA options (i.e. illustration, repetition, addition and contrast) found in the texts of the corpus. Ultimately the detailed analysis of these findings offers a broader repertoire of categories of each MMA system choice. The purpose of Table 5.2 is to display subgroups of each MMA system choice in **bold** accompanied by at least one example from the data source texts.[6]

Table 5.2: Visual–verbal relations: Grouping of data instantiations

Visual–Verbal Relations in MDAs of B1 Level Source Texts		
Types of Intersemiotic Relations	Instantiations	Source Text
Verbal Content Infornation	Visual Content Information	Source Data
Illustration		
an abstract entity		
• the Trojan War	a scene from the Trojan war	*Homer*
• children's life	a scene from children's life	*Dogtooth*
• a problem	not paying attention to the lesson	*Pay Attention*
• interest	green travellers showing their interest: hugging local people	*Traveller's Code 2*

6   The examples are indicative, aimed at illustrating the categories in bold.

Visual–Verbal Relations in MDAs of B1 Level Source Texts		
Types of Intersemiotic Relations	Instantiations	Source Text
a new/unfamiliar concept		
• medical tourism	a comic strip showing some of the participants of medical tourism (hospitals, airplanes and the globe) in interaction	*Medical Tourism*
• new Spain	recently structured areas and futuristic buildings in Spain	*New Spain*
a described process		
• horses walking	wild horses walking in Nestos valley	*Nestos Valley*
a concept		
• body language	a handshake	*Body Language*
Repetition		
an entity		
- an object: satellites	a satellite	*Satellites*
- a person: students	Students	*Pay Attention*
- a building; the Parthenon	the Parthenon	*Parthenon*
- a place: Nestos valley and river	Nestos valley and river	*Nestos Valley*
a gesture	a handshake	*Body Language*
circumstances - conditions of living	people living in a rainforest	*Tropical Rainforests*
Addition		
a symbol	a woman's strength	*Women's History*
a process	people harvesting rice	*Rice*
a person	well-known personalities	*Special Olympics*
a print text	magazine covers with soap opera scenes	*Soap Operas*
Contrast		
a process		
- **a relational process**	not being alone in the Universe	*Are We Alone*
- **a material process**	not paying attention	*Pay Attention*

In Table 5.2, a variety of examples are provided to compare illustrations in order to clarify this quite obscure kind of relation. An abstract entity like a problem under discussion was illustrated with a visual to provide a more tangible depiction of it. A person's life could become better understood through an image showing a scene from the person's day-to-day activity. A concept which might be unfamiliar for readers was illustrated, such as in the example of New Spain which contrasts with the more familiar existing notion of Spain, in 'TEXT: New Spain'. A concept such as, for example, body language, which is quite abstract was illustrated through a more concrete example from people's actions, for example, the act of shaking hands. A process described in the written text was also depicted as well (e.g. wild horses walking in Nestos valley, in 'TEXT: Nestos Valley').

To continue with the second comparative relation category (i.e. repetition), entities such as persons, animals or objects were referred to in the verbal text and were shown in the accompanying visuals, contributing to the depiction of what the text was talking about. Moreover, circumstantial information was translated from the written mode to the visual mode. Regarding addition, new information about what was discussed in the text was provided through the accompanying visual. The depiction of a symbol, a process or an object could give test-takers extra information which could assist them in the meaning-making process. Other instances of addition include a visual which depicted well-known personalities, who were not mentioned in the text, and the visuals of print texts like leaflets or magazine covers which were relevant to the topic under discussion. With reference to contrast, both instances detected in the data are included here since, interestingly, different kinds of processes were contrasted (i.e. material processes and relational processes).

Finally, having explored the visual-verbal relations in the source texts, the participants were analysed in order to investigate which were presented both verbally and visually. Special interest was paid to the main participant of each text and the frequency with which that participant was presented intersemiotically. It was found that the main participant of each verbal text was represented in the visual mode in the vast majority of the source texts. Therefore, source texts included in reading comprehension test tasks at B1 language competence level seem typically to depict the main participant of the verbal text in their main visual display.

In summary, the source texts included a variety of visual-verbal relations (i.e. illustration, repetition, addition and contrast) which contributed to the source text ideational meaning potential. This finding indicates that the visual mode actively participates in the representation domain of the source texts. The relations were further grouped into sub-categories on the basis of the instances of intersemiotic relation which were found in the source texts. This sub-classification of visual-verbal relations offered more specific types of each relation. On the whole, the analysis of visual-verbal relations underlines how the visual mode acts in co-operation with the verbal mode. Thus, it has a contribution to the meaning potential of the source text by adding intersemiotic meanings. But the question of whether reading comprehension test items that accompany the source texts require elements of this visual contribution to the ideational meaning potential triggered the following analysis of gist items.

Analysis of gist items

The gist items that accompanied the B1 source texts of the data used here were classified according to their content and purpose into Types of Gist Items (TGIs). Since preliminary findings showed that some gist items shared a common purpose, the gist items were grouped and TGIs were listed for practical reasons. This classification helped in discovering the frequency of occurrence of each gist item type. In this way, conclusions regarding the most frequently found TGIs in B1 level exams could be made. The grouping of similar gist items in a list of TGIs could be further employed for other gist items included in other reading comprehension test tasks of the same or a different level. The analysis of the forty-five gist items showed that they belonged to the following twelve TGIs (see Table 5.3).

The findings presented in the previous section showed that the visual mode contributes to the source text meaning potential as the visual and the verbal are intersemiotically related through illustration, repetition, addition or contrast. However, in the context of reading comprehension

Table 5.3: Types of Gist Items (TGIs)

Types of Gist Items		
Questions		Frequency of occurrence %
TGI1.	What the aim of the text is	23.4%
TGI2a.	What a possible/alternative title for the text would be	2.13%
TGI2b.	What the full title of the text would be	2.13%
TGI3.	What the source of the text is	6.38%
TGI4a.	What the writer's attitude towards the main theme/ participant of the text is	6.38%
TGI4b.	What impresses the writer about the main topic	2.13%
TGI5.	What the target audience is	19.15%
TGI6.	Who the writer of the text might be (role/occupation)	2.13%
TGI7.	What conclusion can be drawn from the text	6.38%
TGI8.	Who the writer of the text might be (personal life)	4.25%
TGI9.	Where the text pays emphasis	2.13%
TGI10.	What the text is about	12.77%
TGI11.	What the reader will probably do after reading the text	4.26%
TGI12.	What the writer does in the text	4.26%

testing, apart from the analysis of the source text itself, the analysis of test item requirements is also necessary. Test-takers are expected to be engaged in the reading comprehension process in order to respond correctly rather than merely read and comprehend a text as they would do in a real-life context. Since the reason why the gist items were analysed was to investigate whether and to what extent the visual mode is required for the successful completion of reading comprehension test tasks, each gist item was treated separately and used to determine whether test-takers would necessarily derive meanings from the visual mode in order to provide the correct response, or if it confirmed that the content information of the verbal text was sufficient for the correct multiple choice answer to be selected. It was then examined whether visual and intersemiotic literacy requirements were posed by gist items which belonged to the same type, in order to draw conclusions about each TGI. Analysis at this stage focused on answering the following questions: are there TGIs which directly require intersemiotic meanings in order to be answered successfully? Can the meanings of the visuals contribute to test-takers' processing of the text with the aim of answering a gist item correctly? Is the visual mode alone sufficient for the test-taker to answer an item? Is the verbal mode sufficient for a test-taker to answer all the TGIs without taking the visuals into consideration?

Twelve different types of gist items were detected in the data. The TGIs were about various issues concerning the whole text, such as the aim of the text, the title, the source of the text, the writer's attitude, the target audience, the topic of the text. While all three strata of meaning (i.e. ideational, interpersonal and textual) are expected to construe meaning simultaneously, in the data it seems that certain TGIs are strongly related to a particular kind of meaning. For example, TGI10 (i.e. What is the text is about?) directly asks for the text content information (i.e. ideational meanings), TGI4a (i.e. What is the writer's attitude towards the main theme or participant of the text?) requires interpersonal meanings related to positive, negative or neutral attitudes, and TGI3 (i.e. What is the source of the text?) is strongly connected with the textual metafunction given that the design of the text plays an important role. The ideational metafunction, which is the focus in the present study, seems to be important for the majority of TGIs.

With regard to the frequency of occurrence of each TGI, the most frequent types of gist items were TGI1 (i.e. What the aim of the text is), TGI5 (i.e. What the target audience is) and TGI10 (i.e. What the text is about) which necessarily require ideational meanings to be answered. Regardless of the metafunctional focus of each TGI, the overall examination of test item stems and their available options in relation to the source text content indicated that the role of the visual seems to be supportive rather than fundamental for the selection of the correct option choice for the majority of the TGIs. It was not possible to answer any gist item by deriving meanings only from the visuals. The verbal always provided sufficient content information. Therefore, the visual offers a choice for meaning making but is not directly or necessarily required by the gist items. There was no gist item which only required meanings derived from the visual elements, and no gist item was found in the source text which directly asked for the detection of an intersemiotic relation.

Overall, the study investigated visual-verbal relations of similarity and difference in source texts. It found that the visual and the verbal do indeed co-act rather than merely co-exist since they are linked through illustration, repetition, addition and contrast. The detection of these inter-semiotic relations, coupled with the absence of displacement, renders the source texts supportive of the multimodal coherence of the source texts. This finding indicates that the visual contributes to the overall ideational meaning of the source text. Despite the importance of the visual in the meaning potential of the texts, gist item analysis showed that the meanings derived from the verbal were sufficient and the role of the visual was supportive for the successful completion of the test. No gist item was directed towards intersemiotic relations per se or the meanings that could be derived from a visual.

Discussion about ideationally oriented intersemiotic literacy requirements and implications

This chapter aims to contribute to the ongoing discussion about intersemiosis by adding insights into the visual-verbal relations of reading comprehension texts used in KPG English exams. This research supports Unsworth's (2007:1166) claim that students should extend their critical reading to images and engage in 'intermodal meaning making', or other meanings made through visual-verbal relations. Furthermore, the research presented in this chapter has shown that KPG test-takers should be able to comprehend visual-verbal interaction so as to construct further ideational meanings.

The study supports that KPG test-takers are required to design meaning in multimodal contexts for the great majority of the source texts, given that only a small minority of them do not contain images. For this reason, the main purpose of the chapter was to draw attention to the examination of the intersemiotic texture of the data. The vast majority of the data included an average of two instances of similarity per text. The regular existence of these intersemiotic cohesive ties adds to the multimodal coherence of the texts. Source text multimodal coherence is further enhanced by the fact that displacement instances were not found in the data, which proves that source texts typically include visuals which are conceptually and ideologically relevant to the verbal text. Moreover, the main visual display of B1 level source texts is always related to the main issue under discussion through illustration, repetition, addition and contrast. Hence this demonstrates that test-takers can count on both the verbal and the visual in the process of making ideational meanings while reading KPG multimodal source texts. In general, images are used for the reformulation and repetition of central ideas in the written text or for the addition of new but relevant information. Yet test-takers should be cautious with regard to the fact that sometimes ideas which are presented in the visual may contrast with what is written. Thus, careful meaning making based on the critical balance of both the visual and verbal input is recommended before test-takers' can make the correct response to the accompanying test items.

A distinguishing feature of current research in comparison to previous studies is the fact that no image in the data used here was followed by a caption, as for instance in Roth et al. (2005). Even without a caption, however, the ideational connection between the visual and the verbal is quite direct in most texts. The role of the image should not be characterised as merely decorative (Roth et al. 2005) since the visual builds an intersemiotic relation with the text and adds an aesthetically positive effect at the same time. Moreover, in contrast to Roth et al.'s (2005) and Unsworth's (2007) work which concentrated on a set of thematically relevant texts from science books, the current research was not confined to a measurable amount of thematic units. KPG reading comprehension source texts embrace a great variety of topics and have a large number of different participants involved in their main text or story. The range of topics and participants per text justifies the variety of visual-verbal relations reported in the study. Each visual played a different role and contributed in a unique way to the meaning potential of each source text.

Apart from the analysis of source text intersemiotic meaning potential, a closer look at gist item requirements can also underline the significance of the visual mode. The gist item analysis indicates that both verbal and visual ideational meanings can be helpful for the majority of TGIs as these meanings are typically related to the main issues under discussion. Thus, the role of the ideational meanings of visuals is to assist and their contribution strongly depends on the test-taker's awareness of possibilities for visual and intersemiotic meaning. There is no item that is solely directed towards the visual or a particular visual-verbal relation.[7]

This study shows that intersemiosis seems to make a considerable contribution to the ideational stratum of source text meaning potential. The fact that meanings are multiplied through visual-verbal co-action has several implications for the field of language testing and teaching. Teachers are expected to raise their students' awareness towards the synergistic work of visual and verbal modes. More specifically, students should be made aware that ideational meanings are offered through illustration, repetition, addition, contrast as well as their subcategories. It is suggested that KPG test-takers' repertoire of test-taking strategies should include the activation of visual and intersemiotic literacies as a tool to assist efficient meaning making. Moreover, since KPG source texts seem to be typically intersemiotically coherent, test-takers should be able to identify different types of intersemiotic linkages in the source texts. Language test developers are expected to be aware of the importance of intersemiotic texture and make a conscious selection of source text visuals in order to design coherent multimodal texts that have an intersemiotic effect. Moreover, visual and intersemiotic literacies should be systematically developed

---

7   Interestingly, the ideational meanings of the visuals together with the visual design of the source text, with its layout, typeface choices and arrangement in space (i.e. textual meanings), are very important or even necessary for the selection of the correct response for TGI₃ (i.e. What the source of the text is). This is the only TGI that cannot be answered correctly unless the test-taker takes visual elements into consideration. However, since the textual metafunction is very important for TGI₃, the contribution of the visual mode to this TGI was not elaborated on in this analysis.

by EFL learners since they are indispensable requirements for everyday communication.

Conclusion

From the research that has been conducted on the intersemiotic texture of KPG source texts, it is possible to conclude that well-founded visual-verbal relations exist in the source text multimodal discourse. The frequent detection of intersemiotic cohesive ties, such as instances of illustration, repetition, addition and contrast, proves that visual meaning resources do matter in terms of a source text's meaning potential from an idea-tional metafunction perspective. Thus, test-takers as meaning makers are urged to be involved in 'an ongoing process of contextualization' (Liu and O'Halloran 2009: 35), in which meanings are made through the interplay of verbal and visual modes. For this reason, test-takers are expected to not only develop verbal language awareness but also visual and intersemi-otic awareness in order to adequately comprehend a multimodal source text. Furthermore, the aforementioned conclusion concerning the signifi-cance of the visual mode is strengthened by the fact that the completion of the test tasks can be facilitated by the ideational meaning made on the basis of the visuals and their intersemiotic relations with the verbal texts. Therefore, the visual can play an important role not only for test-takers' holistic comprehension of the source text but also for reading based on gist item requirements. Overall, this study suggests that multimodal literacy be perceived as a prerequisite for effective meaning making in the context of KPG language testing.

In future research, ideational intersemiotic meanings should be further examined through the investigation of more KPG past papers. The subcat-egories of similarity and difference, presented in Table 5.2, could be further investigated, elaborated or even standardised. Apart from intersemiosis in the ideational metafunction, intersemiotic relations in interpersonal and textual metafunctions could be explored further. Finally, interesting outcomes are expected from the comparative investigation of visual-verbal relations between KPG exams for English and KPG exams for other languages or other exam batteries.

Bibliography

Bateman, J. (2008). *Multimodality and Genre: A Foundation for the Systematic Analysis of Multimodal Documents*. New York: Palgrave Macmillan.

Halliday, M. A. K. (1979). *Language as a Social Semiotic: the Social Interpretation of Language and Meaning*. London: Edward Arnold.

——(1994). *An Introduction to Functional Grammar*. London: Edward Arnold.

Halliday, M. A. K., and Hasan, R. (1976). *Cohesion in English*. London: Longman.

——(1985). *Language, Context, and Text: Aspects of Language in a Social-semiotic Perspective*. Geelong: Deakin University Press.

Hasan, R. (1985). 'The Texture of a Text'. In M. A. K. Halliday and R. Hasan (ed.), *Language, Context, and Text: Aspects of Language in a Social-semiotic Perspective*, pp. 70–96. Geelong: Deakin University Press.

Holsanova, J. (2012). 'New Methods for Studying Visual Communication and Multimodal Integration', *Visual Communication*, 11 (3), 251–7.

Jewitt, C., Bezemer, J., and O'Halloran, K. L. (2016). *Introducing Multimodality*. New York: Routledge.

Kress, G., Jewitt, C., Ogborn, J., and Tsatsarelis, Ch. (2001). *Multimodal Teaching and Learning: The Rhetorics of the Science Classroom*. London and New York: Continuum.

Kress, G. (2010). *Multimodality: A Social Semiotic Approach to Contemporary Communication*. London: Routledge.

Kress, G., and van Leeuwen, T. (1996). *Reading Images: The Grammar of Visual Design*. London: Routledge.

——(1998). 'Front Page: (The Critical) Analysis of Newspaper Layout'. In A. Bell and P. Garrett (eds), *Approaches to Media Discourse*, pp. 186–219. Oxford: Blackwell.

Lim Fei, V., O'Halloran, K. L., Tan, S., and Marisa, K. L. E. (2015). 'Teaching visual texts with the multimodal analysis software', *Educational Technology Research and Development*, 63, 915–35.

Liu, Y., and O'Halloran, K. L. (2009). 'Intersemiotic Texture: Analysing Cohesive Devices between Language and Images', *Social Semiotics*, 19 (4), 367–88.

Martin, J. R. (1992). *English Text: System and Structure*. Amsterdam: John Benjamins.

Martin, J. R., and Rose, D. (2003). *Working with Discourse: Meaning Beyond the Clause*. London: Continuum.

O'Halloran, K. L. (2005). *Mathematical Discourse: Language Symbolism and Visual Images*. London: Continuum.

—— (2007). 'Systemic Functional Multimodal Discourse Analysis (SF-MDA) Approaches to Mathematics, Grammar and Literacy'. In A. McCabe, M. O'Donnell and R. Whittaker (eds), *Advances in Language and Education*, pp. 77–102. London: Continuum.

O'Halloran, K. L., Podlasov, A., Chua, A., and Marisa, K. L. E. (2012). 'Interactive Software for Multimodal Analysis', *Visual Communication: Special Issue: Methodologies for Multimodal Research*, 11 (3), 363–81.

O'Halloran, K. L., Podlasov, A., Chua, A., Tisse, C.-L., Lim-Fei, V., and Smith, B. A. (2014). 'Challenges and solutions to multimodal analysis: Technology, theory and practice'. In Y. Fang and J. Webster (eds), Developing systemic functional linguistics: Theory and application, pp. 271–97. London: Equinox.

O'Halloran, K. L., Tan, S., and Marisa, K. L. E (2017). 'Multimodal analysis for critical thinking', *Learning, Media and Technology*, 42 (2), 147–70.

Roth, W., Pozzer-Ardhenghi, L., and Han. J. (2005). *Critical Graphicacy Understanding Visual Representation Practices in School Science*. Dordrecht: Springer.

Royce, T. D. (1998). 'Synergy on the Page: Exploring Intersemiotic Complimentarity in Page-Based Multimodal Text', *JASFL. Occasional Papers*, 1 (1), 25–49.

—— (1999). *Visual-Verbal Intersemiotic Complementarity in the Economist Magazine*. Unpublished PhD Thesis, University of Reading, UK.

—— (2007). 'Inter-semiotic Complementarity: A Framework for Multimodal Discourse Analysis'. In T. D. Royce and W. L. Bowcher (eds), *New Directions in the Analysis of Multimodal Discourse*, pp. 63–109. Mahwah, NJ: Lawrence Erlbaum Associates.

Royce, T. D., and Bowcher, W. (2007). *New Directions in the Analysis of Multimodal Discourse*. London: Routledge.

Tan, S., Marisa, K. L. E., and O'Halloran, K. L. (2012). *Multimodal Analysis Image (Teacher Edition)*. Singapore: Multimodal Analysis Company.

Unsworth, L. (2007). 'Image/Text Relations and Intersemiosis: Towards Multimodal Text Description for Multiliteracies Education'. In L. Barbara and T. B. Sardinha (eds), *Proceedings of the 33rd International Systemic Functional Congress (33rd ISFC) PUCSP*, pp. 1165–205. São Paulo, Brazil.

van Leeuwen, T. (2008). *Discourse and Practice: New Tools for Critical Discourse Analysis*. Oxford: Oxford University Press.

TRISEVGENI LIONTOU

6 Test-takers' strategies in responding to KPG English language reading comprehension tasks: Evidence from retrospective think-aloud protocols

ABSTRACT

Extensive research in EFL reading comprehension supports the view that a satisfactory understanding of the reading process not only depends on an accurate identification of the various text elements and the connections among them but also on a better description of the interaction between reader and text (Bachman 2000; Bailin & Grafstein 2001; Freebody & Anderson 1983). Motivated by these studies, this chapter reports on a one-year longitudinal study that aimed to investigate the reading comprehension strategies employed by 25 advanced EFL learners when preparing to take the Greek State Certificate in Language Proficiency, Reading Comprehension C1 test paper (KPG). To this end, the present study attempts, through the collection of retrospective think-aloud protocols, to shed light on the reading and test-taking strategies used by advanced EFL learners when responding to specific reading comprehension items of the KPG English Language Reading Comprehension paper and measure the extent to which successful EFL readers differentiate themselves from less successful ones in terms of their reading comprehension and test-taking strategies. The findings of the study add to the construct validity of the KPG English language exams and further provide practical guidance to EFL teachers, material developers and test designers as to the kind of reading comprehension strategies EFL learners develop in relation to their language competence level.

Introduction

Recent research in reading comprehension processes, when dealing with a foreign language from a psycholinguistics perspective, has highlighted the significant effect of reader factors on comprehension (Crossley et al. 2008a: 477; Drucker 2003: 25; Freebody & Anderson 1983: 278). At the same time, it has supported the view that a satisfactory understanding of the reading process, which involves operations at a number of different levels of processing, that is, lexical, syntactic, semantic, and discoursal, depends not only on an accurate identification of the various text elements and the connections among them, but also on the strategies used to actively reconstruct text meaning (Gürses & Bouvet, 2016: 22; Khalifa & Weir 2009: 19–20; Krekeler 2006: 121; Phakiti 2003: 651; Rayner et al. 2012: 246–7; Rupp et al. 2006: 445).

Test designers' knowledge of the variables that can influence the reading process and product is, thus, in many respects linked to the validity of the reading tests (Phakiti 2003: 651); test designers need to focus on making their test items as relevant as possible to described levels of difficulty on an a priori basis, and further ensure that these are not biased against particular test-takers nor affected in an unexpected way by readers' test-wiseness strategies (Lee & Kozminsky & Kozminsky 2001: 187; Parker et al. 2001: 308). By following such an approach, they will be able to provide evidence that the methods they employ to elicit data are appropriate for the intended purposes, that the procedures used provide stable and consistent data and, consequently, that the interpretations they make of the results are justified, since they are based on a valid and reliable exam system (Douglas 2001: 448). To this end, a number of testing scholars have called for more research in order to enhance our knowledge in terms of actual reader performance on specific text types (cf. Bailin & Grafstein 2001; Chalhoub-Deville & Turner 2000; Phakiti 2003). To answer the research calls in the literature, the current study, through the collection of retrospective think-aloud protocols, empirically investigates the effect specific reading and test-taking strategies have on the nature and product of the reading comprehension process in the context of the Greek State Certificate in Language Proficiency, Reading Comprehension C1 exam paper.

Literature review

Reading strategies and their impact on the process of constructing text meaning have received much attention over the last two decades (cf. Anderson 1991; Carrell et al. 1993; Salataci & Akyel 2002). According to Block (1986:

463), 'knowledge about the process, not just the product of reading, is needed, if we are to move from head-scratching to designing programs that truly meet the needs of our students', while Cohen (1994: 211) has noted that 'in order to assess reading comprehension in a second or foreign language, it is necessary to have a working knowledge of what that process entails'.

Especially in relation to language testing, a number of researchers have used think-aloud protocols (cf. Anderson et al. 1991; Cohen & Upton 2007; Nikolov 2006) or questionnaires (cf. Brand-Gruwel et al., 1998; Nevo 1989; Purpura 1997), while trying to gain a more in-depth understanding of the difficulties test-takers might experience when coping with a specific task, since test designers' assumptions concerning what they are testing often do not coincide with the actual processes respondents follow when taking a test (Anderson et al. 1991: 42). With specific reference to reading comprehension, research has shown that readers do exert a significant level of active control over their reading process through the use of strategies, which are conscious procedures that are deliberate and purposeful (Williams & Moran 1989; Urquhart & Weir 1998). In other words, while processes are general, subconscious or unconscious, and more automatic, strategies are subject to control, intentional and used to act upon the processes (Cohen 2005). Reading strategies in the context of second language reading have been grouped into three broad categories: (a) planning and identifying strategies that help in constructing the meaning of the text, (b) monitoring strategies that serve to regulate comprehension and learning, and (c) evaluating strategies by which readers reflect or respond in some way to the text (Upton & Lee-Thompson 2001; Carrell & Grabe 2002). At the same time, test-taking strategies have been defined as those strategies learners consciously select to apply when solving specific language tasks and can be best viewed as strategies purposefully employed when responding to a specific test item (Cohen 1998: 92; Phakiti 2003b: 28). At times, test-taking strategies may constitute short-cuts for arriving at answers, such as performing surface matching of identical information in the passage and in one of the response choices or not reading the text as instructed but simply looking immediately for the answers to the reading comprehension questions (Cohen & Upton 2007: 211). In such cases, the respondents may be using test-wiseness to circumvent the need to tap their actual language knowledge or lack of it and in this way not proceed via the text but rather around it (Allan 1992: 102, Cohen 1998: 92; Cohen & Upton 2007: 211–12).

Drawing on the existing literature, there is an increasing number of studies on L2 reading and test-taking strategies, which is beyond the scope of the present review to present in detail. However, a few characteristic examples of seminal research on L2 reading comprehension strategies under testing conditions are presented in an attempt to better understand their contribution to overall reading performance and test score variation. To begin with, a seminal and much quoted study regarding the use and effect of test-taking strategies on a multiple-choice test of foreign language reading comprehension was carried out by Nevo (1989). Aimed at ascertaining the strategies used by foreign language learners when taking a multiple-choice reading test, this research was based on the fundamental premise that it is possible to gain feedback from the subjects themselves concerning the strategies used when completing each test item. Although mentalistic procedures in the form of introspective and retrospective verbal reports had been employed in a number of previous studies, the innovation of Nevo's study lies in the fact that the research introduced a test format which enabled respondents to report on their strategies immediately after completing each test item. Thus, feedback was received in close sequence to the reading process itself. More specifically, 42 tenth-grade students of French, whose mother tongue was Hebrew, took a multiple-choice reading comprehension test in both languages. The test consisted of four passages with five multiple-choice questions per passage and participants were asked to answer each item separately and indicate in the strategy checklist which strategy was the most instrumental at the very moment of arriving at an answer (primary strategy) and, if possible, the second most frequently employed strategy (secondary strategy). This way Nevo secured a record of how respondents arrived at each chosen alternative and was able to ascertain which patterns of strategies respondents employed in order to handle the combination of text plus multiple-choice items in both their native and non-native language. The data analysis revealed that, in both languages, most of the correct responses were obtained by the use of similar contributory strategies, such as 'returning to the passage after reading the question and the multiple-choice alternatives in order to look for the correct answer', or 'locating the area in the text that the question referred to and then looking for clues to the answer in the context' (1989: 199, 208).

Interestingly, in the foreign language, there was greater use of strategies that did not lead to the selection of a correct response than in the first language. In fact, the principal difference between strategies employed in the first language and those used in the target language was with regard to the strategy designated 'guessing not based on any particular rationale', which was rarely used in first language but more frequently reported in foreign language reading (206). As Nevo speculated, 'it is possible that subjects' relative lack of command of the language could have led to lack of confidence, inadequate linguistic basis and incomplete understanding, which in turn caused them to guess without any particular rational considerations' (206). All in all, Nevo's research showed that there was a transfer of strategies from first to foreign language, in particular of contributory ones.

In an older study, Block (1986) used think-aloud protocols to examine the comprehension strategies used by college-level students, including both native and non-native speakers of English, as they read two different passages from a college textbook. Each passage was a self-contained selection that was rated at approximately the ninth grade readability level by the Fry readability formula. Strategies were categorised by Block into two types: general comprehension, which included comprehension-gathering such as anticipating content, recognising text structure and making inferences, and local linguistic strategies, which dealt with attempts to understand specific linguistic units through paraphrasing, rereading parts of the text or solving vocabulary problems by using context, a synonym or some other word-solving behaviour. Interestingly, the analysis showed that there did not seem to be a different pattern of strategy use between native and non-native readers, which, according to the researcher, suggested that strategy use was a stable phenomenon across learners, that is, second language readers bring with them their knowledge of language in general and then apply this knowledge to learning the specific features of another language. These results were confirmed in a subsequent study by Block (1992) who investigated the comprehension monitoring processes used by native and non-native readers of English as they read expository prose. Once again, think-aloud protocols from 25 college freshmen were collected (11 native speakers and 14 non-native ones) and no discrepancies were traced in their application of specific strategies. Carrell et al. (1993) also investigated the strategies of native and non-native learners on a random deletion cloze text in the first and second languages. Similarly to Block, results indicated that native and non-native speakers used the same strategies when dealing with a cloze text.

More recently, Purpura (1997: 293; 1998: 333) used structural equation modeling and exploratory factor analysis to investigate the relationships between test-takers' perceived strategy use and actual performance on foreign language tests. The 1,382 subjects that took part in his study answered an eighty-item cognitive and metacognitive strategy questionnaire before taking a standardised language test with thirty multiple-choice reading comprehension items. In contrast to his original hypothesis, Purpura found no significant effect of perceived cognitive or metacognitive[1] strategy use on second language test performance (Purpura 1997: 311). However, it was noted that successful and unsuccessful test-takers invoked strategies differently, that is, low performers showed an extremely high degree of metacognitive strategies (i.e. deliberate mental behaviors to direct and control their cognitive strategy processing for successful performance) in retrieving information from their long-term memory, whereas high performers used metacognitive strategies to help them understand and remember relevant text information (311). In line with Wesche (1987: 41) and Chamot and Kupper (1989: 14), Purpura concluded that the relationships between perceived strategy use and second language proficiency are extremely complex and at times very subtle, given the multidimensional nature of the constructs involved and the number of possible interactions that could occur between and among variables. As their use depends on

1   Cognitive strategies include making predictions, translating, summarising, linking
     with prior knowledge or experience, applying grammar rules and guessing meaning
     from contexts. Metacognitive strategies include planning and monitoring strategies.
     Planning strategies refer to L2 learners' actions of previewing or overviewing tasks to
     develop directions of what needs to be done, and how and when to do it. Monitoring
     strategies are learners' actions undertaken to check, monitor and evaluate their think-
     ing and reading performance (Phakiti, 2003). Metacognitive strategies are, thus,
     conceived as higher order conscious and deliberate mental processes that provide a
     cognitive management function in language use and other cognitive activities.

test-takers' characteristics, the setting in which testing occurs and the nature of test tasks, more research with a range of test-takers in different settings is needed to confirm or refute current claims.

Following Purpura's suggestion, Nikolov (2006) attempted to investigate twelve- and thirteen-year-old children's uses of strategies, while solving reading and writing test tasks in English as a foreign language. Verbal protocols on a series of tasks were collected from a random sample of fifty-two high, intermediate and low achieving EFL learners in public schools all over Hungary and two major trends regarding employed strategies were noticed. On the one hand, some participants used the same strategies, that is, reading text in English and translating item by item throughout the test booklet, whereas others applied the same ones only occasionally. On the other hand, strategies did not occur in isolation, but usually in combination with one another. For example, translating was often combined with a phonetic reading of unfamiliar vocabulary items. In line with Purpura, Nikolov pointed out that although participants were observed using a variety of cognitive and metacognitive strategies, their relationship was so complex that it remained unclear how they might have contributed to a better performance (2006: 33).

In a more recent study, Cohen and Upton (2007: 209) set out to explore the reading and test-taking strategies that EFL learners used on the reading section of the *LanguEdge Courseware* (2002) materials developed to familiarise prospective test-takers with the new TOEFL format. The investigation focused on strategies used to respond to both the more traditional, single selection multiple-choice formats and the new format of multiple selection reading comprehension items (2007: 209). Verbal report data were collected from 32 students representing various language groups and the analysis revealed that the strategies deployed were generally consistent with TOEFL's claims that the successful completion of this test section required academic reading-like abilities, since, instead of resorting to test-wiseness strategies, subjects generally drew on their interpretation of the passage in order to gain both a local and general understanding of it and answer pertinent reading comprehension questions (2007: 237).

To sum up, studies on reading strategies have shed some light on the different strategies readers resort to when trying to reconstruct text meaning, such as rereading or rephrasing parts of the text (Cross & Paris 1988: 131). However, given the limited amount of think-aloud research regarding the relationship between reading test performance and perceived strategy use by EFL learners (Anderson 2005; Johnstone 2006; Endley 2016; Nikolov 2009; Trendak 2015) further validation studies in this area are needed that will help test designers and test-takers alike become aware of the nature of such processes and their contribution to successful exam performance. In effect, data drawn from this study can be used to gain insights into advanced EFL learners' reading behaviour with an emphasis on decoding difficulties for lower performers.

Research methodology

The current study explored the relationship between reading comprehension performance and strategy use by advanced EFL readers in the context of the Greek State Certificate in Language Proficiency, C1 Reading Comprehension test paper. To this end, the following research questions were formed:

> Research Question 1: What kind of reading and test-taking strategies do advanced EFL learners report using when responding to the Greek State Certificate in Language Proficiency, C1 Reading Comprehension test tasks?

> Research Question 2: Are successful EFL readers differentiated from less successful ones in terms of their reading strategies and/or test-taking strategies when responding to the Greek State Certificate in Language Proficiency, C1 Reading Comprehension test tasks?

To answer those research questions, the following methodology was applied:

a. Retrospective Think-Aloud Protocols: in order to explore how advanced EFL readers process KPG C1 reading comprehension test prompts and respond to test questions, retrospective verbal protocols were employed. As already discussed in the previous section, verbal protocols have been extensively used as an instrument of data collection in the study of reading test strategies (Cohen 1984, 1986; Cohen & Upton 2007). Verbal protocols can be 'introspective' (occurring concurrently with the testing procedure) or 'retrospective' (occurring after the testing procedure is completed). While introspective protocols are more desirable since they are not limited by memory constraints or open to reconstructive modifications, a caveat exists in that the process of collecting them may, to some extent, alter the task being undertaken. This is so because 'the think-aloud data collection method itself acts as an additional task that must be considered carefully when examining learner performance' (Jourdenais 2001: 373). Bearing in mind this limitation, it was decided that retrospective protocols, which do not have a direct impact on the actual reading process when a task is undertaken, should be collected as follows: advanced EFL learners were asked to explain in their native language (L1: Greek) why they chose a particular answer once they had completed a reading question based on a specific text. The retrospective think-aloud protocol data was recorded and transcribed verbatim. Following that, two judges independently evaluated the presence of specific reading and test-taking strategies.

b. Twenty-five learners of English (12 males and 13 females) were recruited to participate in the study. The median age was twenty-two years of age and all participants were preparing for the KPG C1 English language exams having achieved a certified English language proficiency at intermediate level (B2). The participants had been taught English as a Foreign Language for five to six years before taking part in the research. Their native language was Greek. Before each session, the researcher trained the participants in the production of verbal reports. To avoid influencing the way participants would interact with actual reading questions and the way they would explain their thought processes later on in the project, a series of non-language tasks were used for training (e.g. conversations about their school experiences, hobbies, daily routine, etc.). For the main study, individual appointments were arranged. To avoid fatigue or lack of concentration on the part of the participants, individual sessions were adjusted to learners' abilities with a minimum of thirty minutes per session and a maximum of sixty minutes per session. Special care was taken to complete a set of items related to each text before closing the session to avoid repetition of the same text in a subsequent session.

c. Reading Comprehension Test Materials: ten official reading comprehension texts of the Greek State Certificate in Language Proficiency, C1 Reading Comprehension test paper administered between April 2005 and November 2009 examination periods were used in the main study.

d. Procedures for Data Analysis: while the study was by its very nature primarily a qualitative one, it was felt that some effort at quantifying the verbal report data would help to lend more rigour to statements about the frequency of reading and test-taking strategy use. Hence, a coding scheme was developed to count the occurrence of both reading and test-taking strategies in as finely tuned a manner as possible (see Appendix). The principal variables in the study, such as strategy types and item types, were measured as nominal variables and the total number of times a strategy was verbalised or otherwise indicated was tallied. Since it was possible that there was variety in the total number of questions per item type sampled in this study, a simple count of strategy frequencies would have distorted the importance of any given strategy. Hence, the raw strategy totals were converted into ratio scores using a type/token analysis: the ratio of number of occurrences of each strategy type in relation to the total number of items of a type used in data collection. The ratio scores derived from this analysis were then categorised by frequency in a partly empirical and partly intuitive way following Cohen and Upton's similar methodology (2006). The reason for this was that the finest distinctions seemed to be between low, moderate and high frequency of strategy use. At the highest frequency level, the numbers tended to become inflated by multiple uses of the same strategy by the same individual because multiple counting was allowed. The cut off points used in the present study were as follows:

- very high (VH) frequency ≥ 7.50
- high (H) frequency ≥ 5.00

- moderate (M) frequency ≥ 2.50
- low (L) frequency ≤ 2.49

Such a quantitative analysis reflects trends rather than hard and fast numbers. However, once significant relationships were determined between item types, the specific patterns of strategy use were more carefully examined, bearing in mind that reading and test-taking strategies invariably cluster together in response patterns, sometimes in sequence and sometimes in groups. The analysis focused on the patterns of strategy use that best characterise correct and incorrect responses for each item type but also paid close attention to whether the reported processes for responding to a given item were consistent with the test-constructors' aims and hence indicated that the item tests what it is meant to.

Following Cohen's work (2006), the process for identifying the strategies used by subjects in the present study was approached in much the same way as moves in a discourse genre are identified. A genre move refers to a section of a text that performs a specific communicative function; each move not only has its own purpose but also contributes to the overall communicative purpose of the genre (Bhatia 1993; Swales 1990). While a genre move represents a recognisable communicative event characterised by a communicative purpose, a reading or test-taking strategy represents a specific and recognisable choice made by the subject that is deliberate and purposeful and is intended to facilitate the reading or test-taking task (Cohen & Upton 2006). Verbalisations were classified into various strategies by determining what strategic function they revealed, including explicitly stated as well as obviously implied strategies. Consequently, strategy units had no set length. Most strategies tended to be represented by sentences, but some were signalled by single words, others by multiple sentences. It was also the case that multiple strategies (e.g. a reading and a test-taking strategy) could be signalled by the same verbalisation. Accurately identifying the different strategies and segmenting the transcribed verbalisations was a high priority. All strategy coding was checked by a second researcher, with any discrepancies in coding addressed through discussion.

Findings

Item type classification

The 25 advanced EFL learners that took part in the present study responded to a total of 100 reading comprehension items, that is, ten multiple choice reading comprehension items from ten C1 reading comprehension texts used between the April 2005 and November 2009 examination periods. The classification of item types was based on the general reading comprehension descriptors included in the KPG Exam Specifications booklet (Table 6.1). For the purposes of the present chapter, the analysis focused on a total of eight items (8×25 = 200 responses) representing two specific reading comprehension task types: four Main Idea items that are intended to measure test-takers' ability to understand main ideas, including ones that are not explicitly stated, and four Factual Information items that are intended to measure test-takers' literal comprehension, that is, ability to identify responses to questions about important factual information that is explicitly stated in a text (Table 6.1).

Table 6.1: Sample of KPG reading comprehension test item types

Specific Item Types	
Main Idea	Another possible title for the text would be ... The purpose of the text is ...
Factual Information	Saffron was used ... The experiment showed that ...

Strategy use in main idea items

In reviewing the reading and test-taking strategies that occurred at very high (≥7.50), high (≥5.00), and moderate (≥2.50) rates for the Main Idea items, the following notable strategy trends emerged as regards correct responses.

As can be seen in Table 6.2, among those who managed to choose the correct response, a strategy that occurred at a very high rate was a test-taking (T) one, namely, T21: 'selecting option through elimination of other option(s) as unreasonable based on overall passage meaning' followed by T7: 'predicting or producing own answer after reading the question and looking at the options'. A reading strategy (R) also occurred at a high rate, namely, R5: 'reading the whole passage one time rapidly', followed by R11: 'identifying an unknown word or phrase' and T19: 'selecting options through a sentence, paragraph, or passage's overall meaning'. It is worth pointing out that seven more reading strategies occurred at high and moderate rates for this item type such as R3: 'considering prior knowledge of the topic',

Table 6.2: Strategies for correct responses to main idea items

Strategy code	Strategy description	Frequency rate
T21	Selects options through elimination of other option(s) as unreasonable based on vocabulary, sentence, paragraph, or overall passage meaning.	10.0
T7	Predicts or produces own answer after reading the question and then looks at the options (before returning to text).	9.50
R5	Reads the whole passage one time and rapidly.	9.00
R11	Identifies an unknown word or phrase.	8.50
T19	Selects options through a sentence, paragraph, or passage's overall meaning.	8.50
R3	Considers prior knowledge of the topic.	7.00
R27	Translates from English into mother tongue to improve understanding	6.00
R17	Looks for sentences that convey the main ideas	5.50
R16	Identifies the key words of the passage	5.50
R14	During reading asks self about the overall meaning of the passage	5.50
R4	Reads the whole passage more than one time	5.00
R10	Repeats or paraphrases words, phrases, or sentences to aid or improve understanding	4.00

R17: 'looking for sentences that convey the main ideas', R16: 'identifying the key words of the passage', R4: 'reading the whole passage more than one time', R27: 'translating from English into mother tongue to improve understanding', R10: 'repeating or paraphrasing words, phrases, or sentences to aid or improve understanding' and R14: 'during reading asks self about the overall meaning of the passage'.

The following are some examples of these strategies:

T21:   Selecting an option through the elimination of other option(s) as unreasonable based on vocabulary, sentence, paragraph, or overall passage meaning.

Participant 8, Text 6, Question 1
Researcher: Question Number 1. Did you read the question?
Participant: Yes. 'The main purpose of the text is to ...'
Researcher: OK.
Participant: I have chosen, 'B- inform readers about Sofia'.
Researcher?   How did you come up with this answer?
Participant: I've read the whole text one time and option A-'criticize Sofia' doesn't seem correct because criticize is bad and the text says good things about Sofia. The third option C-record Sofia's history is not right because the text is not only about history. So, option B is more general ...

R4:   Reading the whole passage more than one time.

Participant 3, Text 2, Question 2
Researcher: I saw that you went back to the text.
Participant: Yes.
Researcher: Why?
Participant: To check if the answer is the correct one.
Researcher: How did you do that?
Participant: I read the whole passage one more time to get the general idea.

On the other hand, in exploring the reading and test-taking strategies that occurred at very high (≥7.50), high (≥5.00), and moderate (≥2.50) rates for incorrect responses in this item type, the following notable strategy trends emerged. As can be seen in Table 6.3, among those who did not manage to choose the correct response, two reading strategies occurred at a very high rate, namely, R11: 'identifying unknown sentence meaning' and 'identifying an unknown word or phrase' and R24: 'reading aloud to better understand the text'. Two test-taking strategies also occurred at a moderate rate, namely, T1: 'rereading the question for clarification' and T28: 'discarding options because of unknown words and opting for one of the other options'. Another test-taking strategy followed, namely, T25: 'selecting the option because it appears to have a word or phrase from the passage in it'. It is worth pointing out that two more test-taking strategies occurred at moderate rates for this item type such as T22: 'selecting options through elimination of other options as not comprehensive' and T18: 'selecting options through elimination of other option(s) as unreasonable based on vocabulary, sentence, paragraph, or overall passage meaning', both of which seem to focus more on specific vocabulary knowledge rather than overall text comprehension.

Table 6.3: Strategies for incorrect responses to main idea items

Strategy code	Strategy description	Frequency rate
R11	Identifies unknown sentence meaning and identifies an unknown word or phrase.	11.0
R24	Reads aloud to better understand the text.	9.00
T1	Rereads the question for clarification.	6.50
T28	Discards options because of unknown words and opts for one of the other options.	6.00
T25	Selects the option because it appears to have a word or phrase from the passage in it.	5.50
T22	Selects options through elimination of other options as not comprehensive.	4.00
T18	Selects options through elimination of other option(s) as unreasonable based on vocabulary, sentence, paragraph, or overall passage meaning.	4.00

The following are some examples of these strategies:

R11: Identifying an unknown word or phrase

Participant 19, Text 4, Question 1
Participant: I had too many unknown words. I couldn't understand a lot of things in the text.
Researcher: Which are these words?

Participant: yes ... obituary in option B and in the text deftly, re-puberty rituals,
                sanctuary, structuralism, scholarly, rigour, unappealing, cloistered. ...

T25:   Selecting the option because it appears to have a word or phrase from
                the passage in it

Participant 22, Text 9, Question 1
Participant: I chose C.
Researcher: Why?
Participant: I thought that ... because in the first option, there's nothing about
                Crete's historical presence, not about history and not B because the
                text is not about education. I don't know the meaning of the word
                'vision' in option D but the words tradition and culture are everywhere
                in the text.
Researcher: So you found the same words in the text.
Participant: Yes, many times.

Strategy use in factual information items

Factual information items are intended to measure test-takers' ability to
comprehend text details and identify responses to questions about important information that is explicitly stated in texts, including those with a
high level of linguistic complexity. In reviewing the reading and test-taking
strategies that occurred at very high (≥ 7.50), high (≥ 5.00), and moderate (≥ 2.50) rates for this item type, the following notable strategy trends
emerged as regards correct responses. As can be seen in Table 6.4, among
those who managed to choose the correct response, two test-taking strategies occurred at a very high rate, namely, T20: 'selecting option through
elimination of other option(s) as unreasonable based on background knowledge' and T21: 'selecting option through elimination of other option(s) as
unreasonable based on vocabulary, sentence, paragraph, or overall passage
meaning'. Four reading strategies also occurred at a high rate, namely, R10:
'repeating or paraphrasing words to improve understanding' followed by
R7: 'reading a portion of the passage carefully', R17: 'looking for sentences
that convey the main ideas' and R11: 'identifying an unknown word or

phrase'. It is worth pointing out that three more reading strategies occurred at a moderate rate for this item type such as R8: 'reading a portion of the passage rapidly looking for specific information', R16: 'identifying the key words of the passage' and R27: 'translating from English into mother tongue to improve understanding'. Four test-taking strategies were also used, namely, T25: 'selecting the option because it appears to have a word or phrase from the passage in it', T2: 'paraphrasing the question for clarification', T10: 'considering the options and focusing on a familiar option' and T4: 'reading the question and considering the options before going back to the passage' (4.00)

Table 6.4: Strategies for correct responses to factual information items

Strategy code	Strategy description	Frequency rate
T20	Selects option through elimination of other option(s) as unreasonable based on background knowledge.	10.0
T21	Selects option through elimination of other option(s) as unreasonable based on vocabulary, sentence, paragraph, or overall passage meaning.	10.0
R10	Repeats or Paraphrases words to improve understanding.	7.50
R7	Reads a portion of the passage carefully.	6.00
R17	Looks for sentences that convey the main ideas.	6.00
R11	Identifies an unknown word or phrase.	6.40
R8	Reads a portion of the passage rapidly looking for specific information.	4.50
R16	Identifies the key words of the passage.	4.00
R27	Translates from English into mother tongue to improve understanding.	4.60
T25	Selects the option because it appears to have a word or phrase from the passage in it.	6.00
T2	Paraphrases the question for clarification.	4.50
T10	Considers the options and focuses on a familiar option.	4.00
T4	Reads the question and considering the options before going back to the passage	4.00

The following are some examples of these strategies:

T21:   Selecting option through elimination of other option(s) as unrea-
              sonable based on vocabulary, sentence, paragraph, or overall passage
              meaning
R7:   Reading a portion of the passage carefully

Participant 21, Text 10, Question 8
Researcher: What is the question about?
Participant: 'The experiment showed that dogs ...?' I think it's (B) because '(A)
              are jealous when other dogs are present' is not correct because it says
              in the text that it was not the presence of the second dog. ... Also (C)
              is not mentioned. 'avoid eye contact with people. So B seems correct
              because in the text it says reactions to a sense of injustice so the dog
              had a sense of justice ...

T10:   Considering the options and focusing on a familiar option

Participant 23, Text 5, Question 49
Participant: Here I didn't know the meaning of 'introverted' in option A so I read
              the rest of the options ... my answer to this question is by chance
              because there were a lot of unknown words. ... I don't know the mean-
              ing of the word 'spirited' in option B so I chose 'C-mysterious because
              I know what is means ...

On the other hand, in reviewing the reading and test-taking strategies that occurred at very high ($\geq$ 10.00), high ($\geq$ 7.00), and moderate
($\geq$ 3.00) rates for incorrect responses in this item type the following notable strategy trends emerged. Among those who did not choose the correct
answer, the strategies that occurred at a very high rate (8.00) were once
again two reading ones, namely, R11: 'identifying an unknown word or
phrase' and R12: 'identifying unknown sentence meaning', followed by two
test-taking ones, namely, T27: 'discarding options because of unknown
words' and T25: 'selecting the option because it appears to have a word
or phrase from the passage in it', all of which once again seem to indicate
that advanced EFL learners were not always able to cope with unfamiliar
vocabulary through the elicitation of sentence or paragraph meaning
but rather discarded options because of the presence of unknown words

and opted for one of the other options that contained familiar words or phrases.

Table 6.5: Strategies for incorrect responses to factual information items

Strategy code	Strategy description	Frequency rate
R11	Identifies an unknown word or phrase.	8.00
R12	Identifies unknown sentence meaning.	8.00
T27	Discards options because of unknown words.	4.50
T25	Selects the option because it appears to have a word or phrase from the passage in it.	4.00

The following are some examples of these strategies:

T22:   Selecting the option because it appears to have a word or phrase from the passage in it

Participant 25, Text 4, Question 6
Participant: 'According to the passage, scientists have proved that?' Ok, I think it is A-dogs feel jealous of their owners because it says in the text that scientists have proved what many dog owners suspected: man's best friend is capable of feeling the human emotions of envy ...
Researcher: Did you read the rest of the text?
Participant: No because I found this at the beginning of the text ...

R11:   identifying an unknown word or phrase
R12:   identifying unknown sentence meaning.
T27:   discarding options because of unknown words.

Participant 22, Text 2, Question 8
Participant: I found this text very difficult. I don't know anything about soya and the words were difficult. I chose (C) because I don't know what versatile means in option A and manufacturers in option B. I'm not sure about this but the text says that more than 60% of all processed food in Britain today contains soya in some form so I think C is the same with the text ...

Discussion

The aim of the present research was to empirically investigate the effect specific reading and test-taking strategies have on the nature and product of reading comprehension in the context of language testing with specific reference to the Greek State Certificate in Language Proficiency exam. The focus was on the reading and test-taking strategies used by 25 advanced EFL learners when answering four Main Idea and four Factual Information reading items from the KPG C1 Reading Comprehension Test paper and measuring the extent to which successful readers differentiated themselves from less successful ones in terms of their reading strategies. To this end, 200 retrospective think-aloud protocols were collected. By asking the test-takers to think-aloud as they worked through these two item types, it was possible to analyse the resulting protocol and identify the cognitive processes involved in carrying out these tasks.

The first general finding was that the primary goal of the participants was to get the answers right. This was confirmed by the fact that among those who managed to choose the correct response in both item types, two test-taking strategies occurred at a very high rate, namely, 'selecting option through elimination of other option(s) as unreasonable based on overall passage meaning' and 'predicting or producing own answer after reading the question and looking at the options'. The second finding was that the strategies deployed were generally consistent with the KPG Exam Specifications that completion of this test section requires test-takers to have both a local and general understanding of the test passages. To be more specific, the Main Idea items were found to require understanding of the text at the passage level. The data revealed significant efforts on the part of test-takers to gain this understanding while working with these item types, including rereading, reading purposefully and carefully, and paraphrasing or translating to facilitate comprehension. In addition, this item type indeed challenged the test-takers to use powers of inference to recognise a general idea that was strongly implied but not explicitly mentioned. Related to the point above, high-performers clearly drew on their understanding of overall passage meaning while selecting or discarding options. Moreover, the length of the texts required that test-takers draw more on their memory of what they had read, as well as on what they had learned about the passage by responding to previous questions. Finally, it is worth pointing out that participants in the present study were clearly engaged in problem-solving activities, since they not only made efforts to gain a clear understanding of the text, but also worked to understand and evaluate the test question itself and the options that were given in light of the text. Especially when responding to Main Idea items, participants resorted to specific reading strategies such as: a) 'selecting options through a sentence, paragraph, or passage's overall meaning', b) 'considering prior knowledge of the topic', c) 'looking for sentences that convey the main ideas' and d) 'identifying the key words of the passage'.

As regards Factual Information items, data analysis revealed that advanced EFL learners were not always able to cope with unfamiliar vocabulary through the elicitation of sentence or paragraph meaning but rather discarded options because of the presence of unknown words and opted for one of the other options that contained familiar words or phrases. More specifically, Factual Information items were found to less often require understanding at the sentence level and most often at the paragraph level. In addition, test-takers seemed to be challenged to use powers of inference when they did not recognise vocabulary, a caveat they tried to overcome through test-taking strategies such as 'selecting option through elimination of other option(s) as unreasonable based on background knowledge' or even 'selecting the option because it appears to have a word or phrase from the passage in it'.

Finally, it should be noted that participants in the present study seemed to be more familiar with a limited number of planning and identifying strategies (e.g. planning how to read the passage, checking for prior knowledge of the topic, reading through the whole text, reading portions selectively), which they repeatedly used when processing texts or carrying out specific tasks. On the other hand, monitoring strategies that serve to regulate comprehension (e.g. predicting what will follow in the passage, and modifying comprehension based on new information) as well as evaluating strategies by which readers reflect on the text (e.g. inferring the meaning of unknown words based on textual clues) were reported at a much lower percentage. Based on these findings, it might be useful to draw EFL teachers' attention to the fact that more effort should be made to guide and train students in using a wider range of strategies, especially when processing texts that appear more difficult than expected. In addition, it might be useful to make EFL users more aware of some test-taking strategies, such as reading instructions attentively and rechecking questions before submitting their test papers. This way they may achieve their best performance and even feel less anxious when taking an exam.

As with all studies the implementation of the present one presented a number of challenges and limitations that will hopefully be overcome in future research. To begin with, since this was essentially a qualitative analysis, with some effort made to quantify the verbal report data for the purpose of comparing strategies for frequency of use, we must be wary of putting too much faith in the strategy frequency counts. At best, the data indicate trends in strategy use as reported by the respondents or clearly observable to the researcher who coded the collected data. It should be noted that, undoubtedly, there were other strategies in use that were not described in the verbal reports. In addition, there could have been strategies appearing in the verbal report that were actually used more or less often than indicated. It is also possible that respondents were making an effort to respond to each item more conscientiously than they would under normal circumstances. For one thing, the completion of the test was not timed, as it would be under normal circumstances. This was also a low-stakes task since their score was of no consequence to the respondents. In that sense, the conditions were different for those in place when respondents actually take the test. Nevertheless, it is believed that the data are clearly reflective of the kinds of strategic moves that advanced EFL learners make in an effort to answer the different types of reading items on the KPG English Language C1 Reading Comprehension exam paper. Finally, although the relationship between specific reading and test-taking strategies and mean task scores in pertinent reading comprehension questions was examined, it did not fall within the scope of the present study to include a more detailed analysis of individual text characteristics and their possible effect on actual performance. In other words, the correlation between lexicogrammatical complexity and average reading comprehension performance was not investigated but should form part of future research.

Conclusion

There is no doubt that reading comprehension is no easy task. On the contrary, it is a very complicated act essentially involving the text, the reader, the purpose of the reading action and the context in which the reading occurs. For example, reading to answer test questions in an exam situation – as the one investigated in this study – is very different from a situation where reading is done for pleasure, or where reading and understanding what a text says may be a matter of life or death at the moment that the action is occurring. However, even within the same context, such as in a test situation, what readers are asked to do largely determines what they will do with the text, how they will do it and how difficult the text will be for them. Factual test questions, for example, require a very different kind of reading process than inferential questions. That is to say, questions such as 'According to the text, scientists have proven that ...' involves readers in very different processes and places different cognitive demands on them than questions such as 'What is the author's position on the problem described in the text?'. This view confirms Anderson et al.'s original argument that there is no simple relationship between particular strategies and successful foreign language reading comprehension (1991). In line with Nikolov (2006), the present study showed that successful second language reading comprehension is not a matter of the reader possessing a single set of processing strategies, but rather a matter of controlling a wide and flexible repertoire of strategies and knowing how to use them effectively. Being fully aware of this, it is suggested that future research into the Greek State Certificate in Language Proficiency exams should also systematically investigate the impact of systematic strategy instruction on exam performance. The findings of the present research should be of considerable help in this endeavour.

Bibliography

Alderson, C. (2000). *Assessing Reading*. Cambridge: Cambridge University Press.

Anderson, J. (1991). 'Individual Differences in Strategy Use in Second Language Reading & Testing', *The Modern Language Journal*, 75 (4), 460–72.

Anderson, N., Bachman, L., Perkins, K., and Cohen, A. (1991). 'An Exploratory Study into the Construct Validity of a Reading Comprehension Test: Triangulation of Data Sources', *Language Testing*, 8 (1), 41–66.

Akyel, A., and Erçetin, G. (2009). 'Hypermedia Reading Strategies Employed by Advanced Learners of English', *System*, 37 (1), 136–52.

Bachman, L. (2000). 'Modern Language Testing at the Turn of the Century: Assuring that What We Count Counts', *Language Testing*, 17 (1), 1–42.

Bachman, L., and Palmer, A. (1996). *Language Testing in Practice: Designing and Developing Useful Language Test*. Oxford: Oxford University Press.

Bailin, A., and Grafstein, A. (2001). 'The Linguistic Assumptions Underlying Readability Formulas: A Critique', *Language & Communication*, 21 (3), 285–301.

Baumann, J., Seifert-Kessell, N., and Jones, L. (1992). 'Effect of Think-Aloud Instruction on Elementary Students Comprehension Monitoring Abilities', *Journal of Literacy Research*, 24 (2), 143–72.

Bernhardt, E., and Kamil, M. (1995). 'Interpreting Relationships Between L1 and L2 Reading: Consolidating the Linguistic Threshold and the Linguistic Interdependence Hypotheses', *Applied Linguistics*, 16 (1), 15–34.

Block, E. (1986). 'The Comprehension Strategies of Second Language Readers', *TESOL Quarterly*, 20 (3), 463–94.

Brand-Gruwel, S., Aarnoutse, C., and van Den Bos, K. (1998). 'Improving Text Comprehension Strategies in Reading and Listening Settings', *Learning & Instruction*, 8 (1), 63–81.

Brantmeier, C. (2005). 'Effects of Reader's Knowledge, Text Type and Test Type on L1 and L2 Reading Comprehension in Spanish', *The Modern Language Journal*, 89 (1), 37–53.

Carrell, P., Carson, J., and Zhe, D. (1993). 'First and Second Language Reading Strategies: Evidence from Cloze', *Reading in a Foreign Language*, 10 (1), 953–65.

Carrell, P. (1991). 'Second Language Reading: Reading Ability or Language Proficiency', *Applied Linguistics*, 12 (2), 159–79.

Chalhoub-Deville, M., and Turner, C. (2000). 'What to Look for in ESL Admission Tests: Cambridge Certificate Exams, IELTS and TOEFL', *System*, 28 (4), 523–39.

Cohen, A. (1984). 'On Taking Language Tests: What the Students Report', *Language Testing*, 1 (1), 70–81.

——(1986). 'Mentalistic Measures in Reading Strategy Research: Some Recent Findings', *The ESP Journal*, 5 (2), 131–45.

Cohen, A., and Upton, T. (2007). 'I Want to Go Back to the Text': Response Strategies on the Reading Subtest of the New TOEFL', *Language Testing*, 24 (2), 209–50.

Crossley, S., and McNamara, D. (2008). 'Assessing Second Language Reading Texts at the Intermediate Level: An Approximate Replication of Crossley, Louwerse, McCarthy, and McNamara (2007)', *Language Teaching*, 41 (3), 409–29.

Dabarera, C., Renandya, W., and Zhang, L. (2014). 'The Impact of Metacognitive Scaffolding and Monitoring on Reading Comprehension', *System*, 42, 462–73.

Douglas, D. (2001). 'Performance Consistency in Second Language Acquisition and Language Testing Research: A Conceptual Gap', *Second Language Research*, 17 (4), 442–56.

Drucker, M. (2003). 'What Reading Teachers Should Know About ESL Learners', *The Reading Teacher*, 57 (1), 22–9.

Endley, M. (2016). 'Proficiency as a variable in Gulf EFL students' employment of reading strategies', *Reading in a Foreign Language*, 28 (2), 183–223.

Farr, R., Pritchard, R., and Smitten, B. (1990). 'A Description of What Happens When an Examinee Takes a Multiple-Choice Reading Comprehension Test', *Journal of Educational Measurement*, 27 (3), 209–26.

Garner, R. (1987). 'Strategies for Reading and Studying Expository Text', *Educational Psychologist*, 22 (3), 299–312.

Grabe, W. (2009). *Reading in a Second Language: Moving from Theory to Practice*. Cambridge: Cambridge University Press.

Griffiths, C. (2003). 'Patterns of Language Learning Strategy Use', *System*, 31 (3), 367–83.

Gürses, M., and Bouvet, E. (2016). 'Investigating reading comprehension and learning styles in relation to reading strategies in L2', *Reading in a Foreign Language*, 28 (1), 20–42.

Hong-Nam, K., and Leavell, A. (2006). 'Language Learning Strategy Use of ESL Students in an Intensive English Learning Context', *System*, 34 (3), 399–415.

Israel, S., and Duffy, G. (2009). *Handbook of Research on Reading Comprehension*. New York: Taylor & Francis.

Janzen, J. (2003). 'Developing Strategic Readers in Elementary School', *Reading Psychology*, 24 (2), 25–55.

Jourdenais, R. (2001). Protocol Analysis and SLA. In P. Robinson (ed.), *Cognition and Second Language Acquisition*, pp. 354–75. New York: Cambridge University Press.

Khalifa, H., and Weir, C. (2009). *Examining Reading: Research and Practice in Assessing Second Language Reading*. Cambridge: Cambridge University Press.

Kozminsky, E., and Kozminsky, L. (2001). 'How Do General Knowledge and Reading Strategies Ability Relate to Reading Comprehension of High School Students at Different Educational Levels', *Journal of Research in Reading*, 24 (2), 187–204.

Krekeler, C. (2006). 'Language for Special Academic Purposes (LSAP) Testing: The Effect of Background Knowledge Revisited', *Language Testing*, 23 (1), 99–130.

Macaro, E., and Erler, L. (2008). 'Raising the Achievement of Young-Beginner Readers of French through Strategy Instruction', *Applied Linguistics*, 29 (1), 90–119.

Nevo, N. (1989). 'Test-taking Strategies on a Multiple-choice Test of Reading Comprehension', *Language Testing*, 6 (2), 199–215.

Nikolov, M. (2006). 'Test-taking Strategies of 12- and 13-year-old Hungarian Learners of EFL: Why Whales Have Migraines', *Language Learning*, 56 (1), 1–51.

O'Malley, J., and Chamot, A. (1990). *Learning Strategies in Second Language Acquisition*. Cambridge: Cambridge University Press.

Parel, R. (2004). 'The Impact of Lexical Inferencing Strategies on Second Language Reading Proficiency', *Reading & Writing*, 17 (9), 847–73.

Phakiti, A. (2003). 'A Closer Look at the Relationship of Cognitive and Metacognitive Strategy Use to EFL Reading Achievement Test Performance', *Language Testing*, 20 (1), 26–56.

—— (2006). 'Modelling Cognitive and Metacognitive Strategies and their Relationships to EFL Reading Test Performance', *Melbourne Papers in Language Testing*, 1, 53–95.

Politzer, R., and McGroarty, M. (1985). 'An Exploratory Study of Learning Behaviors and their Relationship to Gains in Linguistic and Communicative Competence', *TESOL Quarterly*, 19 (1), 103–23.

Pressley, M., and Afflerbach, P. (1995). *Verbal Protocols of Reading: The Nature of Constructively Responsive Reading*. Hillsdale, NJ: Erlbaum.

Pulido, D. (2007). 'The Effects of Topic Familiarity and Passage Sight Vocabulary on L2 Lexical Inferencing and Retention through Reading', *Applied Linguistics*, 28 (1), 66–86.

Purpura, J. (1997). 'An Analysis of the Relationships Between Test Takers' Cognitive and Metacognitive Strategy Use and Second Language Test Performance', *Language Learning*, 47 (2), 289–325.

—— (1998). 'Investigating the Effects of Strategy Use and Second Language Test Performance with High- and Low- Ability Test Takers: A Structural Equation Modeling Approach', *Language Testing*, 15 (3), 333–79.

—— (1999). *Learner Strategy Use and Performance on Language Tests: A Structural Equation Modeling Approach*. Cambridge: University of Cambridge Local Examinations Syndicate and Cambridge University Press.

Rayner, K., Pollatsek, A., Ashby, J., and Clifton, C. (2011). *The Psychology of Reading (2nd edition)*. New York: Taylor & Francis Ltd.

Rupp, A., Ferne, T., and Choi H. (2006). 'How Assessing Reading Comprehension with Multiple Choice Questions Shapes the Construct: A Cognitive Processing Perspective', *Language Testing*, 23 (4), 441–74.

Salataci, R., and Akyel, A. (2002). 'Possible Effects of Strategy Instruction on L1 and L2 Reading', *Reading in a Foreign Language*, 14 (1), 1–17.

Salehi, M. (2011). 'Test Taking Strategies: Implications for Test Validation', *Journal of Language Teaching and Research*, 2 (4), 850–8.

Sheorey, R., and Mokhtari, K. (2001). 'Differences in the Metacognitive Awareness of Reading Strategies Among Native and Non-native Readers', *System*, 29 (4), 431–49.

So, Y. (2014). '"Are Teachers' Perspectives Useful?" Incorporating EFL Teacher Feedback in the Development of a Large-scale International English Test', *Language Assessment Quarterly*, 11, 283–303.

Storey, P. (1997). 'Examining the Test-taking Process: A Cognitive Perspective on the Discourse Cloze Test', *Language Testing*, 14 (2), 214–31.

Trendak, O. (2015). *Exploring the role of strategic intervention in form-focused instruction*. New York: Springer.

Zhang, L. (2001). 'Awareness in Reading: EFL Students' Metacognitive Knowledge of Reading Strategies in an Acquisition-poor Environment', *Language Awareness*, 10 (4), 268–88.

Zhang, L., Goh, C., and Kunnan, A. (2014). 'Analysis of Test Takers' Metacognitive and Cognitive Strategy Use and EFL Reading Test Performance: A Multi Sample SEM Approach', *Language Assessment Quarterly*, 11 (1), 76–102.

Acknowledgements

I would like to express my deepest gratitude to my mentor and PhD supervisor Professor Bessie Dendrinos for all the patience and care with which she nurtured the emergence and continuation of this project. Most of all I wish to thank her for placing her trust in me and setting an example for me with her professionalism, strength and determination to complete the study regardless of its difficulties. I would also like to extend my appreciation and special thanks to the volume editors Associate Professors Evdokia Karavas and Bessie Mitsikopoulou for their insightful comments and valuable suggestions, all bearing on the substantive improvement of this chapter. Statements expressed in this paper do not reflect the official policy of the RCeL and responsibility for all expressed views rest entirely with the author.

Appendix

Table 6.6: Reading strategies coding system (adapted from Cohen and Upton 2007)

Strategy Code	Strategy Description
R1	Looks at drawings/pictures before reading the passage.
R2	Plans a goal for the passage
R3	Considers prior knowledge of the topic.
R4	Reads the whole passage more than one time.
R5	Reads the whole passage one time rapidly.
R6	Reads the whole passage one time carefully.
R7	Reads a portion of the passage carefully.
R8	Reads a portion of the passage rapidly looking for specific information.
R9	Uses definitions, examples, indicators of key ideas as markers for meaning in the passage.
R10	Repeats or paraphrases words, phrases, or sentences to aid or improve understanding.
R11	Identifies an unknown word or phrase.
R12	Identifies unknown sentence meaning.
R13	During reading rereads to clarify an idea.
R14	During reading asks self about the overall meaning of the passage/portion
R15	Uses terms/words already known in building an understanding of new terms/words.
R16	Identifies the key words of the passage.
R17	Looks for sentences that convey the main ideas.
R18	Reads ahead to look for information that will help in understanding what has already been read.

Strategy Code	Strategy Description
R19	Goes back in the passage to review/understand information that may be important to the remaining passage.
R20	Verifies the referent of a pronoun.
R21	Infers the meanings of new words by using work attack skills: Internal (root words, prefixes, etc.).
R22	Infers the meanings of new words by using work attack skills (neighbouring words/sentences/overall passage).
R23	Takes notes while reading to better understand text.
R24	Reads aloud to better understand text.
R25	Underlines text information to remember it.
R26	Re-reads text parts/whole text to improve understanding.
R27	Translates from English into mother tongue to improve understanding.
R28	Uses knowledge of the passage/portion: Notes the discourse structure of the passage /portion (cause/effect, compare/contrast, etc.).
R29	Uses knowledge of the passage/portion: Notes the different parts of the passage (introduction, examples, transitions, etc.) and how they interrelate
R30	Uses knowledge of the passage/portion: Uses logical connectors to clarify content and passage organisation (e.g. 'First of all', 'On the other hand', 'In conclusion').
R31	Adjusts comprehension of the passage as more is read: Asks if previous understanding is still accurate given new information.
R32	Adjusts comprehension of the passage as more is read: Identifies the specific new information that does or does not support previous understanding.
R33	Confirms final understanding of the passage based on the discourse structure.

Table 6.7: Test-taking strategies coding system (adapted from Cohen and Upton 2007)

Strategy Code	Strategy Description
T1	Goes back to the question for clarification: Rereads the question.
T2	Goes back to the question for clarification: Paraphrases (or confirms) the question or task.
T3	Goes back to the question for clarification: Wrestles with the question intent
T4	Reads the question and considers the options before going back to the passage/portion.
T5	Reads the question and then reads the passage/portion to look for clues to the answer.
T6	Predicts or produces own answer after reading the portion of the text referred to by the question.
T7	Predicts or produces own answer after reading the question and then looks at the options (before returning to text).
T8	Considers the options and identifies an option with an unknown vocabulary.
T9	Considers the options and checks the vocabulary option in context.
T10	Considers the options and focuses on a familiar option.
T11	Considers the options and selects preliminary option(s) (lack of certainty indicated).
T12	Considers the options and defines the vocabulary option
T13	Considers the options and paraphrases the meaning.
T14	Considers the options and postpones consideration of the option.
T15	Considers the options and wrestles with the option meaning.
T16	Makes an educated guess (e.g. using background knowledge).
T17	Reconsiders or double-checks the response.
T18	Looks at vocabulary items and locates items in context
T19	Selects options through a sentence, paragraph, or passage's overall meaning.

Strategy Code	Strategy Description
T20	Selects options through elimination of other option(s) as unreasonable based on background knowledge.
T21	Selects options through elimination of other option(s) as unreasonable based on vocabulary, sentence, paragraph, or overall passage meaning.
T22	Selects options through elimination of other option(s) as similar or overlapping and as not comprehensive.
T23	Selects options through their discourse structure.
T24	Uses clues in other items to answer an item under consideration.
T25	Selects the option because it appears to have a word or phrase from the passage in it.
T26	Focuses on the main idea (i.e. gist) of the message to understand what it is about in order to respond to test items.
T27	Underlines key lexical items in options to understand what they require while reading them.
T28	Discards options because of unknown words and opts for one of the other options.
T29	Combines information from different parts of the text in order to answer the questions.
T30	Focuses on the pictures of the passage to get an idea of what the text is about.
T31	Reads questions and options before reading the passage in order to get an idea of what the text will be about.
T32	Focuses on the grammatical and syntactic structure of the options (e.g. declarative, imperative, modals, passives) to understand the type of information requested.
T33	Attributes meaning to unknown vocabulary in options.

PART III

Producing written texts

VIRGINIA-MARIA BLANI

7 A comparative study of cohesion in L2 candidates' texts

ABSTRACT

This study investigates the role of cohesion in texts produced under examination conditions by Greek learners of English. It uses a corpus of ninety texts from the KPG English exams in order to explore the extent to which grammatical and lexical cohesion affect writing quality and, as a consequence, the marking of the texts. The results suggest that lexical rather than grammatical cohesion differentiates texts with high marks from texts with lower marks. The findings offer a better understanding of the role of cohesion in L2 writing and assessment and they suggest that contrary to current practices, lexical cohesion descriptors should be added to rating scales.

Introduction

The organisation of discourse is a central issue in L2 writing studies and language testing. Cohesion and coherence are text properties usually examined together that contribute to the organisation of discourse and affect the unity and the connectedness of a text. These two terms are often mistakenly used interchangeably in related literature and educational contexts, but cohesion in this study is defined as the connectedness manifested when the interpretation of an element of a text depends on the interpretation of another element creating 'semantic ties' within the text thus leading to a meaningful whole (Halliday & Hasan 1976). On the other hand, coherence is a link between the text and the outer world, the environment it was written for (Halliday & Hasan 1989:7). This study thus focuses exclusively on cohesion and addresses it from a systemic functional linguistic perspective by analysing texts produced under examination conditions (hence scripts) by non-native speakers of English and, specifically, it attempts to examine whether the choices made by the candidates in terms of cohesive devices affect the quality of their scripts; in other words, whether there are types of cohesive devices that characterise and differentiate scripts that have received high marks from the ones that have received low marks. This study is part of a larger project investigating through the notion of text grammar, which involves the concepts of text organisation, coherence and cohesion, those features of grammar above the sentence level that relate to text unity and texture and may affect writing quality.

The importance of cohesion in understanding texts has been an issue of concern in several works (see McNamara et al. 2010) and it has been suggested that it affects writing quality (see, for instance Collins 1998; De Villez 2003), but there is not enough empirical evidence to support the role of cohesion in writing quality (Crossley & McNamara 2010: 984). Similarly, in L2 writing research, there have been some studies exploring cohesion and coherence in L2 academic writing (i.e. Liu & Qi 2010; Ahmed 2010; Jin 2001) and comparing L1 and L2 writing (i.e. Hinkel 2002; Kafes 2011; Leo 2012), but research focusing exclusively on L2 candidates' output is rather limited. This study therefore aims to contribute to related literature with further empirical evidence that concerns EFL candidates and the scripts they produce under examination conditions.

The chapter starts with a brief overview of works that have concentrated on the notion of cohesion in L1 and L2 writing. The overall aim of the study and the research questions that it addresses will first be presented followed by the research methods adopted for both the qualitative and the quantitative analysis of the scripts. Next, the qualitative and quantitative findings resulting from the cohesion analysis will be presented and discussed. The chapter will end with the conclusions of the study and the implications for both language test development and L2 writing.

Literature review in L1 and L2 research on cohesion

Cohesion is a notion that has attracted attention in discourse studies and as a result, an extensive body of research has been carried out. A considerable number of these studies have explored the connection between the use of cohesive devices and text quality in L1 contexts. Most of them have focused on data from academic settings mainly because of the important role of writing in tertiary education in the United States and other English-speaking countries, and the interest on improving students' writing skills. The results have mainly highlighted the positive correlation between lexical cohesion and writing quality but limited positive correlation with grammatical cohesion. One such a study was conducted by Witte & Faigley (1981) with 90 L1 English freshman essays marked by two raters and found that lexical collocation was an indication of better overall writing quality. This is similar to the results of research conducted by Neuner (1987), who analysed L1 English freshman compositions and found that longer cohesive chains and other measures of lexical quality were characteristic of high-rated essays.

Similar studies in L1 writing have been conducted in school contexts and have also yielded positive results in relation to the connection of lexical cohesive devices to writing quality. For example, McCulley (1985) examined a random sample of 493 persuasive papers produced by high-school students during the National Assessment of Educational Progress writing evaluation (1978–9). The results of the analysis revealed that lexical cohesion and particularly the categories of synonymy, hyponymy and collocation affect writing quality significantly. Similarly, Crowhurst (1987) applied Halliday & Hasan's (1976) model of cohesion analysis in order to investigate cohesion in two types of writing, argumentative and narrative, at three grades (grade 6, 10 and 12) and found that more instances of collocation and synonyms – which are signs of a more mature vocabulary – are used by students in higher grades and this is an indication that more skilled writers use lexical cohesive devices instead of grammatical ones to produce effective texts. Taking the above findings into consideration, we could say that collocation and reiteration seem to be the type of cohesive devices that relate to the quality of L1 texts.

Another body of research focuses on comparative studies investigating cohesion. For instance, in an academic context, Liu & Qi (2010) explored the textual cohesion of academic abstracts in engineering discourse, thirty of them produced by Chinese EFL writers in English and another thirty by English native speakers. The results suggest that while Chinese EFL writers used simple repetition extensively (which is also used in their mother tongue for emphasis and power), native speakers of English preferred the use of synonyms instead of simple word repetition (a finding also supported by Lian 1993). A similar study was conducted in the school context by Kafes (2011) who examined similarities and differences in terms of lexical cohesion devices used in the texts produced in Turkish and English by forty Turkish EFL learners. The results showed that simple repetition was the prevailing type of lexical cohesion in both Turkish and English texts.

Moving to L2 writing contexts, some studies have examined the types of cohesive devices employed by L2 writers in their effort to produce effective texts in an academic context. All of the studies presented below have revealed a high reliance of L2 writers on lexical cohesion. Khalil (1989) found that reiteration, and more specifically simple repetition, is a predominant linking device used in expository essay writing by Arab EFL college students. Similarly, Johnson (1992) found that good essays written by Malay students also included more instances of reiteration than weak essays. In his analysis of argumentative essays written by Filippino college students, Castro (2004) supported the finding that repetition and synonymy were the most commonly used sub-types of lexical cohesion. In addition, Liu and Braine (2005) concluded that the scores of undergraduate students' essays correlated positively with the number of lexical cohesive devices used. Finally, Pearson & Speck (2005) conducted research on English essays written by non-native speakers in sociology and found that skilled writers used more antonyms, hyponyms and meronyms, which suggest a finer knowledge of vocabulary (lexical cohesion). Similar findings were also recorded in studies that took place in a school context. Ferris (1994) analysed a corpus of 160 ESL student compositions to determine the lexical and syntactic features used at different levels of second language proficiency and concluded that lexical repetition is a feature used more often in less advanced levels.

Another body of research used computational tools (e.g. Coh-Metrix) to analyse the relation between lexical cohesion and writing quality in corpora which consist of rated academic texts. These studies explored lexical cohesion through the feature of lexical proficiency or sophistication which emphasises the importance of vocabulary in L2 writing. Crossley et al. (2012), for instance, investigated lexical proficiency in L2 writing using different measures based on the indices provided by the computational tool Coh-metrix. Using data from undergraduate students (240 written texts) their study revealed that the indices of lexical diversity, hypernymy and content word frequency can predict human ratings in terms of lexical proficiency in the analysed sample with a percentage of 44 per cent success. Thus, these three measures were considered to be related to L2 writing quality since the higher these indices were, the higher the grade the texts received.

As has already been noted, most of the previously conducted studies yielded positive results for the connection of lexical cohesion and writing quality. However, there were studies that also revealed positive results for grammatical cohesion. These studies focused exclusively on the use of connectives in L2 writing (Scollon & Scollon 1995; Shibatani 1987; Sneddon 1996; Kim 1987; Ostler 1987; Sa'adeddin 1989; Levinson 1983) and found that more advanced writers used more cohesive devices (Jin 2001). They also reported that the use of connectives indicated higher proficiency in writers (Connor 1990). In addition, Grant & Ginther (2000) noted that two grammatical cohesive devices, conjunctions and demonstratives, were used significantly more often in high-scored essays produced for the Test of Written English (TWE). With regards to reference, pronominals were also found along with additive conjunctions to be the most frequently used grammatical cohesive devices in Filipino college students' L2 writing (Castro 2004), but they were not found to affect the quality of the writing. Finally, within the school context, Bae (2001) also found that reference in young learners' writing was an indicator of writing quality.

To conclude, the results of previous studies reveal that some subsets of cohesive devices have a positive correlation with writing quality and that it is more often lexical and not grammatical cohesion that is related to writing quality.

Research context, data and methodology

In order to investigate correlations between the use of cohesive devices and writing quality in English scripts produced by Greek candidates sitting for the KPG exams, this chapter presents the findings of both a qualitative and a quantitative statistical analysis in its attempt to provide answers to the following research questions:

1) Is there a significant difference in the number of grammatical and lexical cohesive devices in L2 English scripts that are rated, low, mid and high in terms of quality?
2) What is the role of lexical and grammatical cohesive devices in determining candidates' scripts writing quality?

Corpus

The corpus consists of ninety rated scripts which were extracted from the English script Database of the Research Centre for Language Teaching Testing and Assessment (RCeL) of the Faculty of English Studies, National and Kapodistrian University of Athens under the supervision of Professor Bessie Dendrinos. These scripts were produced in exam conditions by Greek learners of English for Activity 1 of the C1 level writing test of the KPG exams in May 2006. The selection of C1 level was not random. C1 level candidates are expected to produce well-structured scripts (Council of Europe 2001:24) which provide more useful data for the purposes of this study than lower level candidates' scripts (e.g. B1 and B2 level) which are expected to be simple, connected texts on a topic (B1 level) or clear, detailed texts on a wide range of subjects related to their interests (B2 level).

Activity 1 of the C1 level writing test of the KPG integrates reading with writing and ask candidates to perform interactively (i.e. read a text in English which may be accompanied by illustration, graphs or tables, understand it and react to it in some way) in order to produce their own texts in English. The topic of the selected C1 writing task was about the average marrying age in different European countries in different decades. Candidates were given the beginning of an article with the title 'Better late than never ...' accompanied by a table with some statistics about the percentages of mean marriage age per sex and per decade for each country and were asked to continue writing a script of about 180–200 words, discussing the data in the table (e.g. making comparisons and assumptions about the situation today) and explaining the situation using the same discourse as the initial paragraph.

Each one of the scripts in the corpus was rated by two experienced evaluators and their marks were saved in the database together with the script itself. The rating was based on the KPG holistic scale designed for assessing writing (with marks ranging from 5 to 15) which involved three main criteria: task completion, which relates to contextual features, that is, the communicative purpose of the text to be produced, the appropriateness of the genre, register and style; text grammar, which includes text organisation, coherence and cohesion; and sentence grammar and lexical features, which refers to the grammatical and syntactical competence of the candidate and vocabulary range and appropriateness. On the basis of these three criteria, scripts were rated as fully satisfactory scripts (satisfying all three criteria and having received a mark from 12–15), moderately satisfactory scripts (the ones that partly fulfill the evaluation criteria and received a mark from 8–11), and unsatisfactory scripts (the ones that do not fulfill the evaluation criteria and received marks from 5–7).

It should be highlighted that the use of rated scripts from two trained raters ensures reliability and renders the data more reliable. The corpus (n = 90) consists of three sub-corpora, each including thirty scripts. The total size of the corpus is 23,026 words (N = 90) with the three sub-corpora divided as follows: the fully satisfactory sub-corpus amounts to 8,248 words (n = 30), the moderately satisfactory sub-corpus to 7,655 words (n = 30) and the unsatisfactory corpus to 7,123 words (n = 30).

Methodology

The adopted model for the cohesion analysis

To analyse candidate scripts in terms of cohesion, this study adopted the model proposed by Halliday & Hasan (1976). This model was chosen because it provides the analyst with a tool for a systematic analysis of grammatical and lexical cohesion and is considered a seminal work in the field of cohesion analysis. According to this model, grammatical cohesion consists of the following categories: reference (where one word or phrase in a text points to another element in order to be interpreted, e.g. a pronominal or a demonstrative pronoun), substitution (replacement of a part of a sentence with a substitute word or phrase in the same grammatical slot), ellipsis (the omission of parts of a clause which can be presumed from what has already been stated in a text), and conjunction (additive, adversative, causal, temporal and continuative) for grammatical cohesion. Lexical cohesion, on the other hand, consists of lexical reiteration (repetition of the same item, use of a synonym or a near-synonym, superordinate or general item) and collocation (achieved by the association of items that regularly occur in the same lexical environment).

It should be noted that, similarly to other studies on cohesion (Liu & Braine 2005; Tierney & Mosenthal 1983; Witte & Faigley 1981), substitution and ellipsis were found to have limited instances in the analysis of the texts in this study, probably due to the fact that both are characteristic of spoken not written discourse. Consequently, regarding grammatical cohesion, this chapter will only present the findings for the categories of reference and conjunction. Analysis of lexical cohesion was conducted for both categories on the basis of Halliday & Hasan's cohesion analysis model with the addition of the category of complex repetition adopted from Hoey's model (1991) for lexical cohesion analysis.

Hoey (1991:10) claimed that lexical cohesion is the dominant mode of creating coherence and based on that argument, constructed his model of lexical repetition. The main categories of this model are: simple lexical repetition (lexical items used in an identical form in text), complex repetition (lexical items sharing a lexical morpheme e.g. marry-marriage, antonymy formed by affixes, and identical forms with different grammatical functions, e.g. (n) debate – (v) debate), simple lexical paraphrase (a lexical item may substitute another in context with no discernible change in meaning and grammatical function, e.g. (n) change – (n) alteration), and finally, complex paraphrase (a lexical item may substitute another with no discernible change in meaning but different grammatical function, e.g. (v) change – (n) alteration). The incorporation of Hoey's category of complex repetition was considered important in order to investigate lexical cohesion in depth, as in past studies simple repetition was found to correlate with low quality texts and complex repetition to be an indication of linguistic variety and high writing quality.

Data analysis procedure

The research methodology combines qualitative and quantitative analysis. The scripts were first qualitatively analysed manually by the researcher taking one text at a time and recording the cohesive devices used in each. N-Vivo software was used to import and organise data into folders according to the overall mark they received and the cohesion devices used in each script, based on the taxonomy of Halliday & Hasan's cohesion analysis model with the incorporation of Hoey's sub-type of complex repetition. WordNet (2010), the online lexical database, was used as a guide for the valid annotation of lexical cohesion in order to avoid personal judgement. This tool is used extensively to annotate a corpus with potential cohesive ties or develop algorithms for faster text annotation (see Morris & Hirst 1991; Barzilay & Elhadad 1997; Silber & McCoy 2000).

Next, the results of the qualitative analysis of the three scripts categories in terms of the cohesive devices used were recorded in an Excel file. This file included the main categories (grammatical cohesion: reference, substitution, etc.) and all the subcategories (personal reference, zero substitution, etc.) of the cohesive devices and the lexical items that were annotated in the scripts under a specific category of cohesive devices (i.e. they – under the category of personal reference). This record of the data facilitates the calculation of the frequency of each type and sub-type of cohesive devices for all the script categories through filtering and allows comparisons within the different categories.

Finally, the qualitative data emerged from the cohesion analysis were converted into numbers in order to be processed statistically, a procedure known as data transformation (Miles & Huberman 1994). The quantification of the data aimed at comparing the three script categories and the cohesive devices used in them. In addition, the significance of the results from these comparisons was tested afterwards by conducting non-parametric tests (e.g. Chi-square test, Mann-Whitney U test, Kruskal-Wallis test). In order to investigate which types of cohesive devices differentiate the three script categories, an analysis of variance (ANOVA) was also conducted.

Presentation of the results and discussion

Grammatical cohesion

Upon completion of the cohesion analysis of the candidate scripts, the overall quantitative results were used in order to record the most common cohesive categories employed by candidates. This section discusses the role of grammatical cohesion in candidates' scripts and more specifically identifies the prevailing grammatical cohesive devices used. Previous studies investigating cohesion reported that conjunction and reference were the grammatical categories of cohesion with the highest frequency in L2 writing (e.g. Connor 1990; Johnson 1992; Khalil 1989). However, only limited findings support a connection between the use of conjunctions and writing quality (Connor 1990). According to the results of the cohesion analysis conducted in this study (Table 7.1), the prevailing types of grammatical cohesion are conjunction and reference, in similar lines to previous studies. To investigate the weight of conjunction and reference within the grammatical cohesion types used, the relative frequency was calculated by dividing their absolute frequency (total number per category) with the total number of values for grammatical cohesion. The results of their relative frequency show that conjunction covers 46 per cent of the instances of grammatical cohesion for unsatisfactory scripts and about 30 per cent for the other two script categories (34 per cent for moderately satisfactory and 32 per cent for fully satisfactory scripts). However, the difference in terms of the use of conjunction among the three script categories was not

Table 7.1: Grammatical cohesion analysis results

Grammatical cohesion	Script category						
	F	Relative frequency	M	Relative frequency	U	Relative frequency	Total
Conjunction	448	0.3286	444	0.3257	471	0.3455	1363
Ellipsis	2	1	0	0	0	0	2
Reference	906	0.3954	831	0.3627	554	0.2418	2291
Substitution	10	0.333	14	0.466	6	0.2	30
Grand Total	1366		1289		1031		3686

found to be statistically significant.[1] Thus, contradicting Connor's finding, although conjunction was found to be a prevailing cohesive device in the corpus, it does not seem to correlate with writing quality in this corpus.

Conjunctions

Despite the fact that overall the use of conjunctions did not seem to correlate with writing quality, it was considered important to analyse each one of its sub-types separately, taking into account that it was the most widely used category of grammatical cohesion. Focusing on the different types of conjunction (Table 7.2), the most common type in the corpus was additive conjunction. Although additive conjunctions were found to be the most frequent conjunction in previous studies too (Castro 2004), their use in this study does not correlate with writing quality. The chi-square tests conducted to investigate the significance of the difference observed among the script categories in relation to the different types of conjunction yielded

---

1   Statistically significant difference refers to the cases where the tests (chi-square tests) have shown a $p \leq .05$ (probability value) and this indicates strong evidence against the null hypothesis. The null hypothesis refers to a general statement that there is no relationship between the two groups examined.

positive results only for adversative and causal conjunction (Table 7.2). As can be observed, adversative conjunctions are used more in the corpus of fully satisfactory than in unsatisfactory scripts. Regarding causal conjunctions, the findings are the opposite, with more instances in the corpora of unsatisfactory and moderately satisfactory scripts. As a result, the use of this category of conjunctions does not correlate with writing quality. However, the types of conjunctions used in the different script categories relate to the communicative purpose of the task candidates were assigned. More adversatives relate to the achievement of the communicative purpose of the writing task which required the interpretation of the data in terms of some parameters and more specifically, the comparison and contrast of the data provided by the task in terms of the decade, the country and the sex (male/female).

Table 7.2: Types of conjunction per script category and statistical significance chi-square test results

Type of conjunction	F	M	U		Chi-square	p-value		Chi-square	p-value
Additive	301	278	302						
Adversative	70	61	43	F-M-U	6,517	.0384	F-U	6,451	.011
Causal	41	76	75	F-M-U	12,406	.0020	U-F	9,966	.0015
							M-F	10.47	.0012
Temporal	34	27	38						
Total	446	442	458						

Examining more closely the sub-types of adversative conjunctions and causal conjunctions, the prevailing ones for fully satisfactory scripts are adversative proper simple (i.e. yet, though) and adversative proper emphatic conjunctions (i.e. however, even so), whereas both moderately satisfactory and unsatisfactory scripts have higher frequencies for adversative proper, and conjunctions (i.e. but). Chi-square significance tests were conducted for each script category and each type of adversative conjunctions in order to examine the significance of the differences observed. The results of the chi-square test are presented in Table 7.3. According to these, fully satisfactory scripts used the sub-type of adversative proper emphatic (i.e. however) conjunction more than unsatisfactory scripts. A significant difference between fully satisfactory and unsatisfactory scripts can also be observed for the sub-type of adversative proper simple conjunctions (i.e. though) (Table 7.3) with unsatisfactory scripts using significantly fewer instances than fully satisfactory scripts.

Table 7.3: Chi-square significance test results for adversative conjunctions

		Chi-square	p-value		Chi-square	p-value
adversative proper, emphatic	F-U	6	.014			
adversative proper, simple	F-M-U	12,743	.0017	F-U	11.56	.00067

As far as causal conjunctions are concerned, there were fewer instances of this type of conjunction in all script categories. The most prevalent sub-type of causal conjunctions in the corpus are reversed causal (i.e. because) and general simple (i.e. so, thus). The tests (chi-square) carried out to examine the significance of the difference identified in terms of causal conjunctions in the three script categories, showed that general simple and reversed causal conjunctions seem to negatively affect the quality of the scripts (Table 7.4). More specifically, unsatisfactory scripts and moderately satisfactory scripts were found to use significantly more general simple and reversed causal conjunctions in comparison to fully satisfactory scripts. This difference in the terms of the sub-type of causal conjunctions used may indicate that the types of conjunctions applied are related to the communicative purpose of the text to be produced. As a result, in opposition to fully satisfactory scripts, the other two script categories provided more reasons about the situation to be discussed and fewer arguments and this may explain the extensive use of causal conjunctions. In other words, they did not adequately discuss the data they were provided with in relation to the problematic situation at hand, but instead discussed the situation per se in order to provide reasons and possible explanations.

In fact, in addition to the chi-square results, qualitative analysis revealed that unsatisfactory scripts may have extensively used the two types of causal conjunctions mentioned above, but they did not use a great variety of them. The majority of candidates' unsatisfactory scripts used 'so' in order to express general simple causality and 'because' for reversed causality, but did not regularly use more complex examples such as 'due to'. On the other hand, fully satisfactory scripts might have employed fewer instances of reversed causal conjunctions, but there was greater variety. To conclude, it seems that the quality of the scripts is not related to the frequency of the conjunctions but to the variety of causal conjunctions used which was found to be associated with higher quality, probably because the use of a variety of causal conjunctions indicates a writer's ability to employ a wider range of conjunctions and thus indicates increased language sophistication.

These findings are similar to the results of other studies (Crownhurst 1987; Khalil 1989; Connor 1990; Johnson 1992; Crossley & McNamara 2010; McNamara et al. 2010) which confirm that the overuse of grammatical cohesive devices does not lead to high-quality scripts and thus their frequency may in fact be a negative predictor of writing quality. For instance, instead of using the explicit causal conjunction 'because', scripts of higher quality might use expressions such as, 'another reason why this happens', etc., to provide potential explanations and reasons. An additional finding of this study regarding conjunctions is that the choice of the types or sub-types to be employed is affected by the communicative purpose of the writing task, as the writers attempt to connect ideas or arguments effectively in their texts in order to achieve it.

Table 7.4: Chi-square significance tests results for causal conjunctions

		Chi-square	p-value		Chis-quare	p-value
general, simple	F-M-U	11,488	.0032	M- F	8,909	.002
				U-F	11.56	.0006
reversed causal	F-M-U	9,901	.007	M-F	6,373	.011
				U- F	9,449	.0021

Reference

Previous studies have suggested that reference is one of the most common grammatical categories of the cohesive devices used in writing (Khalil 1989; Johnson 1992; Castro 2004), although there were contradictory findings concerning the effect of reference on writing quality. Crowhurst (2004), for instance, found more instances of reference in weak essays arguing that it could not be considered an indicator of high writing quality. On the other hand, Bae (2001) supported the notion that the use of reference can affect writing quality. However, her study focused on texts produced by very young learners and at a level that reference could be related to writing quality.

The results of cohesion analysis conducted in this study (Table 7.5) reveal that reference is the prevailing category of grammatical cohesion for all categories of scripts. Moreover, fully satisfactory and moderately satisfactory scripts were found to have more instances of reference than unsatisfactory scripts. However, a statistically significant difference was only identified between fully satisfactory and unsatisfactory scripts ($p < .01$). Consequently, contrary to Crowhurst's (2004) study, the findings here suggest that the use of reference could be considered an indicator of writing quality.

Having identified reference as an indicator of writing quality, the next step of the analysis was to conduct a detailed investigation of its sub-types, namely comparatives, demonstratives and pronominals (Table 7.5). In previous studies, comparatives were the least used category in the analysed data (Zhang 2000), which was also confirmed here. Nonetheless, it is important to note that comparative reference is used more in fully satisfactory and moderately satisfactory scripts and, according to the chi-square test, the difference especially between moderately satisfactory and unsatisfactory scripts in terms of the instances used is statistically significant. In other words, in the analysed data comparative reference has been found to be an indicator of writing quality. Demonstrative reference was also identified as an indicator of writing quality in this study as it was employed more frequently in fully satisfactory and moderately satisfactory than in unsatisfactory scripts and this difference was reported to be significant according to the statistical tests that were conducted (Table 7.5). On the contrary, pronominal reference was the only type of reference where the frequency in unsatisfactory scripts outweighed the other two script categories. As a result, the use of pronominals does not indicate high writing quality in the texts of the current corpus.

Table 7.5: Types of reference per script category (raw frequency per type) and chi-square test significant difference results

Types of reference	F	M	U		Chi-square	p-value		Chi-square	p-value
Comparatives	126	129	91	M-U	6,564	.0104			
Demonstratives	520	438	190	F-M-U	154,293	0	F-M	7,019	.008
							F-U	153,38	0
							M-U	97,936	0
Pronominals	260	264	273						
Total	906	831	554						

Lexical Cohesion

Previous studies have suggested that advanced writers use more instances of lexical cohesion devices to link their ideas in their texts than grammatical ones (McNamara et al. 2010; Crossley & McNamara 2012). This section discusses the role of lexical cohesion in candidates' scripts and examines the use of lexical cohesion versus grammatical cohesion across the three script categories. The results of the cohesion analysis (Table 7.6) regarding lexical cohesion reveal that the sub-types used most extensively are repetition and collocation.

Collocation was found to be used more in the corpus of fully satisfactory scripts whereas repetition was more common in moderately satisfactory and unsatisfactory scripts. However, the frequency of each of these lexical cohesion sub-types should be investigated taking into consideration the total number of lexical cohesion patterns for each script category in order to see how important each of them is within lexical cohesion. As

Table 7.6: Raw and relative frequencies of lexical cohesion types

Lexical cohesion	Script category						Grand Total
	F	Relative frequency	M	Relative frequency	U	Relative frequency	
Collocation	335	0.478	198	0.282	167	0.238	700
Complex paraphrase	2	0.666	0	0	1	0.333	3
Complex repetition	189	0.413	146	0.319	122	0.266	457
General item	0	0	0	0	4	1	4
Repetition	521	0.303	615	0.357	582	0.338	1718
Superordinate	53	0.337	58	0.369	46	0.292	157
Synonymy hyponymy	207	0.343	222	0.368	173	0.287	602
Grand Total	1307		1239		1095		3641

a result, the relative frequencies of each lexical cohesion sub-type were calculated. The relative frequencies of repetition (Table 7.6) for moderately satisfactory and unsatisfactory scripts are 50 per cent and 53 per cent respectively in comparison with fully satisfactory scripts where the relative frequency is 40 per cent. In opposition, the relative frequency of collocation is high for fully satisfactory scripts (26 per cent) and low for moderately satisfactory and unsatisfactory scripts (16 per cent and 15 per cent respectively).

To assess the significance of the differences between the script categories in terms of the sub-types of lexical cohesion, chi-square tests were conducted and the results were positive for four out of the six lexical cohesion sub-types (see Table 7.7). More specifically, in terms of collocation, fully satisfactory scripts have a significantly higher frequency distribution than moderately satisfactory and unsatisfactory scripts and this reveals that there is a positive correlation between the quality of the script and the use of collocation. This finding confirms the outcomes of the studies

Table 7.7: Chi-square test results for lexical cohesion sub-types

Lexical cohesion		Chi-square	p-value		Chi-square	p-value
Collocation	F-M-U	68,506	0	F-M	36,567	0
				F-U	57,903	0
Complex repetition	F-M-U	15,129	.0005	F-U	14,434	.00014
Repetition	M-F	7,778	.0052			

conducted by Witte & Faigley (1981) and McCullay (1985) which related the use of collocation to good writing quality.

With regards to the rest sub-types of lexical cohesion, a significant difference was identified between fully satisfactory and unsatisfactory scripts in terms of complex repetition ($p < .001$). In this case, fully satisfactory scripts were found to use more instances of complex repetition. Complex repetition may be an indication of greater lexical variety in candidates' scripts since it occurs when 'two lexical items share a lexical morpheme, but are not formally identical, or when they are formally identical, but have different grammatical functions (i.e. marriage-> get married)' (Hoey 1991: 55). On the contrary, simple repetition, which occurs when a lexical item that has already occurred in a text is repeated with no greater alternation, was found to have fewer instances in fully satisfactory scripts, in comparison to moderately satisfactory scripts with a significant difference proven after conducting a chi-square test ($p = .0052$).

When examining the relationship between complex repetition and simple repetition with writing quality it is interesting to report the results regarding the weight these two sub-types have within the three script categories. For instance, dividing the raw frequency of simple repetition instances with the total number of lexical cohesion instances (i.e. for F = 521/1307 = 0.39), we can see that 39 per cent of lexical cohesion instances fall under the type of simple repetition, and this percentage is constantly getting higher as the script quality declines. Thus, in moderately satisfactory and unsatisfactory scripts almost half of the identified instances (namely 49 per cent and 53 per cent) for lexical cohesion fall under the category of simple repetition. It can be stated that the reason the use of complex repetition in candidates' scripts correlates with writing quality is because in this way candidates create lexical networks throughout their texts thus avoiding redundancy. On the other hand, the findings for simple repetition confirm Ferris's (1994) suggestion that simple repetition is a feature of low-rated scripts.

In conclusion, in terms of lexical cohesion, collocation seems to have a positive correlation with the quality of candidates' scripts whereas simple repetition has a negative correlation. Unsatisfactory scripts seem to have lower linguistic variety since they exhibit a high frequency of simple repetition – which may sometimes create redundancy – and a low frequency of collocation and complex repetition. Collocation can be considered a means of achieving more complex linguistic expression since it demands use of vocabulary which tends to appear in a similar context in order to generate a cohesive force in the text (Halliday & Hasan 1976: 286). Thus, it is not surprising that unsatisfactory scripts lack this type of lexical cohesion. This finding lends support to the study conducted by McNamara et al. (2010) which claims that higher-quality essays were the result of the use of more sophisticated language.

Conclusion and implications

This study examined cohesion in L2 candidates' texts and demonstrated that candidates' choices in terms of the cohesive devices they use in their scripts can affect the quality of their scripts. Similarly to the study conducted by Crossley & McNamara (2011), an essential outcome here is the fact that the frequency of the cohesive devices does not guarantee high-quality writing. More specifically, the findings of this study suggest that there are particular types of cohesive devices which indicate writing quality and these are mainly related to lexical cohesion. For instance, collocation and complex repetition were found to be an indication of high writing quality in opposition to simple repetition which correlates negatively with writing quality as it is an indication of lower linguistic variety and greater redundancy. Regarding the role of grammatical cohesion in determining candidates' scripts writing quality, some sub-types of grammatical cohesive devices had a positive correlation with writing quality. For instance, the analysis yielded positive results for some sub-types of reference and conjunctions. In terms of reference, comparatives and demonstratives were found to correlate positively with writing quality. In terms of conjunctions, the total number of conjunctions used was not an indication of cohesive texts. An interesting finding of this study is that the writing quality is related to some sub-types of conjunctions which were found to support the achievement of the communicative purpose of the text produced.

Overall, it can be claimed that in determining writing quality, lexical cohesion plays a more significant role than grammatical cohesion. This occurs due to the fact that more skilled writers use a greater degree of sophisticated language and more complex syntactical and grammatical structures in order to develop their ideas and link them implicitly with phrases or expressions and not necessarily with explicit grammatical cohesive devices.

Unlike previous studies in L2 writing which have investigated cohesion without taking into account the communicative purpose of the writing task, this study discusses the findings that result from the cohesion analysis in relation to the communicative purpose of the writing task highlighting its importance. This is a parameter which is crucial for marking and subsequently the characterisation of the scripts in terms of their writing quality because candidates must respond to the writing task given to them following the task rubric (i.e. the instructions of the writing task) which provide the candidates with the necessary information with regards to: (a) what kind of text they have to produce and where it is to appear; (b) who the addressees of the text are; (c) what their role is as writers of the text; and, (d) what the communicative purpose of the text to be produced is. Based on the writing task instructions provided by the rubric, they have to make appropriate choices in terms of the language they will use and in this case in terms of the cohesive devices they will employ to achieve unity and connectedness in their scripts. This procedure is followed by candidates or L2 writers within the context of a language proficiency examination system; however, this is also the procedure followed by the users of a language for the production of any text in real-life situations. The production of any text in daily interaction is a purposeful activity serving a particular communicative purpose, with language users making appropriate choices dictated by this communicative purpose (Halliday & Hasan 1989). In similar lines to real-life texts, the KPG writing tasks fully specify communicative features (concerning who writes what to whom and for what purpose) and therefore it is suggested that when investigating scripts produced under this examination suite, researchers should take into account all these contextual features. Specifically for cohesion analysis, the communicative purpose of the produced script seems to affect the use of cohesive devices and it should therefore be included in the research agenda of similar investigations.

Another point to be made is that this study differs from the majority of others since it is one of the very few (i.e. Grant & Ginther, 2000) to use empirical evidence produced under language proficiency examination conditions by L2 candidates. This is an important factor because these candidates' scripts have officially been marked by experienced raters rendering their marking accurate and their categorisation more valid.

The findings of this study have several implications for L2 writing assessment and instruction. To begin with, L2 writing assessment at C level should place more emphasis on lexical cohesion devices. The KPG rating scales (but also the rating scales of other large-scale examination systems) used for the marking of candidates' scripts should incorporate descriptors of lexical cohesion. The focus of the rating scales in terms of cohesion should not be only on the use of connectives and their frequency because as the results of the study showed, the frequency of the connectives is not a valid predictor of writing quality. This study proposes the incorporation of descriptors including collocation and complex repetition as an indication of good writing quality and simple repetition as an indication of lower quality and redundancy.

Regarding L2 writing instruction, the emphasis in relation to cohesion should also be placed on lexical cohesion which seems to characterise high-quality scripts. The extensive use of connectives and conjunctions is probably supported by textbooks which provide learners with lists of connectors and linking devices. The results here indicate that L2 candidates or writers use repetition and conjunctions in their effort to connect their ideas to form unified texts but this does not contribute to the production of cohesive and unified texts. It is necessary to raise learners' and teachers' awareness that cohesion in texts is achieved with the use of different types of cohesive devices and that the use of conjunctions should not be considered the only way for learners to connect their sentences and their ideas.

Future studies should be conducted to consider whether similar results occur in lower language proficiency level candidates (i.e. A and B level) regarding the significance of lexical and grammatical cohesion. Based on the findings here we could perhaps expect lower level candidates to use grammatical and lexical cohesion devices differently from more advanced candidates who rely on lexical cohesion devices in order to link their ideas. For instance, it would be interesting to explore whether lower level candidates turn to grammatical cohesion devices more often in order to achieve unity in their writing and to note the extent to which they do this successfully. Another research direction could examine the types of cohesive devices employed in different text types produced by L2 candidates of C level in English for different communicative purposes. Overall, although well-researched, the fact remains that cohesion constitutes a complex feature of writing for research related to text-grammar rather than sentence-grammar, and this study has attempted to shed light on one aspect of cohesion analysis of rated texts produced in exam conditions.

Bibliography

Ahmed, A. H. (2010). 'Students' Problems with Cohesion and Coherence in EFL Essay Writing in Egypt: Different Perspectives', *Literacy Information and Computer Education Journal*, 1 (4), 211–21.

Bae, J. (2001). 'Cohesion and Coherence in Children's Written English: Immersion and English-only Classes', *Issues in Applied Linguistics*, 12, 51–88.

Barzilay, R., and Elhadad, M. (1997). 'Using Lexical Chains for Text Summarization'. In Mani, I., and Maybury, M. (eds), *Proceedings of the Intelligent Scalable Text Summarization Workshop*, pp. 10–17.

Bell, J., and Burnaby, B. (1984). *A Handbook for ESL Literacy*. Toronto, Ontario: Ontario Institute for Studies in Education Press.

Bialystok, E. (1978). 'A Theoretical Model of Second Language Learning', *Language Learning*, 28 (1), 69–83.

Brown, G., and Yule, G. (1983). *Discourse Analysis*. Cambridge: Cambridge University.

Castro, C. D. (2004). 'Cohesion and the Social Construction of Meaning in the Essays of Filipino College Students Writing in L2 English', *Asia Pacific Education Review*, 5 (2), 215–25.

Council of Europe (2001). *Common European Framework of Reference for Languages: Learning, Teaching, Assessment*. Cambridge: Cambridge University Press.

Collins, J. L. (1998). *Strategies for Struggling Writers*. New York: The Guilford Press.

Connor, U. (1984). 'A Study of Cohesion and Coherence in English as a Second Language Students' Writing', *Research on Language & Social Interaction*, 17 (3), 301–16.

——(1990). 'Linguistic/Rhetorical Measures for International Persuasive Student Writing'. *Research in the Teaching of English*, 24, 67–87.

Cox, B. E., Shanahan, T., and Sulzby, E. (1990). 'Good and Poor Elementary Readers' Use of Cohesion in Writing', *Research Quarterly*, 25, 47–65.

Crossley, S. A., and McNamara, D. S. (2009). 'Computationally Assessing Lexical Differences in Second Language Writing', *Journal of Second Language Writing*, 17 (2), 119–35.

Crossley, S. A., and McNamara, D. S. (2010). 'Cohesion, Coherence, and Expert Evaluations of Writing Proficiency'. In R. Catrambone and S. Ohlsson (eds), *Proceedings of the 32nd Annual Conference of the Cognitive Science Society*, pp. 984–9. Austin, TX: Cognitive Science Society.

——(2011). 'Text Coherence and Judgments of Essay Quality: Models of Quality and Coherence'. In L. Carlson, C. Hoelscher & T. F. Shipley (eds). *Proceedings of the 29th Annual Conference of the Cognitive Science Society*, pp. 1236–41. Austin, TX: Cognitive Science Society.

——(2012). 'Predicting Second Language Writing Proficiency: The Role of Cohesion and Linguistic Sophistication', *Journal of Research in Reading*, 35, 115–35.

Crossley, S. A., Salsbury, T., and McNamara, D. S. (2012). 'Predicting the Proficiency Level of Language Learners Using Lexical Indices', *Language Testing*, 29, 240–60.

Crowhurst, M. (1987). 'Cohesion in Argument and Narration at Three Grade Levels', *Research in the Teaching of English*, 21 (2), 185–201.

De Villez, R. (2003). *Writing: Step by Step*. Dubuque, IO: Kendall Hunt.

Ferris, D. R. (1994). 'Lexical and Syntactic Features of ESL Writing by Students at Different Levels of L2 Proficiency', *TESOL Quarterly*, 28 (2), 414–20.

Frase, L., Faletti, J., Ginther, A., and Grant, L. (1999). *Computer Analysis of the TOEFL Test of Written English*: *TOEFL Research Report 64*. Princeton, NJ: Educational Testing Service.

Graesser, A. C., McNamara, D. S., Louwerse, M. M., and Cai, Z. (2004). 'Coh-Metrix: Analysis of Text on Cohesion and Language'. *Behavioral Research Methods, Instruments, and Computers*, 36, 193–202.

Grant, L., and Ginther, A. (2000). 'Using Computer-tagged Linguistic Features to Describe L2 Writing Differences', *Journal of Second Language Writing*, 9 (2), 123–45.

Halliday, M. A. K., and Hasan R. (1976). *Cohesion in English*. London: Longman.

——— (1989). *Language, Context, and Text: Aspects of Language in a Social-semiotic Perspective*. Oxford: Oxford University Press.

Hinkel, E. (2002). *Second Language Writers' Text: Linguistic and Rhetorical Features*. Mahwah, NJ: Erlbaum.

Hoey, M. (1991). *Patterns of Lexis in Text*. Oxford: Oxford University Press.

Jarvis, S., Grant, L., Bikowski, D., and Ferris, D. (2003). 'Exploring Multiple Profiles of Highly Rated Learner Compositions', *Journal of Second Language Writing*, 12 (4), 377–403.

Jarvis, S. (2002). 'Short Texts, Best-fitting Curves and New Measures of Lexical Diversity', *Language Testing*, 19 (1), 57–84.

Jin, W. (2001). *A Quantitative Study of Cohesion in Chinese Graduate Students' Writing: Variations Across Genres and Proficiency Levels*. <https://eric.ed.gov/?id=ED452726> accessed 14 April 2017.

Johnson, P. (1992). 'Cohesion and Coherence in Compositions in Malay and English', *RELC Journal*, 23, 1–34.

Kafes, H. (2011). 'Lexical Cohesion: An Issue only in the Foreign Language?', *English Language Teaching*, 5, 83–94.

Khalil, A. (1989). 'A Study of Cohesion and Coherence in Arab EFL College Students' Writing', *System*, 17 (3), 359–71.

Kim, N. L. (1987). 'Korean'. In B. Comrie (ed.), *The World's Major Languages'*, pp. 881–98. Oxford: Oxford University Press.

Leo, K. (2012). 'Investigating Cohesion and Coherence Discourse Strategies of Chinese Students with Varied Lengths of Residence in Canada', *TESL Canada Journal/ Revue TESL du Canada*, 29 (6), 157–79.

Levinson, S. (1983). *Pragmatics*. Cambridge: Cambridge University Press.

Lian, S. (1993). *Contrastive Studies of English and Chinese*. Beijing: Higher Education Publisher.

Liu, M., and Braine, G. (2005). 'Cohesive Features in Argumentative Writing Produced by Chinese Undergraduates', *System*, 33 (4), 623–36.

Liu, L., and Qi, X. (2010). 'A Contrastive Study of Textual Cohesion and Coherence Errors in Chinese EFL Abstract Writing in Engineering Discourse', *Intercultural Communication Studies*, 19 (3), 176–87.

McCulley, G. A. (1985). 'Writing Quality, Coherence and Cohesion', *Research in the Teaching of English*, 19, 269–82.

McNamara, D. S., Louwerse, M. M., McCarthy, P. M., and Graesser, A. C. (2010). 'Coh-Metrix: Capturing Linguistic Features of Cohesion', *Discourse Processes*, 47, 292–330.

Morris, J., and Hirst, G. (1991). 'Lexical Cohesion, the Thesaurus, and the Structure of Text', *Computational linguistics*, 17 (1), 21–48.

Neuner, J. L. (1987). 'Cohesive Ties and Chains in Good and Poor Freshman Essays', *Research in the Teaching of English*, 21 (1), 92–105.

Nunan, D. (1989). *Designing Tasks for the Communicative Classroom*. Cambridge: Cambridge University Press.

Ostler, S. (1987). 'English in Parallels: A Comparison of English and Arabic Prose'. In U. Connor and R. Kaplan (eds), *Writing Across Languages: Analysis of L2 Text*, pp. 169–86. Reading, MA: Addison-Wesley.

Palmer, J. (1999). 'Coherence and Cohesion in the Language Classroom: The Use of Lexical Reiteration and Pronominalisation', *RELC Journal*, 30 (61), 61–85.

Pearson, R., and Speck, B. P. (2005). 'Coherence in English Essays Written by Non-native Students of Sociology', *Quaderns de Filologia, Estudis Linguistics*, 10, 261–78.

Reid, J. (1986). 'Using the Writer's Workbench in Composition Teaching and Testing'. In C. Standfield (ed.), *Technology and Language Testing*, pp. 167–88. Alexandria, VA: TESOL.

——(1990). 'Responding to Different Topic Types: A Quantitative Analysis from a Contrastive Rhetoric Perspective'. In B. Kroll (ed.), *Second Language Writing Research*, pp. 191–210. Cambridge: Cambridge University Press.

Reppen, R. (1994). *Variation in Elementary Student Language: A Multi-Dimensional Perspective*. Unpublished PhD Thesis, Northern Arizona University, Flagstaff.

Sa'adeddin, M. A. (1989). 'Text Development and Arabic-English Negative Interference', *Applied Linguistics*, 10 (1), 36–51.

Scollon, R., and Scollon, S. (1995). *Intercultural Communication: A Discourse Approach*. Oxford, UK: Blackwell.

Shibatani, M. (1987). 'Japanese'. In B. Comrie (ed.), *The World's Major Languages*, pp. 855–80. Oxford: Oxford University Press.

Silber, H. G., and McCoy, K. F. (2000). 'Efficient Text Summarization Using Lexical Chains'. In *Proceedings of the 5th International Conference on Intelligent User Interfaces*, pp. 252–5. New York: ACM 2000 Proceeding.

Silva, T. (1993). 'Toward an Understanding of the Distinct Nature of L2 Writing: The ESL Research and its Implications', *TESOL Quarterly*, 27 (4), 657–76.

Sneddon, J. (1996). *Indonesian: A Comprehensive Grammar*. New York: Routledge.

Tierney, R., and Mosenthal, J. (1983). 'Cohesion and Textual Coherence', *Research in the Teaching of English*, 17 (3), 215–29.

Todd, R. W., Khongput, S., and Darasawang, P. (2007). 'Coherence, Cohesion and Comments on Students' Academic Essays', *Assessing Writing*, 12 (1), 10–25.

Witte, S., and Faigley, L. (1981). 'Coherence, Cohesion and Writing Quality', *College Composition and Communication*, 32, 189–203.

WordNet (2010). Princeton University. <http://wordnet.princeton.edu> accessed 14 April 2017.

Zhang, M. (2000). 'Cohesive Features in the Expository Writing of Undergraduates in Two Chinese Universities', *RELC Journal*, 30 (1), 61–95.

VASSO OIKONOMIDOU

8 The effect of source text on read-to-write task difficulty

ABSTRACT

This chapter focuses on the effect of source text on the difficulty of a specific type of writing test task which contains text-based prompts, known as 'read-to-write' tasks. Drawing data from KPG exams in English, the study is concerned with the read-to-write tasks of B1 level writing test papers. B1 level read-to-write tasks contain a source text in the target language, the role of which is to act as a model for test-takers' written response. In order to investigate the effect of source text on the difficulty of B1 level read-to-write tasks, the study considered the relationship between two facets: source texts and test-taker scores. The investigation uses data from two different sources – test tasks and scores – and combines two different types of analysis: source text analysis and scoring analysis. The findings reveal that source texts seem to have an effect on the difficulty of B1 level read-to-write test tasks of the Greek State Certificate in Language Proficiency exams.

The aim and context of the study

In foreign language writing assessment, the issue of what makes one writing task more difficult or easier than another is quite complex since each type of task entails different demands and creates different kinds of difficulty for test-takers (cf. Purves 1992). Various factors have been considered as affecting the difficulty of writing test tasks, one of these being the nature of the writing task itself. This chapter focuses on the kinds of difficulty entailed in a particular type of writing task which contains text-based prompts known as 'read-to-write'. Read-to-write tasks require that test-takers base their output on a text which is part of the prompts – a source text.

Resting on the hypothesis that a source text may have a strong effect on the difficulty of writing test tasks, this chapter focuses on findings derived from the investigation of the effect of a source text on the difficulty of read-to-write tasks. The data have been drawn from a particular examination battery, the Greek State Certificate in Language Proficiency exams and the chapter draws on a broader postgraduate research project exploring the factors that affect read-to-write task difficulty through a multi-faceted investigation using different sets of data analysed through various methodological tools.

In order to investigate the role of source texts in read-to-write task difficulty, the relationship between two facets, or variables, was considered: source text and test-taker scores. Assuming that tasks leading to lower-scored scripts are more difficult than others (cf. Weigle 1999), the aim was to investigate whether 'difficult' tasks, as reflected in task scores, contain source texts that are more complex and difficult to process.

This chapter consists of eight sections. This section presents the aim and context of the study. The section that follows introduces read-to-write tasks and, in particular, the read-to-write tasks used in the Greek State Certificate in Language Proficiency exams. The third section presents previous research on read-to-write task difficulty, while the subsequent sections specify the research questions this investigation addresses as well as the data used and the methods of analysis employed. A discussion of research findings with regard to both source text and scoring analysis follows, together with a summary of the findings, suggestions for test task writers and implications for further research.

Read-to-write tasks in foreign language exams

Read-to-write tasks are writing tasks which contain a reading source text. Their special characteristic is that they integrate reading with writing in the sense that test-takers are provided with a source text on the basis of which they are expected to produce their written response. Read-to-write tasks actually differ from independent writing tasks in that they measure a different construct of writing ability (Lee & Kantor 2005: 2). Ascensión (2008: 140) refers to this type of tasks as an independent construct rather than the sum of test-takers' reading and writing abilities. In these tasks reading comprehension and composing writing co-exist and are interdependent (Ackerman 1991: 134).

Read-to-write tasks are quite frequently used in the academic context where university students are required to write summaries, response essays, argument-based essays or reviews using information drawn from various different sources. Depending on the goal of read-to-write tasks, the role of source texts varies (Ascensión 2008: 148). For instance, in summary writing the source text provides test-takers with the content of their output. In response essays it stimulates ideas and may also serve as a model for text structure and form. What is more, each type of read-to-write task requires different connections to be made with source texts. Ascensión (2004: 27) refers to five processes involved in performing read-to-write tasks: selecting, organising and connecting, and two metacognitive ones, planning and monitoring. Also, some read-to-write tasks may require connecting information included in source texts with test-takers' background knowledge. This entails an additional demand on test-takers, especially the ones who lack the necessary knowledge.

In the Greek foreign language examination context, read-to-write tasks have made their appearance quite recently through the Greek State Certificate in Language Proficiency Examination battery. In particular, read-to-write tasks are included in the writing test papers of two different proficiency levels, B1 and C1. The role, as well as the demands, of the read-to-write tasks is different at the two proficiency levels. At B1 proficiency level, the source text included in the writing task is to be used as a model for test-takers. In other words, test-takers are expected to produce their written response which should be in the same genre, register and style as the source text but on a different topic. At C1 proficiency level, the role of the source text included in the writing task is interactive. In this sense, test-takers are either expected to draw relevant information from the source text or continue the source text.

This chapter focuses in particular on B1 level read-to-write tasks where the source text indicates what the discoursal and generic features of test-takers' written output should be. For example, a B1 level task (November 2010) asks test-takers to produce a magazine text explaining why their best friend should get the best friend award based on a source text which describes the best dad. The provided source text serves as a model for text discourse, genre and organisation. This facilitates B1 level test-takers who have not yet been exposed to a variety of genres and usually need some guidance for the production of their own texts. As regards content, a B1 level source text does not serve as a resource for ideas; instead test-takers are expected to draw on their background knowledge in order to produce satisfactory responses in terms of content. While source texts seem to have a facilitating role, read-to-write tasks do not always appear easy to test-takers. The section that follows presents and discusses studies conducted on read-to-write task difficulty.

Research on read-to-write task difficulty

Research on read-to-write tasks has been quite limited and mostly concerned with the tasks included in language tests used for academic purposes, since read-to-write tasks are more prevalent in the academic context (cf. Plakans 2007; Plakans 2009; Plakans & Gebril 2013; Watanabe 2001; Weigle, 2004; Yang & Plakans 2012). Read-to-write tasks have only recently been used in foreign language proficiency tests for certification purposes, as is the case of the Greek State Certificate in Language Proficiency exams, and therefore, the area has not yet been explored in depth.

Specifically, research conducted on read-to-write tasks has been concerned with the nature of read-to-write tasks, read-to-write task processes and the differences between read-to-write and independent (or writing-only) tasks. A main point has been the concern expressed over the use and the role of source texts. On the one hand, the inclusion of a source text has been considered a means of making tasks appear more authentic through the provision of input, as it occurs in real life (cf. Plakans 2008; 2009). Their role appears helpful since they provide learners with a common information source and, therefore, even test-takers who lack the necessary background knowledge are not in a disadvantaged position (Weigle 2004: 30). On the other hand, it has been found that less proficient writers tend to rely heavily on the source text and resort to copying. Shi (2004) compared two types of essays (summary and opinion) written by native speakers of English and Chinese learners of English. The comparison revealed that the Chinese learners of English borrowed significantly more words from the provided source text than the native speakers of English. It also revealed that more copying occurred in the summary writing than in the opinion writing. One possible justification for this is that in opinion essays writers combined the ideas provided in the source text with their own background knowledge, while in summary essays it was necessary for writers to base their responses on the source text. Keck's (2004) findings illustrate a similar pattern. Investigating the use of paraphrasing by both L1 and L2 writers, Keck found that L2 writers resorted to 'near copying' to a greater extent than L1 writers.

Other researchers were concerned with the differences between read-to-write and independent tasks (cf. Lewkowicz 1994; Esmaeili 2002, Gebril 2006). Findings appear contradictory. The studies conducted by Lewkowicz (1994) and Gebril (2006) revealed high correlations in the performance on both types of tasks. On the other hand, the study conducted by Esmaeili (2002) showed that the writers performed better on the read-to-write tasks as they were assigned higher scores.

Generally, from the related literature it is evident that the source text included in read-to-write tasks has a significant effect on performance. However, previous studies have not systematically investigated the effect of source texts which are used as models for the written product – as in the case of B1 level read-to-write tasks of the Greek State Certificate in Language Proficiency exams.

Source text related factors affecting read-to-write task difficulty

Researchers who have studied the factors affecting task difficulty have mainly referred to three broad categories: task related, learner related and text related factors. Task related factors are linked to the characteristics of tasks while learner related factors are connected to the individual character-istics of the learners or test-takers when it comes to considering the testing situation (cf. Bachman 2002). Text related factors, which are the focus of this chapter, are associated with the complexity of the texts included in tasks (Brindley 1987; Nunan 1989).

Text related factors of task difficulty, as pinpointed by Brindley (1987) and Nunan (1989), are not just restricted to writing tasks but refer to all types of language tasks. These include a number of characteristics of texts given as input: text length, density of information, text content and the amount of support provided (e.g. photographs, graphs and cues) (see Table 8.1). Additionally, through the use of a more detailed list than Brindley's, Nunan pinpoints the importance of text genre, grammatical complexity and the amount of low-frequency vocabulary.

Table 8.1: Text-related factors affecting task difficulty

Text related factors (or input factors)	
Brindey (1987)	Text size and density Text format and presentation The number and type of contextual cues provided Text content
Nunan (1989)	Grammatical complexity Text length Propositional density The amount of low-frequency vocabulary Information explicitness Discourse structure and clarity The amount of support provided (e.g. photographs, graphs) Text genre Topic

The investigation reported in this chapter focuses on factors based on Brindley's (1987) and Nunan's (1989) list of text related factors and is adapted on the basis of B1 level read-to-write task characteristics. Therefore, the list created here includes discoursal or generic and textual features relating to content, genre, length, format and presentation and amount of visual cues provided in the source text. In addition, considering the factors investigated by researchers dealing with reading text difficulty (cf. Fulcher 1997; Rupp et al. 2001), the list includes certain text complexity features: text readability, syntactic and lexical complexity including lexical density, sophistication and variation (see Table 8.2). Readability relates to the 'ease of understanding a particular text' (Horning 1993, qtd in Mickan et al. 2000: 32). Syntactic complexity refers to the variety and degree of sophistication of forms characterising language production (Foster & Skehan 1996; Lu 2010; Ortega 2003; Wolfe-Quintero et al. 1998). Lexical complexity relates to lexical richness of texts and in particular, lexical density, lexical sophistication and lexical variation including type or token ratio of the words in a text (Engber 1995; Read 2000) as well as lexical diversity relating to 'the number of words a writer knows' (Crossley et al. 2011: 293).

Table 8.2: Source text-related factors in this investigation

Source text related factors for B1 level
Text content
Text genre
Text format and presentation
The amount of support provided (e.g. photographs, graphs)
Text length
Text readability
Syntactic complexity
Lexical complexity (lexical density, sophistication, variation)

Research methods: Two types of analysis

Aim and research questions

The study reported in this chapter aims at investigating the effect of source texts on the difficulty of read-to-write tasks. Focusing on B1 level read-to-write tasks of the Greek State Certificate in Language Proficiency exams where the role of the source text is to act as a model for test-takers' responses, the study addresses the following main research question: to what extent does the source text affect the difficulty of B1 level read-to-write tasks?

In order to investigate the effect of source text on read-to-write task difficulty, two facets and the interaction between them were analysed: source text and test-taker scores. The analysis was conducted in two phases: source text analysis and scoring analysis. Source text analysis was the most important part of the investigation since it was expected to reveal the differences among B1 level source texts in terms of discoursal or generic, textual and complexity features. In particular, complexity measures in the source texts were expected to pinpoint the source texts that were more difficult or easier to process than others. The source texts of B1 level read-to-write tasks were analysed in terms of the text related factors described in the previous section (see Table 8.2). In particular, the source texts were analysed in terms of discoursal or generic and textual features by considering content, genre, format and presentation, and amount of support provided. They were also analysed in terms of length and complexity measures such as source text length, readability, syntactic complexity and lexical complexity.

Assuming that more difficult source texts increase the difficulty of tasks, a hypothesis was formed regarding which source texts might have affected task difficulty. Scoring analysis came to examine whether this hypothesis was verified. This actually constituted the second phase of the investigation and aimed to pinpoint which read-to-write tasks were more difficult or easier than others, based on task scores. A comparison of both analyses was then expected to reveal whether task difficulty was associated with source text difficulty; in other words, whether the most difficult task included the source text that was the most difficult to process or vice versa.

On the basis of the above, two secondary research questions emerged:

- Are there any B1 level source texts that appear more difficult or easier than others based on discoursal or generic, textual and complexity features?
- To what extent is there a relation between source text difficulty and read-to-write task difficulty, as reflected in test-taker scores?

The data: B1 level source texts and task scores

Data drawn from the writing test paper of the Greek State Certificate in Language Proficiency Exams were used to address the research questions. Specifically, two sets of data were used, one for each type of analysis: B1 level source texts and test-taker scores. The first set of data, B1 level source texts, accompanied the task rubrics (or instructions) of six B1 level read-to-write tasks of six exam administrations.[1] As was outlined earlier, B1 level source texts were to be used as models for test-takers' responses.

The second set of data, that is, test-taker scores, were drawn from the scores data bank of the Research Centre for Language, Teaching, Testing and Assessment (RCeL).[2] The scores given to each script were assigned by two raters on the basis of three assessment criteria adhering to a functional view of language, as determined by the B1 level 'global' scoring grid:[3] a. discourse grammar, b. text grammar and c. sentence grammar. Discourse grammar focuses on task completion and specifically, on whether test-takers have produced texts with the appropriate content, genre, register and style. Text grammar relates to text organisation, cohesion and coherence, while sentence grammar focuses on whether test-takers have managed to produce scripts which are appropriate in terms of lexicogrammatical features depending on generic constraints and accurate in terms of grammar, vocabulary, syntax and spelling. A script was considered fully satisfactory (score: 12–15/15) only if it satisfied all three criteria, moderately satisfactory (score: 8–11/15) if it satisfied some or part of the criteria and

---

1   The study covers the exam administrations from May 2008 to November 2008. The B1 level read-to-write tasks can be found at the RCeL website: <http://rcel.enl.uoa.gr/kpg/gr_B_Level.htm>.

2   I would like to thank the director of the RCeL, Prof. B. Dendrinos, for providing me with access to the RCeL scores data bank.

3   Since 2011, when the intergraded B level exam was introduced, another scoring grid has been used. For the scoring grid applied for the assessment of the scripts this study focuses on, readers can visit <http://rcel.enl.uoa.gr/kpg/script_train.htm> (see script rater booklet May 2010).

unsatisfactory (score: 4–7/15) if it partly responded to a limited number of criteria. What is more, scripts received a score of 3, 2 and 1 if they were judged to be 'irrelevant', 'unintelligible' or written 'with scattered words', respectively.

Methods of data analysis

Considering the nature of the data, a different method of investigation was employed for each type of analysis. The source texts were analysed both qualitatively and quantitatively. With regard to the qualitative part, the source texts were analysed in terms of discoursal or generic and textual features. Specifically, the discourse environment (e.g. magazine), text type (e.g. article) and communicative purpose (e.g. to complain) were considered along with text format, presentation and the amount of support provided (e.g. photographs, graphs and cues). This analysis aimed to pinpoint the similarities and differences among the six test tasks and allow assumptions to be made regarding the kinds of difficulty each one entailed for B1 level test-takers.

The most important part of source text analysis, the quantitative part, is related to the measurement of source texts in terms of complexity (see Table 8.3). To this end, as explained previously, the methodology adopted here was applied in studies related to reading text difficulty in order to measure the source texts in terms of readability, syntactic complexity and lexical complexity. Specifically, readability was measured through two web-based text-analysis tools, Coh-Metrix 2.0 and Text-Analyzer, 'UsingEnglish'. Through the two tools, nine readability indices were measured, which mainly rely on number of words, syllables and sentence length. Syntactic complexity was measured through the web-based text analysis tool, Coh-Metrix 2.0. Specifically, four syntactic complexity indices related to the amount of modifiers in word phrases were measured, signifying density of information. Finally, lexical complexity was measured through Lu's (2010) web-based L2 Lexical Complexity Analyzer. Through Lexical Complexity Analyzer, three types of lexical complexity were also measured, all of which are dimensions of lexical richness: lexical density, that is, the ratio of the

Table 8.3: Source text complexity indices

Readability	
Tool	Index
Coh-Metrix	Flesch Kincaid Grade Flesch Reading Ease
UsingEnglish	hard words (with more than three syllables) long words (with over six characters) Gunning Fog Index Coleman-Liau Grade ARI (Automated Readability Index) SMOG LIX number of words

Syntactic complexity	
Tool	Index
Coh-Metrix	logical operator incidence score mean number of modifiers per noun-phrase mean number of higher level constituents per word mean number of words before the main verb of main clause in sentences

Lexical complexity	
Tool	Index
Lu's Lexical Complexity Analyzer	*lexical density* *lexical sophistication*: lexical sophistication I & II, verb sophistication I & II, corrected vertical sophistication 1 *lexical variation*: number of different words, type/token ratio, uber index, verb variation I & II, lexical word variation, noun variation, adjective variation, adverb variation, modifier variation

number of lexical words to the total number of words in a text, lexical sophistication and lexical variation. This type of analysis sought to pinpoint the source texts that were harder in terms of readability and more syntactically and lexically complex than others. On the basis of these measures, it was then possible to make some assumptions regarding the difficulty that each source text might create to B1 level test-takers, based on the hypothesis that the harder and more complex the source text of the tasks the more difficult a task seems to be for test-takers.

Test-taker scores were then analysed in order to verify the aforementioned hypothesis. Scoring analysis was expected to pinpoint the tasks that led to lower-scored scripts than others. The statistical program SPSS was used to analyse the test-taker scores in terms of quantitative measures. Then, a comparison was made across the statistical measures of the six read-to-write tasks. Specifically, mean scores, mode, that is, the scores that appear most often, standard deviation and range of scores were all considered. It was expected that the test tasks leading to lower-scored scripts would be more difficult for B1 level test-takers. Ultimately, consideration of the findings from both source text and scoring analysis findings was expected to reveal whether more difficult and complex source texts are associated with more difficult read-to-write tasks. In other words, the findings from scoring analysis were expected to verify the assumptions made on the basis of the findings of source text analysis.

Research findings

Source text analysis

The qualitative part of source text analysis revealed more similarities than differences among the six B1 level source texts. With regard to discourse, genre and text format, the six B1 level read-to-write tasks contain source texts that generally exhibit similar features (see Appendix). However, the differences among the source texts have led to certain assumptions.

With regard to the similarities, five out of the six read-to-write tasks contain source texts of the same type: texts in magazine columns. What is more, the communicative purposes of all the source texts are the expected ones for the B1 level, considering B1 level illustrative descriptors: to describe, explain, narrate or complain. All source texts are also multimodal, accompanied by visual cues. Finally, they are all characterised by a similar text format given the short nature of these texts; with the exception of the Acting source text, which has three short paragraphs, the others contain just one paragraph.

With regard to the differences, the source text of the Acting task is different from the other source texts in terms of text type, as it is a personal statement. Specifically, test-takers are expected to read the personal statement source text and produce a text of the same type. Although the discoursal or generic features of a personal statement text are provided to test-takers through the source-model text, it could be argued that a lack of familiarity with the specific text type might increase the difficulty of the task. On the other hand, test-takers might be more acquainted with magazine texts, which is the text type of the other five source texts.

The six source texts also differ in terms of their topics, which belong to three thematic areas: relations, education and experiences. Some source texts relate to more familiar everyday topics than others. Specifically, due to their age, proficiency and literacy level, B1 level test-takers would feel more acquainted with the topics relating to the person who has influenced them, the victory of a school team, waking up early for school and best dad, than topics which are outside their everyday experiences like the personal statement for taking an architecture course at an English college or the experience of someone being bitten by a dog (the task analysis is included in the appendix at the end of this chapter). Another aspect to consider is that while both the source and the target text of each test task belong to the same thematic area (e.g. relations), their topics are different – with the exception of one task, Influence. Unavoidably, the degree of familiarity with the source and target text topics cannot always be the same. In particular, the target text topic of the Tree planting task is probably less familiar to test-takers than the source text topic, which renders the task more difficult. Specifically, while the source text refers to the victory of a school team, the target text should be about a tree planting event. Describing a school team victory must be easier than describing a tree planting event especially for test-takers who have not experienced a tree planting event. Similarly, in the case of the Wallet task it must be quite difficult for B1 level test-takers to talk about their experience of losing a wallet if it is outside of their experience. In the case of this task, however, the source text, that is, about being bitten by a dog, appears more difficult than the target text in terms of degree of familiarity with topic. As regards the topics of the other three tasks, that is, Acting, Free time and Best friend dad, the topics of both the source and target texts appear to be the same in terms of degree of familiarity. While the Acting source text is a personal statement for attending an architecture course, the target text should be a personal statement for attending an acting course. Both the source and target text might create difficulty for younger test-takers or school students with regard to content because attending a course might not be an immediate concern of theirs. On the other hand, the Free time and Best friend topics of both source and target texts appear familiar for B1 level test-takers. Specifically, in the Free time source text a student complains about having to wake up early for school and in the target text test-takers are asked to complain about not having enough free time because of homework. Also, while the Best friend source text describes the best dad, the target text should describe the best friend.

On the whole, the qualitative part of the analysis led to the assumption that task difficulty might be affected by text type and text topics. Specifically, it was expected that the text type of a personal statement might create greater difficulty than magazine texts especially since B1 level test-takers are not so familiar with the particular text type. It was also expected that the topics of the three tasks – Acting, Tree planting, Wallet – would seem more difficult to test-takers because they might be outside some test-takers' experience.

The quantitative part of source text analysis has shown the text complexity features of the six source texts; in particular, readability, syntactic complexity and lexical complexity. With regard to readability measures, the Acting source text which is of a different text type, that is, a personal statement, seems to be the hardest (see Table 8.4). This is not surprising if we consider the features of a personal statement text in comparison with the features of teen magazine texts, which are rather more informal. With regard to text length, however, another source text, Tree planting, is the longest (n = 144). It is also much longer than the target text which should be about 100 words. Since its role is to be used as a model for the target text, the fact that it is longer might confuse test-takers as to the length required of their texts. Besides text length, the Tree planting source text appears harder in comparison to the other five magazine texts especially in terms of the use of difficult and longer words. On the other hand, the Free time and Best friend source texts appear easier than the others in terms of readability measures (see Table 8.4). So, there seems to be some agreement between the assumptions made on the basis of the qualitative part of the analysis and the readability measurement. Specifically, two out of the three tasks that were assumed to have caused greater difficulty to test-takers were found to contain harder source texts. On the other hand, two tasks that were assumed to have been 'easier' were found to contain easier texts.

Table 8.4: Readability indices of source texts

Source / Indices	Magazine texts				Personal statement	
	Influence	Tree planting	Free time	Wallet	Best friend	Acting
Flesch-Kincaid Grade Level	5.12	4.59	3.04	4.47	3.68	7.48
Flesch Reading Ease*	82	83.39	89.18	84.52	91.4	62.82
hard words	8	14	6	5	3	17
long words	14	24	13	15	16	25
Gunning Fog Index	7.73	8.38	5.36	6.34	5.83	10.47
Coleman – Liau Grade	14.3	16.5	14.9	14.49	13.4	18.95
Ari	9.3	10.36	7.61	8.84	8.28	12.36
Smog	7.9	8.68	6.46	6.69	5.63	10.14
Lix	23.8	27.41	18.63	23.37	22.4	32.83
Text length						
words	107	144	109	107	129	117

*The lower the Flesch Reading Ease Index the harder the text in terms of readability.

As regards syntactic complexity, the measurement did not reveal a source text that is more syntactically complex than the others because each source text was found to be characterised by different prevailing syntactic complexity indices (see Table 8.5). Specifically, the source text of the Influence task seems to be more syntactically complex than the other source texts in terms of the logical operator incidence score, which signifies density and abstractness (cf. Costerman & Fayol 1997) and the mean number of words before the main verb of main clause in sentences, which is a good index of working memory load. The source texts of the Acting and Free time tasks contain a larger number of higher level constituents than the other source texts. Texts which tend to have a higher index of high order syntactic constitutes per word have many levels of structure and contain structurally dense sentences (Schaeffer & Dykema 2010). In addition, the source text of the Tree planting task contains the largest number of modifiers per noun-phrase, which indicates text complexity and shows the density of information within a sentence (Biber & Gray 2010). Finally, the Wallet and Best friend source texts do not exhibit any indices that are higher in comparison with the other texts, which indicates a smaller degree of

Table 8.5: Syntactic complexity indices of source texts

| Source / Indices | Magazine texts | | | | | Personal statement |
	Influence	Tree planting	Free time	Wallet	Best friend	Acting
logical operator incidence score	66.6	44.3	28.8	36.77	41.67	24.39
mean number of modifiers per noun-phrase	0.58	0.96	0.61	0.62	0.58	0.5
mean number of higher level constituents per word	0.77	0.67	0.83	0.77	0.80	0.83
mean number of words before the main verb of main clause in sentences	2	1.75	1.1	1.67	1.8	0.88

syntactic complexity. So, on the basis of the syntactic complexity measures, it cannot really be argued that one source text is more syntactically complex than another since there is no consistency in the measurement among the four syntactic complexity indices. We could, however, pinpoint the most prevalent syntactic complexity features of each source text.

Similarly, the lexical complexity measurement did not reveal a source text that is more lexically complex than the others, as each source text was found to be characterised by different prevailing lexical complexity indices (see Table 8.6). Specifically, the source text for the Influence task is the most lexically sophisticated and has the greatest variety of lexical words,

Table 8.6: Lexical complexity indices of source texts

Source text / Indices	Magazine texts					Personal statement
	Influence	Tree planting	Free time	Wallet	Best friend	Acting
lexical density	0.38	0.42	0.37	0.39	0.37	0.41
lexical sophistication						
lexical sophistication I	0.25	0.24	0.07	0.24	0.21	0.21
lexical sophistication II	0.25	0.21	0.23	0.22	0.21	0.19
verb sophistication I	0.09	0.17	0.06	0.15	0.07	0.00
verb sophistication II	0.09	0.33	0.06	0.31	0.07	0.00
corrected vertical sophistication I	0.21	0.41	0.17	0.39	0.18	0.00
lexical variation						
number of different words	71	85	82	78	77	83
type/token ratio	.61	.57	.71	.67	.60	.65
uber index	19.9	19.37	28.9	24.7	19.88	23.6
verb variation I	.91	.92	.83	.85	.87	.94
lexical word variation	.89	.77	.86	.84	.83	.83
verb variation II	.23	.18	.35	.24	.27	.28
noun variation	.84	.74	.94	.81	.81	.77
adjective variation	.20	.16	.09	.18	.06	.11
adverb variation	.09	.03	.09	.07	.06	.02
modifier variation	.30	.19	.19	.24	.12	.13

adjectives, adverbs and modifiers. The source text for the Acting task contains the largest ratio of the number of verb types to the total number of verbs in a text (verb variation I). The Tree planting task has a source text that appears to be the most lexically complex in terms of lexical density, verb sophistication and number of different words, which is an index of lexical variation. What is more, the source text for the Free time task seems to be the most lexically complex due to the presence of five lexical variation indices and in particular, the type/token ratio, the uber index (which is an algebraic transformation of type token ratio), verb variation II (i.e. the ratio of the number of verbs to the number of lexical words in a text), noun variation and adverb variation. Finally, the Wallet and Best friend source texts do not exhibit any indices that are higher in comparison to the other texts, which indicates that they have a smaller degree of lexical complexity. Considering the lexical complexity measures of B1 level source texts, it cannot really be argued that one source text is more lexically complex than another as in the case of syntactic complexity measurement. We can, however, pinpoint the most prevalent lexical complexity features of each source text.

To sum up, the analysis of the six source texts sought to answer the first research question, that is, to see if there are any B1 level source texts that appear more difficult or easier than others based on discoursal or generic, textual and complexity features. With regard to discourse, genre and text format, certain differences among the six source texts were identified and it was concluded that text type and topic might be two basic factors affecting read-to-write task difficulty. There were three tasks in particular that might have created greater difficulty to test-takers due to a lack of familiarity with text type and topic, namely in the Acting, Tree planting and Wallet texts. With regard to source text complexity analysis, the 'harder' and 'easier' source texts could be identified through a readability measurement rather than syntactic and lexical complexity measurement. Specifically, the readability measurement allowed two source texts to be identified that appeared harder than the others, namely the Acting text, which appeared to be the most difficult and Tree planting, which was the longest of all the source texts but also the hardest magazine text in terms of readability. The two source texts that appeared easier than the others, Free time and Best friend, could also be identified. It seems interesting that the readability measurement findings are in agreement with the assumptions made on the basis of the qualitative analysis with regard to the discoursal or generic and textual features of the source texts. However, through syntactic and lexical complexity measurement we could not really pinpoint any source text that was more complex than others since there was no source text deemed to be the most complex in terms of all or most of the syntactic and lexical complexity features; each source text was actually characterised by different prevalent syntactic and lexical complexity features. The Acting source text, for instance, which was found to be the hardest in terms of readability measures (which mainly rely on counting the number of difficult and long words, syllables and sentence length), was not the most complex text in terms of syntax and lexis. Specifically, it only exhibited the highest measures in terms of the number of higher level constituents per words and the number of verb types of the total number of verbs of the text (verb variation I).

Scoring analysis

Scoring analysis was a means of verifying the findings of the source text analysis discussed in the previous section. Specifically, the analysis of test-taker scores aimed to pinpoint the test tasks that led to lower-scored scripts and which would determine these tasks as 'difficult' based on the assumption that tasks leading to lower-scored scripts are more difficult than others. Ultimately, the analysis sought to answer the second research question, that is, to what extent a relation exists between source text difficulty and read-to-write task difficulty as is evident from test-takers' performance.

Scoring analysis included the estimation of the mean score (average), mode (the score appearing most often), standard deviation and range (maximum/minimum) (see Table 8.7). The results showed that three read-to-write tasks led to scripts with a relatively low mean score signifying unsatisfactory performance (scores: 3.1–7/15) or a low medium performance (scores: 7.1–11/15): Tree planting (mean score: 6.7/15), Wallet (mean score: 7.8/15) and Acting (mean score: 7.87/15). Two of these tasks – Tree planting

and Wallet – also led to scripts with a relatively low mode, that is, the score
that appears most often, and a relatively high standard deviation signifying
scores that are far from the mean score. In particular, both tasks led to scripts
characterised by a mode that is a score of 3/15 which is given to irrelevant
scripts. These results indicate that the three tasks created greater difficulty
to test-takers than the other three tasks. On the other hand, the results
showed that the other three read-to-write tasks led to scripts with a mean
score that signified medium performance: Influence (mean score: 9.33/15),
Free time (mean score: 8.46/15) and Best friend (mean score: 9.38/15). The
Best friend task, in particular, led to the scripts with the highest scores.
This is evident from the highest mean score (score: 9.37), the highest mode
(score: 10) and the low standard deviation (2.43) (see Table 8.7).

Table 8.7: Test-taker performance on read-to-write tasks

Tasks \ Statistics	Influence	Tree planting	Free time	Wallet	Best friend	Acting
N	822	385	1076	1090	347	343
Mean	9.33	6.7	8.46	7.8	9.38	7.86
Mode	9.0	3.0	9.0	3.0	10.0	7.5
Std. Deviation	2.81	3.46	2.82	3.12	2.43	2.82
Minimum	1.0	1.0	1.0	1.0	2.5	1.0
Maximum	15.0	15.0	15.0	14.5	14.5	15.0

Considering the aforementioned findings, there seems to be a relation
between source text analysis and scoring analysis findings. Specifically,
three source texts which were assumed to have created some difficulty to
test-takers based on Task Analysis – the qualitative part – belonged to
tasks leading to lower-scored scripts. Two of these source texts, Acting and
Tree planting, were also found harder in terms of readability measures. In
particular, the Acting task that led to unsatisfactory performance contained
a source text that was of a different text-type, a personal statement, which

B1 level test-takers are not so familiar with; at B1 level test-takers are not exposed to a great variety of text types as is the case with more advanced proficiency levels. Also, the topic of the source text would be more appropriate for university students who are more familiar with personal statements for attending university courses. In addition, the fact that the source text was also 'hard' to read – compared to the other five source texts – seems to have increased the difficulty of the Acting task. The Tree planting task which led to the lowest-scored scripts was also found 'hard' to read – compared to the other 'magazine' texts. In the case of this task, the text type does not seem to have created difficulty to the test-takers but it is rather the task topic. Actually, the required topic of the target text, that is, the Tree planting event, seems less familiar to test-takers than the topic of the source text, that is, school team victory. In this task, test-takers are asked to produce a text of a more difficult topic than the source text provided as a model. The fact that the task led to many irrelevant responses (mode: score 3) verifies the above considerations. Therefore, in the case of the Tree planting task, source text difficulty along with test-taker familiarity with the required topic seem to have affected task difficulty. The third task found 'difficult' by scoring analysis is the Wallet, which, contrary to the other two 'difficult' tasks, was found neither 'harder' to read nor more syntactically or lexically complex than the other B1 level source texts. However, the topic of both the source and the target text was found to be outside the test-takers' everyday experiences. The fact that the task led to many irrelevant responses (mode: score 3) seems to verify the assumption that topic must have affected the difficulty of this task.

On the other hand, the other three source texts that were considered 'easier' belonged to tasks leading to higher-scored scripts, namely those of Influence, Free time and Best friend. The text type, that is, magazine texts, and topics of the source texts of these tasks seemed to be familiar to B1 level test-takers. Especially, with regard to the Best friend task which led to the highest-scored scripts, the topic of the source text appears simple and appropriate for the test-takers' age and proficiency level. Along with the Free time source text, it was also found to be 'easier' than the other source texts in terms of readability measures. Another aspect to consider is that the Best friend source text is neither syntactically nor lexically complex in comparison to the others in terms of any indices. So, it appears that the 'easy' source texts along with the use of familiar topics and text types are associated with higher-scored scripts.

On the whole, through scoring analysis not only were the tasks that were more difficult than the others highlighted but the relation between source text difficulty and read-to-write task difficulty was explored. The findings revealed that there does seem to be some relation between source text difficulty and read-to-write task difficulty since difficult tasks were found to contain difficult source texts and vice versa. However, the source of difficulty was not the same in every case and was dependent on different factors: text type, topic, source text complexity and length.

Discussion of findings

This investigation combined two different types of analysis, source text analysis and scoring analysis, in order to explore the effect of source text on the difficulty of B1 level read-to-write tasks. Source text analysis identified the source texts of the tasks that might have affected difficulty based on discoursal or generic, textual and complexity measures. The scoring analysis then verified the source text analysis findings.

According to these findings, there seems to be a relation between source text difficulty and read-to-write task difficulty as evident from test-taker performance. In particular, the tasks which led to either lower or higher-scored scripts were found to contain more difficult or easier source texts respectively. Different aspects of the tasks seemed to have affected task difficulty in each case, namely text type, topic familiarity and source text complexity. Specifically, it appeared that the test-takers had greater difficulty with the personal statement text type and topics that were outside their immediate environment such as the Tree planting event, while the source texts of the 'difficult' tasks were found to be harder in terms of readability measures. In particular, with regard to the task that led to the lowest-scored scripts (Tree planting), the source text was found to be harder in terms of readability and also longer in terms of text length when compared to the other source texts of the same type of magazine texts. It also contained the largest number of modifiers per noun-phrase and appeared to be the more lexically dense and sophisticated in terms of verb use. So, besides the difficult topic of the task, the complexity of the source text can be said to have increased task difficulty.

Another issue to consider based on these findings is that readability measures appeared more reliable for indicating source text difficulty than syntactic and lexical complexity measures. It is also important that read-to-write task difficulty was associated with source text difficulty based on readability measures. Readability measures are used to characterise texts with regard to difficulty or ease of processing based on the number of long and difficult words and sentence length. In this investigation, it was easier to pinpoint the source texts that were harder or easier to process on the basis of readability measures. On the other hand, the syntactic and lexical complexity measures did not help in distinguishing the complex from the less complex source texts because each source text was found to be more complex in terms of certain indices and less complex in terms of others.

On the whole, the findings of this investigation provide evidence that source text seems to affect the difficulty of B1 level read-to-write tasks. The findings thus confirm Brindley's (1987) and Nunan's (1989) claims that task difficulty is affected by text related factors among others.

Conclusions and implications

This investigation focused on exploring the effect of source texts on read-to-write task difficulty. The context of the study was the Greek State Certificate in Language Proficiency exams. The study was particularly concerned with B1 level read-to-write tasks where the source text serves as a model for test-takers' written responses. In order to respond to the main research question, that is, to what extent the source texts affect read-to-write task difficulty, the investigation considered two variables and the interaction between them: source text and test task scores. To this end, two types of analysis were conducted and combined, namely, source text analysis and scoring analysis.

The results of the study suggested that source texts seem to have an effect on the difficulty of B1 level read-to-write tasks. Specifically, it was found that source text difficulty seems to be associated with task difficulty. In particular, text type, topic, text length and source text complexity appeared to play a role in read-to-write task difficulty. Especially among text complexity measures, readability measures appeared to be the most reliable indicators of text difficulty.

The findings are of practical use to test task writers as they provide important implications for the design of read-to-write tasks. In selecting the appropriate source texts, test task writers should consider discoursal or generic features and text length but mainly readability and complexity measures. It is important for read-to-write tasks of a specific level to contain source texts that are equivalent in terms of readability, syntactic and lexical complexity measures.

In conclusion, read-to-write tasks are quite complex since they integrate reading with writing. Due to their nature, several aspects of read-to-write tasks contribute to making them difficult to students. This chapter focused on only one aspect, the source text, but other aspects of read-to-write tasks such as rubrics, that is, instructions, genre or the type of source text, may also play a role in task difficulty and should be investigated.

Bibliography

Ackerman, J. M. (1991). 'Reading, Writing, and Knowing: The Role of Disciplinary Knowledge in Comprehension', *Research in the Teaching of English*, 25 (2), 133–78.

Ascensión, Y. D. (2004). *Validation of Reading-to-write Assessment Tasks Performed by Second Language Learners*. Unpublished PhD Thesis, Northern Arizona University.

——(2008). 'Investigating the Reading-to-write Construct', *Journal of English for Academic Purposes*, 7 (3), 140–50.

Bachman, L. F. (2002). 'Some Reflections on Task-based Language Performance Assessment', *Language Testing*, 19 (4), 453–76.

Biber, D., and Gray, B. (2010). 'Challenging Stereotypes About Academic Writing: Complexity, Elaboration, and Explicitness', *Journal of English for Academic Purposes*, 9 (1), 2–20.

Brindley, G. (1987). 'Factors Affecting Task Difficulty'. In D. Nunan (ed.), *Guidelines for the Development of Curriculum Resources for the Adult Migrant Education Program*, pp. 45–56. Adelaide: National Curriculum Resource Centre.

Costerman, J., and Fayol, M. (1997). *Processing Interclausal Relationships: Studies in Production and Comprehension of Text*. Hillsdale, NJ: Laurence Erlbaum Associates.

Crossley, S. A., Weston, J. L., McLaim Sullivan, S. T., and McNamara, D. S. (2011). 'The Development of Writing Proficiency as a Function of Grade Level: A Linguistic Analysis', *Written Communication*, 28 (3), 282–311.

Engber, C. A. (1995). 'The Relationship of Lexical Proficiency to the Quality of ESL Compositions', *Journal of Second Language Writing*, 4 (2), 139–55.

Esmaeili, H. (2002). 'Integrated Reading and Writing Tasks and ESL Students' Reading and Writing Performance in an English Language Test', *The Canadian Modern Language Review*, 58 (4), 599–622.

Foster, P., and Skehan, P. (1996). 'The Influence of Planning and Task Type on Second Language Performance', *Studies in Second Language Acquisition*, 18 (3), 299–323.

Fulcher, G. (1997). 'Text Difficulty and Accessibility: Reading Formulae and Expert Judgement', *System*, 25 (4), 497–513.

Gebril, A. M. (2006). *Independent and Integrated Academic Writing Tasks: A Study in Generalizability and Test Method*. Unpublished PhD Thesis, The University of Iowa.

Horning, A. S. (1993). *The Psycholinguistics of Readable Writing: A Multidisciplinary Exploration*. New Jersey: Ablex Publishing Company.

Keck, C. (2006). 'The Use of Paraphrase in Summary Writing: A Comparison of L1 and L2 Writers', *Journal of Second Language Writing*, 15 (4), 261–78.

Lee, Y., and Kantor, P. (2005). 'Dependability of New ESL Writing Test Scores: Tasks and Alternative Rating Schemes', *TOEFL Monograph Series No. 31*. Princeton, New Jersey: Educational Testing Service.

Lewkowicz, J. (1994). 'Writing From Sources: Does Source Material Help or Hinder Students' Performance?'. In N. Bird (ed.), *Language and Learning: Papers presented at the Annual International Language in Education Conference*, pp. 204–17. Hong Kong [ERIC Document Reproduction Service No. ED386050].

Lu, X. (2010). 'Automatic Analysis of Syntactic Complexity in Second Language Writing', *International Journal of Corpus Linguistics*, 15 (4), 474–96.

Mickan, P., Slater, S., and Gibson, C. (2000). 'Study of Response Validity of the IELTS Writing Subtest]', *IELTS Research Report*, 3 (2), 29–48.

Nunan, D. (1989). *Designing Tasks for the Communicative Classroom*. Cambridge: Cambridge University Press.

Oikonomidou, V. (2017). *Factors Affecting Read-to-write Task Difficulty*. Unpublished PhD Thesis. The University of Athens.

Ortega, L. (2003). 'Syntactic Complexity Measures and their Relationship to L2 Proficiency: A Research Synthesis of College-level L2 Writing', *Applied Linguistics* 24 (4), 492–518.

Plakans, L. (2007). *Second Language Writing and Reading-to-write Assessment Tasks: A Process Study*. Unpublished PhD Thesis, The University of Iowa.

——(2008). 'Comparing Composing Processes in Writing-Only and Reading –to-Write Test Tasks', *Assessing Writing*, 13 (2), 111–29.

——(2009). 'Discourse Synthesis in Integrated Second Language Writing Assessment', *Language Testing*, 26 (4), 561–87.

Plakans, L., and Gebril, A. (2013). 'Using Multiple Texts in an Integrated Writing Assessment: Source Text Use as a Predictor of Score', *Journal of Second Language Writing*, 22 (3), 217–30.

Purves, A. (1992). 'Reflection on Research and Assessment in Written Composition', *Research in the Teaching of English*, 26 (1), 108–22.

Read, J. (2000). *Assessing Vocabulary*. Cambridge: Cambridge University Press.

Rupp, A., Garcia, P., and Jamieson, J. (2001). 'Combining Multiple Regression and CART to Understand Difficulty in Second Language Reading and Listening Comprehension Test Items', *International Journal of Testing*, 1 (3&4), 185–216.

Schaeffer, N. C., and Dykema, J. (2010). 'Response 1 to Fowler's Chapter: Coding the Behavior of Interviewers and Respondents to Evaluate Survey Questions'. In J. Madans, K. Miller, A. Maitland and G. Willis (eds), *Question Evaluation Methods: Contributing to the Science of Data Quality*, pp. 23–40. New York: Wiley.

Shi, L. (2004). 'Textual Borrowing in Second Language Writing', *Written Communication*, 21 (2), 171–200.

Watanabe, Y. (2001). *Read-to-write Tasks for the Assessment of Second Language Academic Writing Skills: Investigating Text Features and Rater Reactions*. Unpublished PhD Thesis, University of Hawaii.

Weigle, S. C. (1999). 'Investigating Rater/Prompt Interactions in Writing Assessment: Quantitative and Qualitative Approaches', *Assessing Writing*, 6 (2), 145–78.

——(2004). 'Integrating Reading and Writing in a Competency Test for Non-native Speakers of English', *Assessing Writing*, 9 (1), 27–55.

Wolfe-Quintero, K., Inagaki, S., and Kim, H. (1998). *Second Language Development in Writing: Measures of Fluency, Accuracy and Complexity*. Honolulu: Second Language Teaching and Curriculum Center, University of Hawaii at Manoah.

Yang, H. C., and Plakans, L. (2012). 'Second Language Writers' Strategy Use and Performance on an Integrated Reading-Listening-Writing Task', *TESOL Quarterly*, 46 (1), 80–103.

Appendix

Table 8.8: Task analysis*

	Influence (May 2008)	Acting (November 2008)	Tree planting (May 2009)
Task Description	This task asks candidates to write about the person who's had the biggest influence on their life, based on a given model.	This task asks candidates to express their interest in taking up a course in Acting	This task asks candidates to write about a tree planting event their school participated in.
Source text type / Target text type	text in a magazine column	personal statement	article
Communicative purpose of source text / Communicative purpose of target text	describe	explain	describe
Discourse environment of source text / Discourse environment of target text	magazine	educational institution	magazine
Source text topic / Target text topic	the person who's had the biggest influence on your life /the person who's had the biggest influence on your life	course in architecture / course in acting	volleyball team victory /tree planting event
Source text organisation / Target text organisation	continuous text	paragraphing	continuous text

*Except for a topic which is different in the source and target text of each B1 level task, the other features coincide.

	Free time (November 2009)	Wallet (May 2010)	Best friend (November 2010)
Task Description	This task asks candidates to write a text complaining about not having enough free time because of too much homework.	This task asks candidates to write their story about losing and then finding their wallet.	The task asks candidates to write their text about their best friend.
Source text type / Target text type	text in a magazine column	text in a magazine column	text in a magazine column
Communicative purpose of source text / Communicative purpose of target text	complain	narrate	describe and explain
Discourse environment of source text / Discourse environment of target text	school magazine	school magazine	teens magazine
Source text topic / Target text topic	waking up early before school / lack of free time due to homework	bitten by a dog / losing (and then finding) a wallet	best dad award / best friend award
Source text organisation / Target text organisation	continuous text	continuous text	continuous text

MARIA STATHOPOULOU

9   Assessing cross-language mediation in the Greek
     national multilingual exam suite: Test-takers'
     language performance and strategy use

ABSTRACT

This chapter is concerned with the notion of cross-language mediation, which appeared in the foreign language teaching context through its inclusion in the *Common European Framework of Reference for Languages* (CEFR) (Council of Europe 2001). Drawing data from the KPG exams, that is, the Greek State Certificate in Language Proficiency exams which include both oral and written mediation activities, this study explores which mediation strategies differentiate successful from less successful mediators (and to what extent) by comparing fully and moderately satisfactory scripts produced by B1, B2 and C1 level test-takers in the KPG written exams in English. This study forms part of a larger research project (Stathopoulou 2013a, 2015), the aim of which was to investigate what types of strategies lead to successful mediation performance and to ultimately discover the mechanisms of cross-language mediation.

Introduction: The context of the study

This chapter presents part of a longitudinal study which was carried out in order to achieve a multileveled understanding of the mechanisms of interlinguistic mediation. The project, which involved Greek users of English sitting for the National Foreign Language exams leading to the Greek State Certificate in Language Proficiency (henceforth KPG), investigated what mediation entails by focusing on candidates' use of mediation strategies in written tasks. A major driving force for this research was the innovative inclusion of mediation tasks in the

KPG exams in 2003, following the publication of the CEFR (Council of Europe 2001), which considers mediation as one of the four basic communicative activities (i.e. along with reception, production, and interaction).

For the purposes of the project, KPG candidates' scripts of written mediation activities, that is, activities requiring relaying of information from Greek texts into English, were textually analysed in order to identify which mediation strategies led to successful mediation practices. The final product of the research is an Inventory of Mediation Strategies (IMS) which acts as a guide for effective mediation. This is one of the most valuable contributions of this project as it ultimately provided empirically based conclusions which have informed to some extent the construction of levelled descriptors (can-do statements) relevant to mediation, something which was absent from the *Common European Framework of Reference for Languages* (CEFR) (Council of Europe 2001) and other international curriculum documents[1] when the project had begun (see Stathopoulou 2015 for the Inventory and Appendix I at the end of this chapter for definitions of the strategies). On the basis of the IMS, mediation strategies were identified in the corpus, and the statistical analysis of the data derived from this identification procedure allow an understanding of a) which mediation strategies triggered by specific tasks lead to successful mediation performance at different levels of proficiency and b) to what extent mediation-strategy use is dependent upon task requirements.

This chapter moves a step forward and presents data regarding the correlation between mediation strategy use and the test-takers' performance. The particular study explores which strategies differentiate successful from less successful mediation scripts (and to what extent) by comparing those which were rated by trained KPG assessors as fully satisfactory with others

---

[1]   In fact, in response to the gap regarding mediation descriptors in the CEFR (2001), from 2013 to 2017 the Council of Europe and the authoring group (Brian North (co-ordinator), Enrica Piccardo, Tim Goodier, and Maria Stathopoulou) worked towards the development and validation of a new set of illustrative descriptors for mediation (North & Panthier 2016). See the recent publication here: <https://www.coe.int/en/web/common-european-framework-reference-languages>.

which were rated as moderately satisfactory. Fully satisfactory scripts are those which have successfully responded to all (linguistic and mediatory) requirements set by the task (e.g. content, genre, register, style, text grammar and sentence grammar), while moderately satisfactory scripts are those which have only partly responded to the aforementioned parameters.

Cross-language mediation in foreign language didactics

Mediation: A neglected area?

Mediation is a totally uncharted area; research is extremely limited while foreign language curricula and materials do not include a mediation component. The notion of mediation in foreign language didactics became more widely known with its inclusion in the CEFR (Council of Europe 2001) which considers mediation activity to be an important aspect of someone's language ability. The CEFR (2001: 87–8) defines mediation as a process where 'the language user is not concerned to express his/her own meanings, but simply to act as an intermediary between interlocutors who are unable to understand each other directly –normally (but not exclusively) speakers of different languages'. Mediation, according to the CEFR, is therefore the production of a text on the basis of a source text which is in a different language. However, probably because of the lack of research in the field, no illustrative descriptors (or can-do statements) relevant to mediation are included therein (cf. Alderson 2007; Little 2007; North 2007; North 2014) and this is the main reason why mediation is not generally developed, taught or tested across Europe (cf. Ntasi and Stathopoulou, 2017; Stathopoulou 2013b).

The creative exploitation of L1 in foreign language teaching was generally not discussed in the past by applied linguists, due to the cultural politics of English which had excluded L1 from the classroom (Dendrinos 2006). The 'English-only' paradigm dictated pedagogical practices with the 'native speaker' of English considered the ideal speaker. Regarding testing, even today, international examination batteries do not usually favour the inclusion of multiple languages and do not assess test-takers' multilingual competence. Multilingual testing, in other words, is overlooked as language assessment is dominated by the monolingual paradigm (Lopez et al. 2017; Shohamy 2011) and is based upon monolingual constructs rather than oriented towards assessing mediation and translanguaging skills (Dendrinos 2012; Gorter and Cenoz, 2017; Shohamy 2011; Stathopoulou 2015). In fact, this is probably another reason why mediation in the area of testing has been neglected.

However, in the Greek context the issue of parallel use of languages is not new. In the 1980s, issues regarding the parallel use of languages appeared in the foreign language teaching scene (cf. Dendrinos 1988, 1997, 2000, 2003). Tasks which made use of Greek for a variety of purposes were included in the materials (see, for instance, textbooks such as *Task Way English 1, 2* and *3*) used in public primary schools (Dendrinos 1986).

In 2003, mediation became a basic component of the KPG exams, which include the assessment of candidates' oral and written mediation performance across proficiency levels. It is assessed through tasks in speaking and writing tests from B1 level onwards. Candidates are provided with a written text in Greek and are given a task which provides the communicative context (who is speaking or writing to whom, with what purpose, what topic, and what text type they are required to produce). An example of a written mediation task is provided below:

> Your friend Sue, who has lived in Greece for three years, has learnt to communicate in Greek but has not proof of her competences. You see the advertisement below. Use the information and write an *email* to her (80 words). *Suggest* that she take the exam to get a certificate and *explain* why she needs it. (KPG, Module 2, November 2014)

What is labelled as mediation in the KPG exams involves verbal activity intended to bridge the gap between a source text in Greek and a target text in L2 (Dendrinos, 2014), in our case in English.[2] This 'mingling-of-

---

2   For examples of written mediation tasks, visit <http://rcel.enl.uoa.gr/kpg/B_Level. htm>.

languages idea' (among other characteristics) makes this system glocal, thereby differentiating it from the majority of international examination systems which are administered only in the target language. Multilingualism is thus promoted by assessing test-takers' mediation performance and their ability to simultaneously draw on multiple linguistic resources from a variety of contexts in order to make meaning.

In 2011, the new Integrated Foreign Languages Curriculum for primary and secondary schools (IFLC) in Greece was launched including a number of mediation skills descriptors (cf. Stathopoulou 2013c, 2014), thus helping teachers to create their own oral and written mediation tasks for teaching and testing purposes (see Dendrinos & Stathopoulou 2014).[3] Both the IFLC and the KPG exams view mediation in exactly the same way, while the former has been developed on the basis of the KPG experience and research.

Towards an understanding of the notion of cross-language mediation

The practice of mediation seems to involve 'a self-effacing bridging effort to get something across and facilitate the (mutual) understanding of other people' (North & Docherty 2016: 24). Similarly, Coste & Cavali (2015: 12) claim that 'the aim of the mediation process, defined in the most general terms, is to reduce the gap between two poles that are distant from or in tension with each other'. The practice of mediation between discourses, languages and cultures is considered to be an important aspect of contemporary human intercultural communication. In today's multilingual societies, being able to communicate in translinguistic contact situations, to deal with multiple intercultural experiences and to effectively shuttle between languages and cultures seem to be a prerequisite for individuals' successful participation in them. As a matter of fact, the ability to take part in an intercultural encounter, which involves relaying information from one language

---

3   To find (in Greek) the mediation descriptors which specify what mediators should be able to do with the language across proficiency levels, see <http://rcel.enl.uoa.gr/xenesglosses/analdiktes.htm>.

to another for a given communicative purpose, is seen to form part of the mediator's interlingual competence, which also entails the simultaneous drawing on different linguistic and cultural resources (Stathopoulou 2015).

Cross-language mediation is a communicative undertaking which entails selective extraction of information by the mediator from a source text in one language and relaying this information into another language with the intention of bridging the communication gap(s) between interlocutors who do not share the same language. The sections that follow emphasise the social role of mediators to create linguistic bridges.

MEDIATORS AS INTERMEDIARIES

Retaining his or her own identity and participating at the same time in two worlds, two languages and two cultures, the mediator acts as an intermediary and his or her role is to make the target audience understand information that otherwise would be impossible for them to understand, thus facilitating communication (Stathopoulou 2015). The mediator, who actually bridges linguistic and cultural gaps, is not considered a neutral third party but an active participant in the communicative encounter, one who takes an active and responsive attitude towards the source text (Stathopoulou 2013a). Mediators, whose actions are situated in a social context, employ knowledge they have developed through social experience, including their knowledge of discourse conventions and their socio-cognitive knowledge of language's possible effect on an audience (Stathopoulou 2015). This is actually the basic reason why Dendrinos (2006) sees mediation as a social practice and mediators as social agents.

MEDIATORS AS TRANSLANGUAGERS

As it is concerned with the purposeful transfer of information from one language to another and passing from one culture to another, mediation is also considered to be a form of translanguaging, a language practice which involves the interplay of linguistic codes (Stathopoulou 2015). Translanguaging, the term chosen to 'describe language fluidity and movement' (Creese & Blackledge 2010: 112), accounts for the capacity of a language user to cross linguistic borders and draw on his or her multiple linguistic and cultural resources in order to communicate. Mediation is also seen as a form of translanguaging and thus emphasises the relationship amongst the languages involved which are not seen as separate. Canagarajah (2006a: 603) characteristically states that in the classroom culture should be treated as a resource rather than a problem and that diverse literacy traditions should be accommodated and not kept divided and separate (cf. García et al. 2017). Besides, 'the concept of language as separable into distinct languages' is being increasingly rejected by sociolinguistics as a valid representation of real-life language use (Ag & Jørgensen 2012: 526). If we consider that speakers are languagers and what they do is languaging (Ag & Jørgensen 2012; Jørgensen 2010), then when they move from one language to another as in the case of mediation, they translanguage.

MEDIATORS AS DECISION-MAKERS

Shifting our attention to another equally important role of mediators, it is important to highlight the fact that in order to be successful in their task they need to consider a variety of contextual factors and employ a variety of strategies. As a matter of fact, when mediation occurs, 'meanings and information in the source text are not only transferred to the target text but they are also transformed in order to fit the new context of the target text' (Stathopoulou 2015: 3). Each time parts of a text and source meanings are used in another text, in a different language and in a different context, the source content is inevitably 'recontextualized' (Fairclough 2003) or reconstructed, and is thereby given new meaning in the new context, a procedure that is carried out unconsciously and so sometimes goes unnoticed. This reconstruction and movement of meanings from one text to another and the creation of new meanings[4] definitely entails certain decisions on

---

4   As North (2016: 133) aptly puts it, mediation involves 'constructing new meaning, encouraging others to construct or understand new meaning, passing on information in an appropriate form, and simplifying, elaborating, illustrating or otherwise adapting input in order to facilitate these processes'.

the part of the mediator, which need to be compatible with the (generic) conventions of the target text. The mediator is, in other words, involved in a decision-making process at every stage of the mediation process, in relation to (i) what information to choose from the source text – on the basis of the context of situation – and (ii) how the relayed information is to be lexicogrammatically realised to fit the new linguistic environment (Stathopoulou 2014). Furthermore, in order to achieve his or her communicative goal, the mediator also needs to employ a number of mediation strategies and mediate between two different linguistic codes, as the following section suggests.

Mediation tasks and mediation strategies

In the KPG writing test paper, which is the focus of this study, candidates from B1 level onwards are asked to complete mediation tasks which involve a Greek text which they have to process in order to write another text in English. The candidates are actually required to produce a text in the target language by extracting and using the relevant source information taking into account the required context of situation (i.e. what the purpose of the text is, who the addressor and addressee are, in what discourse environment the text to be produced is to appear, etc.).

In the KPG exams, mediators' performance is assessed on the basis of how well they respond to the task at hand, that is, whether they produce the appropriate text type with the appropriate register and style, whether the text organisation and the language used is compatible with the context of situation and finally whether they have effectively transferred relevant source information from the Greek text.

It is not just the linguistic competence of the test-takers that will determine their performance but also their ability to effectively use a variety of mediation strategies, which are defined as techniques or choices on the part of the mediator in order to perform as effectively as possible in mediation tasks. In fact, mediation strategies are concerned with how source content is handled and ultimately incorporated into the target text, how added content (i.e. content not included in the source text but introduced by the mediator) has been incorporated at the textual or sentential level, by what means extracted and added information has been mixed up and, finally, how relayed information has been organised in the target environment.

Note that the term 'mediation strategy' firstly appeared in the field of foreign language didactics when mediation was included in the CEFR in 2001 (Council of Europe 2001: 87). As stated therein, mediation strategies 'reflect ways of coping with the demands of using finite resources to process information and establish equivalent meaning'. Developing background knowledge, locating supports, preparing a glossary, previewing, noting equivalences, bridging gaps and checking congruence of two versions or refining by consulting dictionaries are some of the strategies mentioned in the CEFR. However, the definition given by the CEFR does not coincide with the way mediation strategies have been researched for the purposes of this study. This study does not regard mediation strategies as techniques used in order to learn how to mediate as the CEFR suggests; it considers strategies as choices on the part of the mediator, choices which are manifested in mediation scripts while the mediator uses the target language with the aim of being effective in his/her task of relaying information.

In the context of the large scale project, a distinction was made between Type A and Type B mediation strategies – a distinction adopted in this paper as well (see also Stathopoulou 2015, 2016). While Type A strategies require more sophisticated skills on the part of the mediator because they deal with how (extracted or added) information is handled, Type B strategies, only concern mere linguistic transformation of source (or extra-textual) messages (see Table 9.1). Specifically, Type A strategies require selecting and integrating the relevant information either by means of summarising information or blending it with extra-textual information, or combining information found in different parts of the text, or reorganising source content. On the other hand, Type B mediation strategies mainly refer to syntactic and grammatical transformations (see the definitions of mediation strategies in Appendix I). Type A and Type B strategies may be employed simultaneously in the context of a mediation task, meaning that they are not mutually exclusive.

Table 9.1: Types of mediation strategies

TYPE A

01. Creative blending between extracted and extra-textual information
    - at the text level
    - at the sentence level

02. Combining information
    - at the text level
    - at the sentence level

03. Summarising
    - at the text level
    - at the sentence level

04. Reorganising extracted information
    - at the text level
    - at the sentence level

TYPE B
05. Condensing (at sentence level) by combining two (or more) short sentences into one (sentence fusion)

06. Expanding
    - breaking one sentence into two
    - piece of information followed/preceded by an inserted general statement
    - piece of info followed/preceded by another transferring the same information

07. Paraphrasing
    - syntax level paraphrasing
    - phrase level paraphrasing
    - word level paraphrasing

As the table above suggests, it is not only the distinction between the two types of strategies that is important but also their distinction between text and sentence level strategies. Text-level strategies concern the way that source messages are organised across paragraphs or across sentences when transferred into the target environment. Sentence-level strategies, on the other hand, are focused on the way that source information is presented, structured or combined within a single sentence. The strategies presented in Table 9.1 are further subdivided and form the Inventory of Written Mediation Strategies (IMS) which includes 53 strategies in total (see Stathopoulou 2015).

Aim of the study

Research has shown that various factors may affect mediation strategy use.[5] This chapter focuses on test-takers' language performance and explores the extent to which it correlates with mediation strategy use by comparing such use in scripts produced by two groups of test-takers, that is, a low- and a high-performance group. The question addressed is: which are the most and least popular and frequent mediation strategies in fully (high-performance group of test-takers) as opposed to moderately satisfactory scripts (low-performance group)? The discovery of the most and least popular mediation strategies was initially attempted by counting the number of scripts containing each mediation strategy (i.e. popularity of each mediation strategy in the total number of scripts). To find out how frequently strategies were used in each script of the different subcorpora the number of occurrences of each mediation strategy in each script (rather than the number of scripts as in the previous case) was recorded. In order to respond to the initial question concerning how the two subcorpora differ in terms of mediation strategy use, a third analysis was also carried out which involved counting the words used to realise each strategy in order to discover whether the number of words could be considered a discriminating feature in the two subcorpora investigated.

Data collection methods

For the purposes of this study, a corpus of approximately 50,000 words, that is, 600 mediation scripts produced by KPG candidates sitting for the B1, B2 and C1 level exams over a period of six years (2008–13) was analysed

---

5   Stathopoulou (2016) explains how mediation strategy use is dependent upon task requirements (i.e. the linguistic and the mediatory features of the tasks) showing (through textual analysis of scripts) that task parameters affect mediation strategy use. Stathopoulou (2015) also demonstrated that mediation strategy use is heavily dependent on the test-takers' proficiency levels.

with a view to identifying the written mediation strategies they contained. The corpus was comprised of two equally sized main subcorpora, namely scripts that were either fully satisfactory (300 in total) or moderately satisfactory (also 300). Statistical and data analyses were performed using the Statistical Package for Social Science (SPSS), version 20.0 for Windows and provided information about the mode, median, mean and standard deviations related to mediation strategy use.

The analyses and the charts below make a distinction between a) Type A *or* Type B mediation strategy use and b) Type A *and* Type B. The first case refers to the incidence of Type A (or Type B) strategies only, whereas the second one is concerned with the simultaneous use of both Type A and B strategies in the same script.

Presentation and discussion of results

The popularity and frequency of mediation strategies in successful and less successful scripts

The statistical analysis demonstrated that the overall incidence of Type A in combination with Type B strategies (i.e. Type A and Type B strategies occurring simultaneously) is much higher in fully satisfactory scripts compared to moderately satisfactory scripts (see Table 9.2).

This finding shows that the combination of Type A and Type B strategies requires more sophisticated skills on the part of the mediator, who has to successfully incorporate source text information into the target text. Interestingly enough, the lower the performance, the more scripts include only Type B strategies (11.5 per cent in fully satisfactory scripts as opposed to 27 per cent in moderately satisfactory ones). In contrast, the number of fully satisfactory and moderately satisfactory scripts containing only Type A strategies is the same (5.9 per cent).

The investigation of the variable of language performance (fully versus moderately satisfactory) in combination with proficiency level (B1, B2 or C1

Table 9.2: Degree of popularity of mediation strategies in fully satisfactory
and moderately satisfactory scripts

Strategies		Performance band			
		Fully satisfactory		Moderately satisfactory	
		Count (of scripts)	% of fully satisfactory	Count (of scripts)	% of mod. satisfactory
Strategy type	Type A	16	5.9	16	5.9
	Type B	31	11.5	73	27.0
	Type A & B	220	81,5	173	64.1
	None	3	1.1	8	3.0

level) also led to interesting findings. The statistical analysis which focused
on the frequency of strategies in each script generally revealed differences
between fully and moderately satisfactory scripts in terms of Type A and
Type B mediation strategy use across proficiency levels (see Table 9.3 for
descriptive statistics). Shown below is how frequently in each script certain
mediation strategies appear (from 0 to 24 times).

If we look at the mean scores at all proficiency levels (B1, B2 and C1),
we see an overall increase in the mean use of mediation strategies of both
types in the fully satisfactory scripts irrespective of the proficiency level.
In other words, both Type A and Type B mediation strategies are more
frequently used by higher performing candidates. However, the discrepancies between fully and moderately satisfactory scripts become even greater
in the use of Type A strategies.

For each level, statistical tests were conducted in order to discover
whether and to what extent the mean use of Type A and Type B strategies
differed in the two subcorpora. The results of these tests are illustrated in
Table 9.4. The findings seem to substantiate the initial assumption that
fully and moderately satisfactory texts differ in terms of how frequently
mediation strategies are present. Specifically, the greatest differences are
identified for the strategies of creative blending between extracted and
extra-textual information and summarising (Type A), and paraphrasing
(Type B), which are also the most popular strategies in the corpus.

Table 9.3: Type A and Type B mediation strategies in fully and moderately satisfactory scripts across levels: Frequencies

Proficiency level		Performance band	Min	Max	Median	Mode	Mean	Std Error of Mean	Std. Dev
			Type A strategies						
Proficiency level	B1	fully satisfactory	0	5	1.0	1	1.4	.12	1.15
		mod. satisfactory	0	4	1.0	0	.7	.10	.93
	B2	fully satisfactory	0	7	2.0	1	2.4	.17	1.64
		mod. satisfactory	0	5	1.0	1	1.3	.14	1.29
	C1	fully satisfactory	0	6	3.0	2	2.8	.15	1.42
		mod. satisfactory	0	5	2.0	1	1.9	.14	1.29
			Type B strategies						
			Min	Max	Median	Mode	Mean	Std Error of Mean	Std Dev
Proficiency level	B1	fully satisfactory	0	24	4.5	3	5.1	.39	3.66
		mod. satisfactory	0	12	4.0	4	3.9	.25	2.41
	B2	fully satisfactory	0	13	3.0	3	4.1	.34	3.23
		mod. satisfactory	0	12	4.0	0	3.8	.33	3.15
	C1	fully satisfactory	0	16	6.5	6	6.8	.44	4.15
		mod. satisfactory	0	17	6.0	4	6.7	.41	3.87

A closer analysis of each strategy (see Appendix II) leads to the following conclusions. Creative blending between extracted and extra-textual information at B1 level is more frequently detected in fully satisfactory scripts, with a higher number of text level occurrences (as opposed to at the sentence level). At B2 and C1 levels, the number of scripts including text level

Table 9.4: Mediation strategy use in fully satisfactory and moderately satisfactory scripts across levels: Frequency

	Proficiency level											
	B1				B2				C1			
	Performance band											
	Fully satisfactory		Mod. satisfactory		Fully satisfactory		Mod. satisfactory		Fully satisfactory		Mod. satisfactory	
	Mean	Med	Mean	Med	Mean	Med	Mean	Med	Mean	Med	Mean	Med
C.b.	.4	0.0	.2	0.0	.6	0.0	.3	0.0	1.6	1.0	1.0	1.0
C	.1	0.0	.1	0.0	.3	0.0	.1	0.0	.2	0.0	.2	0.0
S	.8	0.0	.4	0.0	1.4	1.0	.9	.5	1.0	1.0	.7	1.0
R	.1	0.0	.1	0.0	.2	0.0	.1	0.0	.0	0.0	.1	0.0
E	.1	0.0	.1	0.0	.1	0.0	.2	0.0	.2	0.0	.2	0.0
Co	.0	0.0	.0	0.0	.0	0.0	.0	0.0	.1	0.0	.0	0.0
P	4.9	4.5	3.7	4.0	3.9	3.0	3.7	4.0	6.5	6.0	6.5	6.0

Note. Cb: Creative blending; C: Combining; S: Summarising; R: Reorganising; E: Expanding; Co: Condensing; P: Paraphrasing.

blending is obviously higher in fully satisfactory scripts, with frequency distributions even higher at C1 level. Creative blending seems to require linguistic maturity on the part of the learners and this may account for the high frequency of the particular strategy in high proficiency levels and in the scripts produced by the high-performance group.

Textual and sentential combining have similar frequency distributions across performance bands, with textual combining less frequent in both subcorpora compared to sentential. At B2 level, while sentential combining is more frequently detected in fully satisfactory scripts, combining at text level appears both in fully and moderately satisfactory scripts with similar frequency. Sentence and text level combining at C1 level is more frequently detected in the sub-corpus of fully satisfactory scripts. Generally speaking, this particular strategy does not seem to be a discriminating feature of the two groups of scripts.

In relation to summarising, at B1 level, the number of scripts that exhibit this strategy is higher in fully satisfactory scripts compared to moderately satisfactory ones. Within the same fully satisfactory script, this strategy may occur from 1 to 4 times more frequently than in a moderately satisfactory one. Similarly, at B2 and C1 level, the number of occurrences of this strategy per script is higher in fully satisfactory scripts.

The number of scripts frequently including reorganising at the level of the sentence is also higher in the B1 level corpus of fully satisfactory scripts, while at text level the frequency distribution almost coincides. At B2 level, while the number of occurrences of text level reorganising is higher in fully satisfactory scripts, reorganising at the sentence level does not exhibit any pattern of differentiation between the two sub-corpora. As for C1 level scripts, reorganising at text level is almost absent in the two subcorpora.

Shifting attention to Type B strategies and focusing on paraphrasing, which is the most common strategy in the corpus, the comparison of frequency distributions between fully and moderately satisfactory scripts does not show any pattern of significant differentiation. As regards syntax level paraphrasing, at all levels, there is no discrimination between fully and moderately satisfactory scripts. At B1 and B2 levels, phrase-level paraphrasing is much more referenced in fully satisfactory scripts, while at C1 level there is no great disparity between the two subcorpora. In relation to word-level paraphrasing, surprisingly enough, it is more frequently detected in moderately satisfactory B1 level scripts and less frequently found in moderately satisfactory B2 level scripts. At C1 level, frequency distributions are very similar in the two subcorpora.

As regards the strategy of expanding, at B1 level the frequency of the sub-strategy of breaking one sentence into two (or more) simpler ones is higher in the sub-corpus of moderately satisfactory scripts. This is a strategy used by the low-performance group probably to compensate for their limited linguistic competence. Generally, it is not a common strategy and the number of occurrences is rather limited in all three subcorpora (of B1, B2 and C1 level). In relation to the other sub-strategy of expanding (i.e. the insertion of a piece of information to transfer the gist), it is frequently used in the sub-corpus of fully satisfactory B2 and C1 level scripts as opposed to the sub-corpus of moderately satisfactory scripts.

Finally, regarding the strategy of condensing (i.e. combining two sentences into one) no pattern emerges when comparing fully with moderately satisfactory scripts. The only exception to this is in the C1 level, where this particular strategy is more frequently used in successful scripts.

An additional analysis, based on counting the words used to apply strategies in fully and moderately satisfactory scripts, confirms the differential mediation strategy use in the two sub-corpora. Although the number of words used in the majority of strategies is higher in fully satisfactory scripts, the significance test shows (see Table 9.5 for results) that the differences are not statistically significant at B1 and B2 levels. At C1, however, it can be concluded that in successful scripts, creative blending

Table 9.5: Mean number of words used to realise mediation strategies

Strategy			Performance band	
			Fully satisfactory	Moderately satisfactory
			Mean	
Proficiency level	B1	Creative blending (sentence level)	18.2	16.5
		Creative blending (text level)	28.9	26.2
		Summarising	48.5	39.0
		Phrasal paraphrasing	4.2	4.0
		Syntactic paraphrasing	7.8	7.0
	B2	Creative blending (sentence level)	22.8	23.5
		Creative blending (text level)	36.4	31.6
		Summarising	37.7	33.6
		Phrasal paraphrasing	3.8	4.7
		Syntax paraphrasing	8.6	8.4
	C1	Creative blending (sentence level)	26.3	24.5
		Creative blending (text level)	47.0	40.3
		Summarising	82.4	86.1
		Phrasal paraphrasing	5.5	3.9
		Syntax paraphrasing	8.2	8.5

at the text level and phrasal paraphrasing are realised through the use of more words, meaning that high-performance test-takers use more words to paraphrase source phrases.

Generally speaking, the number of words used to realise Type A strategies is higher in fully satisfactory scripts, which may support the notion that the particular strategies require more sophisticated skills. Nevertheless, this needs to be further investigated.

The specific quantitative analysis contributed to a deeper understanding of the nature of mediation and raised awareness of which mediation strategies are successful. The most important contribution of the comparison between fully and moderately satisfactory scripts is the fact that the initial distinction between Type A and Type B mediation strategies has been empirically confirmed. Type A strategies, mostly used by the high-performance group, require the writer to have control over the source text and creatively deal with the meanings conveyed both through the paragraphs and within and across sentences (Stathopoulou 2013a). By contrast, Type B strategies (i.e. paraphrasing, condensing and expanding), which refer to textual borrowing and syntactic transformations focusing on the language aspects of the relaying process (i.e. on the level of lexico-grammar and syntax), require less effort and less sophisticated skills which are mainly at the level of language rather than content. This is the reason why it is mainly preferred by less successful mediators. The increasing popularity and frequency of Type A strategies in high-performance (fully satisfactory) scripts also supports the aforementioned statements. Generally, knowing which strategies lead to effective mediation helps gain a better understanding of the particular process which has implications for the teaching and testing of the particular ability.

Conclusion

Drawing its data from an examination system (i.e. KPG) aligned to the descriptors provided by the CEFR, this study demonstrated that there are certain patterned differences between scripts produced by more and less successful mediators across levels. It is not only the nature of the task (Stathopoulou 2016) and the proficiency level (Stathopoulou 2015) that differentiates strategy use but also the test-takers' language performance. In other words, there is evidence that specific mediation strategies discriminate between texts written by low- and high-performance writers.

Specifically, the analysis of mediation strategy use by successful and less successful mediators has led to the following conclusions:

- The more successful the script, the higher the frequency of mediation strategies of both types. In other words, irrespective of the proficiency level of the test-takers, the overall incidence of Type A in conjunction with Type B strategies is much higher in fully satisfactory scripts compared to moderately satisfactory scripts. The writers who simultaneously employ strategies of both types seem to be more effective mediators.
- The lower the performance, the more scripts include Type B strategies exclusively. Type B strategies are easier for the less successful to use since the particular category of strategies demands skills and competence only at the lexicogrammatical level. The number of fully and moderately satisfactory scripts containing only Type A strategies coincides.
- The number of words used to realise Type A strategies has been shown to be higher in fully satisfactory scripts, which may be a supportive indication that the particular strategies require more sophisticated skills.

Generally, apart from the task and the proficiency level of the candidates as previous research has shown, their performance also correlates with mediation strategy use. The findings presented in this chapter, which has attempted to demystify some aspects of the unexplored area of mediation, may contribute to a better understanding of the factors affecting mediation strategy use and mediation performance in general. If combined with previous results (cf. Stathopoulou 2015, 2016), they will be useful for the development of curricula, syllabi and materials aimed at developing learners' mediation skills. Needless to say, the development and implementation of multilingual curricula along with the assessment of multilingual competence constitute significant steps in an effort to secure mediation the attention it deserves in the field of language education (Lopez et al. 2017; Stathopoulou 2017a, 2017b).

Bibliography

Ag, A., and Jørgensen, J. N. (2012). 'Ideologies, Norms, and Practices in Youth Poly-languaging', *International Journal of Bilingualism*, 17 (4), 525–39.

Alderson, C. (2007). 'The CEFR and the Need for More Research', *The Modern Language Journal*, 91 (4), 659–63.

Canagarajah, S. A. (2006). 'Toward a Writing Pedagogy of Shuttling Between Languages: Learning from Multilingual Writers', *College English*, 68 (6), 589–604.

Coste, D., and Cavalli, M. (2015). *Education, Mobility, Otherness: The Mediation Functions of Schools*. Strasbourg: Council of Europe DGII–Directorate General of Democracy, Language Policy Unit.

Council of Europe (2001). *Common European Framework of Reference for Languages: Learning, Teaching, Assessment*. Cambridge: Cambridge University Press.

——(2018). Common European Framework of Reference for Languages: Learning, Teaching and Assessment. Companion Volume with New Descriptors. Language Policy Programme Education Policy Division Education Department Council of Europe.

Creese, A., and Blackledge, A. (2010). 'Translanguaging in the Bilingual Classroom: A Pedagogy for Learning and Teaching?', *The Modern Language Journal*, 94 (1), 103–15.

Dendrinos, B. (1986). *Task Way English 1, 2 & 3*. Athens: State Schoolbook Publishing Organization.

——(2006). 'Mediation in Communication, Language Teaching and Testing', *Journal of Applied Linguistics*, 22, 9–35.

——(2012). 'Multi- and Monolingualism in Foreign Language Education in Europe'. In G. Stickel and M. Carrier (eds), *Education in Creating a Multilingual Europe*, pp. 47–60. Frankfurt: Peter Lang.

Dendrinos, B., and Stathopoulou, M. (2011/2014). Η διαμεσολάβηση ως σημαντική επικοινωνιακή δραστηριότητα [Mediation as a Major Communicative Activity]. In B. Dendrinos and E. Karava (eds), Ξενόγλωσση Εκπαίδευση για την Προώθηση της Πολυγλωσσίας στην Ελλάδα σήμερα [Promoting Multilingualism through Foreign Language Education in Greece], pp. 142–68. Athens: Pedagogic Institute, Ministry of Education and Religious Affairs.

Fairclough, N. (2003). *Analysing Discourse: Textual Analysis for Social Research*. London/New York: Routledge.

García, O., Johnson, S., and Seltzer, K. (2017). *The Translanguaging classroom. Leveraging student bilingualism for learning*. Philadelphia, PA: Caslon.

Gorter, D., and Cenoz, J. (2017) 'Language education policy and multilingual assessment', *Language and Education*, 31 (3), 231–48.

Jørgensen, J. N. (2010). *Languaging. Nine years of Poly-lingual Development of Young Turkish-Danish Grade School Students, Vol. I–II*. Copenhagen Studies in Bilingualism. Copenhagen, Denmark: University of Copenhagen.

Little, D. (2007). 'The Common European Framework of Reference for Languages: Perspectives on the Making of Supranational Language Education Policy', *The Modern Language Journal*, 91 (4), 645–53.

Lopez, A. A., Turka, S., and Guzman-Orth, D. (2017) 'Assessing Multilingual Competence'. In E. Shohamy, I. Or and S. May (eds), *Language Testing and Assessment*, pp. 91–102. Cham: Springer International Publishing.

North, B. (2007). 'The CEFR Illustrative Descriptor Scales', *The Modern Language Journal*, 91 (4), 656–9.

——(2014). *The CEFR in Practice*. Cambridge: Cambridge University Press.

——(2016). 'Developing CEFR Illustrative Descriptors of Aspects of Mediation', *International Online Journal of Education and Teaching*, 3 (2), 132–40.

North, B., and Docherty, C. (2016). *Validating a Set of CEFR Illustrative Descriptors for Mediation, Research Notes No 63*. Cambridge: Cambridge University Press.

North, B., and Panthier, J. (2016). *Updating the CEFR Descriptors-The Context, Research Notes No 63*. Cambridge: Cambridge University Press.

Ntasi, P., and Stathopoulou, M. (2017). 'The Linguistic and Cultural Integration of Refugees In Greece: A Toolkit for Foreign Language Teachers'. Paper presented in the GALA Conference *Migration and Language Education*. Thessaloniki, 6–8 October 2017.

Shohamy, E. (2011). 'Assessing Multilingual Competencies: Adopting Construct Valid Assessment Policies', *The Modern Language Journal*, 95 (3), 418–29.

Stathopoulou, M. (2013a). *Task Dependent Interlinguistic Mediation Performance as Translanguaging Practice: The Use to KPG Data for an Empirically Based Study*. Unpublished PhD Thesis, Department of English Language and Literature, University of Athens.

——(2013b). 'Investigating Mediation as Translanguaging Practice in a Testing Context: Towards the Development of Levelled Mediation Descriptors'. In J. Colpaert, M. Simons, A. Aerts & M. Oberhofer (eds), *Proceedings of the International Conference Language Testing in Europe: Time for a New Framework?*, pp. 209–17. University of Antwerp.

——(2013c). 'The Linguistic Characteristics of KPG Written Mediation Tasks Across Levels'. In N. Lavidas, T. Alexiou and A. M. Sougari (eds), '*Major Trends in Theoretical and Applied Linguistics: Selected Papers from 20th ISTAL*', pp. 349–66. London: Versita de Gruyter.

—— (2014). 'Written Mediation Tasks in the Greek National Foreign Language Exams: Linguistic Analysis and Description'. In J. Aguilar, C. Brudermann and M. Leclère (eds), *Complexité, diversité et spécificité: Pratiques didactiques en contexte*, pp. 248–71. Universite Sorbonne Nouvelle Paris III.

—— (2015). *Cross-Language Mediation in Foreign Language Teaching and Testing*. Bristol: Multilingual Matters.

—— (2016). 'Task Dependent Translanguaging Performance: An Empirical Study in a Testing Context'. In C. Docherty and F. Barker (eds), *Language Assessment for Multilingualism. Proceedings of the ALTE Paris Conference*, pp. 45–74. Cambridge: Cambridge University Press.

—— (2016b). 'From Languaging to Translanguaging: Reconsidering Foreign Language Teaching and Testing Through a Multilingual Lens'. In M. Mattheoudakis and K. Nicolaidis (eds), *Selected Papers of the 21st International Symposium on Theoretical and Applied Linguistics*, pp. 759–74.

—— (2017a). 'Integrating Refugees: The Importance of the New CEFR Illustrative Descriptors for the Development of Multilingual Programmes'. Paper presented in the GALA Conference *Migration and Language Education*. Thessaloniki, 6–8 October 2017.

—— (2017b). 'The Mingling-of-Languages Approach to Testing: The Challenge of Assessing Learners' Translingual Literacy'. Paper presented in the International Conference on Educational Research *Confronting Contemporary Educational Challenges through Research*. Patras, 30 June-2 July.

Appendix I

Table 9.6: Mediation strategies spotted in the corpus (Stathopoulou 2015)

Mediation Strategies
TYPE A
01. Creative blending between extracted and extra-textual information: Given that mediators compose from sources, the texts they produce are blends of content from two kinds of content pools; the source text and their own stored or background knowledge. This strategy refers to how effective the blending of new or extra-textual information with source information is.
02. Combining information: Refers to the successful mixing of information selectively extracted from different parts of the source text. It may involve exclusion and/or regrouping of certain pieces of source information
03. Summarising: Refers to the condensation of source content by excluding parts of the source text that do not add new information according to the communicative purpose set by the task
04. Reorganising extracted information: This is related to the change of the order in which the transferred information is presented in the target context. Whole paragraphs, sentences or clauses may be reorganised and for this reason the typology distinguishes between reorganising at the text (i.e. paragraphs and sentences) and the sentence level (i.e. clauses, phrases and words)
TYPE B
05. Condensing (at sentence level): Combining two (or more) short sentences into one (sentence fusion)
06. Expanding: Refers to conveying the same source text information in the target text but in a longer form or by using more words. Types of expanding: - breaking one sentence into two - piece of information followed/preceded by an inserted general statement - piece of info followed/preceded by another transferring the same information
07. Paraphrasing: Reflects an effort to integrate source information into the target text without depending on the source wording by using different words with a similar meaning. Types of paraphrasing: - syntax level paraphrasing - phrase level paraphrasing - word level paraphrasing

Appendix II

Table 9.7: Mediation strategy use in fully satisfactory and moderately satisfactory scripts across levels: Frequency

Strategy	Frequency (times)	B1 Fully satis-factory	B1 Moderately satisfactory	B2 Fully satis-factory	B2 Moderately satisfactory	C1 Fully satis-factory	C1 Moderately satisfactory
		Count					
Creative blending (sentence level)	0	78	82	73	77	58	68
	1	9	8	14	11	27	19
	2	2	0	3	2	5	3
	3	1	0	0	0	0	0
Creative blending (text level)	0	70	81	65	83	42	49
	1	18	7	17	6	19	24
	2	0	2	8	1	12	11
	3	2	0	0	0	7	4
	4	0	0	0	0	9	2
	5	0	0	0	0	1	0
Combining (sentence level)	0	87	87	75	85	84	86
	1	3	3	10	5	6	4
	2	0	0	5	0	0	0
Combining (text level)	0	87	88	86	87	76	80
	1	3	2	4	3	14	10
Summarising	0	47	62	32	45	27	42
	1	25	22	25	25	42	37
	2	12	4	9	8	15	10
	3	5	1	12	6	5	1
	4	1	1	12	6	1	0

Strategy	Frequency (times)	Proficiency level					
		B1		B2		C1	
		Fully satis-factory	Moderately satisfactory	Fully satis-factory	Moderately satisfactory	Fully satis-factory	Moderately satisfactory
		Count					
Reorganising (sentence level)	0	83	89	89	89	87	86
	1	6	1	1	1	3	4
	2	1	0	0	0	0	0
Reorganising (text level)	0	86	85	77	86	90	89
	1	4	5	12	4	0	1
	3	0	0	1	0	0	0
Expanding (Breaking one sentence into two)	0	86	86	85	79	90	87
	1	3	4	4	8	0	3
	2	1	0	1	3	0	0
Expanding (piece of info followed/ preceded by an inserted general statement)	0	87	86	86	90	81	83
	1	3	4	4	0	9	6
	2	0	0	0	0	0	1
Expanding (piece of info followed/ preceded by another transferring the same info)	0	89	89	90	89	86	86
	1	1	1	0	1	3	3
	2	0	0	0	0	1	1
Combining 2 sentences into 1	0	88	89	89	89	82	89
	1	2	1	1	1	7	1
	2	0	0	0	0	1	0

Strategy	Frequency (times)	Proficiency level					
		B1		B2		C1	
		Fully satis-factory	Moderately satisfactory	Fully satis-factory	Moderately satisfactory	Fully satis-factory	Moderately satisfactory
		Count					
Syntactic paraphrasing	0	4	11	36	37	19	18
	1	9	11	41	24	21	21
	2	23	21	7	11	10	18
	3	17	15	4	10	8	6
	4	14	11	1	3	13	8
	5	9	11	1	5	9	5
	6	5	5	0	0	4	6
	7	2	4	0	0	1	2
	8	1	0	0	0	3	1
	9	1	1	0	0	2	3
	10	2	0	0	0	0	0
	11	1	0	0	0	0	1
	12	1	0	0	0	0	0
	13	0	0	0	0	0	1
	14	1	0	0	0	0	0
Syntactic paraphrasing (bullets to complete sentences)	0	90	90	60	61	59	60
	1	0	0	2	3	3	1
	2	0	0	6	4	2	2
	3	0	0	7	6	2	2
	4	0	0	5	6	5	8
	5	0	0	5	6	2	4
	6	0	0	2	3	6	5
	7	0	0	2	1	1	2
	8	0	0	1	0	4	3
	9	0	0	0	0	5	2
	11	0	0	0	0	1	1

Strategy	Frequency (times)	Proficiency level					
		B1		B2		C1	
		Fully satis-factory	Moderately satisfactory	Fully satis-factory	Moderately satisfactory	Fully satis-factory	Moderately satisfactory
		Count					
Phrasal paraphrasing	0	59	68	67	74	37	43
	1	21	19	16	15	26	29
	2	10	2	7	1	14	13
	3	0	1	0	0	10	2
	4	0	0	0	0	1	1
	5	0	0	0	0	2	1
	6	0	0	0	0	0	1
Word level paraphrasing	0	52	50	37	54	43	37
	1	18	34	27	15	26	27
	2	10	5	8	3	12	10
	3	4	1	4	8	6	8
	4	3	0	4	5	3	6
	5	2	0	4	3	0	1
	6	1	0	3	2	0	1
	7	0	0	1	0	0	0
	8	0	0	1	0	0	0
	10	0	0	1	0	0	0

PART IV

Electronic developments

VOULA GOTSOULIA

10 Documenting language proficiency levels using learner data from the KPG examinations suite

ABSTRACT

This chapter reports on ongoing research carried out at the Research Centre for Language Teaching, Testing and Assessment (RCeL), which aims to make language proficiency levels explicit in terms of linguistic data representing various types of developing competences. We set out to provide detailed, transparent descriptions of how learners are supposed to do what they are expected to at different learning stages, and we make these descriptions comparable across foreign languages. Closely related to the national Integrated Foreign Languages curriculum – a curriculum advocating a substantial shift to a multilingual paradigm of language learning, teaching and assessment or testing at a local level – the work presented in this chapter implements a framework for studying the expanding nature of interrelated language competences, incorporating multilingual corpus datasets acquired from the KPG examination suite. Language features are identified in texts produced by KPG candidates in different languages, across levels, and their distribution is studied in order to supplement the prescriptive, expert-based lists of levelled properties that specify the curriculum's language content.

Enriching language proficiency descriptions

Learning a foreign language (FL) involves complex processes including mastering a range of elements of a structured system and being able to use them appropriately in various social (discursive) contexts. Accordingly, the reliable assessment of a learner's ability to perform socially meaningful tasks in a FL is an undertaking that requires clearly specified criteria for evaluating the development of language properties in their communicative environments. Through the Common European Framework of Reference for Languages (CEFR) (Council of Europe 2001), a first but significant step was made towards an objective basis for the description of language attainment, on a six-level scale. The CEFR contains levelled descriptors articulated as functional characterisations (can-do statements), linked to several types of language-related (e.g. grammatical, lexical, semantic, pragmatic, sociolinguistic) competences. These illustrative descriptors specify what learners are expected to be able to do with the language they are learning at different stages (cf. Little 2007). What a general framework like the CEFR does not do is to specify exactly how (i.e. with which linguistic means) learners are supposed to do what they are expected to.

Given the increasingly important role of the CEFR, in Europe and beyond, as language exam batteries and school language curricula are aligning their components to the descriptors included in this document, it becomes urgent to ask how it can be fully operationalised in terms of precise linguistic data representing developing competences in each single language. Along these lines, our work aims to add details to the CEFR levels by collecting data for more than one language. We seek to make the descriptions of this data comparable across languages using a common meta-language. We crucially refrain from the idea that learning languages means developing parallel monolingualisms (cf. Dendrinos & Gotsoulia 2014: 34–5), thus our goal is to develop a multilingual framework for documenting the descriptors of language proficiency, enabling comparisons and links of language-specific data.

The documentation process combines various sources of evidence. We emphasise, in particular, the significance of empirical data, shedding light on proficiency scaling in terms of the correct (appropriate) or erroneous instantiations of language properties in learners' texts. For this purpose, we use the corpora developed at the RCeL, comprising language data acquired from the KPG exams. The KPG corpora include collections of written texts (called scripts) produced by candidates in English, German and Spanish, at all CEFR levels (from A1 up to C2). KPG candidates are proficient speakers of Greek, living, studying, or working in Greece. Greek is the first language (L1) for the majority of them. With such empirical evidence at hand, we focus on specific aspects of language performance. Features of performance are treated as approximations of language competences. We collect corpus extracted features representing the language use performed by learners with a homogeneous linguistic background (i.e. learners with a common L1) in a specific educational (testing) context, in order to supplement lists of developing language properties, articulated by linguists and experts, targeting learners with underspecified L1 characteristics, in underspecified learning contexts. Corpus data enable meaningful observations of how Greek learners, in particular, learn and use FLs. We also expect that our multilingual data will allow us to abstract over performance features across languages with typological similarities and differences, so as to capture cross-linguistic sequencing (i.e. developmental) patterns, comprising valuable evidence with which to consider critical questions about language learning.

This chapter presents the framework we implement for adding specificity to the levels of proficiency. The range of data collected and associated with the proficiency scale will ultimately be of use not only to practitioners of FL teaching, learning and assessment or testing, especially at a local level, but also to language curriculum planners, language education policy makers, and also second language acquisition scholars, interested in the relationships between first language and foreign languages. We develop a multilingual database to organise and link language data from various resources, employing common models for the representation of competences across languages. In what follows, we give details about this database, which has been designed to document the functional descriptors provided by the national FL curriculum; we present the KPG corpora from which we acquire our learner data, to inform the curriculum database, and we subsequently describe the model we implement for representing interrelated (i.e. lexical, semantic, and syntactic) competences. The building blocks of this model are generic meanings, associated with the lexical and grammatical means expressing them. Finally, we report on illustrative empirical analyses that are based on the KPG English Corpus – a corpus semi-automatically annotated using the aforementioned model; corpus distributions of annotated lexical, semantic and grammatical features are recorded to determine the level(s) at which each feature appears to be learned and used productively. Note that linguistic features are studied in relation to the discursive environments in which they appear, modelling the contextual use of the FL.

A multilingual database with descriptions of levelled language competences

The educational context of our work is tied to the development of the national FL curriculum – the Integrated Foreign Languages Curriculum (IFLC). The IFLC was developed as a component of the new National School Curriculum by a team of experts commissioned by the Greek Ministry of Education in 2010–11, under the supervision of Professor Bessie Dendrinos (cf. Karavas 2012). The design of this curriculum was envisioned by Professor Dendrinos as a response to the emerging role of FLs in the dynamic landscape of modern, multilingual societies. The IFLC treats FLs as a coherent discipline, with common language performance goals to be achieved at key learning stages in school, equivalent to the CEFR proficiency levels (Dendrinos & Gotsoulia 2014).

The pilot version of the IFLC has entailed systematic efforts to specify and empirically trial functional descriptors of language performance, aligned to the descriptors included in the CEFR. What is novel about the IFLC descriptors is that they are constantly being documented with grammatical, lexical, semantic, textual, and other details, i.e. linguistic properties that characterise learners' communicative competences at each stage. The IFLC has been designed as a data-driven curriculum, aspiring to offer language content that is not based solely on intuition. It thus furnishes extensive datasets associated with each type of competence for each of the FLs included in the Greek school curriculum (English, French, German, Italian, and Spanish). These data are represented in the Curriculum Language Database (CLD), which currently comprises the following components:

i.   Language functions that learners are expected to be able to perform (and/or comprehend) at each level (approximating the learners' functional competence)
ii. Grammatical structures that learners are expected to be able to use (and/or comprehend) at each level (approximating their grammatical competence)

iii. Lexical units that learners are expected to be able to use (and/or comprehend) at each level (approximating their lexical semantic competence)
iv. Genres (types) of texts that learners are expected to be able to produce
(and/or comprehend) at each level, when communicating with a FL
(approximating their discourse competence).

Linguistic features of the type represented in each of the above components are described with metadata, such as the language, level, communicative activity (production, comprehension, or mediation), etc., with
which they are associated. The detailed structure of the database is discussed in Dendrinos & Gotsoulia (2014). The data included in the CLD
were collected from a variety of resources: (i) 'Profiles' available for each
language (cf. the T-series, for English, Van Ek & Trim 1991a, 1991b, 2001;
Instituto Cervantes 2006, for Spanish; Spinelli & Francesca 2010, for
Italian; Beacco et al. 2004, Beacco & Porquier 2007, Beacco et al. 2011,
for French; Glaboniat et al. 2005, for German), (ii) FL coursebooks that
are in use in Greek state (primary and secondary) schools, (iii) the KPG
exam specifications. Currently, empirical data (with emphasis on grammatical, lexical and semantic features) acquired from the KPG corpora
are also being collected and analysed to inform the database.

We include datasets from different resources, seeking to ensure that
the curriculum descriptors are documented in an exhaustive and, at the
same time, objective fashion. All sets of levelled features (for each language
and from each resource) are aligned and linked to the descriptors. These
links are the basis for the development of syllabi and learning materials.
That is, selected can-do statements, or sets of can-do statements, associated with related language functions, grammatical and lexical properties,
and types of texts, can form the basis for the development of learning
units addressing specific competences in a FL, or, more interestingly, con-
trasting knowledge in different FLs, in a truly multilingual curriculum.
Table 10.1 shows examples of links between descriptors at A1 level with
features representing lexical and grammatical competences in English.

Linguistic knowledge is usually described in different ways, depending
on the approach to language a given resource adopts. To enable contrastive
analyses of our datasets, we represent features corresponding to each kind

Table 10.1: Language proficiency descriptors linked with lexico-grammatical data

Level	Descriptor	Linguistic data
A1	To identify simple words and phrases to signify time and quantity.	*yesterday, today, tomorrow, January* [months], *Monday* [days of week], *much, many, a lot*, etc.
	To be able to identify specific information in lists or short texts with restricted vocabulary, simple grammatical structures and schematic sentences.	Transitive verb (NP-V-NP) Intransitive verb (NP-V) Intransitive verb with adverb (NP-V-ADV)

of competence in a unified manner. A common meta-language for each kind of competence has emerged from the mapping of descriptions from different resources. Unified representations are comparable across languages and can serve as criteria for supplementing and refining our descriptors. For details on the representations of individual competences, the reader is referred to Gotsoulia & Dendrinos (2014). Later on in this chapter we focus on the model we implement for the representation of lexical, semantic and grammatical competences across languages.

Language performance data

Within the context presented above, we call attention to the significance of empirical evidence for supplementing, and calibrating expert-based descriptions of language proficiency. Note that our approach crucially differs from the work carried out by a notable project furnishing learner data making the CEFR levels explicit – the English Profile Programme (EPP). The EPP is a large-scale project operated by the Cambridge ESOL group of Cambridge Assessment, in collaboration with Cambridge University Press and other stakeholders. It is perhaps the most systematic work undertaken since 2005, adding linguistic information to the CEFR levels and creating a 'Profile', that is, sets of Reference Level Descriptions, for English. The

EPP has been using the Cambridge Learner Corpus (CLC), a resource that amounts to 45 million words of written English, produced by learners from around the world at different levels.

In contrast to the EPP methodology, our focus is on data produced by learners with a homogeneous linguistic background, in different FLs (we use English, German and Spanish as example languages). Besides working on making functional descriptions of language attainment explicit, we also seek to come up with meaningful conclusions about how Greek learners, in particular, learn and use languages. Taking up the perspective of the learner, we investigate the developmental characteristics reflected in language performance, enabling the development of a language user Profile (rather than, simply, separate language profiles specifying the material configuration of proficiency descriptors for each single language). Note that from a theoretical and ideological viewpoint, our approach follows the valued tradition of localised studies in language learning and assessment (cf. Macedo et al. 2003).

In the next section, we discuss in detail the representation of learners' competences in terms of linguistic features that are typed and linked to one another, modelling aspects of language performance in a coherent fashion. For our analyses, we rely on data drawn from the KPG corpora, comprising collections of scripts produced by KPG candidates in English, German and Spanish, from A1 up to C2 level. We initially carry out paradigmatic analyses of the English Corpus, to be followed by similar analyses for the German and Spanish corpora, all adhering to common specifications. The KPG English Corpus is a resource that has been developed over a period of more than seven years and, to date, totals to more than four million words (Gotsoulia & Dendrinos 2011). It includes texts produced by candidates of all ages, sitting for the written production and mediation module of the KPG exam. The test tasks that candidates are asked to complete always circumscribe (as part of the rubric) the situational and discursive context of the text to be produced. The scripts are marked using the KPG grading grid, specifying three performance zones (grading bands) across proficiency levels (Fully satisfactory, Moderately satisfactory, Unsatisfactory).

Work related to the KPG corpora has involved the development of two databases: one includes candidates' scripts – which are being collected and digitised on an ongoing basis – and another includes source texts associated with the test tasks. Scripts as well as source texts are described in terms of bundles of features encoding their genre, communicative environment and function:

i.   The thematic (semantic) domain to which a text pertains (e.g. environment, entertainment, sports, etc.) along with its more specific topic;
ii. The discourse environment to which a text pertains (e.g. newspaper, magazine, encyclopedia, dictionary, web page, literature, etc.), which is specified in terms of the communicative identities or roles of the author and the addressee;
iii. The text type (e.g. article, announcement, report, advert, novel excerpt, etc.), which is specified in terms of the structure of the text and its communicative purpose(s);
iv. The text process by means of which the communicative purpose of the text is fulfilled; text processes include description, narration, explanation, argumentation, instruction.[1]

The notions of discourse and genre are central in the theory of grammar that the exams conform to, consciously avoiding focus solely on assessment of the formal properties of language. Drawing on semiotic perspectives (cf. Kress & van Leeuwen 2001; Martin 2009), it is acknowledged that communicatively competent users of a FL comprehend and produce texts in relation to their contexts and that the realisation of context should be evident in the language produced. Genres are understood to be tied to learners' communicative and functional competences as well as to linguistic

---

1   Text processes are defined in accordance with the genre model proposed by Knapp & Watkins (2005). This model identifies genres that 'describe' through the process of ordering things into common sense or technical frameworks of meaning, 'explain' through the process of sequencing phenomena in temporal and/or causal relations, 'instruct' through the process of logically sequencing actions or behaviors, 'argue' through the process of expanding a proposition to persuade readers to accept a point of view, 'narrate' through the process of sequencing people and events in time and space (Knapp & Watkins 2005: 27, Knapp 1992: 13).

choices in their texts. Language performance is thus related to the features above. The values of the genre features are listed in extensive taxonomies in the KPG specifications.

A substantial portion of the English Corpus has been manually annotated with learners' errors pertaining to distinct levels of linguistic analysis (i.e. orthographic, grammatical, lexical, semantic, and pragmatic errors). Error coding is initially carried out on a word basis. That is, a lexical unit is annotated with one or more error labels, indicating negative properties associated with distinct types of competences. Certain error labels often co-occur: the combination of a lexical and a semantic error label, for example, indicates the erroneous selection and use of a word associated with a meaning that is inappropriate for a given linguistic context. Similarly, lexical items that erroneously realise grammatical dependencies are marked with both lexical and grammatical error tags. Note that errors in our taxonomy are classified in increasingly refined types, hierarchically related to one another, so that conclusions at different levels of abstraction can readily be drawn from the annotated data.

The representation of interrelated language competences

Right from the outset we opt to emphasise the linguistic expression of meaning in the learner data. This spans three levels of analysis: the lexical, semantic and grammatical (syntactic) level. The precise question we wish to investigate is: how are meanings (word senses) and the lexico-grammatical features expressing them learned and used by FL learners in various communicative (discursive) contexts, at different levels of proficiency? While grammatical knowledge is essential for the language user to achieve efficient communication at each level of attainment, we view language production as essentially semantically and lexically driven and we attempt to describe its developing nature in terms of the expanding range of words and denoted meanings. These are, in turn, tied with the grammatical (syntactic) patterns in which they are realised.

Our representation and analysis of the lexical semantic and grammatical interface add to existing analyses, such as the one carried out by the Cambridge EPP. Reporting on analyses of the CLC data, Hawkins & Filipović (2012) provide preliminary summaries of grammatical features of English distinguishing each CEFR level. The EPP criterial features for A2, for instance, include items such as simple intransitive clauses, verbs with a finite complement clause, direct *wh*-questions, postnominal modification with -ed, modals 'may', 'can' and 'might' in the 'possibility' (epistemic) sense, etc.[2] Grammatical and lexical patterns of this sort may serve as useful checklists for examiners, teachers and learners. Yet we believe that language teaching and learning will essentially benefit from lists of semantically driven features, such as groups of semantically similar or related words, consistently linked with the syntactic means expressing their arguments.

Consider, for example, the use of 'admire' in (1): its semantics involves a participant admiring, the entity admired and, optionally, a reason or a property for which the entity is admired.

(1)   I *admire* her very much for her honesty, you know.

We distinguish the use of 'admire' in (1) from that in (2), and we seek to reveal how knowledge of the semantic and syntactic structure associated with each sense develops across learning stages.

(2)   They found several people *admiring* the view across the river.

Possible realisations of the meaning expressed in (1) are shown in (3a-d): in (3a) the reason of admiring is not lexically expressed; in the rest of the sentences, it appears either in a prepositional phrase introduced by 'for' (3b) or as a noun phrase (3c, 3d). The entity admired is realised as a noun

---

2   The lexical and grammatical features in the EPP preliminary lists of criterial reference
     level features are not systematically linked to one another. The English Vocabulary
     Profile includes examples of word usage for the lists of lexical items specified per level,
     but the connection between words and the lists of grammatical patterns characteris-
     ing each level is not explicit (with the exception of certain grammatical patterns, e.g.
     the 'tough' movement, associated with specific lexical items). The EPP currently also
     lacks links between words sharing related senses.

phrase (3a, 3b), as a prepositional phrase introduced by 'in' (3c), or as a possessive determiner (3d). The question we generally ask is: at which proficiency level does a given lexico-grammatical pattern first appear to be used productively? The frequencies of both positive (correct) and negative (incorrect) occurrences allow us to place a given pattern at certain level(s), at which we assume it is learned, and therefore, should be tested.

(3) a. Adam continued to *admire* [ADMIRED him] above all men.
   b. [ADMIRED Piper's designs] *were admired* [REASON for their beauty].
   c. They *admire* [REASON skill] [ADMIRED in a poet].
   d. I *admire* [REASON [ADMIRED your] taste].

In a related vein, we are also interested in investigating the usage distribution of semantically related words across learning/proficiency stages. For example, the verb 'admire' has similar semantic properties with verbs such as 'appreciate', 'respect', 'disapprove', 'blame', etc., and also with nouns such as 'admiration', 'contempt', 'esteem', and the adjectives 'critical', 'disapproving', etc. Our goal is to identify the level or levels at which each of these words is used appropriately. On the basis of individual frequency distributions, we can draw meaningful conclusions on the development of a generic meaning which subsumes the semantics of 'admire', and that of related verbs, nouns, and adjectives. Generic meanings are used to break down the learners' semantic competence. For each of these meanings, we aim to identify the new knowledge (i.e. the lexical items and grammatical patterns) associated with subsequently higher levels. Again, the question asked is: which words distinguish each reference level from another? Are there common sequencing patterns reflecting the development of grammatical knowledge for related verbs?

A lexical semantic model for corpus annotation

The linguistic expression of lexical meaning has recently received much attention in the field of computational linguistics. Algorithms that automatically identify meanings (senses) of words along with their semantic and syntactic dependents (arguments) have been developed for English and other languages, to support a variety of applications. The representation of lexical semantic knowledge is addressed as a prerequisite for the development of such systems. One resource furnishing such representations is FrameNet. The Berkeley FrameNet project (Baker et al. 1998) is an ongoing project creating an online lexical database with annotated sentences for English drawing on Fillmore's (1985) theory of frame semantics. Frame semantics is an empirical paradigm emphasising the continuities between linguistic expression and experience (Petruck 1996). It represents lexical meaning in terms of conceptual structures, related in such a way that to understand any one concept it is necessary to understand the entire system. The basic unit of analysis is the semantic frame, that is, a schematic representation of a stereotypical scene or situation. A semantic frame is a linguistic entity that structures experiential entities and a frame is associated with a set of lexical units (i.e. verbs, nouns, adjectives, adverbs, multi-word expressions, etc.) that evoke it and a set of semantic roles (called frame elements) corresponding to participants and props in the designated event or situation. FrameNet contains approximately 1,200 frames covering more than 13,400 lexical units in more than 202,000 annotated sentences. Table 10.2 shows the 'Judgment' frame, evoked by 'admire' in (1).

Table 10.2: The Judgment frame

Frame: Judgment	
Definition	A Cogniser makes a judgment about an Evaluee. The judgment may be positive (e.g. respect) or negative (e.g. condemn) and this information is recorded in the semantic types Positive and Negative on the Lexical Units of this frame. There may be a specific Reason for the Cogniser's judgment, or there may be a capacity or Role in which the Evaluee is judged.
Frame Elements	Cogniser: [The boss] *appreciates* you for your diligence. Evaluee: The boss *appreciates* [you] for your diligence. Expressor: She *viewed* him with an appreciative [gaze]. Reason: I *admire* you [for your intellect]. Role: I *admire* you [as a composer].
Lexical Units (LUs)	accolade.n, accuse.v, admiration.n, admire.v, admiring.a, applaud.v, appreciate.v, appreciation.n, appreciative.a, approbation.n, approving.a, blame.n, blame.v, boo.v, contempt.n, etc.*

*LUs are listed along with their parts-of-speech ('v' indicates verbs, 'n' indicates nouns, 'a' indicates adjectives).

The FrameNet lexicon furnishes a theoretically well-founded framework, useful for empirical research related to the expression of lexical meaning. Semantic representations are coupled with descriptions of the grammatical properties of words, as shown in (5) for the sentence in (4).

(4)   [COGNISER She] *admires* [EVALUEE her father] [DEGREE greatly] [REASON for his patience].

(5)   Cogniser: Noun Phrase (NP), Subject
       Evaluee: Noun Phrase (NP), Object
       Degree: Adverbial (Adv), Dependent
       Reason: Prepositional phrase (PP), Dependent

We use frame semantics for the representation of meaning in our learner data as it is a paradigm drawing on cognitive knowledge. Frames are firmly grounded in linguistic intuition, capturing the relationship between language and communication in a straightforward manner. Successful communication involves a speaker and an addressee, sharing conceptions of frames pertaining to certain domain or topic, and being able to structure their relationships. Each frame includes a number of related words, of which only a subset is chosen and used in each instance of communication. Frame semantic representations capture the interface between world knowledge and its linguistic expression, modelling events, participants and their relationships, as they are lexicalised by words and their grammatical dependents.

Frame semantic structures are also cross-linguistically valid. The FrameNet representations have been used as the basis for building similar resources in German (Burchardt et al. 2006), Spanish (Subirats & Petruck 2003), and Japanese (Ohara et al. 2004). It has been shown that frames can serve as 'interlingua' for the description of word meaning (Boas 2005), despite differences in the grammatical realisations of semantic properties. Espousing this paradigm, we are thus able to develop annotated corpora with comparable information across target languages. We are also fortunate to have at our disposal algorithms (semantic parsers) that automatically assign frames (senses) to lexical items and extract structured frame semantic features from texts.[3]

---

3   Several systems are currently available, performing the sort of automatic semantic analysis involved in the frame semantics paradigm: Shalmaneser (Erk & Padó 2006),

Finally, frames and their semantic components encode aspects of the semantic competence, as specified by the CEFR, that is, the relation of a word to some general context, inter-lexical relations such as synonymy, antonymy, hyponymy, part/whole relations, componential analysis, translation equivalence. Since they group together words with similar meanings, they are valuable for the description of semantic knowledge, in association with lexical knowledge. Words are not taught or learned independently of one another, but rather linked on the basis of shared semantic properties. These properties are also reflected in shared grammatical (syntactic) patterns in which words appear.[4] We hypothesise that the teaching and learning process will significantly benefit from systematic associations of different types of features and in what follows, we discuss how frame annotations of our corpora are used to model learners' distinct but related competences, across learning stages and discursive contexts.

Illustrative corpus analyses for English

Corpus annotation enables the extraction of the following features from learners' scripts: (i) generic meanings (frames or word senses), (ii) words evoking frames, (iii) frame semantic structures (i.e. sets of frame elements), and (iv) phrase structure patterns. That is, lexical, semantic and grammatical features are jointly identified in the learners' texts, as input to our analyses. The scripts in the KPG English Corpus are parsed with a robust semantic parser – the Semafor parser (Das & Smith 2011) – which assigns semantic

---

LTH (Johansson & Nugues 2007), Semafor (Das & Smith 2011). It should be noted that annotations produced by such systems lack the precision required for valid linguistic analyses; some degree of manual inspection and correction is necessary for ensuring reliability of results drawing on this data.

4   A close association between syntax and semantics has been advocated by various theoretical studies in lexical semantics; among others, Levin (1993) investigates how words sharing a portion of their semantics appear in similar syntactic environments.

frames and frame components to words and their dependents. We study the distribution of the extracted features across levels of proficiency and grading bands. We additionally associate linguistic features with categories of scripts distinguished in terms of the genre features discussed earlier. Table 10.3 shows the output of the parser for the sentence in (6).

(6)   But there still aren't enough ringers to ring more than six of the eight bells.

Table 10.3: Output of the Semafor parser

Frame	Lexical Unit (LU)	Frame Element	Phrase Type	Constituent
Noise_makers	bell.n	Noise_maker	NP	Bells
Cause_to_make_noise	ring.v	Agent	NP	enough ringers
Cause_to_make_noise	ring.v	Sound_maker	NP	more than six of the eight bells
Sufficiency	enough.a	Item	NP	Ringers
Sufficiency	enough.a	Enabled_situation	VP-to	to ring more than six of the eight bells
Existence	there be.v	Entity	NP	enough ringers to ring more than six of the eight bells

Automatically acquired annotations are manually inspected and corrected. Note that these annotations cover only a portion of the words and meanings used in the corpus data. The parser identifies frames and frame evoking elements, as represented in the FrameNet lexicon, a resource which currently has restricted coverage of the English vocabulary. Below we give a rough estimation of the FrameNet lexical coverage in the KPG data, on the basis of a sample sub-corpus comprising ninety rated scripts, randomly selected from scripts with maximum inter-rater agreement, representing all grading bands at B1, B2 and C1 level in a balanced way. Table 10.4 shows average numbers of lemmas per script and grading band, and average numbers of lemmas whose lexical meanings are coded in the FrameNet database.[5] The frame semantic annotations consistently cover more than 60 per cent of the meanings and words in the scripts, but they still will not capture the complete picture. To remedy this coverage issue, our analyses are supplemented with frequencies of word forms (tokens) and lemmas at each level and each grading band, associated with the grammatical patterns in which they appear and with frequencies of tokens and lemmas filling their syntactic argument slots. Grammatical and lexical information is jointly represented, to capture basic sense distinctions in the portion of the data for which no frame annotations are available.

Table 10.4: Lexical coverage of FrameNet (FN) in sample KPG sub-corpus

Level	Grading band	Lemmas per script	Lemmas in FN
B1	FS	65	42
	MS	57	39
	US	65	43
B2	FS	116	81
	MS	85	58
	US	113	92
C1	FS	142	99
	MS	148	112
	US	140	102

Table 10.5 reports on the number of discrete frames attested in the sub-corpus, representing learners' semantic competences at B1, B2 and C1 level. The differences between grading bands at each level indicate that scripts graded as fully appropriate consistently involve a wider range of lexical meanings, compared to those graded as moderately satisfactory or unsatisfactory. Table 10.5 includes additional information about average numbers of sentences per script, across levels and grading bands.

---

5   These numbers ignore articles, pronouns, proper nouns, particles, and interjections. We only count words with lexical content (i.e. nouns, verbs, adjectives, adverbs, prepositions, conjunctions, multi-word expressions) that can be frame evoking elements in the FrameNet lexicon.

Table 10.5: Discrete frame occurrences in sample sub-corpus and sentences per script

	B1			B2			C1		
	FS	MS	US	FS	MS	US	FS	MS	US
Discrete frames in sub-corpus	101	79	47	140	88	97	175	151	133
Sentences/ script (avg)	7.3	8.1	8.0	14.0	13.9	13.6	12.1	13.1	14.6

The frame-based analyses we carry out address occurrence frequencies for each type of extracted feature. On the basis of their distribution, linguistic features characterise a given level uniquely or not. For instance, a lexical unit appearing with characteristic frequency at A1 and A2 level might be used to distinguish both A levels from B and C levels. Alternatively, a word that is used productively at a single level may distinguish that level from the rest. Note that the level associated with the characteristic use of a frame-evoking lexical item may be different from the level associated with the characteristic use of the frame: while the verbs 'applaud', 'esteem', and 'stigmatise', evoking the Judgment frame, are used with characteristic frequency at C1 level, the meaning encoded by Judgment is first used productively at B levels, lexicalised by verbs such as 'admire', 'blame', 'accuse', 'approve', 'disapprove', 'appreciate', 'respect', etc. An interesting aspect of analyses related to frame distributions has to do with frames that are ontologically linked in the FrameNet lexicon, for example, the judgment and the judgment_communication frame. Frequencies of their corpus attestations are investigated in connection to one another, indicating how closely related meanings are learned and differentiated across levels.

Corpus attestations are analysed for both correct and erroneous instantiations of linguistic features. We consider a given feature to be learned at certain level(s) (and to persist at subsequent, higher levels), if its use is consistently correct (appropriate) at the level(s) in question, in the situational contexts in which it functions. The sentences below exemplify some of the types of errors annotated in our data, in accordance with our error taxonomy.

(7)   Incorrect choice of verb, incorrect meaning evoked (error labels LEX1, SEM1)
      If you don't *realise* [recognise] a dish from the menu you ask the waiter's help.

(8)   Incorrect choice of noun, incorrect meaning evoked (error labels LEX1, SEM1)
      If you need anything, you nod or make a *sigh* [sign] to waiter.
(9)   Missing determiner (error label GRAMM2)
      If you need anything, you nod or make a sigh to *waiter* [to the waiter].
(10) Incorrect subject-verb agreement (error label GRAMM1)
      One of those rules *are* [is] that you wait for the host to start dining.
(11) Incorrect determiner-noun agreement (error label GRAMM1)
      Many *student* [students] answered that they would help a person in need.

Each word, in each of its senses (i.e. frames evoked), is associated with the level(s) of proficiency at which it is used appropriately and productively and, additionally, with the genre features of the texts in which it appears to be characteristically frequent. We document learners' levelled lexical and semantic competences in close association to their situational contexts, emphasising the distribution of lexical items across thematic (semantic) domains and discourse environments, as exemplified in Table 10.6.

Table 10.6: Levelled, contextual lexical use in Judgment

Lexical Unit (LU)	Frame	Level	Genre feature	
			Thematic domain	Discourse environment
admire.v	Judgment	B1	Personal relationships	Informal correspondence, Youth magazine, School newspaper
applaud.v	Judgment	C1	Politics, Finance, Science, Technology	Newspaper, Blog, Electronic encyclopedia, Forum
stigmatise.v	Judgment	C1	Politics, Finance, Institutions	Newspaper, Blog
esteem.v	Judgment	C1	Education, Institutions, Culture	Newspaper, Music magazine

Frame semantic annotations link the meaning of lexical items with the grammatical patterns in which they appear. The distribution of correct and erroneous, semantic and syntactic (phrase structure) patterns, at different levels, sheds light on identifiable developmental changes in closely related competences. Examples (12)-(14) show how instantiations of the Judgment meaning may differ across levels, that is, how learners of English at different stages gradually tend to use more complex semantic structures incorporating an increasingly wider range of semantic components.

(12) B1,   Cogniser – Evaluee: [COGNISER He] admires [EVALUEE his father].

(13) B2,   Cogniser – Evaluee: [COGNISER Her mother] disapproves [EVALUEE of her friends].

Cogniser – Evaluee – Reason: [COGNISER Your boss] will appreciate [EVALUEE your] [REASON good manners].

(14) C1,   Cogniser – Evaluee: [EVALUEE The PM] was applauded [COGNISER by the Parliament].

Evaluee – Reason: At school, [EVALUEE he] was stigmatised [REASON for not having parents].

Cogniser – Evaluee – Degree: [COGNISER Critics] highly esteem [EVALUEE this band] [REASON for its inspired compositions and improvisations during concerts].

We also record the use of gradually more complex syntactic (phrase structure) patterns, associated with words and their meanings, or independently of them. Corpus attested patterns (15)-(17) exemplify developmental changes in grammatical competences at B1, B2, and C1 level, with respect to the Judgment frame. Again, we enable links between grammatical features and genre features of scripts, looking for recurring syntactic choices or preferences consistently characterising certain genre (e.g. discourse environment, text type, text process).

(15) B1,   NP-V-NP, *admire*: He admires his father.

(16) B2,   NP-V-NP-PP[for], *admire, blame*: The blamed him for the fire.

NP-V-PP[of], *approve, disapprove*: Her mother disapproved of her friends.

NP-Vpassive-PP[by], *admire, approve, disapprove, appreciate, blame*: He was admired by his colleagues.

NP-V-NP-PP[of], *accuse*: The accused him of racism.

(17) C1,   NP-Vpassive-PPing[for], *stigmatise*: At school, he was stigmatised for not having parents.

NP-ADV-V-NP-PP[for], *esteem, stigmatise*: Critics highly esteem this band for its inspired compositions and improvisations during concerts.

The semantic and syntactic features of words are incorporated in the descriptions documenting levelled lexical competences. Table 10.7, for example, expands the information included in Table 10.5 as regards the use of 'admire' in the judgment frame. It provides an indication about which lexico-grammatical pattern is learned at which level, and in which contexts it has been observed to be used productively, on the basis of the empirical data collected so far.

Table 10.7: Levelled, contextual use of 'admire' in Judgment

Lexical Unit	Level	Semantic-syntactic pattern	Genre feature	
			Thematic domain	Discourse environment
admire.v	B1	NP-V-NP/ Cogniser-Evaluee [She admires her father.]	Personal relationships	Informal correspondence, Youth magazine, School newspaper
	B2	NP-V-NP-PP[for]/ Cogniser-Evaluee-Reason [She admires her father for his patience.]	Personal relationships, Culture and Art	Newspaper, Blog, Informal correspondence, Formal correspondence
		NP-V-NPpossessive/ Cogniser-Evaluee-Reason [She admires her father's patience.]	Personal relationships, Culture and Art	Newspaper, Blog, Informal correspondence,Formal correspondence
	C1	NP-V-NP-PP[in]/ Cogniser-Evaluee-Reason [She admires patience in her father.]	Politics, Finance, Science, Technology, Education, Institutions	Newspaper, Scientific journal, Blog

In the immediate future, extensive analyses of the sort presented in this section will be carried out not only for English, but also for the German and Spanish data. As more data are annotated and analysed our goal is to cast light on the joint development of interrelated competences in a given language, complementing the existing, prescriptive information on how contextual language use should evolve across learning (proficiency) stages. Frame-based descriptions are comparable across languages and will allow us to contrast the developmental patterns observed in each language.

Conclusion

The aim of this chapter has been to describe aspects of an ongoing project adding details to levelled descriptors of proficiency, across languages. Corpus-attested features approximating various types of competences of FL learners, at distinct learning stages, are identified to supplement prescriptive lists of levelled language properties, specified by language experts, teachers, and exam designers. Drawing on diverse sources of data, we deliver increasingly refined descriptions for each proficiency level, making them unambiguous for use in educational practice.

We intend to make a substantial amount of data available, encoding comparable linguistic information about developing linguistic knowledge in three European languages. This will enable systematic, contrastive analyses casting light on how FLs are learned and used in various contexts. We offer descriptions of the competences of Greek learners, in particular, aimed to support the development of teaching, learning, and assessment or testing models as well as learning materials targeted to their profile and needs. We also seek synergies so that such a local model of documentation is replicated with other groups of FL learners, enabling the collection of data that will advocate a shift from the development of general language profiles towards the study of the idiosyncratic use of languages performed by coherent groups of learners. Assuming that a data-driven user or learner profile will also add specificity to the notion of 'plurilingual competence' – a notion that was introduced by the CEFR –, we aspire to make the results of this research available for future developments, if 'the aim of language education is [to be] profoundly modified', in the manner suggested by the CEFR:

It [language education] is no longer seen as simply to achieve 'mastery' of one or two, or even three languages, each taken in isolation, with the 'ideal native speaker' as the ultimate model. Instead, the aim is to develop a linguistic repertory, in which all linguistic abilities have a place. This implies, of course, that the languages offered in educational institutions should be diversified and students given the opportunity to develop a plurilingual competence. (CEFR: 5)

Bibliography

Baker, C. F., Fillmore, C. J., and Lowe, J. B. (1998). 'The Berkeley FrameNet Project'. In *Proceedings of the 36th Annual Meeting of the Association for Computational Linguistics and 17th International Conference on Computational Linguistics (COLING-ACL)*, pp. 86–90. Montreal, Canada.

Beacco, J., and Porquier, R. (2007). *A1 Level for French/A Reference Book and CD Audio*. Paris: Les Editions Didier (in French).

——(2008). *A2 Level for French/A Reference*. Paris: Les Editions Didier (in French).

Beacco, J., Bouquet S., and Porquier, R. (2004). *B2 Level for French/A Reference Book and CD Audio*. Paris: Les Editions Didier (in French).

Beacco, J., Blin, B., Houles, E., Lepage S., and Riba P. (2011). *B1 Level for French/A Reference Book and CD Audio*. Paris: Les Editions Didier (in French).

Boas, H. C. (2005). 'Semantic Frames as Interlingual Representations for Multilingual Lexical Databases', *International Journal of Lexicography*, 18 (4), 445–78.

Burchardt, A., Erk, K., Frank, A., Kowalski, A., Padó, S., and Pinkal, M. (2006). 'The SALSA Corpus: a German Corpus Resource for Lexical Semantics'. In *Proceedings of 5th International Conference on Language Resources and Evaluation (LREC)*, pp. 969–74. Genoa, Italy.

Council of Europe (2001). *Common European Framework of Reference for Languages: Learning, Teaching, Assessment*. Cambridge: Cambridge University Press.

Das, D., and Smith, N. (2011). 'Semi-supervised Frame-semantic Parsing for Unknown Predicates'. In *Proceedings of the 49th Annual Meeting of the Association for Computational Linguistics: Human Language Technologies (ACL-HLT)*, pp. 1435–44. Portland, Oregon.

Dendrinos, B. (2005). 'Certification de Compétences en Langues Étrangères, Multilinguisme et Plurilinguisme' ['Certification of Foreign Language Competences, Multilingualism and Plurilingualism']. In *Langue Nationales et Plurilinguisme: Initiatives Grecques*, pp. 95–100. Athens: The Ministry of National Education and Centre for the Greek Language.

—— (2013). 'Social Meanings in Global-glocal Language Proficiency Exams'. In C. Tsagari, S. Papadima-Sophocleous and S. Ioannou-Georgiou (eds), *Language Testing and Assessment Around the Globe: Achievements and Experiences*, pp. 46–67. Frankfurt: Peter Lang.

Dendrinos, B., and Gotsoulia, V. (2014). 'Setting Standards for Multilingual Curricula to Teach and Test Foreign Languages'. In B. Spolsky, O. Inbar-Lourie and M. Tannenbaum (eds), *Challenges for Language Education and Policy, Making Space for People*, pp. 23–39. New York: Routledge.

Erk, K., and Pado, S. (2006). 'Shalmaneser: A Flexible Toolbox for Semantic Role Assignment'. In *Proceedings of the 5th International Conference on Language Resources and Evaluation (LREC)*. Genoa, Italy.

Fillmore, C, J. (1985). 'Frames and the Semantics of Understanding', *Quaderni di Semantica*, 6 (2), 222–54.

Glaboniat, M., Müller, M., Rusch, P., Schmitz, H., and Wertenschlag, L. (2005). *German Profile. Common European Framework of Reference for Languages. Description of Learning Objectives, Can-do Statements, Communicative Resources: Levels A1-A2, B1-B2, C1-C2*. Berlin/München/Wien/Zurich/New York: Langenscheidt.

Gotsoulia, V., and Dendrinos, B. (2011). 'Towards a Corpus-based Approach to Modeling Language Production of Foreign Language Learners in Communicative Contexts'. In *Proceedings of the 8th International Conference on Recent Advances in Natural Language Processing*, pp. 557–61. Hissar, Bulgaria.

Hawkins, J. A., and Buttery, P. (2010). 'Criterial Features in Learner Corpora: Theory and Illustrations', *English Profile Journal*, 1 (1), 1–23.

Hawkins, J. A., and Filipović, L. (2012). *Criterial Features in L2 English: Specifying the Reference Levels of the Common European Framework. English Profile Studies 1*. Cambridge: Cambridge University Press.

Johansson, R., and Nugues, P. (2007). 'LTH: Semantic Structure Extraction Using Nonprojective Dependency Trees'. In *Proceedings of the 4th International Workshop on Semantic Evaluations*, pp. 227–30. Prague, Czech Republic.

Instituto Cervantes (2006). Curricular Plan of Cervantes Institute: Levels of Reference for Spanish. Madrid: Instituto Cervantes – Biblioteca Nueva (in Spanish).

Karavas, E. (2012). 'Introducing Innovations in Periods of Financial Crisis: Obstacles in the Implementation of the New Integrated Foreign Languages Curriculum in Greece'. In *Proceedings of the 5th International Conference of Education, Research and Innovation (ICERI)*, pp. 5534–42. Madrid, Spain.

Knapp, P., and Watkins, M. (2005). *Genre, Text, Grammar: Technologies for Teaching and Assessing Writing*. Sydney: UNSW Press.

Knapp, P. (1992). *Resource Book for Genre and Grammar*. Metropolitan West Literacy and Learning Program, Parramatta, NSW Dept of School Education.

Kress, G., and van Leeuwen, T. (2001). *Multimodal Discourse: The Modes and Media of Contemporary Communication*. London: Hodder and Stoughton.

Kurtes, S., and Saville, N. (2008). 'The English Profile Programme. An Overview', *Research Notes*, 33, 2–4. Cambridge, Cambridge ESOL.

Levin, B. (1993). *English Verb Classes and Alternations: A Preliminary Investigation*. Chicago: University of Chicago Press.

Little, D. (2007). 'The Common European Framework of Reference for Languages: Perspectives on the Making of Supranational Language Education Policy', *The Modern Language Journal*, 91 (4), 645–55.

Macedo, D., Dendrinos, B., and Gounari, P. (2003). *The Hegemony of English*. Boulder, CO: Paradigm Publishers.

Martin, J. R. (2009). 'Genre and Language Learning: A Social Semiotic Perspective', *Linguistics and Education*, 20 (1), 10–21.

Ohara, K., Hirose, S., Fujii, T. O., Ryoko, S., Hiroaki, S., and Shun, I. (2004). 'The Japanese FrameNet Project: An Introduction'. In *Proceedings of the Satellite Workshop 'Building Lexical Resources from Semantically Annotated Corpora' in the 4th International Conference on Language Resources and Evaluation (LREC)*, pp. 9–12. Lisbon, Portugal.

Petruck, R. L. M. (1996). 'Frame Semantics'. In J. Verschueren, J. O. Östman, J. Blommaert and C. Bulcaen (eds), *Handbook of Pragmatics*, pp. 1–13. Amsterdam: John Benjamins.

Spinelli, B., and Francesca, P. (2010). *Profile of the Italian Language: CEFR levels A1, A2, B1, B2*. Milano: La nuova Italia (in Italian).

Subirats, C., and Petruck, R. L. M. (2003). 'Surprise: Spanish FrameNet'. Paper presented in *International Congress of Linguists. Workshop on Frame Semantics*. Prague, Czech Republic.

Van Ek, J. A., and Trim, J. L. M. (1991a). *Threshold 1990*. Cambridge: Council of Europe/ Cambridge University Press.

——(1991b). *Waystage 1990*. Cambridge: Council of Europe/Cambridge University Press.

——(2001). *Vantage*. Cambridge: Council of Europe/Cambridge University Press.

BESSIE MITSIKOPOULOU, EVDOKIA KARAVAS AND
SMARAGDA PAPADOPOULOU

11   KPG e-school: The diffusion and implementation of an educational innovation

ABSTRACT

This chapter presents the rationale permeating the development of the educational web-site called KPG e-school in the context of a European and state-funded project. During a period of dire socioeconomic crisis in Greece, the KPG e-school aimed at becoming a locus of digital educational materials for the foreign language educational community in the country, connecting the KPG exam to formal education. Adopting the perspective and ideology of open educational resources, the KPG e-school addresses four key stakehold-ers related to the KPG exams: teachers, students, parents and KPG assessors. The chapter deals with the digital materials developed for the first three categories of stakeholders. It describes the selected design process of the educational resources produced, presents the rationale for the adopted pedagogical approach and discusses the potential and the contribution of these materials for the preparation of language learners in the foreign languages taught in Greek schools.

Introduction: Setting the context

The learning of foreign languages forms a significant component of Greek students' education from their very early years. Generally speaking, foreign languages are very important for the present generation of Greek parents since the Greek language is one of the least widely spoken languages outside of Greece (European Commission 2006). English is the primary foreign language spoken by more than 48 per cent of the population, as it is consid-ered to be the key for social mobility and professional development open-ing the door to important educational, professional and socioeconomic opportunities, followed by German (9 per cent able to converse in the language), French (8.5 per cent) and Italian (8 per cent).[1] These are also the languages offered in primary and secondary schools in Greece (with English being introduced in the first grade of primary school and French and German from the fourth grade).

Foreign language education in Greece is highly exam and certificate oriented, with Greek parents having a predominantly utilitarian and materialistic view towards foreign language learning which focuses on the acquisition of a language certificate. This view affects both parents' and learners' attitudes towards languages and raises learners' instrumental motivation towards learning a foreign language. According to Mattheoudakis & Alexiou (2013), the number of Greek students who sit for EFL exams upon completing their primary education is the highest in Europe. Cummins & Davison (2007) also support this finding, stating that Greece comes first in the number of candidates sitting for those exams.

Although within the Greek educational system systematic attempts have been made over the years to provide comprehensive foreign language education to its students in public primary and secondary schools, the vast majority of Greek parents choose to send their children to private foreign language centres (called *frontistiria*) in order to prepare for foreign language certificates as a child's future career development is considered to be inextricably linked to certified knowledge of foreign languages (Mitsikopoulou 2007). Due to the fact that foreign language education in schools did not, until recently, prepare students for foreign language certification, offered fewer contact hours and less intensive courses than private language institutes, parents preferred to pay for extra intensive foreign language instruction so their children can obtain the much coveted language certificate. According to recent research (see Angouri et al. 2010), about 80 per cent of Greek school children attend foreign language institutes and Greek families spend on average about 880 million euros on foreign language school fees and textbooks. Thus, private language institutes have become a burgeoning business in Greece and are almost exclusively oriented towards preparing

[1]   <http://www.worldatlas.com/articles/what-language-do-they-speak-in-greece.html>.

students for language certification exams. A recent survey reports that there are 6,564 foreign language schools in Greece with 510,575 students, the vast majority of whom (448,822) are preparing for English language certificates.[2] Within *frontistiria*, international foreign language teaching and learning materials, rather than local ones, are used for the preparation of students for international foreign language certificates, which are largely dependent on monolingual ideologies and a monocultural ethos of communication (Dendrinos 2009). This practice of financial exertion reflects parents' perennial lack of trust in the quality of foreign language provision in Greek public schools and is a result of their deep-seated belief that foreign language instruction equals foreign language certification. Greek parents' passion for foreign language certification explains why so many low income families pay for their children to have language support classes after school. This of course creates an additional problem in school foreign language classes because students have substantially different knowledge and communication skills in the target language – a problem which is not dealt with easily by teachers when the infrastructure of a school does not support differentiated teaching.

Major changes have recently been introduced in Greece aimed at providing more and better opportunities for foreign language learning within state schools and to facilitate the achievement of the European objective for multilingualism and plurilingual citizenry. The introduction of the KPG exam system in 2003 (see introduction to this volume) aimed to support the idea of European multilingualism and plurilingual citizenry, to legitimate community languages, to have a washback effect on how additional languages are taught or learnt and how literacies are used to access information (Dendrinos 2009). Moreover, in line with European developments in ELL (early language learning) and EU policy recommendations, in 2010 the Greek Ministry of Education introduced English as a Foreign Language in the first and second grades of public all day primary schools. The program, which has come to be known with the Greek

---

2   <http://www.esos.gr/article/frontistiria/510.575_mathites_6564_lkentra_xenon_
     glosson_13650_kathigites_eparkeia_8187_ptyxio_aei_pinakes_kata_nomo> accessed
     February 2013.

acronym 'PEAP', was developed within the context of a European funded project entitled 'New Foreign Language Education Policy in Schools: English for young learners' and was implemented experimentally in 960 primary schools throughout Greece but has now been implemented in all primary schools in Greece (see Karavas 2014). In addition, a new curriculum for foreign language teaching in schools, the Integrated Foreign Languages Curriculum (IFLC), was developed in 2011 within the framework of the new National Curriculum and implemented on a national scale in 2016. The IFLC is common for all foreign languages that are currently offered in Greek state schools, that is, English, which is the so-called 'first' foreign language taught in Greek schools, and also French, German, Spanish, and Italian, referred to as 'second' foreign languages, comprising an integrated framework applying to both primary and secondary education. More precisely, the new IFLC adopts a generic approach to language learning and the use of foreign languages for communication and is intended to apply to all languages that may, at some time, be included in the school curriculum (either as obligatory or as optional). This in itself constitutes a major breakthrough since until recently languages were treated in the Greek school curriculum as separate clearly defined subjects, and curricula for each foreign language were developed adopting different aims and promoting different approaches to language learning. Foreign language curricula for primary education were developed independently of curricula for secondary education adding to the incoherence and unsystematic nature of foreign language education in Greece (see Karavas 2012). With the IFLC, foreign language learning, teaching, and assessment conform to the six-level scale specified by the Council of Europe comprising the European standard for language proficiency (A1-C2 levels). With descriptors for each level of language proficiency that are matched against the Common European Framework of Reference (CEFR), during the piloting phase of its implementation, the administrative practice of levelling students on the basis of their language proficiency, on the scale set by the Council of Europe, has been instituted (see Dendrinos et al. 2013).

Many more changes are taking place with the aim of creating and adopting a well-articulated (foreign) language education strategy and of setting standards to align foreign language curricular policy and practices in Greece. Efforts are being made to link the KPG exams to the foreign languages school curriculum since both adopt the six level scale of the Council of Europe and are based on common illustrative descriptors of language proficiency. This is done with the aim of establishing the connection between the KPG and the school system in the hope that this connection will have a positive washback effect on classroom practice. In 2016 the Ministry of Education officially announced that public school students would be prepared for the KPG exams in school, responding to the longstanding request of public school foreign language teachers who have always believed that this practice would elevate the status of the foreign language lesson at school, would boost students' interest in foreign language lessons and alleviate the financial burden of the majority of parents who were 'forced' to send their children to *frontistiria* to gain certification. In this context the KPG e-school was developed as one attempt to connect the KPG exams to school.

Designing the KPG e-school

The KPG e-school is an educational website which was developed by the members of the Research Centre for Language Teaching, Testing and Assessment (RCeL) at the National and Kapodistrian University of Athens as part of a European and state funded project.[3] The main goal of this action was to link the KPG language exams with the state compulsory education system and to give primary and secondary school students the opportunity to prepare in school for the KPG exams in English, German, French, Italian and Spanish. The final outcome was the presentation of a 'Uniform KPG exam preparation programme' which is open to the public and can be visited at <http://rcel.enl.uoa.gr/kpgeschool/>.

---

3   The project entitled 'Differentiated and graded national foreign language exams' was funded by the National Strategic Reference Framework (NSRF 2010–1013).

The KPG e-school is a multi-purpose and multi-functional educational website which addresses the needs of multiple stakeholders. In particular, it caters for:

- foreign language teachers who prepare students wishing to sit for the KPG exams,
- students who are interested in preparing individually for the KPG exams,
- parents who would like to be informed about the opportunities the KPG exams offer,
- foreign language teachers who wish to receive online training in order to be included in the body of certified KPG oral examiners and/or script raters.

In order to address the specific needs of each one of the target groups, we employed different methodologies and used appropriate digital technologies each time. First, however, we conducted a thorough examination of available content management systems to select the one that would allow us to manage the diverse digital content. A content management system (CMS) can be thought of as a special kind of software which builds, organises, manages and stores collections of digital work (text, image, audio, video, multimedia) in a repository (Barker 2016), and includes a set of processes that support the administration of digital content (e.g. by adding, capturing, storing, sorting, integrating, updating or removing and protecting various types of digital content in different formats). However, since our purpose was to deliver our educational digital content through the internet, we specifically needed a web content management system (WCMS) that would facilitate the website building process (Severdia & Crowder, 2009) and facilitate easy content changes and simplified control of digital content (Patel et al. 2011). The selection of the appropriate WCMS for our specific set of requirements took into account the types of content we wanted to create for our KPG e-school website as well as the types of engagement we wished to elicit from our target audiences. After reviewing a number of WCMSs an open source, customisable and easily extendable online publishing platform[4] was decided upon designed for creating highly interactive and flexible multi-language websites in a short time.

From inception to launch and ongoing usage, the KPG e-school CMS involved many people working in our research centre (RCeL), all with different roles and responsibilities. According to the categorisation proposed by Barker (2016), our content management team comprised editors, site planners, developers and administrators. Editors were responsible for creating, editing, and managing the content, whereas site planners were graphic designers and user interface experts responsible for designing the website. Most of their involvement was prior to launch, with continuing involvement as the site developed and changed over time. Developers were responsible for installing, configuring and integrating the CMS to match the requirements of the project, either as back-end developers working on complex content management tasks through a programming language or as front-end developers responsible for the creation of the template logic required to present the content to the viewers. Administrators were responsible for the continued operation of the CMS and the associated infrastructure. They included a CMS administrator responsible for user and permission management, workflow creation and management, licensing management, and all other tasks not related to content creation, and a server administrator responsible for the maintenance and support of the server on which the CMS runs.

The design and development process of the online educational materials for KPG e-school brought together a group of people with different competencies: research and design co-ordinators, instructional designers, subject matter experts, editors, graphic designers, multimedia developers and learning objects specialists. Some roles and responsibilities overlapped,

---

4   We selected *Joomla* CMS for its user friendly interface, its various available extensions that add new features to the website and its rich set of templates which can easily change the website's appearance. In addition, as happens with other open source software, it is supported by a worldwide user community and is further developed by an international team of volunteers (Tiggeler 2013).

as many e-learning tasks are interrelated and interdependent. In particular, according to the classification suggested by Khan and Joshi (2006), the research and design co-ordinator co-ordinated the e-learning research and design processes and informed management and design teams about the latest data pertaining to online learning activities and research. In addition, instructional designers provided consultation on instructional strategies and techniques for e-learning contents and resources, whereas qualified language learning researchers and experienced foreign language teachers served both as (a) content or subject matter experts responsible for writing the course content and transforming existing materials to make them learner centric, and as (b) editors who reviewed the developed e-learning materials for clarity, consistency of style, grammar, spelling, appropriate references and copyright information. Moreover, graphic designers and multimedia developers created 2D/3D graphics, videos, audios, animations and simulations to enhance the learning process, while learning object specialists guided the design, production, and meaningful storage of learning objects by following internationally recognised standards.

Contrary to many educational websites which seem to be locked in a traditional, rigid pattern, the design of the KPG e-school website promotes a pleasant and relaxing atmosphere that opens the door to a whole new world of educational resources and a way of learning and exploring instructional materials. High-resolution images were used together with concrete organisation of content in order to create a clean structure which visitors would appreciate from their first visit to the website.

Overall, the website consists of four main sections each addressing one of the four main stakeholders identified above. The metaphor of the class was adopted in the design of the website, thus the website consists of the students' class, the teachers' class, the parents' class and the assessors' class, each delivering specialised courses for the specific category of users. The following parts of this chapter present the rationale and the electronic materials developed for the first three classes. Although the specifications of the assessors' class have been drawn up, it is not presented here since its content is still being developed.

Strategy apps in the students' electronic class

Purpose

The students' electronic class of the KPG e-school website aims to offer students who are interested in sitting the KPG exam online self-study courses especially designed for the development of their test-taking strategies. Multimedia lessons in the form of strategy apps were developed for these courses in all four modules (Module 1: Reading comprehension and language awareness, Module 2: Writing and written mediation, Module 3: Listening comprehension, and Module 4: Speaking and oral mediation) for the five languages taught in Greek schools (English, German, French, Italian, Spanish).

At this point it is necessary to define what can be included under the umbrella of test-taking strategies. As Cohen (2014: 305) states test-taking strategies involve,

> the consciously-selected processes that the respondents use for dealing with both the language issues and the item-response demands in the test-taking tasks at hand. In reality, the level of conscious attention in the selection of strategies can be on a continuum, starting with general awareness and ending with highly focused attention.

Specifically, Cohen (2012) identifies three types of strategies that may be enlisted during the completion of language assessment tasks:

1. language learner strategies – the ways that respondents operationalise the basic skills of listening, speaking, reading, and writing, as well as the related skills of vocabulary learning, grammar, and translation,
2. test-management strategies – strategies for responding meaningfully to the test items and tasks, and
3. test-wiseness strategies – strategies for using knowledge of test formats and other peripheral information to answer test items without going through the expected linguistic and cognitive processes.

The design of online self-study courses and multimedia lessons (strategy apps) for the development of students' test-taking strategies was guided by Cohen's categorisation of strategies as well as by the findings from systematic research conducted by RCeL in this relatively unexplored field. In fact, for more than ten years, RCeL has been carrying out the Test-Taking Strategies Research Project (TSRP), a project whose aim has been to investigate the strategies used by candidates in each of the four modules of the KPG exams in English which lead to successful test performance. The findings of this research project are systematically analysed by RCeL researchers every year and have offered some useful insights into the preparation of the test itself as well as the preparation of some guidelines for candidates. For instance, given that KPG aims to evaluate language proficiency in a unified manner by focusing on language use – as opposed to usage[5] – it has been useful in determining the most popular test-taking strategies irrespective of proficiency level (Stathopoulou & Nikaki 2009).

As pointed out by several researchers (e.g. Amer 1993; Cohen, 2006; Lee & Alley 1981, among others), identifying the strategies to be used in a test is considered very important when these are to be taught. Knowing which strategies are used in the KPG tests has offered content designers significant information in order to form an online exam-preparation syllabus and to design effective online courses that guide candidates step by step through the format and requirements of each of the tests, while 'teaching' them the relative test-taking strategies, that is, the techniques consciously used by test-takers when responding to test requirements (cf. Cohen 1998, 2014).

---

5   While some international language exam suites emphasise language usage (focusing on grammar, syntax and vocabulary without considering the context in which they may appear), the KPG exams assess candidates' proficiency on the use of language by asking candidates to perform in a variety of contexts and discourse environments, to recognise and use the different conventions of the genres related to these contexts and to be aware of the functions of the linguistic elements they use (see also Chapter 1, this volume).

Structure

The students' e-class of the KPG e-school consists of asynchronous e-learning courses designed for individual self-study. These courses are self-paced, allowing individual learners to access the instructional materials at any time or any location on their own. The e-courses include both content (i.e. information) and instructional methods (i.e. techniques) to guide students through tests. Separate e-courses for each intergraded level (A1-A2, B1-B2) and for each language tested (English, French, German, Italian and Spanish) have been developed. Each course contains four multimedia lessons, each concerning one of the four modules of the exam. Courses of all languages have followed the same structure. Moreover, the lessons within a course share a common architecture but are not linear and can be studied in any order and as many times the student wishes. The lessons across levels and languages also have similar navigation routes.

Key components of each multimedia lesson include: (a) the can-do statements that specify language use, as they are described in the Common KPG Framework (cf. *The KPG Handbook*), (b) general information about each module (e.g. the number of items in each test paper), (c) practical guidelines (e.g. how to complete the answer sheet), (d) guidelines how to deal with the various task types (e.g. multiple choice, matching),[6] (e) information about how each test task is marked (e.g. how many marks are given to each item, how open-ended items are evaluated and marked), (f) general tips (e.g. techniques for time management).

Design and development process

For the design and development of the KPG exam preparation online courses we followed a series of basic steps in order to ensure the high quality and efficiency of the final online learning experience. Taking into account that the process of creating quality e-learning content begins with conducting

---

6   These are based on the typology of tasks the KPG test development team for each language has agreed on for all exam levels (cf. *The KPG Handbook* 2013).

a comprehensive learner analysis (Khan & Joshi 2006), we started the e-learning content design and development process by taking into account the characteristics of the target group for the intended e-courses, namely foreign language learners that wish to sit for the KPG exams.

After formulating the profile of our target group, it was important to determine the learning objectives of the e-courses early in the design process so that objectives could serve as design guidelines (Allen 2011: 122). The expected learning outcomes greatly affected the type, structure and features of the e-course to be developed. Clark & Mayer (2011: 20–21) distinguish two types of e-courses: those which are designed primarily to build awareness or provide information and those which are designed to build specific skills. Our e-courses actually perform both of these functions since they prepare students for the steps required in the test following an 'explanation-example-question-feedback' sequence and guiding learning in a step-by-step manner through multimedia lessons which aim to improve learning through the use of visual and verbal modes.

However, the instructional design, scripting, and interaction design of such e-courses can take a very long time depending on the size of the program, the amount of content, and the intensity of the interactions (Toth 2008).[7] In order to reduce development time, we decided to adopt a hybrid rapid e-learning strategy. In order to develop high-quality interactive multimedia e-learning courses which are generally short to medium length learning units in a minimum amount of time (Brandon 2005), and to take into account that rapid e-learning affects both the development cycle of production and e-learning contents production (Baldassarre et al. 2012), we reviewed several authoring tools to find the one that would give us enough creative control and flexibility without sacrificing user-friendliness. We selected Articulate Storyline as our core authoring tool which allows quick prototyping and template formation, enables easy packaging and flexible publishing and is compatible with all the latest browsers, devices and learning management systems (cf. Harnett 2013). We used it in combination with

---

7   In fact, estimates of development time vary from 200 to 300 hours of authoring for one hour of instruction (Chapman 2010; Kapp & Defelice 2009), depending on the type and requirements of the course.

other tools and attempted hybrid development blending the rapid authoring with some custom Flash elements[8] (cf. Kuhlmann 2011: 6) which allowed us to generate small file sizes while producing high-quality animation with optimal sound reproduction. After creating the first complete version of our multimedia learning applications, we examined their effectiveness by conducting a beta test.[9] Our group of beta testers included mainly foreign language students and teachers who offered valuable feedback that led to improvements regarding the multimedia materials and the embedded interactions. An enhanced version of the multimedia lessons was developed and uploaded on the KPG e-school Web Content Management System in the form of online multimedia applications.

Specifications, principles and features

The instructional principles that guided the design and development process and formed the specifications and features of our e-courses took into account instructional methods that have been shown to be effective based on high-quality research (Clark & Mayer 2011: 50). In our e-courses we focused on what Clark & Mayer (2011) call instructional effectiveness, that is, identifying instructional methods or features that have been shown to improve learning.

In recent years, the multimedia principle, which has been considered one of the most well-established learning principles that can be applied to educational settings, has emerged based on research evidence that people remember better when they are exposed to visual material which is accompanied by oral or written speech than from oral or written speech alone (cf. Fletcher & Tobias 2005). This is why in our e-courses we have used a

---

8   Given that gradually the Flash Player stopped being supported by all browsers, we converted all our Flash animation objects (.swf) to bite-sized animated videos (.mp4).

9   In software development, a beta test is the phase in the development cycle when a relatively complete application is given to real users for testing, a process that often reveals design flaws (Henry 2008) and leads to additional refinements in order to improve the final application (Rutenbeck 2012).

combination of written text and audio, as well as still and motion graphics (animation/video) to communicate our content. During the development stage, our instructional designers considered how words and pictures could work together to create meaning for the learner. This aligned with the contiguity principle which involves the need to co-ordinate printed words and graphics (Mayer 1989; Mayer et al. 1995; Moreno & Mayer 1999). For instance, applying the contiguity principle we avoided scrolling windows, in which graphics and corresponding printed text are separated due to scrolling screens. In cases where the text was long and could not fit on the screen, we preferred to use the mouse-over technique in which a small pop-up message appears describing each action or state when the cursor rolls over the corresponding portion of the graphic. Moreover, when learners place their cursors over different sections of the application screen, a text caption appears that explains that section. Another version of the contiguity principle deals with the need to co-ordinate spoken words and graphics (Clark & Mayer 2011: 102). This is why in our e-courses voice narration has been synchronised with motion graphics. Especially in cases where the graphic is an animated video showing how to perform a task of the test, the narration describing each step is presented at the same time as the action shown on the screen. The rationale behind this decision is based on research evidence (Mayer & Anderson 1991, 1992; Mayer et al. 1999; Mayer & Sims 1994) which proves that when words and pictures are integrated, learners can hold them together in their working memories and make meaningful connections between them. The contiguity principle however needs to work together with the coherence principle, according to which instructional designers should avoid adding any material that does not support the instructional goal.[10] Based on research findings which claim that when pictures and music are used just for decorative purposes with no obvious educational purpose, they are not likely to improve learning (Mayer, Heiser & Lonn 2001) and may even confuse learners (Moreno & Mayer 2000), we omitted irrelevant graphics, sounds and lengthy narrations from our design.

---

10   Mayer & Moreno (2003) have used the term 'weeding' to refer to the need to eliminate any words, graphics, sounds or lengthy narrations that are not significant for the instructional goal of the lesson.

In fact, in order to make our content more comprehensible and digestible we broke it down into small parts and used the metaphor of a tablet (see Figure 11.1) for the design of the user interface and the navigational structure of each lesson. The key of the tablet metaphor is simple navigational structure and a visually appealing icon-based design (Santally, Rajabalee & Cooshna-Naik 2012). In our case the interface of each lesson resembles a tablet home screen on which each bite-sized section is depicted by a representative labelled icon which is clickable and serves as a hyperlink. This representation schema (metaphor) was chosen because we employed small content granularity and did not want the structure to be complex. For instance, when students click on a section they are directed to a segment or a hyperlinked set of segments. At the end of each section, students may be redirected to the home screen from which they can choose the section they prefer to browser next. The sections are accessible independently of each other and can be revisited as many times as students wish.

Figure 11.1: The reading strategy app for KPG exam in English (B level).

This practice is aligned with the segmenting principle which recommends breaking a lesson into manageable segments, that is, parts that convey a maximum of three steps in the process, or describe just a few major relations among the elements (Clark & Mayer 2011: 205). The segmenting principle also suggests that learners can control the rate at which they access these small parts of digital content. Thus, we allowed learners to access each bite-sized segment at their preferred rate using navigation buttons. We also used 'stop', 'pause' and 'replay' buttons on videos and animations. By applying the segmenting principle along with the tablet metaphor we were able to build interactive multimedia applications reducing the cognitive load for the learner while minimising the amount of text displayed on the screen. The learning paths created for each one of the modules depended on the needs and the particular characteristics of each module, as can be seen from the example of two modules in Table 11.1.

Table 11.1:   Contents and modalities used in Modules 1 and 4

Test module	Sections		Modality
Module 1: Reading comprehension and language awareness	Can-do statements		Written Text
	Practical Guidelines		Animated video with voice narration
	General Information		Animated video with voice narration
	Tasks Types	Description	Animated video with voice narration
		Examples	Combination of written text, images and voice narration
	Grading Information		Animated video with voice narration
Module 4: Speaking and oral mediation	Can do statements		Animated video with voice narration
	General Information		Animated video with voice narration
	At the begining of the test	Example	Simulation Video
		Tips	Animated video with voice narration
	Tasks	Description	Animated video with voice narration
		Example	Simulation Video
		Tips	Animated video with voice narration
	In the End	Example	Simulation Video
		Tips	Animated video with voice narration
	Grading Information		Animated video with voice narration

Finally, it is worth noting that our scripts (written and audio) were formed in a conversational rather than a formal style. We used first and second person extensively and all spoken texts have been narrated using a friendly human voice. In fact, our narrator is an experienced radio broadcaster and knows how to sound personable, friendly and compassionate (personalisation principle). This was extremely important given that, according to research findings (Mayer 2005), instruction containing social cues (such as conversational style) activates a sense of social presence in the learners (a feeling of being in a conversation with the author or narrator) motivating them to get more actively involved in deeper cognitive processing during learning and thus leading to a better learning outcome (Clark & Mayer 2011: 205).

E-books and activity database in the teacher's electronic class

Purpose

The teachers' section of the KPG e-school aims to equip primary and secondary foreign language teachers and students with essential educational resources for the KPG exams. Appropriate test preparation not only raises the students' performance on the test but also increases their mastery of the content knowledge itself. Towards this end we have created self-study courses for students who wish to prepare at home (see previous section) as well as a teacher's class for teachers who wish to implement specific test preparation practices in order to effectively prepare their students to sit the KPG exams. According to Popham (1991), test preparation practices can take several forms including previous-form preparation, same-format preparation and varied-format preparation. The rationale underlining the teacher's section is to cover this variety of test-preparation strategies.

Structure

The teachers' section is divided into three distinct subsections, each focusing on different test preparation practices. One subsection includes informational materials on the KPG exams. In particular, visitors to this subsection can find and download: (a) documents which briefly explain the KPG exam specifications (i.e. the can-do statements for all modules and levels of competency and the rating scale), (b) past papers for teachers to use in class as practice tests (previous-form test preparation practices, according to Popham 1991), (c) KPG related presentations, articles and guides, and (d) useful tips that can help teachers effectively prepare candidates.

Another subsection includes e-books specifically designed for KPG test preparation. This subsection helps teachers apply same-format test preparation practices. Same-format preparation provides regular classroom instruction dealing directly with content covered in the test using practice items in the format of the actual test (Popham 1991). Towards this end, we developed six downloadable and printable electronic books for each language: that is, a student's and teacher's book for the A (A1+A2) and B (B1+B2) intergraded[11] levels of competence and for C1.[12] As in the actual test, the items for all levels and languages are subdivided into four test papers (modules), each of which aims to assess the use of the target language for comprehension and production of written and spoken discourse. Electronic practice books were selected over other types of interactive materials for a number of reasons. First, both students and teachers come from an educational culture that values books highly (Mitsikopoulou 2015) and uses them extensively in educational practice. Print textbooks have been used since the beginning of the twentieth century in response to a need for standardised materials (Apple 2004; Dendrinos 2015), and are central to schooling practices, according to Dendrinos (1992), regardless of the subject matter being taught. In the field of English Language Teaching, in particular, the print textbook tradition is so strong that several foreign

---

11   As of 2009, KPG exams have been designed as intergraded exams (A1/A2, B1/B2, C1/C2) with each exam containing an equal number of items from each of the two levels. The intergraded exam offers candidates more opportunities to be certified at one of the two levels within the same exam.

12   During the implementation phase of this project the C2 level exam was still not available. The C (C1+C2) intergraded exam was later introduced.

language teachers in Greece cannot even consider teaching the language without using a specific textbook. Preparing electronic books for KPG preparation was therefore viewed by the development team as a way to approach foreign language teachers with a genre familiar to them, that of the EFL textbook, and guide them smoothly towards the use of digital materials. Second, the electronic books are mainly books with complete practice tests, the use of which in the foreign language classroom to prepare students for a specific exam is another familiar educational practice. Finally, the structure of a book, with a beginning, middle and end, seems to offer language teachers a feeling of security and a sense of continuity. As a result, although practice tests could also be offered electronically in other ways, we decided to place a number of practice tests together in the form of electronic books for teachers to use with their students during the KPG preparation course. This proved a good decision which was warmly welcomed by language teachers and served as a guide for their preparation of the classes for the KPG exams.

However, despite the advantages of a book as outlined above, we were also aware of the restrictions that books entail and wanted to offer language teachers the choice to decide for themselves which digital materials to use and how: for instance, to incorporate individual KPG tasks in their regular lessons as a kind of an indirect preparation for the KPG exams, or even to create their own syllabus using digital resources they could find in the KPG e-school. That is why in the third subsection we developed an external database of searchable and downloadable KPG test preparation activities.

The rationale of the KPG e-school activity database is to gather various test preparation activities in a single area, offering teachers the opportunity to search, find and download test tasks according to multiple criteria that align with the KPG specifications (cf. *The KPG Handbook*). In this case, it is the language teachers who decide what materials to use, when and in what way, instead of simply following the fixed order followed in a preparation textbook. Therefore, the third subsection focuses on varied format preparation, which provides regular classroom instruction on content assessed in the test using practice items of various formats (Popham 1991).

Design and development process of the activity database

A core aspect of software engineering is the subdivision of the design and development process into a series of stages each of which focuses on one aspect of the design and development (Watt & Nelson 2014). The first stage refers to requirements gathering. During this step, our database designer worked together with the RCeL researchers to obtain an understanding of the proposed system and document the functional requirements. The requirements establishment stage involved a mutual agreement amongst the research and development team as to what data were to be stored as well as to the meaning and interpretation of the data elements. This resulted in the formation of a detailed (but not overly formal nor highly encoded) data requirements document.

After the documentation of data requirements, the data analysis phase began to move to the production of a conceptual data model for the database. The aim of analysis was to obtain a detailed description of the data that would suit the documented requirements so that both high and low level properties of data and their use would be dealt with (cf. Watt & Nelson 2014). These included properties such as the possible range of values that could be permitted for attributes such as the task type, the learning objective, the topic, etc. The conceptual data model provided a shared, formal representation of what was being communicated between RCeL researchers and developers. In fact, the conceptual data model made it clear to both sides what data the database should contain and the constraints the data should satisfy.

Therefore, the database design phase started with the conceptual data model and produced a specification of a logical schema which determined the specific type of database system that was required. In particular, we used a relational representation of the conceptual data model as input to the logical design process (cf. Watt & Nelson 2014). The output of this stage was a series of instructions detailing the creation of tables, attributes, domains, views, indexes, security constraints and storage and performance guidelines (cf. Coronel & Morris 2016).

The implementation stage was then initiated – a process which involved the construction of the database according to the design specifications of the logical schema. In general, implementation is heavily influenced by the selection of available database management systems (Watt & Nelson 2014).[13] A relational database was developed with an open source software which offers a flexible programming environment, allowing us to set up rules governing the relationships between different data fields (such as one-to-one, one-to-many, unique, required or optional, and 'pointers' between different tables). In addition, in order to create a user-friendly environment that would allow non-developers to easily access the database management system we created a web-based application[14] which allowed RCeL researchers to easily import or upload more than 500 activities onto the database and characterise them based on specific predefined attributes and values which comply with the KPG exam specifications (language, level, module, task type, communicative competence, learning objectives, text type). Finally, this web application was integrated into the KPG e-school website through a user friendly interface and can be viewed as a dynamic directory of various task types.

Specifications, principles and features

The design of each activity imported in the KPG e-school activity database has taken into account the can-do statements that specify language use as described in the Common KPG Framework, as well as the performance descriptors for each exam level. Since the KPG examination battery is based

---

13   We used MySQL as our database management system in order to create a relational database which provides a greater degree of data independence than the earlier hierarchical and network database management systems (Teorey et al. 2011). As an open source software it allows its users to modify the software, which can be downloaded from the web at no charge.

14   For the web-based application we selected the CakePHP framework, a rapid development framework for PHP programming language, which provides an extensible architecture for developing, maintaining, and deploying web applications (Bari & Syam 2008; Chan et al. 2009). We used it to develop a functional web application that communicates with the MySQL database management system and through that with the database itself.

on the premise that language use depends largely on the context of situation, comprehension and production of written and oral discourse is measured with tasks that create real conditions for language use. Therefore, only tasks that assess the specified uses of language and which conform to the common KPG task typology have been included in the activity database.

Specifically, the KPG exam preparation activities aim at assessing the degree to which candidates, depending on their level of proficiency, can comprehend and produce a suitable written or oral text that includes vocabulary, sentence structure and style appropriate to the circumstances of communication. Generally, the higher the level of proficiency the more candidates are expected to recognise the characteristics of the target language and use it appropriately for different language purposes or under different circumstances. The KPG specifications for each of the levels of proficiency have determined the type of text candidates are asked to comprehend or produce in order to complete a task (cf. *The KPG Handbook*). Each KPG exam preparation activity registered and uploaded on the database is accompanied by respective attributes (language, level, module, task type, learning objectives and text type) and correlated to one or more domains and relevant topics covered within. In addition, teachers are guided in their search by detailed instructions that appear on the screen as they proceed step-by-step through the search process.

The parent's electronic class

Purpose

The KPG is one of the few systems that recognise parents as key educational stakeholders. With the creation of the parent's section we attempted to establish a communication path with students' parents in order to raise their awareness of the KPG exam system in relation to other international language certification systems and to keep them informed about developments and innovations of the KPG exam system.

While designing the KPG e-school, the multiple benefits of parental involvement could not be denied nor overlooked. Research in the last thirty years has overwhelmingly demonstrated the positive effects of parental involvement for children, parents and teachers alike. Findings from international research have clearly established a strong correlation between parental involvement and increased student achievement (Argent 2007; Epstein 2001; Griffith 1996; Marcon 1999). As Esptein (1992: 1141) notes 'students at all grade levels do better academic work and have more positive school attitudes, higher aspirations and other positive behaviours if they have parents who are aware, knowledgeable, encouraging and involved'. Moreover, as Pugliese (2010) states, based on her research on the impact of bilingual programs, the primary inhibitor of the success of educational programs are uninformed and misinformed parents. Thus, the need to engage the support of parents is indisputable for the academic success of learners and for ensuring the effective implementation of educational reforms. Parents not only have the right to be involved in their children's education but they also have the power to alter educational practices at national level (Goldring 1991) and block innovation efforts (Pugliese 2010).

The need to create a separate 'e-class' for parents was triggered by the fact that parents serve an important language model for shaping their children's language behavior (Wong 2000) and that parental attitudes towards the language and its people shape and influence a learner's language development (Chang 2008; Tavil 2009) and even influence the degree of skill which the learner attains in a second language (Gardner 1975). Given parent's perennial lack of trust in the quality of foreign language provision in Greek public schools (Angouri et al. 2010) and their strong preference for foreign language certification offered by international exam bodies, it was imperative to make parental awareness of the KPG program principles a priority area.

Structure

The parents section of the KPG e-school, offers insights into how parents can support their children in their foreign language learning journey and informs them about their children's further foreign language development opportunities in the public school system. This section is structured in terms of FAQs (Frequently Asked Questions). FAQs are organised 'collections' of valuable information that have come from questions (and their corresponding answers) for the most common issues raised by parents.

More specifically, this section provides information in three broad areas. The first includes information about foreign language certification in general explaining issues concerning the significance of foreign language certificates, guiding parents how to choose the appropriate certificate for their children, describing what a 'recognised' certificate actually means in practice, explaining whether a certificate guarantees the acquisition of a foreign language, and giving suggestions about when it is advisable for a child to sit for foreign language exams. The second part provides information about the KPG certificate explaining to parents why to choose the KPG certificate, describing the ways the KPG certificate is recognised in Greece and worldwide, pointing out the significance of intergraded exams, presenting how a KPG candidate can be prepared for the exams and how a candidate can participate in the exam process. The last part of the parent's section focuses on how parents can help their children-KPG candidates at home. This was considered an important step for taking into account Greek parent's involvement in their children's studies.

Conclusion

The KPG e-school serves many purposes. On one level it acts as an awareness raising tool for students, teachers and parents alike facilitating the diffusion of information regarding the nature, validity, structure and content of the KPG exams. On another level it represents a public service reflecting one more aspect of the local character of the KPG exams (see the introduction to this volume). It responds to an urgent and pressing social need. Taking into account the large amounts of money that parents are required to pay for language exam preparation classes at *frontistria* in a period of severe financial crisis, the KPG e-school offers free preparation courses for students and teachers. Students can prepare themselves for the KPG exams autonomously without having to pay for special preparation classes or buy rather expensive test preparation materials. Teachers can also access the various digital materials through the KPG website: they can explore the strategy apps with their students, they can download the KPG practice books in order to prepare students at school for the KPG exams, and they can use the database to select materials and activities for their lessons. Most importantly, they can use the database as the basis for constructing their own KPG preparation syllabus.

On a more general level, though, the KPG e-school also operates as a means to facilitate the implementation of educational policy. It represents a strategic move to facilitate the link between the KPG exam system and the national Integrated Foreign Languages Curriculum (IFLC). The curriculum, as mentioned above, has been aligned to the KPG exam system by adopting the same framework (the six level scale of the Council of Europe) and common learning objectives (as expressed through the illustrative descriptors of communicative performance). Curriculum alignment may promote positive washback which refers to the effects of high-stakes tests on classroom practices – particularly teaching and learning. Thus, positive washback is said to result when a testing procedure encourages 'good' teaching practice (Alderson 2004) and when teaching the curriculum is no different from teaching to the test (Weigle & Jensen 1997).

However, positive washback represents only one of the effects of tests. The term 'impact' refers to all the potential effects of tests. As Taylor (2005) explains, tests and test results may not only impact on the career or life chances of individual test-takers (e.g. access to educational/employment opportunities) but may also impact on educational systems, may affect decisions concerning curriculum planning and the development of language policies while they may also lead institutions to produce test preparation materials and run test preparation courses. Accordingly, the KPG exam system has had an impact not only on curriculum planning and development, but also on the development of language policy, as the decision of the Ministry of Education to prepare public school students for the KPG exams attests. The link between the KPG exam system and the national Integrated Foreign Languages Curriculum not only leads to the development of a more comprehensive foreign language policy in the Greek educational system but also impacts on the quality of teaching and learning in public schools by elevating the status of foreign language teaching in schools and boosting students' instrumental motivation in learning foreign languages at school. The KPG e-school offers resources to teachers which will enable them not only to prepare their students for the KPG exams at various levels but which also acts as a guide for teachers on how to orient their teaching to the theory of language permeating the IFLC and the KPG exams, how to organise their teaching in terms of student levels and how to understand and make use of illustrative descriptors of communicative performance. The KPG e-school can thus potentially facilitate the implementation of the Integrated Foreign Languages Curriculum itself.

Bibliography

Alderson, J. C. (2004). 'Foreword' in L. Cheng, Y. Watanabe and A. Curtis (eds). *Washback in Language Testing: Research Contexts and Methods*, pp. 1–6. London: Lawrence Erlbaum.

Allen, M. W. (2011). *Designing Successful E-learning: Forget What You Know about Instructional Design and Do Something Interesting* (Vol. 2). San Francisco, CA: John Wiley & Sons.

Apple, M. (2004). *Ideology and Curriculum*. New York: Routledge.

Amer, A. A. (1993). 'Teaching EFL Students to Use a Test-taking Strategy', *Language Testing*, 10 (1), 71–7.

Angouri, J., Mattheoudakis, M., and Zigrika, M. (2010). 'Then How Will They Get "the Much-Wanted Paper"?: A Multifaceted Study of English as a Foreign Language in Greece'. In *Advances in Research on Language Acquisition and Teaching: Selected Papers (Proceedings of the 14th International Conference of Greek Applied Linguistics Association)*, pp. 179–94. Athens: Greek Applied Linguistics Association.

Argent, K. (2007). 'Every Child Matters: Change for Parents/Carers and Families? Can Schools Work with Families to Promote Knowledge and Understanding of Government Expectations?', *Education 3–13*, 35 (3), 295–303.

Baldassarre, M. T., Bruno, G., Caivano, D., and Convertini, V. N. (2012). 'Rapid E-learning'. In N. M. Seel (ed.), *Encyclopedia of the Sciences of Learning*, pp. 2762–4. New York: Springer.

Bari, A., and Syam, A. (2008). *CakePHP Application Development*. Birmingham: Packt Publishing Ltd.

Barker, D. (2016). *Web Content Management: Systems, Features, and Best Practices*. Sebastopol, CA: O'Reilly Media.

Brandon, B. (2005). *Exploring the Definition of Rapid E-learning* <http://www.elearningguild.com/pdf/4/rapid_elearning_whitepaper_3-2-05.pdf> accessed 22 August 2016.

Chan, K., Omokore, J., and Miller, R. K. (2009). *Practical CakePHP Projects*. New York: Apress.

Chang, Y. F. (2008). 'Parents' Attitudes Toward the English Education Policy in Taiwan', *Asia Pacific Education Review*, 9 (4), 423–35.

Chapman, B. (2010). *How long Does it Take to Create Learning?* <http://www.chapmanalliance.com/howlong> accessed 28 April 2017.

Clark, R. C., and Mayer, R. E. (2011). *E-learning and the Science of Instruction: Proven Guidelines for Consumers and Designers of Multimedia Learning*. Hoboken, NJ: John Wiley & Sons.

Cohen, A. D. (1998). 'Strategies and Processes in Test-taking and SLA'. In L. F. Bachman and A. D. Cohen (eds), *Interfaces between Second Language Acquisition and Language Testing Research*, pp. 90–111. Cambridge: Cambridge University Press.

—— (2006). 'The Coming of Age of Research on Test-taking Strategies', *Language Assessment Quarterly*, 3 (4): 307–31.

—— (2012). 'Test-taking Strategies'. In C. Coombe, P. Davidson, B. O'Sullivan and S. Stoynoff (eds), *The Cambridge Guide to Second Language Assessment*, pp. 96–104. Cambridge: Cambridge University Press.

—— (2014). *Strategies in Learning and Using a Second Language*. London & New York: Routledge.

Coronel, C., and Morris, S. (2016). *Database Systems: Design, Implementation, & Management*. Stanford, CA: Cengage Learning.

Cummins, D., and Davison, J. (2007). *International Handbook of English Language Teaching*. Norwell, MA: Springer.

Dendrinos, B. (1992). *The EFL Textbook and Ideology*. Athens: N. C. Grivas Publications.

—— (2009). 'Language issues and language policies in Greece'. In G. Stickel (ed.), *National and European Language Policies. Contributions to the Annual Conference 2007 of EFNIL in Riga*, pp. 53–69. Frankfurt: Peter Lang

—— (2015). 'The Politics of Instructional Materials of English for Young Learners'. In X. L. Curdt-Christiansen and C. Weninger (eds), *Language, Ideology and Education: The Politics of Textbooks in Language Education*, pp. 29–49. London & New York: Routledge.

Dendrinos, B., Zouganelli, K., and Karavas, E. (2013). *Foreign Language Learning in Greek Schools: European Survey on Language Competences*. RCeL, National and Kapodistrian University of Athens with Institute of Educational Policy, Ministry of Education and Religious Affairs.

Dendrinos, B., and Gotsoulia, V. (2015). 'Setting Standards for Multilingual Curricula to Teach and Test Foreign Languages'. In B. Spolsky, O. Inbar-Lourie and M. Tannenbaum (eds), *Challenges for Language Education and Policy: Making space for people*, pp 23–39. New York: Routledge.

Epstein, J. L. (1992). 'School and Family Partnerships'. In M. Alkin (ed.) *Encyclopedia of Educational Research* (2nd edn) New York: Macmillan.

——(2001). *School, Family, and Community Partnerships: Preparing Educators and Improving Schools*. Boulder, CO: Westview Press.

European Commission. (2006). *Special Eurobarometer 243: Europeans and their Languages*. Brussels: European Commission.

Fletcher, J. D., and Tobias, S. (2005). 'The Multimedia Principle'. In R. Mayer (eds), *The Cambridge Handbook of Multimedia Learning*, pp. 117–33. Cambridge: Cambridge University Press.

Gardner, R. C. (1975). 'Attitudes and Motivation: Their Role in Second Language Acquisition'. In J. W. Oller and J. C. Richards (eds), *Focus on the Learner: Pragmatic Perspectives for the Language Teacher*, pp. 235–46. Rowley, MA: Newbury House.

Goldring, E. B. (1991). 'Parents: Participants in an Organizational Framework', *International Journal of Educational Research*, 15 (2), 215–28.

Griffith, J. (1996). 'Relation of Parental Involvement, Empowerment, and School Traits to Student Academic Performance', *The Journal of Educational Research*, 90 (1), 33–41.

Harnett, S. (2013). *Learning Articulate Storyline*. Birmingham: Packt Publishing Ltd.

Henry, J. J. P. (2008). *The Testing Network: An Integral Approach to Test Activities in Large Software Projects*. New York: Springer Science & Business Media.

Kapp, K. M., and Defelice, R. A. (2009). 'Time to Develop One Hour of Training', *Learning Circuits: ASTD's Source for E-Learning*. <https://www.td.org/Publi cations/Newsletters/Learning-Circuits/Learning-Circuits-Archives/2009/08/ Time-to-Develop-One-Hour-of-Training> accessed 12 April 2017.

Karavas, E. (2012). 'Introducing Innovations in Periods of Financial Crisis: The Implementation of the New Integrated Foreign Languages Curriculum in Greece', *Proceedings of the 5th International Conference of Education, Research and Innovation, Madrid, Spain 19-21/11/2013*, 5534–42. <http://library.iated.org/view/ KARAVAS2012INT> accessed 10 April 2017.

Karavas, E. (2014) 'Implementing Innovation in Primary EFL: A Case Study in Greece', *ELT Journal Special Issue 2014 'Teaching English to Young Learners'*, 68 (3), 243–53.

Khan, B. H., and Joshi, V. (2006). 'E-Learning Who, What and How?', *Journal of Creative Communications*, 1 (1), 61–74.

The KPG Handbook: Performance Descriptors and Specifications (2013). Athens: RCeL Publications.

Kuhlmann, T. (2011). 'Rapid e-Learning Reality Check'. In M. W. Allen (ed.), *Michael Allen's 2012 e-Learning Annual (Vol. 54)*. San Francisco, CA: John Wiley & Sons.

Lee, P., and Alley, G. R. (1981). *Training Junior High School LD Students to Use a Test-taking Strategy, Research Report 38*. Lawrence, KS: Institute for Research in Learning Disabilities.

Marcon, R. A. (1999). 'Positive Relationships Between Parent School Involvement and Public School Inner-city Preschoolers' Development and Academic Performance', *School Psychology Review*, 28 (3), 395–412.

Mattheoudakis, M., and Alexiou, T. (2013). 'Introducing a Foreign Language at Primary Level: Benefits or Lost Opportunities? The Case of Greece', *Research Papers in Language Teaching and Learning*, 4 (1), 99–119.

Mayer, R. E. (1989). 'Systematic Thinking Fostered by Illustrations in Scientific Text', *Journal of Educational Psychology*, 81 (2), 240–6.

—— (2005). *The Cambridge Handbook of Multimedia Learning*. Cambridge: Cambridge University Press.

Mayer, R. E., Moreno, R., Boire, M., and Vagge, S. (1999). 'Maximizing Constructivist Learning from Multimedia Communications by Minimizing Cognitive Load', *Journal of Educational Psychology*, 91 (4), 638–43.

Mayer, R. E., and Sims, V. K. (1994). 'For Whom is a Picture Worth a Thousand Words? Extensions of a Dual-coding Theory of Multimedia Learning', *Journal of Educational Psychology*, 86 (3), 389–401.

Mayer, R. E., Steinhoff, K., Bower, G., and Mars, R. (1995). 'A Generative Theory of Textbook Design: Using Annotated Illustrations to Foster Meaningful Learning of Science Text', *Educational Technology Research and Development*, 43 (1), 31–41.

Mayer, R. E., Heiser, J., and Lonn, S. (2001). 'Cognitive Constraints on Multimedia Learning: When Presenting More Material Results in Less Understanding', *Journal of Educational Psychology*, 93 (1), 187–98.

Mayer, R. E., and Moreno, R. (2003). 'Nine Ways to Reduce Cognitive Load in Multimedia Learning', *Educational Psychologist*, 38 (1), 43–52.

Mitsikopoulou, B. (2007). 'The Interplay of the Global and the Local in English Language Learning and Electronic Communication Discourses and Practices in Greece', *Language and Education*, 21 (3), 232–46.

—— (2015). 'Digital Textbooks and the Politics of Content Enrichment in EFL Textbooks'. In X. L. Curdt-Christiansen and C. Weninger (eds), *Language, Ideology and Education: The Politics of Textbooks in Language Education*, pp. 181–204. London: Routledge.

Moreno, R., and Mayer, R. E. (1999). 'Cognitive Principles of Multimedia Learning: The Role of Modality and Contiguity'. *Journal of Educational Psychology*, 91 (2), 358–68.

——(2000). 'A Coherence Effect in Multimedia Learning: The Case for Minimizing Irrelevant Sounds in the Design of Multimedia Instructional Messages', *Journal of Educational Psychology*, 92 (1), 117–25.

Patel, S. K., Rathod, V. R., and Prajapati, J. B. (2011). 'Performance Analysis of Content Management Systems – Joomla, Drupal and Wordpress', *International Journal of Computer Applications*, 21 (4), 39–43.

Popham, W. J. (1991). 'Appropriateness of Teachers' Test Preparation Practices', *Educational Measurement: Issues and Practice*, 10 (4), 12–15.

Pugliese, J. K. (2010). *Parental attitudes toward bilingual education programs and policies*. Unpublished manuscript. University at Buffalo. Retrieved from <http://www.acsu.buffalo.edu/~jkp3/ParentalAttitudes_BilingualEducation.pdf>.

Shaeffer S. (1992). 'Collaborating for Educational Change: The Role of Parents and the Community in School Improvement', *International Journal of Educational Development*, 12 (4), 277–95.

Rutenbeck, J. (2012). *Tech terms: What Every Telecommunications and Digital Media Professional Should Know*. Burlingon, MA: CRC Press.

Santally, M. I., Rajabalee, Y., and Cooshna-Naik, D. (2012). 'Learning Design Implementation for Distance E-learning: Blending Rapid E-learning Techniques with Activity-based Pedagogies to Design and Implement a Socio-constructivist Environment',. *European Journal of Open, Distance and e-Learning*, 15 (2), 1–14.

Severdia, R., and Crowder, K. (2009). *Using Joomla: Building Powerful and Efficient Web Sites*. Sebastopol, CA: O'Reilly Media.

Stathopoulou, M., and Nikaki, D. (2009). 'Test-Taking Strategies in the KPG Reading Test: Instrument Construction & Investigation Results', *The Journal of Applied Linguistics, 25*: 129–48.

Taylor, L. (2005). 'Key concepts in ELT: Washback and Impact', *ELT Journal*, 59 (2), 154–5.

Tavil, Z. (2009). 'Parental Attitudes Towards English Education for Kindergarten Students in Turkey', *Kastamonu Education Journal*, 17 (1), 331–40.

Teorey, T. J., Lightstone, S. S., Nadeau, T., and Jagadish, H. V. (2011). *Database Modeling and Design: Logical Design*. Birlington, MA: Elsevier.

Tiggeler, E. (2013). *Joomla! 3 Beginner's Guide*. Birmingham: Packt Publishing Ltd.

Toth, T. (2008). 'Authoring Techniques and Rapid E-Learning'. In E. Biech (ed.) *ASTD Handbook for Workplace Learning Professionals*. Baltimore, MA: ASTD Press.

Watt, A., and Nelson, E. (2014). *Database Design*. B.C. Open Textbook project. Available online at <https://opentextbc.ca/dbdesign01>.

Weigle, S. C., and Jensen, L. (1997). 'Issues in Assessment for Content-based Instruction'. In M. A. Snow and D. Brinton (eds), *The Content-based Classroom: Perspectives on Integrating Language and Content*, pp. 210–12. White Plains, NY: Longman.

EVDOKIA KARAVAS AND BESSIE MITSIKOPOULOU

Conclusion
(G)Local alternatives in testing

> There is no place for universal proficiency in English language testing anymore. Proficiency can be addressed meaningfully in only specific contexts and communities of communication in relation to the repertoire of codes, discourses, and genres that are conventional for that context.
>
> — CANAGARAJAH (2006: 241)

The beginning of the twenty-first century has been marked with radical changes in the nature and focus of language testing and assessment. In 2001, Alderson expressed a longstanding concern of the language testing profession about the dearth of publications and research regarding local and national language tests and the insistence of language testing researchers on focusing exclusively on large scale international tests such as TOEFL, IELTS and Cambridge exams. This concern had already been articulated to the Greek educational authorities by Dendrinos and a team of her colleagues who were finally commissioned in 2002 to begin developing the KPG multilingual examination suite, partly inspired by the Finnish National Certificates of Language Proficiency involving tests intended for adults in English, Finnish, French, German, Italian, Russian, Saami, Spanish and Swedish.

A few years later, Rea-Dickins et al. expressed the need for language testing and assessment to

> address the specificity and contextual features of situated language assessment practices so as to extend our understandings of fair and equitable educational and social processes and develop new insights about language(s) use mediated through diverse socially situated assessment practices and discuss the implications for broadening the constructs that inform valid assessment practices. (Rea-Dickens et al. 2008: 576)

A similar concern was expressed in 2011a by O'Sullivan in his book on language testing in which he highlights two major themes: a) an opposition to the 'ethnocentric' nature of language testing claiming that most research conducted on testing English (as well as standardisation and measurement studies) has been dominated by the two centres of language testing in the United States and the United Kingdom, and b) the tension between local and culturally specific contexts with international components of language testing calling into question the use of international standardised tests in local contexts.

What is evident from these calls is the expansion of the language testing field towards new directions that look at testing within a variety of social, cultural and individual contexts. This volume fits within this new paradigm in language testing and aspires to contribute to the contemporary language testing literature focusing on research within the context of what we call a 'glocal' language testing scheme offering insights into situated language assessment.

Furthermore, this volume is associated with international tendencies emerging with greater frequency to question the value of international language tests (or the 'one size fits all' approach) over local tests which are sensitive to and take into account the specificities of the context which they have been developed to serve and the particular needs or realities of the candidates within that context. This tendency has resulted in a new understanding, conceptualisation and even operationalisation of test validation. A new model of test validation – the socio-cognitive framework – has emerged (O'Sullivan 2011a, 2011c; Weir 2005) which attempts to identify the evidence required to develop a transparent and coherent validity argument, while at the same time addressing the interaction between different types of validity evidence. The model has influenced leading examination boards and testing projects worldwide while the British Council has characterised it as 'the most influential test validation theory in modern assessment'[1] and has adopted it as an approach to language assessment underlining all its recent testing projects.

---

1   <http://www.britishcouncil.org/exams/aptis/research>.

The model comprises a number of components each of which must be attended to by the test developer at one or more points of the test development, implementation and validation cycle. It identifies and comprehensively defines three key elements: the test-taker (i.e. the candidate's cognitive and linguistic resources); the test system, which reflects social and performance variables of the tasks; and the scoring system, which is theoretically linked to the two other elements of the framework. This framework, according to its authors, is highly sensitive to context and also results in tests being *localised* and appropriate for the populations and the skills being assessed (O' Sullivan, 2011b).

'Localisation' has thus become a new term that has been brought into the discussion of the testing literature which is looking at alternatives to expand the market of testing. Of course, localised language testing is different from local or glocal language testing schemes; however, all these terms are sometimes used interchangeably.

Localised language testing

The *localisation* of tests refers to the practice of making adjustments to international tests so that they seem appropriate for the candidates to whom they are marketed. It is a term discussed in relation to the socio-cognitive model of validation which is characterised as the most significant development in language testing and which reflects 'the recognition by developers of factors of the context and the test-taker which can impact on test performance' (O'Sullivan 2011b:270). Localisation is viewed as a critical aspect of validation while language tests that exhibit a high level of concern for both the local test context and for the particular needs or realities of the candidates within that context are considered to constitute good 'localisation' testing practices (O' Sullivan 2014).

A first attempt at developing a localised test was the EXAVER project (Florescano et al. 2011) which has been characterised as 'the first systematic attempt to create a 'local', affordable, and sustainable language test system'

(O'Sullivan 2011c:10). As a matter of fact, EXAVER is the name of a suite of English language certification tests that are administered by the Universidad Veracruzana (UV) in Mexico. The suite was developed in 2000 by a small group of English language teachers from the UV, with the assistance of representatives from the British Council, Cambridge Assessment, and Roehampton University's Centre for Language Assessment and Research (CLARe) (see Ryan 2014).

The experience with the EXAVER project led to the development of an ingenious, highly marketable and profitable testing system by the British Council, called APTIS, which is underpinned by the socio-cognitive framework. With this new system the British Council has developed its own testing products, rather than acting as the distributor of other products.[2] As a result there have been tangible economic benefits, as the product has created a *significant* new revenue stream.[3] Launched globally in August 2012, APTIS is a modular system with fifteen different configurations of four fundamental elements (reading, writing, speaking, listening). It offers an item bank of test tasks and items which 'clients' (i.e. local test developers) can choose precisely what they need to assess and tailor components to local contexts. The system is designed for a wide, mainly young adult population while the contents of the test are designed to be used with learners irrespective of gender, language or cultural background and are monitored at the production stage for these variables (O'Sullivan 2015). The tests are administered in pen-and-paper form but also in digital form, as they can be taken over the phone or on computer. By offering 'customizable content' the British Council works with clients to localise the test (i.e. make it appropriate to the particular context and domain of language uses), 'thus ensuring it will meet the expectations and requirements of the client while maintaining its internal integrity (from a content and a measurement perspective)' (O'Sullivan 2015:10). Other examples of such

---

2   This development coincided with UK's decision to no longer provide public funding to the British Council branches around the world. By and large, they would have to find funding themselves through their own projects.

3   Impact case study (REF3b): 3, <http://impact.ref.ac.uk/casestudies2/refservice.svc/GetCaseStudyPDF/20471>.

localised tests (i.e. testing experts from the international testing business telling local test developers how to design context sensitive tests) can be found in the journal *Language Testing in Asia* while examples of indigenous language testing projects developed with British aid are described in a recent publication by Weir and O'Sullivan (2017). This publication provides a historical evidence-based account of the role played by the British Council in the development of English language testing over the last seventy-five years. It may be interesting for those concerned with the British Council's patronising attitude towards English language proficiency testing, now presented in politically correct terms as the process of localising language tests. In essence, with this new enterprise in language testing, the linguistic hegemony of global international knowledge products is reproduced.

The localisation of international language proficiency tests, whose content (mostly topics and visual input) is adapted to the experiences and needs of the local context by the local *clients*, is another form of 'industrialised language testing' says McNamara (2002) and we agree. Localised tests especially those that measure English proficiency (which is often the case) are one more lucrative product exported around the world, serving both the provider and the English language (cf. Pennycook, 1994: 157). The very practice of localising tests implies that expertise in test development can come from the West while local test developers can only offer insider perspectives on the appropriacy of topics for the local test-takers. The overall assumption here is that local test developers know the context well but lack expertise in language test development and thus need assistance from leading language testers and international testing organisations in order to develop valid and reliable language tests.

Glocal language testing

While the term 'glocal' with reference to language tests has also been used for the localised products discussed above, the term is perhaps more suitable for national or context specific language testing projects, such as the

Finnish National Certificates of Language Proficiency, the EIKEN – Japan's most widely used English language testing program[4] – the GEPT (General English Proficiency Test) which targets English learners at all levels in Taiwan),[5] and the KPG exams. These are actually *rooted* in the local context and are culturally appropriate and relevant to social needs but what is more they employ local testing experts who take into consideration international standards and research findings (see Dendrinos 2013; Canagarajah 2006; Clyne and Sharifian 2008; Lowenberg 2002; Tsou 2015; Wu 2014). Glocal testing, distinctly different from localised international tests, takes into account candidates' cultural experiences, areas of lifeworld knowledge, types of literacies, linguistic and discursive experiences, types of competences, skills and strategies the groups of language learners it addresses need to develop and, most importantly, it is suited to the local context and follows the educational framework in which it operates.

The aforementioned are characteristics of the KPG multilingual examination suite, which has gone through an evidence-based process of alignment with the CEFR, which targets learners of those foreign languages considered important in the Greek context, and which provides institutions or schools with a reference for evaluating the proficiency levels of their job applicants, employees and students. Like other glocal tests, the KPG promotes a balanced learning process, covering the four basic language competences, that is reading, writing, listening and speaking, plus the newly described in the CEFR Companion (2017) competence

---

4   Eiken produces and administers English-proficiency tests with the support of the Japanese Ministry of Education, Culture, Sports, Science and Technology and in co-operation with Japanese prefectural and local boards of education, public and private schools, and other leading testing bodies. More than 2 million people take the tests each year at 18,000 locations in Japan and forty-five other countries. It started in 1963 and has a total number of 80 million examinees.

5   GEPT is developed and administered by a prestigious institution in Taiwan known as the Language Training and Testing Center (LTTC). This test corresponds to Taiwan's English education framework, meets the specific needs of English learners in Taiwan for self-assessment, and provides institutions or schools with a reference for evaluating the English proficiency levels of their job applicants, employees, or students.

of mediation, with the goal of improving Greek language learners' general proficiency. While the KPG shares similarities with other local and national tests, it is distinct from these and from glocal tests such as the EICHEN and the GEPT which deal with a single language, English in particular. This difference is important to the extent that the languages being tested have an impact on test formatting, on testing specifications, and other important traits which have been discussed elsewhere (e.g. Sella-Mazi and Mavropoulou 2015, Tsopanoglou 2009, Tsopanoglou and Dendrinos 2012) concerning the KPG, which like the Finnish exams deal with several languages under the umbrella of common specifications. However, the KPG multilingual suite is characterised by another important difference: a key feature of the exams, as discussed by Dendrinos (2013), is the fact that in the KPG exams attention is relocated from the language itself (as an abstract meaning system) to the user (as a meaning maker). This is a particularly significant shift of attention because it means that there is only modest concern with how the ideal 'native speakers' use the language in their home country. The greatest concern is focused on how language learners, viewed as cultural agents, use the target language with increasing communicative competence in global or local settings, in ways that involve their sociocultural knowledge and allow them to articulate their experiences. Such concern justifies the theory of language adopted by the KPG, as discussed by Mitsikopoulou, Karavas and Lykou (this volume).

Further to the above, the KPG makes every effort, as do many other international and glocal exam schemes, to respond to codes of ethics (Karavas 2013) and international standards regarding principles of transparency, accountability and quality in testing.[6] This process enables test developers to operationalise quality management systems and to offer criterion referenced evidence of their tests' validity.

---

6   Various European and international organisations have published international standards that testing schemes should consider. The most influential standards or guidelines are those published by ALTE 1998, EALTA 2006, ILTA 2007 and, more recently, the standards published by the American Educational Research Association 2014.

The studies included in this volume (and elsewhere) give testimony to the validation research carried out by the KPG team,[7] to the evidence-based study of learner language proficiency for calibration purposes, and to the scaling of competences *across levels* and, most importantly, *across languages*. This is described in 'The Language Learner Profile Project'[8] that Gotsoulia (this volume) discusses – a project whose aim is to describe the linguistic profile of the Greek learner/user of foreign languages, adding details to the CEFR leveled descriptors of language proficiency and, most importantly, across KPG languages. Emphasising the significance of learner data for describing language competences, the project team specifies proficiency scaling in terms of the use of target language properties exhibited by learners with coherent L1 characteristics and asks important questions, such as how language competences of learners are scaled across levels, and to what extent the language use exhibited by learners is similar or different from that generally expected from learners with similar or different characteristics across levels.

The linguistic data which comprise the KPG Corpus (complete with their metadata) useful for several studies that appear in this volume – many of them using advanced natural language processing techniques for automated or non-automated text analysis serving KPG research purposes – has been collected from pen-and-paper tests and the procedure has been both difficult and costly. Therefore, the KPG team is eagerly anticipating the availability of digital learner data for more rigorous validation research and further development of calibration standards through evidence based research. Access to a huge amount of linguistic data will be less of a painstaking process once the KPG exams are carried out, as it is being planned, by way of an electronic platform with a sophisticated testing engine that will

7   For KPG quality assessment and evaluation for test validation appears see: *The KPG Handbook: Performance Descriptors and Specifications* (2013), pp. 109–14: <http://rcel2.enl.uoa.gr/kpg/files/KPG_Handbook_17X24.pdf>.

8   <http://www.rcel.enl.uoa.gr/research/language-education-research/the-language-learner-profile-project.html>.

be administering the KPG exams in all its languages through a computer adaptive testing system.[9]

It should be noted, however, that the findings from validation research associated with glocal tests have implications not only for the fine tuning and further development of the glocal test but also for the international language testing arena more generally. The studies included in this volume provide ample evidence of this fact. Although the studies have as a starting point the investigation of particular features of the KPG exams, their focus is on researching areas where empirical research is lacking or on providing fresh insights into global testing issues through the application of original, alternative research methodologies. For instance, they focus on issues such as on-site observation and investigation of oral examiner discourse (Delieza, this volume); candidates' perceptions of the listening test difficulty both in terms of text and task (Apostolou, this volume) and of reading test difficulty (Liontou, this volume); the investigation of read-to-write test task difficulty (Oikonomidou, this volume); the ideological inscription of texts used in reading comprehension tests (Balourdi, this volume); cohesion analysis as part of the assessment criterion of text grammar (Blani, this volume); visual literacy and multimodal discourse analysis of reading test tasks (Karatza, this volume).

Moreover, the studies included in this volume and related papers have been presented at international conferences and published in international

---

9   The platform being developed using the engine for computer adaptive testing in English, French, German, Italian and French within the context of the KPG exams consists of 1) an authoring tool supporting: a) the production line for the development of test tasks and items and b) their validation for use to test the four competences (reading and listening comprehension, writing and speaking production and cross linguistic mediation); 2) a pretesting or piloting tool, for the realisation of test tasks and item calibration; 3) a test player that is a software program used for the realisation of the exam process. The platform also supports: 1) tools for automated administration processes, such as 'testlet' synthesis, distribution of tests to authorised examination centres, receipt of data from the examination centres, collection of candidate requests, etc.; 2) statistical analysis tools helping to maintain test task pools; 3) a supporting e-learning platform for the training of assessors.

and local journals or books.[10] Some of the research studies comprising PhD theses were later published as books (Liontou 2014; Stathopoulou 2015). Over the years that KPG has been developing as a testing system, many more theses and dissertations have been produced at the two universities involved in the KPG project, the National and Kapodistrian University of Athens and the Aristotle University of Thessaloniki,[11] generating a team of young scholars in language testing and assessment.

The expertise developed through the inclusion of mediation as a component of the KPG writing and speaking modules, mediation task analysis and the investigation of candidates' mediation performance on test tasks, was used in the development of mediation descriptors for the CEFR Companion (2017).[12] Moreover, a selection of KPG tests tasks from all modules have been selected as examples of good practice and have been included in the Council of Europe's collection of illustrative tasks.[13] This collection is intended to help users relate locally relevant test items to the CEFR and to gain insights into developing items that can eventually claim to be related to CEFR levels.

Apart from the studies included in this volume, various developments related to diffusion of the KPG or based on KPG research have taken place with clear implications for testing research, curriculum development and foreign language teaching and assessment. These efforts have contributed to the quality of the KPG exams and perhaps confirm O'Sullivan's (2011a:270) assertion that

> Until now, administrators and policy makers have argued, with a lot of success and some justification, that no local test could match the international examinations for quality. No longer. Nowadays, there are many examples of excellent local examinations

10   <http://rcel2.enl.uoa.gr/kpg/presentations.htm> & <http://rcel2.enl.uoa.gr/kpg/gr_papers.htm>.
11   <http://rcel2.enl.uoa.gr/kpg/papers.htm>.
12   <https://rm.coe.int/common-european-framework-of-reference-for-languages-learning-teaching/168074a4e2)>.
13   <https://www.coe.int/en/web/common-european-framework-reference-languages/using-illustrative-tasks)>.

in which the knowledge of the local domain (culture, language, society etc.) contributes significantly to the format and contents of the test.[14]

Referring in the preceding paragraph to *quality*, it is perhaps interesting to ask what counts as 'quality' in testing. Which are the attributes of an exam suite as a whole and of each test separately that contribute to its worth, that counts towards its being considered a good or beneficial product? Good in terms of what and beneficial for whom? Most certainly, the reliable quality management and assurance of an examination suite weighs heavily toward its value and so do the tests' psychometric properties. But, surely there are other properties and traits in tests which add to their merit. The answer to those of us who are committed to developing socioculturally sensitive foreign language programmes as well as teaching, learning and testing materials is that quality in testing is not measured only by its quantifiable attributes but also by many other characteristics which are the result of qualitative research answering highly relevant questions such as which or whose social needs the testing project serves or the degree of relevance of its contents to the candidates it addresses, the backwash effect it has on language learning and education, the ideological construals in its source texts and the representations of the world that it makes.

Karavas (2013) refers to Bachman (2000) to support the position that 'tests are not value-free, culturally neutral tools developed in psychometric test tube environments. They are, in fact, powerful tools with far-reaching and sometimes detrimental consequences for individuals and society at large'. She also quotes (ibid.) Shohamy (2001) who highlights the symbolic power of tests,

> arguing that they can be used as rites of passage, as a means of socializing the public, and creating a dependency of test takers on tests as a main criterion of worth. While tests represent 'cultural capital', the knowledge contained in tests, on the other hand, represents in the minds of test takers and users what counts as legitimate, worthwhile knowledge, and, thus, tests can provide the means for controlling knowledge.

14 O'Sullivan does not make a distinction between 'local' and 'glocal' testing. Therefore in discussing local examinations he is also talking about the schemes we refer to presently as 'glocal'.

On the other hand, Dendrinos (2013) who discusses the advantages of glocal over global, profit-driven, industrialised language testing, points out that, while one of the most obvious benefits of glocal exam suites is that they are low cost alternatives to international tests, perhaps their most important advantage is 'their socially interested control over forms of knowledge and literacy' (2013:8) and 'the command [glocal exam suites have] over the social values inhabiting tests' and 'the control [they have] over the world embodied in the test texts' (ibid. 19). These, Dendrinos maintains (ibid.), 'might be better off in the care of domestic, non-profit-driven educational and testing institutions that might be better trusted with the power *to regulate the social and pedagogical identity of language learners*'.

In similar line of thought with Bachman and Shohamy, Dendrinos (2013:3) stresses the fact that 'tests are not value-free or ideology-free products, and exam systems are apparatuses involving processes of ideologisation – just as the discursive practices in the texts of language textbooks do' as she specifically analyses in various publications (Dendrinos 1992 and 2014). Ample linguistic evidence of that has been provided by Balourdi (this volume), who carried out rigorous linguistic analysis of source texts used in tests of three different English exams – one of them being the KPG exam in English – providing support to her claim that there are ideological inscriptions in test texts that linguistically construe different realities.

One more point made by Dendrinos (2013:6) is that while global language tests are by default monolingual projects, most local and some glocal tests are not. Offered within the context of a multilingual suite, the KPG exams involve the use of the candidates' common language – which is Greek since it addresses learners living and working in Greece. Actually, Greek is used for the assessment of candidates' B and C level cross-linguistic writing and oral mediation competence, in ways discussed by Dendrinos (2006) and by Stathopoulou (this volume), while at A level testing, it is used at the level of comprehension rather than production. Moreover, especially for A level testing, both in the KPG and other glocal exams, the common language of the candidates is used to ensure that they understand what the test task at hand requires; that is, test task rubrics are in the candidates' language.

The idea of using the candidates' first language (henceforth L1) in language teaching and testing materials is neither new nor uncommon. In Asian and European countries, for example, locally produced textbooks for the teaching of English in school have included the students' L1 in various inventive ways which have been promoting the creative interaction of two languages, rather than merely including add-on translated word lists as many international publications often do in an effort to make their products more appealing to local markets. In fact, the inclusion or exclusion of the L1 in teaching and testing materials, and in the foreign language classroom as a whole, has been an object of debate in the foreign language didactics literature since the early 1990s, long before the concept of 'translanguaging' as discussed by García (2009) became popular in the field. It was around the time that critical applied linguistics was emerging and the 'native' speaking teacher as the perfect pedagogue was being deconstructed.

On the basis of the issues raised above are politicised views of foreign language teaching and assessment and the growing concern in the European context for the promotion of multilingualism (as articulated in the European Commission's multilingualism policies), a move from monolingualism to multiligualism in language teaching and learning, and a paradigm shift in education promoted by the Council of Europe allowing the development of plurilingual competence[15] and intercultural awareness. Plurilingual competence entails the use multiple semiotic resources from speakers' multilingual repertoire in order to communicate (cf. Gorter & Cenoz 2017), while

> the plurilingual approach emphasises the fact that as an individual person's experience of language in its cultural contexts expands, from the language of the home to

---

15   According to the CEFR (2001: 4) 'the aim of language education [should be] profoundly modified. It [should] no longer be seen as simply to achieve 'mastery' of one or two, or even three languages, each taken in isolation, with the 'ideal native speaker' as the ultimate model. Instead, the aim should be to develop a linguistic repertory, in which all linguistic abilities have a place. This implies, of course, that the languages offered in educational institutions should be diversified and students given the opportunity to develop a plurilingual competence'.

that of society at large and then to the languages of other peoples, whether learnt at
school or college, or by direct experience. (CEFR 2001:4)

What is more, language users do not keep these languages and cultures
in strictly separated mental compartments, but rather build up a communicative competence to which all knowledge and experience of language
contributes and in which languages interrelate and interact (ibid.).

As European countries and European schools are becoming increasingly multilingual, the proposals above are gaining currency. It is

> no longer considered enough simply to achieve 'mastery' of one or two, or even three
> languages, each taken in isolation, with the 'ideal native speaker' as the ultimate
> model. Instead, the aim is to develop a linguistic repertory, in which all linguistic
> abilities have a place. (CEFR 2001:4)

Supporting this is the view that languages are not distinct fixed codes
composed of phonetics, grammar and vocabulary but ideological artifacts
that are socially and politically constructed and interrelated (Blommaert &
Rampton 2012; Makoni & Pennycook 2007). Speakers with plurilingual
competence use all their semiotic resources, which include all their linguistic resources, in creative ways to make meaning (Dendrinos & Gotsoulia
2014:24).

Viewing language and ability to communicate as such can facilitate the
language acquisition process by providing students with different resources,
such as the activation of the cognate relationships between languages (cf.
Cummins 2007). As Lin (2015) maintains it allows them to draw on multiple resources in their communicative repertoire, to provide language and
semiotic support when they are learning content using a second or foreign
language. These views are welcomed by Kramsch (2012) because they question the whole monolingual foundation of theoretical and applied linguistics as well as the traditional national underpinnings of foreign language
teaching and testing.

It is against this background that we, who have been working on
language examination schemes such as the KPG multilingual suite,
believe that glocal testing may not only best serve local sociocultural
needs but also the European vision for education. Contrary to international or global examination schemes which are founded on monolingual

premises and views of language and which can have a very negative backwash effect on language education, we view the European citizen as an active agent in communicative events with the ability to perceive and mediate the relationships which exist between multiple languages and cultures.

Bibliography

Alderson, Ch. (2001). 'The Shape of Things to Come: Will it be the Normal Distribution?'. Plenary talk in *European Language Testing in a Global Context Proceedings of the ALTE Barcelona Conference July 2001*.

Bachman, L. (2000). 'Modern Language Testing at the Turn of the Century: Assuring that what we Count Counts', *Language Testing*, 17 (1), 1–42.

Blommaert, J. M. E., and Rampton, B. (2012). 'Language and Superdiversity: A Position Paper'. *Working Papers in Urban Language & Literacies*, pp. 1–36. Tilburg: University of Tilburg.

Canagarajah, S. (2006). 'Changing Communicative Needs, Revised Assessment Objectives: Testing English as an International Language', *Language Assessment Quarterly*, 3 (3), 229–42.

Clyne, M., and Sharifian, F. (2008). 'English as an International Language: Challenges and Possibilities', *Australian Review of Applied Linguistics*, 31 (3), 28.1–28.16.

Council of Europe (2001). *Common European Framework of Reference for Languages: Learning, Teaching and Assessment*. Cambridge: Cambridge University Press.

——(2018). *Common European Framework of Reference for Languages: Learning, Teaching and Assessment. Companion Volume with New Descriptors*. Language Policy Programme Education Policy Division Education Department Council of Europe.

Cummins, J. (2014). 'To what Extent are Canadian Second Language Policies Evidence-Based? Reflections on the Intersections of Research and Policy', *Frontiers in Psychology*, 5, 1–10.

Dendrinos, B. (1992). *The EFL Textbook and Ideology*. Athens: N. C. Grivas Publications.

——(2006). 'Mediation in Communication, Language Teaching and Testing', *Journal of Applied Linguistics*, 22, 5–35.

——(2013). 'Social Meanings in Global-Glocal Language Proficiency Exams'. In C. Tsagari, S. Papadima-Sophocleous and S. Ioannou-Georgiou (eds), *Language*

Testing and Assessment around the Globe: Achievements and Experiences, pp. 47–67. Frankfurt: Peter Lang.

——(2014). 'The politics of ELL and Instructional Materials for EYL in School'. In X. Curdt-Christiansen and C. Weninger (eds), *Language, Ideology and Education: The Politics of Textbooks in Language Education*. London: Routledge.

Dendrinos, B., and Gotsoulia, V. (2014). 'Setting Standards for Multilingual Curricula to Teach and Test Foreign Languages'. In B. Spolsky, O. Inbar-Lourie and M. Tannenbaum (eds), *Challenges for Language Education and Policy*, pp. 35–51. London: Taylor & Francis Group.

Florescano, A., O'Sullivan, B., Sanchez Chavez, C., Ryan, D E, Zamora Lara, E., Santana Martinez, L. A., Gonzalez Macias., M. I. Maxwell Hart, M., Grounds, P. E., Reidy Ryan, P., Dunne, R. A., and Romero Barradas, T. E. (2011). 'Developing Affordable 'local' tests: the EXAVER Project'. In B. O'Sullivan (ed.), *Language Testing: Theory and Practice*, pp. 228–43. Oxford: Palgrave.

García, O. (2009). *Bilingual Education in the 21st Century*. Oxford: Wiley-Blackwell.

Gorter, D., and Cenoz, J. (2017). 'Language Education Policy and Multilingual Assessment', *Language and Education*, 31 (3), 231–48.

Graham, S. (2006). 'Listening Comprehension: The Learners' Perspective', *System*, 34 (2), 165–82.

Green, A. (1998). *Verbal Protocol Analysis in Language Testing Research: A Handbook*. Cambridge: Cambridge University Press.

Karavas, K. (2013). 'Fairness and Ethical Language Testing: The Case of the KPG', *DIRECTIONS in Language Teaching and Testing*. RCeL Publications, University of Athens, 1 (1).

Kramsch, C. (2012). 'Authenticity and Legitimacy in Multilingual SLA', *Critical Multilingualism Studies*, 1, 107–28.

Lin, A. (2015). 'Conceptualising the Potential Role of L1 in CLIL', *Language, Culture and Curriculum*, 28 (1), 74–89.

Liontou, T. (2014). Computational *Text Analysis and Reading Comprehension Exam Complexity: Towards Automatic Text Classification*. Frankfurt: Peter Lang.

Lowenberg, P. (2002). 'Assessing English Proficiency in the Expanding Circle', *World Englishes*, 21 (3), 431–5.

McNamara, T. (2002). *Language Testing*. Oxford: Oxford University Press.

Makoni, S., and Pennycook, A. (2007). 'Disinventing and Reconstituting Languages'. In S. Makoni and A. Pennycook (eds), *Disinventing and Reconstituting Languages*, pp. 1–41. Clevedon: Multilingual Matters.

O'Sullivan, B. (2011a). *Language Testing: Theories and Practices*. Oxford: Palgrave Macmillan,

O'Sullivan, B. (2011b). 'Language Testing'. In J. Simpson (ed.), *The Routledge Handbook of Applied Linguistics*, pp. 259–73. London: Routledge.

——(2011c). 'Theories and Practices in Language Testing'. In Ph. Powell-Davies (ed.), *New Directions: Assessment and Evaluation*, pp. 15–23. London: British Council.

——(2014). 'Adapting Tests to the Local Context', *New Directions English: Role of English Assessment in Internationalisation*. 29–30 Sep 2014. Academic presentation available at <https://www.britishcouncil.jp/sites/default/files/new-directions-powerpoint-barry-osullivan.pdf>.

——(2015) *Technical Report Aptis Test Development Approach* TR/2015/001 English Language Assessment Research Group. London: British Council.

Pennycook, A. (1994). *The Cultural Politics of English as an International Language*. Essex: Longman Group Limited.

Rea-Dickins, P., Scott, K., and Yu, G. (2008). 'Language Testing and Assessment in Applied Linguistics: Identifying Reciprocity in Applied Linguistic Research', *Language Teaching*, 41 (4), 575–80.

Ryan, D. E. (2014). 'Consider the Candidate: Using Test-taker Feedback to Enhance Quality and Validity in Language Testing', *e-TEALS: An e-journal of Teacher Education and Applied Language Studies*, 5, 1–23.

Sella-Mazi, E., and Mavropoulou, M. (2015). 'KPG Turkish: Former and Future Directions'. Paper presented at the 22nd International Symposium of Theoretical and Applied Linguistics, Department of English Language and Literature, Aristotle University of Thessaloniki (in Greek).

Shohamy, E. (2001). *The Power of Tests: A Critical Perspective on the Uses and Consequences of Language Tests*. London: Longman Group Limited.

Stathopoulou, M. (2015). *Cross-Language Mediation in Foreign Language Teaching and Testing*. Bristol: Multilingual Matters.

Tsopanoglou, A. (2009). *Issues in Language Certification. The KPG as a Reference Point*. Thessaloniki: Malliaris Paideia.

Tsopanoglou, A., and Dendrinos, B. (2012). 'KPG Selections for the Appraisal of Language Proficiency'. *DIRECTIONS in Language Teaching and Testing*. RCeL Publications, University of Athens, 1 (1).

Tsou, W. (2015). 'Globalization to Glocalization: Rethinking English Language Teaching in Response to the ELF Phenomenon', *English as a Global Language Education (EaGLE)*, 1 (1), 47–63.

Weir C. (2005). *Language Testing and Validation: An Evidence Based Approach*. Palgrave: Macmillan.

Weir, C., and O'Sullivan, D. (2017). *Assessing English on the Global Stage – The British Council and English Language Testing, 1941–2016*. Sheffield: Equinox eBooks Publishing.

Wu, R. (2014). *Validating Second Language Reading Examinations: Establishing the Validity of the GEPT through Alignment with the Common European Framework of Reference*. Cambridge: Cambridge University Press.

Appendix[1]

The structure and content of the KPG exams

Each KPG exam, regardless of level and language, consists of four modules:

Module 1 tests Reading comprehension and Language Awareness.
Module 2 tests Writing production and written mediation skills (no mediation activities for A1/A2 level).
Module 3 tests Listening comprehension.
Module 4 tests Speaking production and oral mediation skills (no mediation activities for A1/A2 level).

A level exam

Candidates interested in being certified as 'Basic users' of a language are tested through an integrated A1+A2 level exam, whose purpose is mainly to motivate young language learners to build their language learning skills and language testing strategies. The A level intergraded exam consists of four modules or tests:

MODULE 1: READING COMPREHENSION AND LANGUAGE AWARENESS

This module tests candidates' (a) ability to understand written (multimodal) texts, and (b) language awareness with regard to lexical and grammatical elements as used in utterances and brief texts. The test consists of 50 items,

---

1   The editors would like to thank Dr Mary Drossou for her help in collecting information about the KPG exam specifications.

40 multiple choice (20 for A1 and 20 for A2) and 10 short answer items (5 for A1 and 5 for A2). The duration of this test is 65 minutes.

MODULE 2: WRITING PRODUCTION AND WRITTEN MEDIATION SKILLS

This module tests the candidates' ability to produce messages and short texts in writing, given instructions and cues. Writing at this level is very controlled. It consists of 4 activities, 2 activities for A1 and 2 for A2. The duration of this test is 40 minutes.

MODULE 3: LISTENING COMPREHENSION

This module tests candidates' ability to understand spoken language which is linguistically simple. The messages candidates are asked to listen to are on predictable, everyday topics, and they are all studio-recorded so that speech is slow and clear –with no background noise interfering. Candidates always have the opportunity to listen to the recording at least twice before responding. This test consists of 10 multiple choice items (5 for A1 level and 5 for A2 level) and 10 short answer items (5 items for each level). The duration of this test is 20 minutes.

MODULE 4: SPEAKING PRODUCTION AND ORAL MEDIATION SKILLS

This module tests candidates' ability to deliver a message orally and specifically, (a) to respond to personal questions (two questions for each level, i.e. four questions in total), (b) describe or talk about something that they see a picture of (two questions for each level, i.e. four questions in total) and (c) to answer questions about one or more multimodal texts belonging to the same thematic category (two questions for A1 level) and to ask questions relating to missing information in one of the multimodal texts (three questions for A2 level). The duration of this test is 20 minutes.

In modules 1, 2 and 3 of the A level exam, all instructions are provided in both English and Greek. Additionally, one activity in module 1 and one in module 3 check candidates' reading and listening comprehension, respectively, through the use of items written in Greek.

B level exam

Candidates interested in being certified as 'Independent users' of a language are tested through an integrated B1+B2 level exam. The B level intergraded exam also consists of four modules or tests:

MODULE 1: READING COMPREHENSION

Module 1 tests reading comprehension skills and language awareness. It aims at assessing candidates' understanding of the overall or partial meanings in a text, to make inferences or intelligent guesses on the basis of the text. Moreover, some items are designed to assess their ability to make language choices that are correct and appropriate to the linguistic, discursive and social context. The test consists of 60 items, 50 multiple choice items (25 for B1 and 25 for B2) and 10 short answer items (5 for B1 and 5 for B2). The duration of this test is 85 minutes.

MODULE 2: WRITING

This module tests candidates' ability to produce written discourse and function as mediators through written production. It consists of four activities: two activities for written production (one for B1 and one for B2) and two activities for written mediation (one for B1 and one for B2) based on a Greek text. The duration of this test is 80 minutes. Just like the intergraded A level exam, candidates are required to do all four activities if they want to be certified for B2 level proficiency. Candidates who want to be certified for B1 level language proficiency only need to complete the activities marked as B1.

MODULE 3: LISTENING COMPREHENSION

This module aims to assess candidates' ability to understand standard spoken language on both familiar and unfamiliar topics normally encountered in personal, social, academic and vocational life. Candidates always have the opportunity to listen to the recordings twice before responding. This test consists of 15 multiple choice items (seven for B1 level and eight for B2 level) and 10 short answer items (five items for each level). The duration of this test is 25–30 minutes.

MODULE 4: SPEAKING

This module aims to test candidates' speaking production and specifically, candidates' ability to (a) answer questions about themselves and their environment (two sets of questions, each containing a B1 and a B2 level question, i.e. four questions in total), (b) develop a topic on the basis of a visual prompt (one task for B1 level and one for B2 level), (c) relay in English a message conveyed in a Greek text and respond to two tasks related to this text (one task for B1 level and one for B2 level, which belong to the same set). The duration of the test is 25 minutes.

C level exam

Candidates interested in being certified as 'proficient users' of a language are tested through an intergraded C1+C2 level exam. As with all other level exams, the C level exam consists of four modules or tests. Each module aims at assessing specific communicative uses of language.

MODULE 1: READING COMPREHENSION

Module 1 tests reading comprehension skills and language awareness. It requires candidates to skim through or scan complex, demanding texts of different discourses, genres, registers, styles and lengths, aiming at assessing candidates' understanding of the overall or detailed meanings in a text, and their ability to make text or context-related inferences or intelligent guesses, draw conclusions, etc. Moreover, some items are designed to assess their ability to make language choices that are correct and appropriate to the linguistic, discursive and social context. C2 level texts are longer than those used at C1 level and need finer intellectual processing, whereas the questions asked at C2 level are more demanding in terms of the language functions and cognitive processes required. The test consists of 70 items, 50 multiple choice items (25 for each level) and 20 short answer items (10 for each level). The duration of this test is 120 minutes.

MODULE 2: WRITING

This module tests candidates' ability to produce written discourse and function as mediators through written production. It consists of two activities, both of which require the candidates to interact with prompt texts. In Activity 1, candidates are required to understand, interact with and respond to an English text, whereas Activity 2 requires candidates to use mediation strategies to produce a written text based on information in a Greek text. At C2 level, mediation strategies are more demanding in terms of the complexity of messages and the precision required in relaying information. Therefore, candidates' performance is also assessed in terms of the level of literacy they possess and the natural flow of the written output based on the language choices that are correct and appropriate to the linguistic, discursive and social context. The duration of this test is 120 minutes.

MODULE 3: LISTENING COMPREHENSION

This module tests candidates' ability to understand, with relative ease, standard spoken language on both familiar and unfamiliar topics normally encountered in personal, social, academic and vocational life. Texts, at this level, are non-scripted, authentic or simulated-authentic, involving a wide range of speakers speaking different dialects, with different accents and geographical/social varieties of speech. Candidates are tested on their ability to understand the overall and specific meanings in the oral texts, infer meanings, identify finer points, appreciate register shifts, and extract specific information. At C2 level, the oral texts used are heard only once, whereas at C1 level they are heard twice. This test consists of 20 multiple choice items (10 for each level) and 10 short answer items (five for each level). The duration of this test is 30 minutes.

MODULE 4: SPEAKING

This module aims to test candidates' speaking and oral mediation skills, and specifically, candidates' ability to (a) support a point of view based on written prompts, given in the form of a role card, and discuss an issue developing their own arguments), (b) respond to questions requiring their understanding of the content of multimodal or/and literary texts, and (c) function as mediators by relaying orally in English information from a Greek text. At C2 level, the questions and tasks are more demanding and more complex in terms of the ideas included and the issues discussed, than at C1 level. Similarly, mediation strategies are more demanding in terms of the complexity of messages and the precision required in relaying information. The duration of the test is 30 minutes.

Notes on contributors

ELISABETH APOSTOLOU holds a PhD from the Faculty of English Language and Literature of the National and Kapodistrian University of Athens. From 2007–14 she was Research Fellow at the RCeL and a member of the English university team preparing the English exams for the Greek State Certificate in Language Proficiency. She is currently working as an adjunct lecturer at the Hellenic Police Force Academy and the Merchant Marine Academy, School of Engineers. She has participated in research projects associated with foreign language teaching and testing. Her work has been presented at national and international conferences.

AMALIA BALOURDI holds a PhD from the Faculty of English Language and Literature of the National and Kapodistrian University of Athens, where she received her BA and where she has taught as a seconded language teacher from the Greek Ministry of Education. Her thesis investigated world representations in language exam batteries. With an MPhil in Applied Linguistics from Glasgow University, she has been teaching in the state school sector since 1993. Since 2003, she has been an associate of the RCeL and has worked as a member of the test and material development team and as a script rater co-ordinator for the KPG exams.

VIRGINIA-MARIA BLANI holds a PhD from the Faculty of English Language and Literature of the National and Kapodistrian University of Athens. She has been teaching in the private sector since 2006. Her main interests include teaching English to young learners, ESP and the translation of technical texts. She has participated in the design of a Fire Terminology Textbook used in the Greek Fire Brigade Academy. As an associate at RCeL, she has analysed English candidates' scripts produced in the KPG writing module in terms of Text Grammar (i.e. text organization, cohesion and coherence).

XENIA DELIEZA is a graduate of the Faculty of English Language and Literature of the National and Kapodistrian University of Athens. She holds a PhD in Testing and Assessment from the same faculty and an MA in Media Technology for TEFL from the University of Newcastle upon Tyne in the UK. Since 1999, she has been working both in the private and the public sector as an EFL teacher. For four years, she worked in the Faculty of English Language and Literature as a member of the team that carries out research and prepares the English exams for the Greek State Certificate in Language Proficiency (KPG).

VOULA GOTSOULIA, PhD in Linguistics, is Research Fellow at the RCeL. Her interests focus on meaning representations and the syntax-semantics interface, descriptions of language competences, lexical resources and ontologies. As a computational linguist, she has developed and evaluated language technology software for large commercial houses and she has participated in European projects developing monolingual and bi-/multi-lingual lexical databases and annotated corpora. She has been a member of the research team that delivered the national Integrated Foreign Languages Curriculum. Her work has appeared in peer-reviewed journals, conference proceedings and a book in the field of language education and policy.

STYLIANI KARATZA holds a PhD in Language Testing, an MA in Applied Linguistics and a BA in English Language and Literature from the National and Kapodistrian University of Athens. Her research interests include multimodality, social semiotics and systemic functional multimodal discourse analysis. She has worked as an assistant researcher at the RCeL and has been working as an EFL teacher in the public sector since 2008.

EVDOKIA KARAVAS is Associate Professor at the Faculty of English Language and Literature of the National and Kapodistrian University of Athens and Assistant Director of the RCeL (Research Centre for Language Teaching, Testing and Assessment of the University of Athens). Within the wider context of the research, evaluation and development work undertaken by RCeL, she is responsible for the training of oral examiners and markers for the KPG exams in English (Greek State Certificate in Language Proficiency exams) and the development of the KPG speaking test in English. Her research interests include language teacher education and development, language assessment, curriculum/programme evaluation and implementation research. She has publications in these areas in local and international journals.

TRISEVGENI LIONTOU holds a PhD in English Language and Linguistics, with a specialization in EFL Testing and Assessment. She has worked as a research assistant, expert item consultant, freelance item writer, oral examiner and script rater for various national and international EFL examination boards. She has made presentations at national and international conferences and has published papers in the aforementioned fields. Her current research interests include theoretical and practical issues of reading comprehension performance, computational linguistics and classroom-based assessment.

CHRISTINA LYKOU is a researcher in the areas of systemic functional linguistics and social semiotics and holds an MA in Language Studies from the University of Lancaster. Her areas of interest also include critical discourse analysis, literacy and language education. She has worked as a researcher in the RCeL and in the Institute for Continuing Adult Education. She has published in journals and collective volumes. Some of her publications include *The chronicle of an ongoing crisis: Diachronic media representations of Greece and Europe in the Greek press* (2017) and *Metalanguage instruction within an adult literacy program: Lexicogrammar as source for socially meaningful choices* (2014).

BESSIE MITSIKOPOULOU is Associate Professor at the Faculty of English Language and Literature of the National and Kapodistrian University of Athens and Director of the Centre of Self-Access Learning and Materials Development. Her research interests are in the areas of critical discourse analysis, educational linguistics, digital technologies in education and critical literacies. Her more recent projects include the development of the KPG e-school, an online platform with online educational materials that aim to connect the KPG exams to Greek schools, the co-ordination of a group of experts developing learning objects for the teaching of the English language in the context of the Digital School Project and the co-ordination of a group of experts developing digital educational scenarios (The Aesop Project). Her recent book *Rethinking Online Education: Media, ideologies, and Identities* was published by Routledge (2015).

VASSO OIKONOMIDOU holds a PhD and a BA from the Faculty of English Language and Literature of the National and Kapodistrian University of Athens. She also holds an MA in Applied Linguistics from the University of Reading, England. From 1999 to 2006, she taught English in a private language centre. Since 2006 she has been working as a state school EFL teacher. She has also worked at the RCeL as a research assistant. She is an oral examiner, an oral examiner multiplier, a script rater and a script rater co-ordinator for the English KPG exams.

SMARAGDA PAPADOPOULOU holds a BA in Greek Language and Literature from the National and Kapodistrian University of Athens and an MSc in Technology Education and Digital Systems with a specialisation in e-learning from the University of Piraeus. Her scientific interests lie primarily in the fields of technology-enhanced learning, e-learning and online training. Since September 2011 she has been providing her services as an e-learning specialist at the RCeL and has participated in the development of various digital materials, e-courses and online learning environments.

MARIA STATHOPOULOU holds a PhD from the Faculty of English Language and Literature of the National and Kapodistrian University of Athens. She has been a Research Fellow at the RCeL of the University of Athens for the last 11 years. Since 2014, she has been invited to be a member of the ad-hoc committee of experts of the Council of Europe (Strasbourg) concerning the Common European Framework of Reference for Languages. Also since 2014, she has been working at the National Technical University of Athens as an adjunct lecturer and as a tutor at Hellenic Open University. Her book *Cross-Language Mediation in Foreign Language Teaching and Testing* (2015) has been published by Multilingual Matters.

Index

New Approaches to Applied Linguistics

Edited by

DR MARK GARNER
Director, Centre for Language Assessment Research,
University of Roehampton

DR ANNABELLE MOONEY
University of Roehampton

PROFESSOR BARBARA FENNELL
University of Aberdeen

This series provides an outlet for academic monographs and edited volumes that offer a contemporary and original contribution to applied linguistics. Applied linguistics is understood in a broad sense to encompass language pedagogy and second language learning, discourse analysis, bi- and multilingualism, language policy and planning, language use in the internet age, lexicography, professional and organisational communication, literacies, forensic linguistics, pragmatics, and other fields associated with solving real-life language and communication problems. Interdisciplinary contributions, and research that challenges disciplinary assumptions, are particularly welcomed. The series does not impose limitations in terms of methodology or genre and does not support a particular linguistic school. Whilst the series volumes are of a high scholarly standard, they are intended to be accessible to researchers in other fields and to the interested general reader.

New Approaches to Applied Linguistics is based at the Centre for Language Assessment Research, University of Roehampton.